The Woman and the Dynamo

Isabel Paterson

Isabel Paterson
and the Idea
of America

The Woman
and the Dynamo

Stephen Cox

Transaction Publishers
New Brunswick (U.S.A.) and London (U.K.)

Library of Congress Catalog Number: 2004045872
ISBN: 0-7658-0241-4
Printed in the United States of America

Library of Congress Cataloging-in-Publication Data

Cox, Stephen D., 1948-
  The woman and the dynamo: Isabel Paterson and the idea of America /
  Stephen Cox.
      p. cm.
  Includes bibliographical references and index.
  ISBN 0-7658-0241-4
    1. Paterson, Isabel. 2. Novelists, American—20th century—Biogra-
phy.   3. National characteristics, American—Historiography. 4. United
    States—Civilization—Historiography. 5. Journalists—United States.
  I. Title.

PS3531.A774Z53   2004
813'.52—dc22   2004045872

To Muriel Welles Hall

Contents

Acknowledgments ix

1. The View from the Wing 1
2. O Pioneers 7
3. The Unsheltered Life 23
4. Authorship and Exile 41
5. A Matter of Style 65
6. Queen Hatshepsut 83
7. Then or Anywhen 97
8. Never Ask the End 107
9. Let It All Go 125
10. Not Mad—But Atlantean 147
11. The Principle of the Lever Remains the Same 165
12. Spring Day, Too 183
13. Implications of Individualism 193
14. Others 205
15. Attacks and Counterattacks 223
16. War and the Intellectuals 237
17. The Grand Perspective 253
18. The Libertarians of '43 281
19. The Mustard Seed 297
20. The Committee of One Will Now Adjourn 315
21. Completing the Circuit 325
22. Friends 333

23. The Heart and Soul   343
24. Rays of Light   355
Notes   365
Index   411

Illustrations follow page 204

Acknowledgments

I am deeply indebted to people who knew Isabel Paterson or her friends and were willing to share their memories or permit access to historical material: Tom Bevans, Barbara Branden, Nathaniel Branden, John Chamberlain, Muriel Hall, Bernice Henderson, Robert Hessen, Erika Holzer, Henry Mark Holzer, John Hospers, Russell Kirk, John McLaren, Rebecca Metzger, Edmund Opitz, Mabel Owen, Eleanor Perényi, and Gertrude Vogt.

For their gracious permission to quote from unpublished documents, I wish particularly to thank William F. Buckley, Jr., and Annette Kirk. Permission to include excerpts from the writings of Rose Wilder Lane has been granted by the copyright owner, Little House Heritage Trust.

One of the pleasures of writing this book has been the opportunity to learn from professional librarians, curators, and archivists. I want to acknowledge a special debt to Dwight Miller and Lynn Smith of the Herbert Hoover Presidential Library, Rosa Portell of the Stamford Museum and Nature Center, Robin Borglum Carter of the Borglum Archives, Jeffrey Korman of the Enoch Pratt Free Library, and Nancy Shawcross of the Rare Book and Manuscript Library of the University of Pennsylvania.

My relationships with other scholars in the field have been the source of pride and intellectual profit. In this context, I think especially of R. W. Bradford, Barbara Branden, Bettina Bien Greaves, William Holtz, Valerie Legge, Thomas Maeder, Bruce Ramsey, Chris Sciabarra, and Amy Jo Tompkins.

Pamela Clark, Peter Rickgauer, and Paul Hochstetler gave me the inestimable benefit of their computer expertise. My student Cory Craig assisted me greatly in finding and preserving Patersoniana. Garrett Brown and Chris Capen offered untiring support and encouragement. My editor, Laurence Mintz, transformed the process of publication from a grief to a pleasure. As always, Paul Beroza let me test my ideas on him and loyally repressed all impulses to beg for mercy.

Three people were of extraordinary importance to my work: Mrs. Muriel Hall, Isabel Paterson's friend and executor; Dr. Irving Louis Horowitz, Editorial Director of Transaction Publishers; and the late Dr. Russell Kirk, Editor of Transaction's Library of Conservative Thought. Dr. Horowitz and Dr. Kirk invited me to publish my early findings as an introduction to the fiftieth-anniversary edition of Paterson's *The God of the Machine* and warmly encouraged me to write a full account of her life. From their example I learned that individualism, intelligence, and decisive judgment still have a place in publishing. Without Muriel Hall, who preserved the written records and the vital memory of Paterson's life, this book could never have been written. She welcomed my research, gave me unlimited access to Paterson's papers and her own rich recollections, provided wise advice on work in progress, and left me completely free to express my own ideas. From our first meeting, she has been as good a friend to me as she was to Isabel Paterson. The dedication of this book is only a small indication of my debt to her.

1

The View from the Wing

Isabel Paterson summarized her life by saying that she had "lived from the stone age to the air age." She also said that her girlhood "was rather dull, being spent in the Wild West."[1] But if the West wasn't wild enough to suit her, it did have its exciting moments. She saw her neighbors, the Blackfoot Indians, conducting their great Sun Dance, and she saw the huge mogul engines of the transcontinental railroad rushing down the mountains and across the prairies, messengers of a new industrial civilization. Soon she saw the peculiar sight of an automobile "scurrying along the horizon" like "a large black beetle." By the time she encountered her first airplane, she was prepared to think that "of course, people could fly. In this country at that time any one could do anything."[2] And when she got her own chance to fly, she set a record.

The place was New York City; the date was November 5, 1912—an appropriately symbolic moment for her to enter the drama of American progress. November 5 was Election Day, and progress was the issue. The candidates were Woodrow Wilson (Democrat), William Howard Taft (Republican), Theodore Roosevelt (Progressive), and Eugene Debs (Socialist). Roosevelt's party was the only one that named itself "progressive," but all four candidates demanded progress, and all believed that it required, not just the invention of more powerful machines, but the invention of more powerful political machinery, machinery capable of controlling the economic system that had been the maker of progress.[3] The four men denounced and ridiculed one another; still, they agreed that the era of uncontrolled individualism had ended.

Many intellectuals also agreed. Frederick Jackson Turner, the distinguished historian of American progress, put the prevailing

1

idea in its most influential form. He noted that the vast free lands of
the West were now occupied; the frontier was closed; an age of
nearly anarchic freedom had passed away, and an age of limitation
had arrived. Turner foresaw an era of "greater social control." Yet
limitation could also be a means of progress, a means by which
"civic power shall dominate and utilize individual achievement for
the common good."[4]

About such ideas Paterson would later express her own, vigorously dissenting views. She would make her mark on American
history as a political theorist who argued that the extent of progress
is determined by the extent of individual freedom, that "the strength
of a nation" is "directly proportionate to the freedom of the individual."[5] But on that November afternoon in 1912, when she was
twenty-six years old, Paterson had something different in mind.
She wanted to fly.

At Oakwood Heights on Staten Island, the Aeronautical Society
had announced an exhibition. The climax, the last of twenty-five
flights, would be an attempt by a pilot named Harry Bingham Brown
to set an American record for altitude with a passenger on board.
Ten thousand spectators assembled, their imaginations stimulated
by the risk of tragedy. Newspapers regularly reported the grisly
deaths of pilots and passengers who had foolishly meddled with
the new machines. On Staten Island, the only official safety pre-
caution was a posse of mounted policemen who tried to keep spectators off the field.

Isabel Paterson, mysteriously known as "Mrs. Paterson," since
there was no sign of a husband in her vicinity, had heard that Brown
was looking for a woman to fly with him. She immediately volunteered. Now, in the late afternoon of a beautiful Indian summer
day, she seated herself beside him in the cloth and wood framework of his little Wright biplane. A photographer snapped their
picture—Brown posing with both hands on the levers of control,
Mrs. Paterson sitting next to him, wrapped in several layers of cloth-
ing, smiling contentedly.

Then the engine started, the plane picked up speed, and the
ground fell away beneath her feet. It rolled out like a tapestry, she
thought, like a complex work of art; and she felt "triumphant, as if
coming into a deferred heritage," the heritage of the magnificent
land and the power to see it for herself. Higher and higher they

rose, in circle after circle, heading past South Beach and out to sea, far, far out, where there was nothing but the sky and the ocean, and the sky and the ocean merged, as she felt, in "Nirvana." Still they climbed across the sunset, until they reached 5,000 feet. That was a record. Isabel Paterson had flown higher than any woman had ever flown before.

At that point, Brown touched the levers in a businesslike way, and the plane started down. The flight had lasted most of an hour; shadows already extended across the island, and spectators were growing fearful about Brown's ability to find his way home. They kindled bonfires on the landing field, and by the light of those fires he found his course. The plane touched ground, "coming to rest like a duck on the surface of the water," and the crowd sent up a long cheer.

Isabel Paterson was amused. She was being applauded "for getting down rather than going up," but going up was the point, after all. What counted was the adventure of the air, not the security of the ground. While she was flying "it did not matter in the least" to her if she "never walked the earth safe again." "It was the greatest experience of my life," she told a reporter.[6]

Back in the city, the election returns were coming in. A reporter from the *New York World*, which supported Wilson, turned up at the headquarters of the Roosevelt or "Bull Moose" party, where he was happy to find an "air of cheerlessness": "Moose Quarters" were a "Cavern of Gloom."[7] Democrats rushed into the streets to celebrate their first presidential triumph in twenty years. Masses of party faithful collected on Broadway, at City Hall Park, and at Democratic headquarters, Tammany Hall on Fourteenth Street. Fireworks exploded, streetcars were stopped, the police were helpless. Free-spending customers thronged the best hotels and restaurants, and unprecedented numbers of automobiles appeared in the streets, a sign that "class privilege" and "political progress" were not utterly distinct.[8]

Paterson's reaction to the festivities is unrecorded. She made her way homeward, a little woman in an enormous town. During her flight, she considered whether the pilot might "have been wondering who was elected President"; but she herself didn't wonder. She was a partisan of nobody; she had no connection with political life. She thought only of the sky and the sea and the steady climb of the machine.

But the real adventure of her life lay ahead of her. It was the intellectual adventure of discovering, in her own way, what America was about. Taking her own survey of the landscape of ideas, she would try to find the relationship between the achievements of private life and the sustaining principles of public life, of the political machinery that allowed the literal machinery to fly. "The airplane," she would write, "was invented in the United States precisely because this was the only country on earth, the only country that has ever existed, in which people had a right to be let alone." The machine itself wasn't revolutionary; it was merely "an end-product" of a revolutionary "energy system," a system of invention, production and communication that could operate only in conditions of freedom.[9]

While other intellectuals of her time identified progress with an increasingly regulated and regimented world, Paterson identified it with limited government and with individual responsibility for the taking of life's risks and rewards. It was not the loss of "free land" that concerned her; it was the loss of freedom itself. But, she believed, the ideals of liberty could be recovered; they could even be enhanced, if people were adventurous enough to accept the challenge. Limited government could become minimal government; individuals could be made freer than ever before to conduct the experiment of life; "the technology of freedom" could be fully used; and the incalculable energy of the individual self, which is ultimately the energy of God, could create progress far beyond the ability of anyone to imagine.[10]

In the years that followed her flight, Paterson became a well-known columnist and literary critic; a best-selling novelist; and, in her great book, *The God of the Machine* (1943), the author of a unique contribution to American political thought. She developed radical individualism into a philosophy of remarkable richness and explanatory power. She went further. She gave it wit and charm, and a fighting common sense.

She was one of a handful of intellectuals whose rebellion against the modern state created the individualist "right" as we know it today—a complex web of classical liberals, libertarians, and free-market conservatives united by certain ideas about economics and politics and by a certain demotically American style. The question of who first wove that web, and when, remains controversial. Paterson, as I will show, was there at the beginning. She designed the classic pattern of modern political individualism, and she discovered its most colorful materials.

Very little of this story, and none of its fun, appears in conventional historical studies. As a modern liberal historian has said, the American Right has never "received anything like the amount of attention from historians that its role in twentieth-century politics and culture suggests it should." He mentions a lack of "imagination."[11] Certainly you need some imagination if you want to understand the history of the radical individualists and their contribution to American ideas. You need enough imagination to see that the landscape of American history is indeed complex, and that its forms may not always have been determined by professional politicians, corporate leaders, pressure groups, and graduates of the better Eastern colleges. You may even need a taste for paradox.

Radical individualism is an influence without an institution, a power that never grasped at power, a social democracy at war with the concept of social democracy. In Paterson's generation, its leading figures produced more than their share of enigmas and ironies. Their political "conservatism," as it seemed to others, could more accurately be termed an insistence on the fundamental ideals of liberalism, a liberalism that made generous allowance for personal difference and diversity. They were men and (more often) women, natives and immigrants, modernists and antimodernists, Christians and deists and atheists; and they felt free to defend the capitalist system while mercilessly attacking the capitalists who, they thought, were criminally mismanaging it. They were masters of the colloquial American language and enjoyers of vernacular American culture, but they lived at an immense and frequently mysterious remove from normal American life. So private was Mrs. Paterson that a would-be investigator predicted that her biographers would "end in Bellevue."[12] Bellevue was an insane asylum.

I'll take that as a warning. I have discovered many facts about Paterson (beginning with her date of birth) that she preferred no one to know, but some facts are still buried too deep for even a decade of research to reveal. I have tried not to lose my sanity over this, and Paterson's own example has helped me. She suggested that the story of her life was something more than the story of the facts about herself. In her old age, when she made plans to write an autobiography, she said that it would be an account "of the world I have seen."[13] It would be a book about her experience of America, her idea of what had happened to America in its progress "from the stone age to the air age." It would, of course, be a picture of America as seen from a distance, a distance established both by time and by her own highly individual temperament. But there is no sight without distance; it is distance that allows us to see the many patterns of a landscape. And outsiders can make use of their distance, too.

Preparing to write her book, Paterson sorted through boxes of photographs and letters and other souvenirs of the world she had seen, discarding some and preserving others. One of the things she kept was an article from a Staten Island newspaper, reporting on an aeronautical event of 1912; another was the picture of a young woman sitting on the wing of a tiny airplane, smiling into the distance. Paterson died before she could write what she thought about that. But it's easy to see, looking at the picture, that who she was and what she did has something important to say about the risks and possibilities of life in America.

That is the story I've tried to write.

2

O Pioneers

Isabel Paterson's proudest boast was her identity as an American. "Whoever is fortunate enough to be an American citizen," she wrote on the last page of *The God of the Machine*, "came into the greatest inheritance man has ever enjoyed."[1] But for her, that identity was an achievement, not a birthright. She was born a subject of Queen Victoria, in an obscure corner of the British empire. As she told it, she was born "in the middle of Lake Huron," but "[f]ortunately, there was an island on the spot"—Manitoulin Island, just off Huron's northern shore.[2]

The settlement of the Grand Manitoulin, as it is called on old maps, would lead anyone to question the idea that "free land" is an independent force in history. Once intended as an Indian reservation, the glacier-scarred island was thrown open to white occupation in the nineteenth century; but despite determined efforts at salesmanship, which included absurdly low prices and arrangements for purchase on the installment plan, many government properties remained unsold as late as the 1930s.[3] Even when land is almost "free," it means something only if people want it, and know how to profit from it.

Francis (Frank) Bowler evidently thought that he knew. Around 1880 he concluded that conditions were right for him to build a grist mill in Tehkummah ("TACK-ummuh"), a small community on the south side of the island, a few miles from some unceded Ojibwe land. His log house stood just west of the mill, on a little rise; and it was there that a local newspaper (there is always a newspaper in a frontier town) reported the birth of a daughter, on January 22, 1886. This daughter would become Isabel Paterson.[4]

7

The Bowlers—Francis, born 1848, and Margaret, born 1856—had five daughters and four sons. The baby who arrived in 1886 was "about in the middle" of this brood.[5] Though not the youngest of the nine, she was the "smallest," which meant that she got used to being "picked on." She also learned how to defend herself.[6] The name given at birth may have been Mary Isabel; until her dying day, her relations called her "Mary."[7] "Mary" required no special inspiration; "Isabel" repeated the name of an aunt. "And it could have been worse," Paterson would say. "[W]e had lots of aunts, some of them named Bridget and Hannah." There were uncles, too, one of them a policeman; a grandmother who had emigrated from Ireland's County Clare; and a grandfather "who was a Yorkshire man." When Paterson had occasion to summarize her ancestry, she briefly noted that she was "of English, Irish, and American descent"—a mixture that typified the settlers of Manitoulin Island.[8]

Wit ran in the family, and a strong streak of sarcasm. When someone fell down the cellar steps, Paterson's grandfather asked, "'Did you do it to your liking?' And if the answer was no, he remarked, 'Then do it over again.'" Paterson would commend this saying to people who were dissatisfied with the results of World War I but who didn't mind planning for other wars.[9] Unfortunately, her most pertinent lessons in the repetition of mistakes came from her own upbringing. Failure ran in this family too.

It is easiest to characterize the Bowlers by what they lacked. The most obvious deficiency was financial. Paterson said that so far as she knew, "there never was any money in the family."

> I have sometimes thought that being poor is a habit as much as anything. I am sure it's hereditary. As some families are red-headed or left-handed others are poor. Our family is left-handed too.[10]

How and why these left-handed people came to inhabit the Grand Manitoulin is a mystery, though not, perhaps, a very interesting one. The mill was probably just one more shiftless episode in the shiftless life of Francis Bowler, whose good qualities, if any, Isabel never learned to appreciate. He was known by his Manitoulin neighbors as "a great teller of tall tales. One, for instance, was about his red hen which laid two or three eggs a day."[11] This talent for lying seems not to have made a favorable impression on his daughter. Even in her old age she remembered him with contempt. The theme of the irresponsible father or, more generally, the irresponsible figure of authority is everywhere in her work. In her novel *Never Ask the End*, the father of the protagonist's destroys her "confidence in the goodness of the universe," not by violence—"[h]e had not broken any of the commandments"—but "by an incessant tyranny, in ways too petty to describe, a grudging, futile egotism." The protagonist of another novel, *The Golden Vanity*, reflects disgustedly on a stepfather who sits and watches while his wife carries all the burdens of a large family. He complains that he was "born too late for opportunity."[12]

This is the kind of complaining that one might expect from a man like Frank Bowler, who had a way of getting to frontiers—Manitoulin Island and several other places, down the road—just when they were being "closed." In later life, his daughter felt herself pursued by men who had situated themselves in unproductive physical or intellectual territory but kept insisting that they had some miraculous means of making it profitable, if other people would only help them. Would-be inventors of perpetual motion machines, literal or symbolic, figure prominently in her work. In her last published novel, *If It Prove Fair Weather*, the heroine's father gives up working so that he can spend all his time on perpetual motion. He dies after a mere twenty years of fruitless speculation. In *The God of the Machine*, Paterson describes advocates of collectivism as "perpetual motion crank[s]" who think that a socialist economy will run on its own, if only someone else has created the means to get it started.[13]

According to Mysie, Paterson's alter ego in *The Golden Vanity*, the demand for "opportunity" is a judgment on the demander himself, not on the deficiencies of society, the economic system, or the land ("free" or otherwise) that he chose to occupy. Her stepfather's defect is that he is

simply useless. There is that fact which sentimental sociologists do not take into account; some people are useless. It doesn't matter whether they sit in club windows and turn purple over the insolence of workingmen demanding higher wages, or sit in the kitchen grumbling about the injustices of capitalism; they are a dead loss. What are you going to do with them? They are more useless in a job than out of it. They have to be carried. . . . Mysie used to wish disinterestedly that her stepfather would die. He wouldn't, of course. He would never die. His kind are notably long-lived, since they do not deplete their energies by excessive toil or mental exertion. Since for years Mysie had sent money to her mother, his lumbago had become chronic.[14]

While Paterson was preparing this novel, her father looked to her very much like Mysie's stepfather. Paterson was sending money home to her mother and accusing her father of financial incompetence and the exploitation of her brother Mark, who had remained at home to work the family farm:

> Father I suppose will have to die some time, though I've about given up hope. . . . Father was always impossible, and now he is doddering. If I am a half-wit it's no wonder. He has taken the money from the crops, that Mark earned with hard work, and lent it on worthless notes.[15]

One of Paterson's maxims was that "spendthrifts are never generous."[16] Her father seems to have exemplified the saying. He was a strong inspiration for the theories she developed about the sanctity of common sense and personal responsibility.

Her mother offered support for the same theories, in quite a different way. She was a member of what Paterson would come to consider the most important minority group in the country, the inconspicuous people who "always somehow get things done, get some practicable result from whatever material is at hand and whatever other people they must work with. . . . One can't always see how they do it."[17]

Paterson recorded two revealing stories about her mother. In one of them, she recalled Mrs. Bowler saying "casually" to her: "I guess people do the best they can, and they don't know why they do things." Paterson took this as a lesson in individualism. It left her "permanently incapable of regarding any action except as a special case. You do what you do and take the consequences—and the consequences also may be entirely private and personal."[18] A more unsettling kind of individualism emerges in the second anecdote, this one attributed to the mother of the protagonist in Paterson's very autobiographical *Never Ask the End*. The "worn little old woman" tells her daughter, "I don't think I believe in marriage. But I don't know what else people can do." "And," as the daughter recalls, "she had been married nearly fifty years."[19]

Paterson loved her mother, hated her father, and reacted with varying degrees of affection and amusement toward the rest of her family, but she seems to have been most impressed by her mental distance from them all. It is "an obscure and dreadful business," she said, "this being entangled with dozens of strangers who compose one's family."[20] She would do the best she could, but she expected no help from them.

Like other "left-handed" families who had come to Manitoulin Island, the Bowlers soon abandoned it. The immediate cause may have been the destruction of their house, which burned down "soon after" Paterson's birth, in one of the forest fires that regularly swept the island. She had "a vague idea" that she was carried out of the house in a bureau drawer.[21] She would see Manitoulin only once again, when she was forty years old. By then, she was a widely read columnist who was able to give dramatic emphasis to her travel plans. She announced to the nation that she meant to revisit her natal isle, the Grand Manitoulin, the "place of the Manitou," the "equivalent of Olympus in Indian mythology."[22] To a friend, she confided that she had "ten thousand cousins scattered about the place," people whom she had not met and did not wish to meet: "Families are a blight, if not worse." She returned from her pilgrimage with little to report. She had found no radios, which was good, or bookstores, which was bad.[23]

Having failed on one frontier, the Bowlers moved to another one, the closest and cheapest—the Upper Peninsula of Michigan. Their destination was Newberry, a settlement in the center of the peninsula, about fifty miles north of the straits of Mackinac, in a country of low hills and plains and luxuriant marshes. The area was slow to develop. The frontier arrived at the site of Newberry a generation after it had reached the iron and copper ports of Lake Superior and many generations after it had reached the trade zones of the straits. Newberry was the product of a railroad constructed by John S. Newberry and other Detroit capitalists to connect the straits with Marquette on Lake Superior. Newberry and his associates found a place on the line where trees could be used to make charcoal and the charcoal used to make iron. In the year before Paterson was born, a town was incorporated, with streets named after members of the Newberry family.[24] This frontier was anything but a matter of "free land" and artlessly democratic development. It was a matter of money and machines.

Paterson's self-consciousness began with the decisive motion of one of those machines. The little girl was on her first journey by train, probably a train that the Bowlers used on their trip to Newberry, when she uttered her "first clear sentence." From the carriage she saw a boy running along the station platform, and she cried, "Oh, see the young lad running!" Her family remembered that she had attained the "appalling age of thirteen months" when she produced this highly literary exclamation (or something like it, perhaps). And it was in Newberry that she abruptly learned to read. She didn't need to be instructed; she picked it up on her own, when she was three years old: "Nobody ever taught us; we just went ahead and read. Yes, and what of it? Look at the darned thing now. It is fairly obvious that children should be kept back." She found that reading books was easier when she attended only to the conversational parts, "skipping the rest of the text." When she grew up, and the avant garde began its experiments with plotless novels, these naturally seemed "all right" to her.[25]

She was used to things happening in such peculiar ways that the sequence often didn't seem to matter. What she remembered of her life in Newberry reflects the general capacity of North Americans to see themselves simultaneously at a number of places in a fantastically variegated stream of time. She remembered a raw new town with an iron foundry, and she remembered a world as indifferent to change as the scenes on Keats's Grecian urn, an imaginary world with a curious ability to survive independently of the imaginer. In middle age, she was "startled" to receive correspondence from a reader who lived in her childhood home. "After all these years and years and years, to learn that Newberry still exists," she said.

> And do the raspberries still ripen best in the "Swede holes" along the narrow-gauge spur track that runs out to the lumber camp? and are the bumblebees still as thick in the red clover? and the hazel bushes and beech trees vocal with squirrels in October? and does the village grocer still sell little striped candy fishes three for a cent? In winter the dried thistleheads came up like ghosts through the three-foot crusted snow, and we used to race about in the blue moonlight whipping them off with a willow-switch, till we also turned blue with cold and retreated sniffing to the kitchen stove. And then we went away from there, and never went back, and every year in our imagination the elm trees grow taller and the white clover smells sweeter and the fireworks on the Fourth of July go up in an increasing blaze of glory.[26]

These memories and imaginative perceptions were all accurate enough, in their way. Together, they formed a picture of the true frontier, an instantaneous frontier that came equipped with an instantaneous past, several alternative futures, and many indications of the diversity of human life. Newberry was a small town, but it was a social world too "complicated and various" to be stereotyped. There was the Civil War veteran who stopped at the Bowlers' house to give Isabel candy and declare that he was still not ready to forgive the Confederates. There were the Finnish and Swedish workmen who got drunk every Saturday and sang until they fell asleep along the railroad track. There was the doctor with his span of snow-white Arabian horses: how had they gotten to Michigan, the little girl wondered.[27] And how could one account for the strange compatibility of all these people and things and the times and places they represented? Paterson would devote much of her life to thinking that question through.

"And then we went away from there. . . ." Newberry was not the Bowlers' last frontier. They arrived at the height of its boom, but apparently they derived no advantage from it. No trace can be found of Frank's business, whatever it was. Perhaps he kept a store or followed a trade and failed for lack of capital. Perhaps he spent too much time sitting in the kitchen, grumbling about the injustices of capitalism. In any case, the Bowler family "left Michigan to go West" when Isabel was six years old.[28]

They went to Utah Territory, "pioneering" someplace where Isabel enjoyed tracking lizards over the "red-hot sand."[29] She never saw the Mormon capital of Salt Lake City, though she remembered listening to fearful tales of "Danite" warriors and the Mountain Meadows Massacre of 1857, when Mormons liquidated non-Mormon emigrants. The tales were fearful, but Isabel was not afraid. After hearing them, she continued to visit her "Mormon neighbors without a quiver of apprehension." Jean-Jacques Rousseau, the patron of social equality, argued that no one can maintain a social contract with people who harbor "intolerant" religious views; modern patrons of political correctness agree. Isabel knew by experience that the idea was false.[30]

In Utah, it seems, she endured her first, brief trial of school. She attended for a month, then asked to leave, claiming that she knew as much as her teacher. Her reading had already "progressed to a consideration of Bryan's stand on the free silver question," so "the adventures of the little red hen seemed somewhat lacking in spice." The teacher–"capable and kindly"— gave her permission to quit.[31]

When Isabel was eight years old, the family moved again. They packed up a covered wagon and embarked "on the last pioneer trail"—eight hundred miles to their new home, a ranch in Canada's

Northwest Territories. It must have been a hard journey, but what she remembered was the absence of hardship:

> [W]e ate flapjacks cooked by a campfire, and went to sleep in heaps all over the blanket rolls and frying pans when the day was too long. It wasn't a bad life, but somehow six weeks of it provided fewer thrills than a few days as imagined by Miss [Edna] Ferber. There is a kind of monotony about pioneer life, a peacefulness if one takes it that way, which we suspect is what the pioneers wanted. They tried to get away from the hazards of civilization, its demand on their nerves and brains, of competing, adapting, and sharing.[32]

From her point of view, the Bowlers' great trek "wasn't travel, it was leisure." She would never regard the frontier as the breeding ground of puritan virtues. She was aware that other people did. Those people, she could only suppose, had "never lived on the frontier," where freedom to loaf was more highly prized than hard work and stern ambition.[33] She was proof against any conservative tendency to idealize the "heartland" and its pioneers. She was also proof against any economic theory that concerned itself with people's desire for material goods alone. She knew that there are no "free" goods, that everything, even freedom, must be purchased by surrendering something else; but she knew, as well, that there are many kinds of goods, and what can be bought with money is just one kind.

The Bowlers' destination lay about ten miles north of the Montana border, in the Glacier Park district: "that cold, beautiful, strange upland of the Great Divide, the ultimate watershed of the American continent." It was the southwest corner of what would become Alberta. The largest nearby town was Cardston, settled a few years before by Mormons from Utah. Although no one in the Bowler family appears to have been a Mormon, they had followed the Mormons' trail.[34]

By 1894, when Paterson's family crossed what the Blackfoot Indians called the "medicine line" between the United States and Canada, only about 30,000 people lived in the immensity of the future province. Southern Alberta was so thinly settled that people "knew direction not by landmarks but by the sun, the stars and the mountains." The Bowlers' ranch was five miles from their closest neighbor. At the start—and a long start it was, lasting for "months and years"—the Bowlers lived in tents built over board flooring. They had come down a good deal from the days when Francis

Bowler could afford to have a gristmill constructed and hire millers to run it.[35]

Paterson insisted, nevertheless, that the frontier "was not primitive." Even the life of the Blackfoot had not been so. As early as the 1730s, they were using guns and horses, revolutionizing their means of acquiring food and furs and making themselves comparatively wealthy. At last, however, the buffalo herds, their principal source of trade goods, were depleted, victims of a communal system in which resources were owned by everyone and conserved by no one. The Bowlers' Blackfoot neighbors gave Isabel unforgettable lessons in the energy and fragility of cultures. She witnessed the power of their Sun Dance ceremony; she also saw Indian families coming, destitute, to her parents' house for food. She remembered the Indians' "dainty fine-limbed" ponies, "descended from the steeds of the conquistadors"; and she remembered their "vanishing silhouettes against the skyline."[36]

Against that sky, the features of the settlers' society showed up clearly, too. Paterson never idealized the settlers themselves: "they were just average, and it is a moot question how civilized people are at best." To the purveyors of frontier nostalgia, there could be no more offensive word than "average"; but Paterson knew very well that it wasn't just the best people who wound up on the frontier. Civilization, if it meant anything, meant a structure that average people could work with. And it wasn't a mere system of rules. Frontier society offered "the most civilized type of association," if you will, because it had "the absolute minimum of external regulation" and therefore "the maximum of voluntary civility and morality." Reading *Robinson Crusoe* as a child, Paterson was "startled by the indication that Crusoe was alarmed at sight of a footprint in the sand. Our feeling was that he should have been pleased." The people she knew weren't afraid of other people. "[F]or a time" the West was as egalitarian as it was individual; it "was a genuinely classless society." Her experience in this society placed her at a permanent "disadvantage, not knowing how to treat important people with special consideration—and in fact not caring whether they are important or not."[37]

It wasn't that the West was too poor and simple to include representatives of the time-honored social classes. It had plenty of them: "the prairie was lousy with nobility and gentry, and who cared?"

One of Paterson's brothers managed a ranch for Lord Delaval Beresford, a son of the Marquis of Waterford and a man who, she said,

> drank a good deal. And he had a little old dog of nondescript breed which he always took on his travels. Once he was observed distinctly tight, walking and leading his saddle horse, with the little dog on the saddle. He was talking to himself, saying the dog had got tired. No doubt it did. . . . As far as I know he never did any harm and was decent to work for.[38]

To Paterson's way of thinking, Western social equality was a subspecies of American individualism, a way of sizing people up for what they were as individuals and leaving it at that. A practical corollary was a laissez-faire attitude toward other people's business. In the West, if somebody didn't volunteer his name, you didn't ask for it, so as not to "imply that you were measuring hospitality in accordance with the possible 'importance' of the guest—an unthinkable mode of behavior. It was rude to bother anybody or make distinctions except in respect of strictly personal friendships." Really active intolerance, Paterson came to believe, may be natural, in some sense of that word, but it is not spontaneous. It is the product of politics. People are naturally either unconcerned or curious about "seeing a 'different' kind of person," but the imposition of political power has another effect. That is what creates conditions for resentment, hatred, and violence.[39]

Her experience of the West taught her that civilized order need not be formal or legal. When order fails to be imposed from the outside, people "fall back upon" their own "manners and morals." Lack of a rigid social system and an intrusive government provides the best environment for social harmony. The idea of "spontaneous order," which has become a crucial concept for libertarian thinkers, seemed obvious enough to Paterson. She was well acquainted, of course, with the theory that America's chief inheritance from its frontier past is "aggressiveness." "Such nonsense," she replied. "[O]n the frontier you have to be polite to your fellow men, and it won't get you anywhere to be aggressive to a blizzard." What worked out West wasn't aggressiveness but "a peculiarly individual, mind-your-own-business confidence."[40]

To Isabel Bowler, indeed, the West seemed too orderly. She "yearned from the depth of [her] heart to be either a female bandit or a lady faro dealer, or both." She read books about Australia and longed to go there, believing that was where "exciting things happened. We didn't realize that we were living in the Wild West ourself."[41] But the strangeness of the frontier, its simultaneous newness and oldness, made a permanent impression. Recalling the Indians she had known—Crow, Cree, Blood, and Blackfoot—she thought of "a strange sunken world, a real lost Atlantis, which is the element in the American mind that Europeans do not understand."[42] The image of another world, a world lurking just behind the surface of the present, would always be connected in her mind with the idea of America. The image meant freedom—the freedom of a past that had departed but remained real and inviting, the freedom of many possible futures.

In purely physical reality, the West of Paterson's childhood was far from Atlantean. The family had "[h]ard times," very hard times. She could never forget the scars they inflicted. She remembered that she "had to worry about things from the time [she] could notice anything whatever." Visits to the family in her adult years brought back "a lot of painful memories"—not just of poverty, it seems, but of other things as well, things connected with her father's petty tyranny and her unhappy resistance.[43] She had been "a sickly child," and she thought that poverty had left her permanently damaged. She stopped growing, she said, "at the awkward age when some of the bones are grown and some aren't," and she developed "the worst figure and features possible, short of being a hunchback." According to Paterson, her head was square, badly set, and an inch and a half too big; her neck had the wrong shape; her shoulders were narrow and round, but her chest had a ridiculously large expansion; she had "no legs," and when she was standing she leaned crazily forward. None of this was visible to her contemporaries or shows in her pictures—she considered herself a master at disguising herself for the camera—but it showed in her self-consciousness, and she thought it showed in her mirror. Flattery would get you nowhere:

> You know nothing of my troubles, and will say I don't know what I'm talking about. This will really annoy me. . . . I have wept uncounted tears being forced to face the truth, to study it minutely, point by point. I *know*.[44]

Growing up wasn't all hardships, of course. When Isabel was ten years old, as she later claimed, she was "one of the best anglers, with a grasshopper, in the whole Northwest." She kept a pet pig. At some point, she learned how to hop a freight. She sat on a corral fence and watched spontaneous contests of roping and bucking in which there were "no rules or points, except that the rider endeavored to stay on; and spectators were supposed to keep out of the way." She herself became an expert horsewoman. When she revisited Alberta in later years, she put on her riding clothes and headed out to the country.[45]

Paterson was proud to be able to say that she knew how to cook bear meat ("the bear's paws are the best"), fix a log cabin, raise sheep and cattle, make butter ("hundreds of pounds" of it), make jam, make soap, make hay, make her own clothes, make almost anything she needed.[46] Her mother said that Isabel was "the most disagreeable child she ever saw," but she was "dependable when left to do the dishes or any other suitably disagreeable chore." Because she was "a conscientious infant," she was "the one who planted the vegetable garden when there was any."[47] That last phrase sheds some additional light on the Bowler family: they were farm folk, but they did not always have the wherewithal or the organizational impulse even to plant a garden.

Paterson was sixteen years old before she saw an electric light bulb. She left it on all night, imagining that it might kill her if she touched it.[48] Having lived before the machine age completed its predominance in American life, she never felt the haughty sense of entitlement, or the creepy sense of foreboding, that machines now give their masters. She never forgot that whatever a machine does is the result of human thinking, not of some force inherent in the machine itself. To her "early education in the wilderness" she attributed her so-called reactionary politics, which consisted largely of a refusal to believe that risks and fallibilities can ever be planned out of life. Progress, miraculous progress, can be made, but it has to start with the realization that everything must be paid for—"including morality," she said at age forty—and that there is nobody to pay for it but fallible, risk-taking individuals:

> We weren't brought up in a world in which water ran from taps and food came in tin cans, and we know that whatever is done, some one has got to do it.

Having "lived in a shack" gave her an advantage over people who grew up in a better environment. It gave her "good reason to know that such an environment doesn't occur in nature. It has to be earned and invented and made."[49]

When Isabel was about the age of nine, another attempt was made to educate her. It lasted a bit longer this time. Her teacher at the log schoolhouse on Willow Creek was W. Everard Edmonds, who eventually, as she was proud to say, became an important figure in Alberta. Sixty years after Willow Creek, she wrote him to renew the acquaintance and found that he remembered her, too, and had been reading her works.[50] She did well enough in his school to win prizes—Shakespeare plays—but she remained essentially uncooperative. Instead of reading her textbooks, she hid behind a big geography and explored the books she chose herself. She left school at about eleven. All told, she had spent ("lavished, one might say") two and a half years on formal education.[51]

Again, it was informal processes that mattered most to her; reading was obviously more important than schooling. Assured that certain highbrow cultural critics "do at least stimulate an interest in literature," she would reply: "The trouble is that we do not require any external stimulus to literature. We have always been interested in it, to the verge of nosiness and direct action."[52] In childhood, she recalled,

> We read whatever we could get, and our earliest provender included the newspapers, a detective story called "Shadowed to Europe," an even more deplorable tale the name of which we are glad to say we forget—someone else might remember it—the novels of Charlotte M. Braeme, of Dickens, and of Dumas, the Bible, a volume entitled Millennial Dawn, a few of the Pansy Books, the Police Gazette, Shakespeare's "Antony and Cleopatra," the Clairvoyant Revelations of Andrew Jackson Davis, an abridged translation of the Odyssey, and a couple of stories by Ouida. This carried us up to our fifteenth year, when we began to catch up with modern literature in the works of Rudyard Kipling.[53]

Her great wish was to have enough books. When she went visiting with her family, she searched for something to read, then hid herself with it until the visit was over. Not just any book would do. In middle age, she remembered receiving Walter Scott's novel *The Talisman* as a childhood Christmas gift and reported that she was still angry "about being fobbed off with such thin stuff."[54]

The child pestered her elders to answer all the questions that reading can turn up, such as "how astronomers measure the distance to the sun, and what is a preferential tariff, and what became of the Ten Lost Tribes—it didn't seem reasonable that ten whole tribes could be mislaid that way." She found out about Calvinism and rejected it because, given the fine gradations of virtue in the human race, there could be no significant difference between the worst person saved and the best person damned. With the aid of one of the quaint books mentioned above, the supernatural "revelations" of Andrew Jackson Davis, she launched her first investigation of the spiritual importance of the machine age. Davis, a thoroughly American seer, predicted that mechanical invention would create "a kind of material heaven" and "prepare the soul for a natural voyage to post-mundane climes."[55]

The book had belonged to her grandfather, "who took it rather seriously."[56] Isabel probably didn't. But although her ideas about America would never be so doggedly spiritual as Davis's, she was never attracted by the materialist approaches that became fashionable in her own generation. Her way of experiencing the world was essentially intellectual and literary, and she thought that, in general, the world experienced itself in that way, too. She maintained that

> the great body of literature and of information handed down in books actually comprises the world we have lived in, both mentally and physically. Every one who lives in this country lives in books; and that would be true even of an illiterate person. He is living in books he has never read.[57]

She went back to this idea about the importance of books when she tried to explain the "vast disaster" of the modern world. It was implicit, she thought, in "literature, both imaginative and philosophical or historical." Books have consequences. That conviction inspired bitter disputes with her fellow writers, many of whom tried to evade responsibility by arguing that history was shaped, not by ideas, but by material developments, social forces, and the baleful effects of either using the machine or not having the wherewithal to use it. She thought that such writers were denying more than their own responsibility; they were denying human freedom. Despite her vivid memories of childhood hardships, she never claimed that her life was dictated by them. She believed in personal responsibility, including her own. And she stuck to her idea that the West was never *culturally* deprived, frequently protesting against the stereotype of "an uncouth and illiterate frontier": "There never was any place on the frontier, at any time, where culture might not break out."[58]

By "culture" she meant the phony as well as the genuine kind: "Kodiak bears and Arizona gila monsters alike retreated before the advance of the boiled shirt and top hat." In any event, the more one learns about the allegedly uncultured communities of the West, the more cogent her protests appear. Sauk Centre, Minnesota, the home town and principal target of abuse of her friend Sinclair Lewis, witnessed innumerable outbreaks of culture, good, bad, and indifferent—concerts, lectures, recitals, theatrical performances, university extension courses, you name it. Paterson argued, indeed, that "'the West' was never provincial; it had not time to develop the homogeneous character of a regional culture, and drew its population from the world at large." Her childhood source for James Fenimore Cooper's novels of the American frontier was an English neighbor, a "younger son" who had attended university before turning up in the West. She read them all, but she remembered little more about Cooper's vision of the West than the intellectual curiosity of his characters. It confirmed her own impression of the frontier.[59]

Far from being "crudely ignorant," the frontier people whom she knew read "anything they could get." The Bowlers were hardly intellectual, but they were not unlettered: "If one had a book, the others sat around in a circle like—well, we used to say to one another unkindly, like hyenas, waiting to snatch it in an unguarded moment." The family subscribed to a newspaper, a fat weekly edition that arrived at least six days after publication. Isabel volunteered to walk to the post office to get it, so that on the way back she could sit in the grass and read the latest installment of a serialized novel. After dinner, the various sections of the paper—News, Fiction, Poetry, Religion, Sports, and Household Hints—were distributed, and even the people who got stuck with Agriculture were willing to read through it until something else became available. The Miscellaneous section was full of interesting information about gauchos, the Taj Mahal, and peasant fêtes in Brittany. The Children's Corner wasn't nearly as good; in fact, it "was practically a total loss," but Isabel wrote two or three contributions to it on winter nights when she was bored by playing poker.[60]

She did not consider this the beginning of a literary career. When she was nine years old, she heard General Wolfe's famous saying, that he would rather have written Gray's *Elegy* than become the conqueror of Quebec. She was puzzled: what was the point of wishing you had written something? She "had no ambition to become a writer, because [she] didn't know it could be done." She "assumed that a writer was born with the gift fully developed, like red hair or double joints." She would have "walked a mile to see" such a specimen—"and been disappointed, of course."[61]

3

The Unsheltered Life

When she was eighteen, or thereabouts, Isabel Bowler left home to get a job. Her family was poor; she had to support herself. Besides, she had never wanted "a sheltered life."[1] Three decades later, she could report that at "[o]ne time or another," she had "been nearly everything." She had lost count of the number of jobs she had worked.[2]

Her first occupation seems to have been that of a "diningroom girl" in "a small and far from de luxe hotel." The salary was $20 a month; the location may have been Great Falls, Montana. Paterson said that she lived in Great Falls for several months when she was so young that she regarded the place as "practically a metropolis, too large to take in." She navigated its streets in a "cherished and inappropriate hat full-rigged with yards of veiling," while the chinook came down and tried to blow her away, stylish hat and all. She remembered her job, wherever it was, as "such a lot of fun," even though, as she said, it "incapacitated" her "from writing profoundly about the working classes." It taught her so much about the various forms of human life—not all of them pretty to look at, certainly—that she could never pretend to believe in sociological abstractions. In old age, she said with pride that you "can't fool a hotel diningroom girl."[3] It was better than a college.

Her employers had other ideas for her: she must better herself; she must study shorthand and typing. The housekeeper gave her a textbook and got her to take lessons; the manager lent her a typewriter. Isabel had to repay the price of the book (sixty cents) and pay for the lessons (twenty-five cents apiece). The arrangement, she thought, was a real "benefit," because it allowed her to help herself. Prepared to seek her fortune with the aid of stenography, she rode out of town in the caboose of a train carrying passengers and sheep. "Almost [her] first job," she said, was with "a couple of bankers," who appear to have been located in North Dakota.[4] By 1905 she was working in Calgary, the business capital of the newly created province of Alberta.[5] Her life for the next several years would be centered there.

Calgary, a windy little town with wooden sidewalks, was the creature of the Canadian Pacific Railway. It had been laid out by the CPR on a section of land that was owned by the CPR, and it became a city because it became a division point on the CPR. Again, the West was not being built by the unmagnified labor of its pioneers; it was being built by people who could use machines, machines created by capital amassed on a continental scale. Paterson regarded herself as a daughter of "the Rocky Mountain country," used to taking care of herself but also "used to bucking the passes with four mogul locomotives on Number 96 and a rotary snowplow making a blizzard of its own."[6] When she thought of the West, she thought of individual freedom, but she also thought of the CPR—not as an object of worship, to be sure, but as a source of power with which individual lives could gain a new dimension.

Her principal employer in Calgary was R. B. Bennett, attorney for the CPR, whose office was automatically a locus of political power. That power was not unchecked—the system of opposing political parties was fully in play—but it was formidable. An ambitious man could use it to achieve a continental influence, and R. B. Bennett was an ambitious man.[7] A standard-bearer of the Conservatives, he was a member of the territorial legislature from 1898 to 1905 and of the federal parliament from 1911 to 1917 and 1925 to 1939. From 1930 to 1935, he was premier of Canada.

Bennett had qualities to which Paterson could easily adjust, because they were similar to her own. He was hardworking and intelligent; he had the courage to make his own career; he was a determined advocate of his beliefs; and he was moody and complicated, alternating freely between warm generosity and ill-tempered depression. His employees seem to have liked him very well. R. B., as they called him, had a personality, and he recognized that they had personalities, too. To Paterson, he seemed like "a good egg," although, as she remembered, he didn't "smoke, drink, or swear," and "[t]his naturally made him temperamental." Soon after she went to work for him, a young woman named Grace, who was studying law in his office, suddenly asked, "What do you do when he becomes unreasonable?" Isabel replied, "Throw something at him." The next time Grace appeared, she announced that "it worked." When R. B. became premier, Paterson published this incident "as a tip to his Cabinet."[8]

Her job with Bennett taught her a lot about how modern political machinery operated, and how it meshed, or failed to mesh, with modern economic machinery. Her novel *The Shadow Riders* would tell that story, setting it in an environment like that of the Calgary she knew. While learning about politics, however, she was not much influenced by R. B.'s own brand of it. His guiding concept was the imperialism of Cecil Rhodes and Joseph Chamberlain. His friend Lord Beaverbrook remembers the young Bennett talking of the British Empire as "our 'pillar of cloud by day and pillar of fire by night.'" Bennett believed that the empire should become a vast free-trade zone united by tariffs devised to focus its commercial energies inward. Paterson thought that the good thing about the empire was, indeed, its ability to maintain free trade and commercial safety.[9] But the idea of keeping the British dominions British meant nothing to her. Empire, as such, was an interesting historical phenomenon, nothing more.

Bennett's great adventure as premier was his attempt to cure Canada's economic ills by manipulating her tariff policy. Tariffs would be used to connect the Dominion more closely to the Empire, while separating it more firmly from its immediate neighbor and largest trading partner, the United States. This curious scheme was the reductio ad absurdum of Bennett's long-cherished political convictions. In 1932, when he was hosting a great Imperial Conference in Ottawa, Paterson happened to come through town, and he took time out to visit her. She probably seized the chance to tell him what she thought of economic programs like his (she told everybody else), but their disagreements had no effect on their liking for each other. In fact, he took the opportunity to flirt with her.[10]

In 1935, Bennett's final year in office (he had promised that his party would "end unemployment," or "perish in the attempt"), he made a series of national radio addresses in which he blamed capitalism for the Great Depression and even for fascism. He denounced

laissez-faire, attributed improved conditions of economic life to
"the State," and demanded that capitalism be reformed so that government could become its "permanent guide and regulator."[11] His
speeches offered an especially vigorous display of the "progressive" sentiments that many, perhaps most, North Americans were
coming to accept as normal. They were the kind of sentiments that
Paterson attacked when they came from other people. When Bennett
enunciated them, however, she took no public notice. Her only
response to his policies was to stipulate that she was against "pro-
hibitive tariffs." In 1945, long after he had been driven from office
and had gone into voluntary retirement in England, she finally asked
him for a political favor. She had a young friend who wanted to
study at Oxford; could he help her? Amid the immense postwar
demand for entrance to the university, "the idea of giving a cov-
eted space to an American was not popular," but Lord Bennett, as
he then was, "lean[ed] on" the Principal of St. Hilda's College, and
Paterson's friend was admitted.[12] It was probably the last contact
they had; he died in 1947.

During the early days in Calgary, she held a number of jobs
connected in some way with the CPR, including a job with the
Colonization Irrigation Company, a CPR affiliate. This would have
been the outfit for which, as she later said, she spent two years in
the great Western occupation of selling "sections of the boundless
prairie to hopeful settlers." She hoped "it turned out for the best."[13]
Of course, every investment is a risk; there could be no guarantees,
even in the Western land of opportunity. Bennett, it seems, offered
to sponsor her if she wanted to become a lawyer. She declined, and
never regretted it: "[W]e might have become a lawyer, and didn't.
That should be put to our credit." She "just wanted to be allowed to
mooch around quietly on [her] own."[14]

Pictures from this period show Isabel Bowler as a healthy, smiling young woman wearing a mass of dark hair and the voluminous
clothes of the era. She had "a hideous struggle with corsets that
[she] couldn't loll in and collars that choked [her], and hats that
wouldn't stay on and hair that wouldn't stay up." She "was thought
rather fast" for bucking the fashion by wearing low shoes—"anything different was fast!" She was free and she enjoyed her freedom, however mindless the freedom might seem. If she felt like
buying a spring hat, she would get on a train and go down to Min-

neapolis-St. Paul, a two-day journey that seemed like "a mere nothing." When she walked along the platform, the transcontinental train chuffed at her ankles, as if it were inviting her "to climb aboard and go on forever."[15]

Still, she had jobs she enjoyed, and she had friends. Her closest friend in Calgary was a certain Mrs. Booth, a woman five years older, "brilliant" but without "discretion." Isabel, who "was greatly attached" to Mrs. Booth, often had to extricate her from romantic scrapes. Her services sometimes extended to "fish[ing] her out of the river."[16] Grace (later Grace Luckhart) was a particular friend. She had wit; she had conversation;[17] and she had a streak of melancholy darker than Isabel's own. The two women would be fixtures of each other's lives for many years, and Grace would play an important, though for her an unhappy, role in Paterson's *Never Ask the End*. Around Grace and Isabel clustered a group of friends whose faint impressions linger in correspondence: nice young working women who rented a room in someone's house or shared a cottage with someone; and nice young men, ditto. Undoubtedly, they all enjoyed the feeling that they were very fast.

Isabel was happy to find that several of the young men were willing to show her around. One was Napier Smith, "a notable squire of dames, with a deep sympathy for wallflowers." He conceived the idea—based on no evidence, so far as she could tell—that she might have "literary gifts," even while she was devoting most of her thought to more "rational subjects—such as men, dances, and clothes." Yet at some time, as she would briefly and circumspectly recall, she "wrote a lot of short stories for a Calgary weekly." Her contributions have never been located. That would come as a relief to her; she thought that "the less said" about them "the better."[18]

Paterson always retained a sharp sense of the ambiguities of the age in which she was reared, an age that was

at once rigidly respectable and wide open. Novelists scarcely hinted at reality; and with saloons on every corner, it was very bad form and meant being dropped from invitation lists if a young man became intoxicated at a party.[19]

But the peculiar charm of the world before the Great War, as Paterson experienced it, was that "you could do just about what you wanted to, if you didn't go around telling everybody." The

West, in particular, was not yet "Rotarian." Paterson habitually associated freedom with minding one's own business, and she looked back fondly on an era that, she believed, had made the same association. Like it or not, every society had its conventions, and convention deserved a rational, though not a superstitious respect. Yet the prewar conventions could be stretched very far. Paterson laughed at the Victorians' pretensions to respectability, their frequent hypocrisy, and the "great cruelty" that sometimes resulted from the enforcement of their moral codes. But she liked what she regarded as some of their basic assumptions: "There was a recognized right to privacy, personal choice, and individual responsibility. . . . The Victorians drew a rational distinction between sin and crime. Crime is a matter of law, sin is a matter of conscience."[20]

But now comes the anticlimax of Isabel's life, the strange sin against herself by which she almost forfeited her freedom. At Calgary on April 13, 1910, she married one of the young men of the town, Kenneth Birrell Paterson. She had had "vague notions of going on the stage" or marrying a millionaire, but Kenneth Paterson had neither fortune nor romantic occupation. He was a real estate agent; he had been a traveling salesman.[21] The young couple did not have to "stagger" under the "fearful burden" of wedding presents. Then, within a few weeks, Mrs. Paterson was on her way to Spokane, without her husband; the marriage, in effect, was over. By 1918, Kenneth had moved so far out of Isabel's life as to render her incapable of saying where he lived when a lawyer wrote to her seeking information about a Kenneth Paterson who was the legatee of an estate. Naturally, it turned out to be some other Kenneth Paterson.[22]

Not until 1957, however, did she start labeling herself a "widow" on her income tax returns.[23] No one knows whether she had learned of her husband's death, or merely guessed at it. And no one knows why, forty-seven years before, she had married him. She surrounded both her motive and her husband's character with impenetrable secrecy. She once said, perhaps with disparaging intent, that her husband had played the guitar beautifully. This comment represents a significant proportion of the personal information we have of him.[24] Another observation appears in a letter she wrote two decades after her wedding. It relates the story of "the most shocking thing I ever heard"—shocking, that is, for the days when "pro-

priety was still strong" but when "[r]espectable girls . . . knew quite
a lot more than they were supposed to." Two young men called on
two such respectable girls, Isabel and her friend Grace. They talked,
they played the piano, and finally, in an interval of silence, one of
the two young men, who "was lounging on the sofa . . . remarked,
just loud enough to be heard: 'Kiss me, kid, I'm going to sleep
now.'"

> Yes, that was all. Except for the petrified silence which again ensued, you wouldn't
> have known we had heard it. And then we all talked of something else.

The author of that shocking remark was Isabel's future husband.[25]

It seems certain that he was not her first choice. A man who
probably resembles him appears in *Never Ask the End*, where he is
a subject of the poignant reminiscences of Marta, his estranged
wife. She remembers Keith, as he is called, as attractive, weak,
"genuinely amoral, indifferent even to the challenge of virtue or
vanity." She also remembers being in love with another man, a
man she could not have. For reasons that are explicable only in the
most general terms, Marta suddenly consents to marry Keith, then
parts with him. They "had discovered with astonishment that they
were strangers; he could only carry her suitcase to the station."
Paterson may have been thinking about her own marriage when
she said that "[t]he spirit has strange necessities, and failure too is
one of them." In *Never Ask the End*, Marta "suspect[s] that she
married Keith because she knew it wouldn't last. So she would
escape both marriage and the reproach of virginity."[26]

In an earlier novel, *The Magpie's Nest*, Paterson's heroine marries a man she does not love, because she has been rejected by a
man she does love. She too parts with her husband almost immediately. Some years later, he dies in a way that no one bothers to
specify.[27] A much darker sequence of events takes place in Paterson's
last novel, *Joyous Gard*. Here the protagonist is stalked by a husband from whom she separated many years before but whom she
has never divorced.

None of Paterson's friends seems to have pursued these literary
clues. On one of the rare occasions when her husband came up in
conversation, she dismissed the subject with an expressive shrug.
Her writings contain almost no direct references to her marriage.
One of the very few appears in a column in the *New York Herald*

Tribune where she is lightheartedly discussing the theory that men are reluctant to pursue women toward matrimony because they are afraid that their vanity may be hurt by rejection. Then she says, "Why we don't get married ourself is because of a lot of reasons, the recital of which might hurt everybody's vanity, including our own, and besides, it is nobody's business."[28] This must have confused a lot of people who knew that she was Mrs. Paterson. But Mrs. Paterson she remained; her readers were not disposed to ask her why, and she was not disposed to tell them. She continued to be interested in men; her letters regretted her declining ability to attract them; but the details of her marriage did not transpire.

After her death, a telegram and two short, sad letters from Kenneth Birrell Paterson were found among her papers. The telegram was sent from "Pat" in Calgary to Isabel Paterson in Vancouver. The date is April 23; the year is probably 1911.[29] The message is:

> Thank you but am unable to accept,
> Pat

Around this time, Grace wrote to her mentioning the possibility that she might "get Pat out there"—to Vancouver. This may have been the offer that Kenneth was declining. But Grace's letters also refer to Isabel's involvements with other men.[30]

One of Kenneth's letters was sent from Calgary in response to "[y]ours of 6/11." It reports a recent hockey injury and a more serious medical problem, a rupture in the lungs during a fit of coughing. The problem was apparently chronic; the author says he is "patiently awaiting the next installment." Then come the terrible lines:

> As regards my wanting to quit why—that's the only answer. I'm down and out and haven't any ambition to be anything else except extinct.

The writer thanks Isabel for offering to help, but says, "As for doing any thing for me, I'm afraid no one can." He is happy to know that she is "on [her] feet and getting ahead nicely." Yet

> [c]oncerning my people, it does not matter. I know nothing about them whatsoever.
> As for my helping you, of course that's a joke, but if you think I can why let me know. You might right [sic] again and give me the rest of it. In the meantime I shall endeavor to remain in the land of the living.
> Pat.

The return address of the other letter is Lethbridge, Alberta. It was sent on September 17, 1911:

Dear Isabel:—

Would have answered your letter of Sept 6. before, but put off doing so until I had made definite plans for the future. For the past month I have been troubled greatly concerning my health, the lung trouble has returned and has finally become serious. The Doctor has ordered me to the hills & bushes etc, under pain of death etc.

So I am leaving in a day or so. Under the circumstances I can hardly take up the proposition, just at present, that you mention. I appreciate your position, but can do nothing until I have regained some health and have returned to work. Hope you can get along somehow until then. Same address will catch me.
Pat.

Kenneth's illness was probably tuberculosis, a deadly disease but one of notoriously uncertain course and outcome. In the only significant discussion of him in her letters, Paterson remembers that "[t]he only time [she] travelled with [him], he had a touch of pneumonia, coming down from the Crows Nest Pass" (on the border of Alberta and British Columbia). She didn't know what to do, "and he wasn't the kind you could hover over and press your hand on his fevered brow."[31]

The language of Kenneth's surviving communications is that of a man who has lost all vital relationship both to Isabel and to his own life. What she took from the affair was a stronger emphasis on full engagement with life. In her sixties, she advised a young friend to "be patient and keep looking for what you do want." "Most of my numerous mistakes in life I made because of impatience," she said. "Only the old have any patience, which is odd since we have so little time." But she did not itemize her mistakes. Indeed, she was horrified to reflect on the life she would have led if she had always made the right decisions: a really good and sensible life would look "[l]ike a waxworks show, or an absolutely correct 'period room.'"[32]

There is one more piece of literary evidence to be considered here. The heroine of The Magpie's Nest loses track of her husband and neglects to divorce him. She observes that "it's expensive" to procure a divorce from the Canadian Senate; and besides, "I have so many other things to do. . . . You see, my heart has hardened." So, Paterson writes, she "closed her mind and her lips" upon the subject of her husband, "and she saw no reason for rescinding her resolution. . . . She hated women who paraded their woes, anyway."[33]

When she wrote that, Paterson was not exactly parading her woes, since virtually no one in her audience would have understood the connection with herself. But it is interesting to see her deliberating about herself in this way, as if the best means of identifying her intensely private thoughts was the shaping of them for publication. This was the enterprise on which she would spend most of the rest of her life.

Her life as a professional writer began—accidentally, as she insisted—in the aftermath of her marriage. In mid-1910, the new Mrs. Paterson traveled on a "holiday" down to Spokane, Washington. She must have been happy to get out of Calgary. In Spokane, she attended a party where she was introduced to the publisher of the *Inland Herald*, the new paper in town. He offered her a job as his secretary. She had no particular interest in working for a newspaper; at some time in the past, she had been offered a newspaper job and had declined it. But "[t]o avoid argument," she took it.[34] She was on her own again, and she evidently needed the work.

She did not avoid argument for long. As she listened to her new boss's dictation, she could not help showing her aversion to his "mangling" of the English language. When he expressed surprise, referring to the fact that his last secretary had found no fault with him, she informed him that his last secretary must simply have corrected his language without telling him about it. Within two weeks, he became so nervous about the pained expression on Mrs. Paterson's face while he dictated to her that he found "a more tolerant secretary" and gave Paterson a job writing editorials. She objected that she had no interest in politics, but the managing editor thought "that was fine; if she had no convictions she would never embarrass the paper by taking a definite stand."[35] Under these favorable conditions, she decided to write.

The *Inland Herald*'s editorials are unsigned; none can be definitely attributed to Paterson. Two decades later, she told an interviewer that she had written "three columns of editorials a day," which would mean that she wrote all the editorials in the *Inland Herald* (and more, since the paper ran only two columns of editorials a day).[36] Some of these pieces were written much more competently than others, but there is little sign of the sharp, colloquial, aphoristic style that distinguishes Paterson's later work. The subjects are not very distinguishing, either. The editorialist's themes were obviously set by the paper's marketing strategy. He or she abuses the rival paper, extols the potential of the "inland empire," advocates economic and civic progress, and comments on contemporary political issues without display of any divisive ideology.

Paterson remembered one specific piece she wrote, an editorial about an event that took place in Reno, Nevada, on July 4, 1910.[37] The significance of this date, for Paterson, is the evidence it offers about her marriage: in the space of three months, she had married and parted from her husband and had relocated in another country. For the *Inland Herald*, the date had quite another significance. It was the date of the Johnson-Jeffries prizefight, the biggest news the paper ever covered. Jack Johnson, a black man, was opposed by Jim Jeffries, a white; and during the ardently anticipated fight, the "white hope" was decisively defeated. Headlines on July 5 concerned the race riots that followed in cities and towns across the East and South.

On July 6, the *Herald* carried two editorials about the fight, both of which may have been written by Paterson.[38] They compliment Spokane for its good race relations, comparing them favorably to those prevailing in the great cities of the East. The far West is not an uncivilized place, after all. The black soldiers stationed in Spokane "are the most orderly—not colored soldiers only, but of any soldiers—that have ever occupied the fort . . . a splendid example to both white and colored." As for the fight itself, who cares? It "should be viewed as unimportantly as a foot race." There will always be fights for "the empty title of 'champion of the world.'" Sometimes whites will win, and sometimes blacks; it makes no difference. But any "hysterical fool," white or black, who "start[s] to blab loudly of color" and provokes violence should be punished "under the strongest of laws." What the writing lacks in style, it makes up for in its no-nonsense attitude.

The *Inland Herald* existed for only a few months. Paterson may have recognized that it was doomed; she resigned and went to the Coast, where she "inadvertently" got another newspaper job, in the business office of the *Vancouver World*. Soon she was back to writing editorials; the usual writer had died, and it was thought that she would do well enough as a replacement.[39] The *World*, owned and actively managed by Mayor L. D. Taylor,[40] was an organ of the Liberal Party; and it is amusing that a paper so immersed in politics should appoint young Mrs. Paterson as its pythoness. Paterson's style remains undistinguishable, and she would have had to follow the party line in any case, but if she wrote the *World*'s editorials on trade, she was adopting positions for which she would later argue in *The Shadow Riders*, one of her novels of the Canadian West.[41] (The *World* was friendly to the cause of free trade, at least to the extent of reciprocal tariff reduction with the United States.) And if it was she who wrote the *World*'s editorials on women's issues, she regarded the legal inequalities and disabilities of women as "a blot on modern civilization."[42]

Within a short time, the *World* made her a columnist. Her weekly contribution—"Postscripts: Put First Because They Ought To Come Last"—appeared on the first page of the Saturday features section, under the banner headline "What Every Woman Knows." The column—signed with the initials "I.M.P." (Isabel Mary Paterson), an acronym that she would make famous in the pages of the *New York Herald Tribune*—was gaily self-advertised as "An Irresponsible Chronicle" of "People, Books and Events—Gossip of the Passing Hour." That was loose enough to cover anything.

Paterson's first column beats the drum for reciprocity, peace-through-arbitration, and women's suffrage. It assails the idea that women should give up meddling with this world's business and resign themselves to being treated like angels: "Nothing to eat and less to wear, I suppose." Casting her own eye on the world's business, she denounces "second-raters" who think they are entitled to a good living just because they are intellectuals or writers, and makes it clear that she is not laboring under any such delusion about herself.[43]

Little of what this version of I.M.P. has to say is memorable, but there are moments when she starts to show an individual style. One passage suggests that she refused to regard separation from her husband as an insupportable tragedy: "Much innocent pleasure may be derived from reading the ever-recurring articles on 'How to Keep a Husband.' The fact is you couldn't lose the average husband if you tried." Another passage reiterates her disgust with whiners and self-entitlers: "[W]henever any human being, man or woman, is 'misunderstood,' a course in either English or elocution is advisable. . . . After repeated failures to make oneself understood, it is time to be silent."[44]

I.M.P.'s political vision is not so sharply expressed. She agrees with H. G. Wells in lamenting "a humanity bogged in laws and customs, which usually only thwart without directing, and caught in a net of economic conditions which ruthlessly and continually sacrifices one strata [sic] of humanity for another." This is not quite What Every Woman Knows, or what I.M.P. knows either, since she backs it up with nothing more than turgid sentences like the one just quoted. She is much better when she gets down to cases, as when she tells Vancouver's society ladies that they should not expect "gratitude" from their hired girls: "Business contracts should be made on a business basis, wherein gratitude has neither part nor lot."[45]

Alongside I.M.P.'s weekly column, the *World* ran a weekly short story, by-lined "Isabel Paterson." No one would expect a young writer to turn out a story every week and make it any good, and these stories are, for the most part, not any good. In general, they are poorly narrated, thinly characterized accounts of the romantic lives of over-sprightly young people. The only really good story, the only one with which Paterson's imagination is really engaged, is something different—an account of Western individualism called "A Question of Values."[46]

Two cowboys, Jim Lamont and Sandy Douglas, work for a crooked, mean-spirited rancher, Old Man Evans. While Evans is in town, drinking at the American Bar, Jim and Sandy are back home, running out of supplies. So Sandy goes to fetch him. A big snow hits the range. Tending the cattle, Jim discovers the footprints of a man who is lost in the storm. He tracks the man down, puts him on a horse, and takes him thirty-five miles to a hospital. (Yes, the old West was civilized enough to have hospitals.) It is a deed of mercy; but while Jim is accomplishing it, the herd wanders off, and Jim and Sandy have to find it, round it up, and bring it back. Their enraged employer, who cares nothing about Jim's reason for leaving the ranch, lets him and Sandy do all the work, and it is terrible work—but not so terrible as to preclude a second deed of mercy. Hungry and desperately cold, the two friends see a ten-point buck within easy shooting range. Sandy aims, then drops his gun: "We don't want him," he says. The buck is too beautiful to shoot.

That is the second deed of mercy. The third occurs when they have managed to work the herd back to the ranch. Evans, an incompetent horseman, is thrown by his mount and is about to be dragged to his death when Jim, who has borne the brunt of Evans' rage for his act of generosity to the man lost in the snow, succeeds in rescuing him, too. When Jim realizes what he has done, "his expression [is] tinged with sadness." Certainly: he acted out of duty, not out of love. At any rate, his sense of duty was his own; it did not result from any pressure from other people. Evans is the one who is swayed by others. Seeing everybody standing around expecting him to present Jim with some kind of reward, he forks over the munificent sum of twenty dollars. Jim looks at it, asks for change, and returns all but ten cents to the reluctant giver: "'All it was worth I assure you,' he said pleasantly." Then he and Sandy mount their horses and ride "into the white dusk." The effect is exactly right. Against the enormous Western sky, the essential human drama has been played out, as pure as a parable—the drama of individual choice and values.

Paterson's columns and stories ran for only eight weeks. There is no indication of why they ended. We do know that at some point, and for some reason, she decided that she preferred the rival paper, the *Province*.[47] She walked over to its office and "wander[ed] around opening doors" until she found the owner and publisher hiding in his untitled, unnumbered "den." She asked him for a job and was told that if there was one, he'd let her know. But she was not to be brushed off.

> At the end of a week we meandered back, and said brightly that we had come to work as he told us to.
>   . . . He gazed at us in gloomy silence for about three minutes and then said: "Umph: all right."[48]

The managing editor, Roy Brown, didn't have a job for Paterson and could hardly bear to speak to her. Eventually he concluded that she "didn't do any actual harm, and in an emergency . . . could always be put to writing editorials." Again, she protested that she "didn't know enough" to write such things, but the owner just gave her "a startled look, as if he had heard a funny noise."[49]

She now found that she enjoyed newspaper work after all. "Nowhere else in the world," she thought, "do men and women work together with such brusque friendliness, so little consciousness of sex." She considered the *Province* her "literary nursery," and she cherished a warm affection for Brown.

No matter what else may change, we cling to the thought of Roy Brown sitting there like Buddha in that particular newspaper office forever, while dynasties pass and kingdoms fall and the Pyramids crumble to dust.[50]

A newspaper office didn't offer much "companionship," however; it was simply a "workshop" for people who "like their work." Her friends in Alberta remained important. She wrote to them frequently and maintained a lively interest in their doings. There was always something of the voyeur and spectacle-lover in Paterson. She was very fond of gossip, and she frequently complained, "[l]ike old James Forsyte," that "nobody ever tells me anything." In her cheerful moods, she thought of human life as "a good show . . . if you have a good seat." Sometimes a good show could make her cheerful, whatever seat she had. During the anxiety of the Great Depression, the acts and sufferings of financial potentates often had her "rolling on the floor, holding [her] sides, and yelling with laughter. . . . You know, the show is almost worth the money." At all times she regarded America, seen from either side of the Medicine Line, as an amazing "spectacle."[51]

A good seat need not be a prominent one. After abandoning her desire to become an actress, she discovered no desire to make a spectacle of *herself.*

What we'd most like is to be something like the First, Second or Third Citizen in the big play. To get in on things without having to make any of the orations. To be independent and active and have some sort of invisible passport that would admit us wherever we had a notion to go.[52]

Her work in Vancouver fulfilled part of that wish. Both the *World* and the *Province*, it seems, employed her as "a proud dramatic critic."[53] Her contributions (again) cannot be distinguished by style or subject, but it is certain that the critic had something to see. In that great age of entertainment, even remote Vancouver was constantly visited by classic plays, melodramas, vaudeville performances, and motion pictures. As Paterson maintained, culture (however you want to define that term) was always breaking out in the West.

Reading back issues of the *Province* and the *World*, one sees how accurately those papers were named. Vancouver had its own brash provincial atmosphere, full of brag and boosterism. The city's progress was an ideal and a certainty; and the machinery of progress—telegraphs and steamships and the great CPR—gave the city a remarkable intimacy with the wider world. The Vancouver papers of Paterson's day treat political events at Whitehall and theatrical events on Broadway as if all of them took place in downtown Vancouver. And whatever happened (on Broadway, at least) was easily exportable to Vancouver, where the proud critic could inspect both the best and the worst that the North American stage had to offer.

Paterson also got the chance to see life as a reporter—often, apparently, on human-interest stories, some of which were of genuine human interest.

> We once interviewed a lifeguard, who rescued hundreds of simpletons from the tiderip at the Narrows in Vancouver Harbor. Being very young and innocent in those days, we said artlessly that the folks he fished out of the briny deep must be profoundly grateful. He said, not at all. They had been warned not to go there in the first place; and when dragged ashore they were usually indignant because he didn't rescue the canoe cushions, too. We then asked him, didn't he get tired of saving people's lives? He said, "yes ma'am, it gets very monopolous, very monopolous."[54]

She would remember that story when it came time to talk about the monopolous workings of the welfare state.

During her working life in the Northwest, Paterson got used to catching late-night lifts from passing trucks, riding in the cabooses of trains and on the handlebars of motorcycles, traversing the backwoods with a rifle-toting escort (watch for the mountain lions), and being "tossed across six feet of water into the freight hatch of a ship by eager bystanders after the gang-plank was pulled up." Fun. But what she liked most of all was her talks with old timers who recalled the drunken, dancing excess of the Northwest's early days, days when people's confidence in life had not been "based on the local banker or the number of churches in town." Here was Atlantis, recalled once more; and here were people who were tough enough to make individual choices of values:

> [T]hey had one pocket lined with buckskin because they preferred gold money to paper—five-dollar gold pieces that they occasionally paid out absently in change as quarters, and double eagles, which were better, because you could tell them by the weight without looking. They'd give a guest turtle soup, but they really preferred pork and beans personally—suit yourself. Well, they're gone. . . .[55]

And she herself would soon be gone. In 1912 she left the Northwest and moved to New York City. She later said that she decided to "devote [herself] seriously to literature," so she "ventured East," but that may have been a joke about her lack of literary success after she arrived there. The best guess is that she wanted more challenging work, perhaps a more challenging environment. The leading character in *The Magpie's Nest* explains that she decided to leave Seattle, where she was very comfortable, and go to New York because she didn't want to keep "doing the little easy things that were nearest. I came on instinct."[56] So Paterson, who would always love the Pacific Northwest more than anywhere else, came East.

4

Authorship and Exile

In late 1912, she was working for the *New York World*, probably as a reporter. One of her few specific comments about this period was that when she "first came to New York" she was sent to interview Howard Chandler Christy (an artist, famous for his illustrations of women) "to ask him the names of the prettiest women he'd ever seen."[1] She did not say whether he divulged the names.

After her job on the *World*, she became a reporter for the *New York American*, a Hearst paper.[2] It is said, on her authority, that "[s]he wrote for the feature page, interviewing people on miscellaneous subjects, etc."—not a very good job. After that (at least from August 1914 until September 1915), she was a member of the editorial staff of *Hearst's Magazine*.[3] She thought that Hearst spent money "insanely," but "he paid good salaries." The magazine job, however, was soon succeeded by an editing job for the Fox Film News Reel. On that occasion, she "lost [her] temper" over something, and never "recovered it entirely." One assumes that was the end of the job.[4]

Her memories of her first years in New York included "moving from one neighborhood to another and usually from bad to worse: El trains and ambulances roaring past [the] windows, boarding-house basement dining-rooms and flats up five flights of stairs."[5] In these circumstances, she developed a strong partiality for New York cops, especially those who gave her their arm and helped her cross the avenues. Her first friends in New York were the women who worked at the Public Library on 42nd Street and were "unofficially kind" to her. She immediately started carrying "the contents of the circulation department" home with her.[6]

The major event of her life in the East was her record-breaking airplane flight. She had seen airplanes out West, and the first time she saw one, she decided to take a ride. She didn't regard the appearance of a lighter-than-air machine as exceptional: "[I]t was a case of why not? Go right ahead. I guess you can fly, if you want to." But that day, she was the only person who wanted to exercise that freedom—and the airplane, very unfortunately, wrecked itself on a fence before it could become airborne. After November 5, 1912, when she finally realized her ambition to fly, people wrote to her and begged her not to do it again; if she kept at it, she would surely be killed. But flying was wonderful fun, particularly when "you sat on a six-inch strip of matchboard and held onto a wire strut, and looked down past your toes at nothing but the earth half a mile away."[7]

The fun was in inverse relationship to the size of the plane. In 1936, Paterson appears to have suffered some nervousness when she was flown over New York in a much larger plane with other literary folk who agreed to participate in a publicity stunt for the Lippincott publishing firm. When she flew to Los Angeles in 1948, the thrill was gone; she was too far up to see anything, and "those durned winged hippopotamuses aren't safe"—unlike primitive biplanes, presumably. Her flight in 1912 was important to her because it was so clearly an individual enterprise, yet also the kind of enterprise that symbolized something of general importance to the American experience. It was a symbol waiting for a book to explain it. Thirty years later, while discussing the origin of the theory of history that she presented in *The God of the Machine*, she mentioned her migration in a covered wagon and her first ascent in an airplane, and she remarked: "[A]ll I can say is—I was there, I saw it happen."[8]

Her literary project in her early days in New York was to explain her experience by putting it in novelistic form. She had taken a long time to get started on a career as novelist. Her seventh novel, *The Golden Vanity*, describes a woman like herself: "Geraldine was unable to account for her persistent impulse to write. She had gone about it unobtrusively, with no special hopes; and she used to wonder what a writer was like, never having seen one." Paterson's work as a novelist began in Calgary, with Napier Smith's mere speculation about her lurking literary talent. A lady (probably the "fast"

Mrs. Booth) also tried to bring out her latent authorial powers. She demanded that Isabel give her a chapter a week. So, "to please a dear friend," she complied. The results, she found, were "simply awful."[9]

The subject of that awful novel, or perhaps of a somewhat later awful novel, was her "family history." It was a "pioneer novel" that included an account of the Bowlers' eight-hundred-mile trek by prairie schooner. This would be of some interest; but Paterson was distracted by her personal knowledge of the people she was writing about, and she failed to achieve perspective. She was also troubled by a feeling that she was violating their privacy, a feeling that "it would be more decent to let them alone." So the novel remained "dim, not significant."[10] It was about individual experience, but it failed to grasp its reality.

In addition, her early writing was plagued by problems of plot and action. These problems would annoy her to the end. It was the vitality of individual character that attracted her; but because she was much more interested in character than in plot, she regarded her characters as congenitally in need of prodding into "some sort of ambition":

> It won't do to accept excuses from them about the wrong environment and all that sort of stuff. We know how characters are. They're just like us. They hate to do anything. They want to sit around and talk forever. When we first tried to write novels the conversational propensities of our characters nearly defeated us. They wouldn't, they would NOT even get up and walk into the next room. We had to mentally put tacks in their chairs—but we did finally make them stir themselves.[11]

When Paterson at last tried to publish a novel—her pioneer novel, or some other—it achieved "only one reader besides myself, a publisher's reader." He rejected it, observing primly that "[t]his is not the kind of novel we expect from the Canadian west." This meant that it lacked the requisite number of mounties and sled dogs. The prevailing idea among publishers was that western Canadians could not be described as they were—as people "with vaudeville and movies and magazines." In Paterson's view, Canadian literature was already far too well supplied with romantic props devised chiefly by non-Canadians. But she didn't complain: "Not enough first novels are rejected."[12] The novel failed to meet her own standards, and she did not allow it to survive.

These early failures were instructive. When she looked at her first effort, the one that she pronounced "simply awful," she

> could see that it lacked everything a novel should have. This roused our curiosity. We began pondering, what should a novel be like? We got to brooding over it. . . . We've never had a carefree moment since we began learning to write.

Out of her brooding evolved a set of guiding literary ideas. One of her first principles was the importance of organic relationships between the parts of a literary work and the whole. Her family-history novel lacked such relationships. In future, she would cite it as a warning to an aspiring writer whose work had similar defects:

> [Y]ou know the necessity of every sentence and word having an edge and a relevance to the other parts, in poetry; but maybe you don't realize, simply for that reason, that prose is the same. You think a *general effect* will emerge, out of a general purpose. It will not. The parts make up the whole.[13]

Paterson agreed with the literary modernists of her generation that fiction should meet the technical demands of poetry. Like them, she believed in the power of direct personal experience, while lamenting its inability to discipline its own expression: witness her loss of perspective in writing about her family. Experience was one thing; technique was another: the problem was to forge a unity between them.

Her desire, as she often said, in varying ways, was to communicate her experience of the world she had seen. She thought that

> Joseph Conrad expressed on behalf of all novelists the whole purpose of fiction, perhaps of literature: "It is to make you see, to make you feel."

There was a world to be seen and felt, but it stubbornly resisted capture and subjection to literary form. This was a subject of chronic complaint:

> I have been struggling desperately and despondently with my own book. Months over a single chapter. . . . How would you describe a hill with willow bushes here and there on it? You know what I mean! That one particular hill, and the rounded knolls of the top, not a conical top, but uneven; and the grass underfoot. Grass is immensely complicated itself. It is full of little plants and flowers you don't know the name of, and it all laces together and really does clothe the earth—we could not love the earth if there were no grass. Grass is the most wonderful thing in the world. You can feel it through your shoes, a vital medium; raw earth is not alive of itself. But under grass it is alive. But there are some people walking on a grassy hill, and that's all I can get

down.—The hill is not any hill, it is a place you'd have to see to believe it could *be* a grassy hill at all, but that's just the point, it is. Well—dammitall— [14]

Life in its intricacy and vigor; life in its energy, subtle though strong; life as she knew it: that was what she needed to express; but this romantic impulse was perpetually at odds with the cool craftiness of modern fiction, in which she also believed.

Paterson the professional journalist knew that there was all the difference in the world between reporting and imaginative writing. A real novelist was not a reporter but an evoker, trying somehow to communicate such fundamental but enigmatic realities as the relations of "color, tone, and accent" between people and their settings. The novelist's aim was to find the true inwardness of individual feeling and choice, to insist on "values beyond the material things of life." This was especially true, Paterson thought, of the novelist of America, a country that "has never been anything but romantic."[15] The romance was there even in the works of such satirists and ostensible realists as Sinclair Lewis. He might be mistaken for a journalist, but he was actually an evoker of essential relations, relations that reveal the soul. His characters, Paterson said,

> are story-and-a-half false fronts like the buildings along Main Street; their minds are narrowed down to the limits of a prairie village; and at moments the beauty of the untouched prairie is glimpsed wistfully in their eyes.

After she had become a successful novelist, Paterson acknowledged that one might, indeed, begin as a journalist and after years of heartbreak arrive at art. But don't bet on it: "Jordan is a hard road to travel, and reporting is rather a side track than a step on the way."[16]

In early 1915, Isabel Paterson, journalist, was haunting the offices of the John Lane Company, publishers of novels. Emma Pope, who worked for Lane, served tea on her desk when people dropped in. Paterson took advantage both of the tea and of the chance to borrow books: "We got a good deal of our education, such as it is, off the Lane shelves." To the Lane Company she submitted the manuscript of what she sometimes called her "first novel."[17]

In fact, she was trying to market two novels: *The Magpie's Nest* and *The Shadow Riders*. *The Magpie's Nest*, the first to be completed and submitted, was going the rounds of publishers by September 1914. By December, it had reached the desk of Sinclair Lewis himself—not yet the famous author of *Main Street* and *Babbitt*, still only a reader for the George H. Doran Company. In Paterson's words, he was a "red-headed young man who lit up George Doran's office like a torch." He rejected her novel, saying that she had "a tremendously complicated character and series of situations" but did not yet have the experience "to put it across." He added, "you certainly have the stuff in you," and encouraged her to send other things.[18]

He had rejected the novel so courteously and enthusiastically that she continued to like him and maintain that he had "charm," which few other people suspected. Conscious that he was universally regarded as remarkably ugly, she declared that he was "very handsome. . . . Yop, handsome! We said it and will stand to it. Good looking, debonair." She liked him even after his drunkenness and obsessions had made most of his other acquaintances heartily sick of him, and after she herself had come to regard him as a "pathetic wreck." When she was in a bad mood with America, she argued that Lewis was a scapegoat, "blasted for the sins of the people"; he was "a human receiving station for all the cross-currents and confusions and absurdities of a most distressful country. It isn't that nothing escapes him so much as that he escapes nothing." He was distressful like America itself, but inside him she detected, as she did in America, "a kind of sweetness, gentleness, gayety and goodwill . . . that persists in spite of the frightful ordeal to which he is subjected."[19]

In June 1915, Putnam's added itself to the list of publishers rejecting *The Magpie's Nest* and expressing interest in her future work. She tore the letter to pieces—then saved the pieces. But the Lane Company had become interested in her second novel, *The Shadow Riders*; and in 1916, they published it. They must have regarded it as a success; in 1917, they published *The Magpie's Nest* as well.[20]

This first novel, *The Magpie's Nest*, opens by describing a girl reading and daydreaming among "the million hills which undulate away from the dark flanks of the Northern Rockies."[21] The girl, Hope Fielding, looks at the mountains and decides that some day she will go "beyond them" (12). She is free-spirited and ingenuous; she is also callow and undirected, always "reaching for something elusive" (274). She seeks "that indefinable goal, the heart of life itself"—not a bad description of Paterson's own goal in writing this book (71). Hope has another quality that Paterson identified with herself: a respect for "reality, however hard one found it" (60). The plot allows for the convergence of romanticism with realism. Hope leaves her parents' ranch in the foothills of the Rockies and finds jobs in the new prairie towns. She works successively as a hotel maid, a schoolteacher, and a commercial artist. In the free though philistine atmosphere of a town that must be Calgary, she encounters a number of men who might be part of that "something elusive": a handsome young chauffeur (Hope likes to ride fast); his employer, a wealthy American businessman, who visits Alberta to invest in land and utilities; and the young scion of a respectable eastern Canadian family who is trying to make his fortune in the West.

This last gentleman falls in love with her, and she with him. They become engaged; then misunderstandings and mistrusts arise, largely because of her independent spirit. He abruptly breaks the engagement. Distressed, she goes for an automobile ride with the wealthy American, Conroy Edgerton. He is a generation older, and unhappily married. It is a classic scene of headlong Western mobility: the young woman who wants to go somewhere, the machine that is both the symbol and the means of going, the man with money. . . . Hope accepts Edgerton's offer to run away with him. "Now, show me how fast you can drive— No, let me!" she shouts (151).

Modern machinery gives Hope the ability to go where she wants; it also gives her the ability to change her plans almost immediately. She and Edgerton leave town on separate trains, but before they can meet, a friend intercepts her and convinces her that the affair is wildly unrealistic. Yet "[t]he thought that obsessed her was that if she failed to do something, and that quickly, some spring of life in her would fail" (159). She is in a desperate, half-suicidal mood when an accident of train schedules throws another man across her path, a weakly handsome young person with the apt name of Ned Angell. Ned responds to her distress by proposing to her. She consents. They are married—then immediately find themselves impossibly ill matched.

Even Ned, who is not the brightest man in the world, feels that he has "done an unforgivable thing" in marrying Hope, although he feels that the ultimate responsibility is not his own, that the universe must be wrong for allowing "any poor weak mortal [to] be able to do just such a thing" (171). So Hope must take the responsibility of leaving him.

> He knew she was going forever. She did not tell him; it was not needed. They could see each other with terrible distinctness. They could not reach each other. He went to the station with her, for what reason they did not quite know; perhaps because it did not seem to matter. At the last moment they clasped hands quickly and fell apart again, looking at each other with a kind of desperation, a silent confession of inability to grapple with the problem each presented to the other. She did not look out of the window as the train drew out. (175)

In some such way, Kenneth Birrell Paterson must have receded from Isabel Paterson's life.

Most novelists of the period would make Hope's flight from marriage the last of her wrong turns; the next scene would disclose her vehicle lying wrecked at the bottom of some convenient hill. But for Paterson, this is only the middle of the journey. Hope migrates to Seattle and then to New York, abjuring love but continuing to seek adventure. She finds both things in Norris ("Nick") Carter, a man of her own age who has good family connections but still needs to work for a living. More to the point, he shares Hope's persistent ingenuousness and good humor. His business, appropriately, is selling high-performance engines: "He liked machinery; he liked anything that would go" (238). The campaign to win Hope's heart is his great adventure at going somewhere. He succeeds.

And here, again, the novel ought to end. The promise of the first chapter is fulfilled: Hope has gone beyond the mountains and has found a reality that exactly suits her romantic dreams. Even poor Ned cooperates; he obligingly dies, saving her the trouble of obtaining a divorce. But that's not the end. The story continues for another forty pages. This part of the plot is worthy of Thomas Hardy at his most preposterously coincidental. Nick suddenly vanishes without a trace, leaving Hope alone and penniless in the great city of New York. He has been injured in (what else?) an automobile accident; and by the time he comes to, she also has vanished without a trace. Never were lovers so perplexed!

The interesting thing is what Hope does in her perplexity. She does not wither away, move back home, or try her luck with a rich

Australian. She gets a job. Specifically, she gets the same job she had when she first left home: she becomes a hotel maid. Looking at her maid's cap, she says, "This is the badge of civilisation, which means servitude" (267). But the Rousseau mood can't last. It is replaced by a Lockean optimism about private property and what libertarian ethicists call "the self-ownership principle." For Hope, even humble work means independence. It's "[e]xpensive, but I like to own myself," she says, in a fine aphorism, expressive of everything that Paterson thought and felt (274). At the end of the novel, a few sentences before Nick finds her and all is well indeed, Hope still possesses both her realism and her romantic spirit:

> She . . . flung out her arms in a gesture of gladness. She would . . . go on with her life, still follow the unknown as her father had. Find Nick, if she could. But if that might never be, she saw her life enriched through him still.[22]

The external complications turn out to be a test, however silly, of what Hope has inside her. She passes the inner test; then she achieves the external reward. The title of the book is derived from a French saying that happiness is found in the magpie's nest; that is, permanently "out of reach" (100). The saying turns out not to be true.

This is a good novel, though far from perfect. The final plot devices are outrageously forced, but the rest of the story responds believably to the characters' motives and options. A repetition of moods and symbols, which is often conducted more subtly than I have indicated, gives the novel depth and roundedness. The qualities that most strongly suggest Paterson's later writing are a sense of humor and, especially, an individualist point of view.

Hope Fielding doesn't rebel against society, but she doesn't let it interfere with her any more than she has to, either. The accepted code of sexual conduct is barely an issue in her decision about whether to elope with Edgerton. What concerns her is whether she is suited to him and whether he will eventually be harmed by his liaison with her. When she determines that he probably will be harmed, she decides to give it up, but not without protest. "Nobody plays a lone hand," her best friend tells her. "You mean," Hope replies, "that someone is always looking over your shoulder and telling you how to play. But you pay your own losses" (158). Hope's thoughts about the difficulty of dissolving her marriage dwell on "the essential brutality of the rigid system that tried to compel all unhappy creatures in like bonds to her own to look only to death for help." This is not a demand to get rid of morals; people in *The Magpie's Nest* are always worrying about whether they *should* do this or that. It is a demand for life, and a lecture about the "strange masks" of social rules by which "morality has been miscalled and defamed" (296-97).

Hope's first fiancé is "harassed by the knowledge that both Edgerton and Hope [are] greater individualists than he." He would have felt better "in the days when there were just two kinds of women," and he wouldn't have had to try to understand women like Hope (116). She takes the opposite view: "People in a crowd aren't interesting" (99). The political relevance of these sentiments comes out in a debate between Hope and an intelligent friend who presents the classical conservative view that people "are not gods," knowing good and evil, although the modern age demands that individuals act as if they were. "I can't think of a time in human history," the friend exclaims, "when every man and woman has been so carelessly entrusted with the charge of his own soul!" Hope responds with the classical individualist argument: "Why should I be more alarmed at having charge of my own soul than at giving it in charge of someone else?" (297).

This is about all that *The Magpie's Nest* has to say about political issues, besides an unsurprised disclosure that it is likely to be "expensive" to get a provincial legislature to grant you a business franchise (106). As for the businessmen themselves: it is interesting, in view of all that Paterson would later have to say about capitalism and the machine age, that Hope should harbor the following thoughts about Edgerton, the capitalist:

> He might set in motion the machines of industry, which would crush a thousand like her, and have no compassion. That was the other side of him. (34)

The image of machines smashing into anonymous multitudes is a cliché of socialist and "progressive" literature; it would be at home in Upton Sinclair's and Frank Norris's novels, and many pages of Theodore Dreiser's. But that is not the side of capitalism that Hope, or any of the other characters in *The Magpie's Nest*, actually sees. What they see is the economic system that created the machines that created their world, the suddenly modern West that they inhabit; they also see a system that enables people to travel far beyond that world. As for Edgerton, the embodiment of capitalism, Paterson's story shows that he and Hope, the working girl, are a lot alike—bright, adventurous, conscientious in keeping to their own ways, more than a little eccentric. Edgerton does not share Hope's intellectual interests; he reads only the newspapers. To the later Paterson, that would seem a large defect in businessmen. For now, however, she is content to observe that capitalists typically have "intelligence" even if they don't have "intellect" (34, 13-14).

And capitalists do have a way of stealing the show. Paterson was so interested in the Edgerton type that she made him the motive force of her next novel, *The Shadow Riders*.[23] Here he becomes a bigger and deeper character, Ross Whittemore, a wealthy eastern Canadian who is both a major investor in the West and a major figure in Liberal Party politics. This man has intellect: he is cultured, refined, humane; he even suffers from guilt over a secret incident of his youth, the suicide of a woman with whom he refused to elope, despite the fact that she was pregnant with his child. How often people in Paterson's novels are minded to run away from conventional society! What is likely to happen if they do is another matter; there is a moral risk on each side.

Whittemore, who did not take the risk of running, now lives without expectations. His only emotional concern is his nephew Chan, to whom he gives a start in life by sending him to Calgary as his business agent. There Chan meets the novel's Patersonesque center of consciousness, Lesley Johns, a young woman who grew up on a ranch, worked in a lawyer's office and the business office of a newspaper, and now writes a weekly column for the paper. Paterson provides enough romantic and financial difficulties to keep Lesley's story moving along, but it is easily summarized: Lesley and Chan fall in love, and eventually they admit it to each other.

The real story is Whittemore's. On a visit to Calgary, he accidentally witnesses a ghastly scene in which a young woman tries to kill her faithless lover. Several years later, he encounters her working as a nurse in Montreal, where she has escaped to bear her child. Determined to make her happy and restore his own connection with life, he proposes marriage—a platonic marriage, since he is sure she does not love him. He accepts his party's gift of the lieutenant governorship of Alberta, so that she can return to the province and humble the local society that exiled her. This proves easy enough to do, but the story only completes itself when Whittemore finally recognizes a fact that had failed to penetrate his intense self-consciousness: his wife actually loves him. The moral of this relationship is the same as the moral of Lesley and Chan's; they have all been "shadow riders," horsemen who keep their eyes on their own shadows instead of the "real things" of the road ahead (78-79).

The real things in this novel are political as well as romantic. Paterson skillfully describes Canadian party politics in the period leading up to the Liberal Party's defeat in the national election of 1911, when Sir Wilfrid Laurier—briefly but effectively introduced as a character in the novel—was turned out of office. This is not a partisan novel; Paterson's political connection, after all, was with the Conservative side. Party politics is portrayed largely as a game, although Whittemore is said to be a Liberal because "he could never have resisted the word itself": the word means freedom (21). The novel's main political conflict is not between Liberals and Conservatives; it is between government and business. "Progressive" thought in both the United States and Canada regarded that conflict as the really basic one, and Paterson seems to share that view: government tries to regulate business, and business tries to have its way with government, often by corrupt means. But the novel is far from treating the problem in a "progressive" way. It does not portray all big businessmen as robber barons, nor does it endorse the progressive ideals of "good government" and state ownership of basic industries.

Paterson's hero, Whittemore, would be a robber baron in anyone else's novel. He is seeking a streetcar franchise from the aldermen of Calgary; if necessary, he will use bribery to get it. Bribery is invited by the local politicians, but Whittemore decides, at last, not to go through with it, partly because he doesn't want to implicate his nephew and more because he doesn't want the action to be used as a campaign issue (169-70). Paterson is not willing to stack the deck. Whittemore is a good man, but he has his flaws, although they are nothing so simple as the tragic flaw of greed. He is not after "the money" but "the creative power, the building of that car line" (145-46).

Corrupt means, to useful ends; and Paterson further complicates the situation by implicating her alter ego, Lesley, in Whittemore's schemes. Lesley invests her little store of money in land that she expects to be made valuable by the streetcar deal, and she uses her influence to keep evidence of the bribery plot from being lodged against Chan in a parliamentary campaign. She knows how "business is." Still, she wonders about "her own responsibility" (133). "Evidently nothing could be done straight anyway; there was an ineradicable kink in human nature to prevent that" (175). And yet: "It's stupid; men trying to build with one hand while they destroy with the other. I suppose they all begin almost imperceptibly, too, and think they can be great men after they get through being little ones" (154). Paterson is not impressed by the simplistic solutions of the progressive good-government crowd, but she remains disturbed by her own moral questions.

The mature Paterson would answer them by arguing that political problems such as the ones in this novel are created by the state's illicit interference with creative power. "Government and business," she wrote in 1933, "can be entwined only in the same way as Laocoon and the python, or whichever breed of snake it was. It doesn't do either of them any good."[24] There would be no occasion for bribery if the state, in its progressiveness, did not attempt to manage business. At present, however, she lacks the analysis that could take her to that solution.

Lesley herself is an advocate of certain progressive or "Radical" views. She regrets the loss of the "democracy" she knew in the frontier youth of the province, a "pure democracy in our social relations." Henry George, the self-taught American economist, had popularized ideas about equal access to land; Mayor Taylor, owner of the *Vancouver World*, had associated himself with those ideas;[25] now Lesley flirts with them, connecting them with a past in which, supposedly, "[e]very one had an equal chance." As for the British Empire, which seemed superbly modern to some political thinkers, she believes that Canada should "get out" of it: "I think we are just a hundred years behind the times in clinging to a word like Empire." When Chan argues that "[w]e have all our liberties," she reminds him that women don't: "Spoils and place and privilege— for money over men—party over principle—men over women. It suffocates me" (85-87, 90).

Paterson's views are developed further in a conversation between Whittemore and his wealthy Liberal friends. They are Eastern financial magnates with Imperial positions; they symbolize the union of economic and political power. In this context, Paterson refers to "the marauding millionaire of the twentieth century, successor to robber barons and pirate vikings of a ruder age." Against these gentlemen, Whittemore argues for truly liberal ideas. Canada, he insists, is denying herself a real life by using political power to isolate herself from economic competition. "Have we got an idea, a real, whole, Canadian idea, to bless ourselves with?" Lesley had asked (85). Whittemore points out that Canada does have one idea, a bad one: the idea of "an enormously high tariff" to sustain Canadian industries against rivalry from the United States (206).

This tariff is currently enriching the very men he's talking to. Nevertheless, he pursues his argument. The problem, he holds, is that "[o]ur [Canadian] manufacturers haven't the enterprise to make as good articles."

> You can get the same raw material if you let down the bars; and as for labour cost, if it is any higher here, why should our young people of Ontario and Quebec go across to work in the New England factories at the shameful wages they get there? (203)

Whittemore tells his friends, the grandees of the Liberal Party, that Canada's current policies are nothing but "hidebound Toryism." It is a conservative folly to try to protect the status quo. Real liberalism demands a dynamic society: "We *need* competition; competition in brains" (206, 203). Another thing that Canada needs is better politicians, and "a Bright and a Cobden," too. John Bright and Richard Cobden were nineteenth-century prophets of laissez-faire economics. "Not much to ask," Whittemore says; laissez-faire is merely common sense (204).

There is passion in these arguments for competitive capitalism, as there is in Lesley's arguments for equality of opportunity. Through reading and reflection, and observation of politics as she knew it, Paterson had completed one of the circuits of thought that would make her distinctive among her contemporaries. She had connected the past with the future, the individualism of a frontier society with the necessities of industrial progress, and she had identified some favorite modern notions as "just a hundred years behind." She found that modern liberals had mistaken, indeed inverted, liberalism's best ideas, preferring control to competition, empire to liberty. She went past the satires of laissez-faire as an outmoded and "Dickensian" philosophy and allied it with the aspirations of adventurous young men and women—particularly women.

This was the omen of something new. Sadly, however, publication of *The Shadow Riders* was greeted by an "extraordinary absence of public parades, banners, brass bands and international reverberations." Paterson's first two novels did receive favorable reviews in good publications, although *The Magpie's Nest* was accused by the *New York Times* of "hold[ing] the reader's interest in spite of its reprehensible characters and very unpleasant situations. Among the former, the word 'Duty' appears to be obsolete; while the latter go far toward indicating that the age-old ideals of feminine conduct are fast crumbling to dust." The protagonist's conduct is troubling; the author's advanced attitude toward marriage and divorce, depressing. Looking back, Paterson said that in *The Magpie's Nest* she had "post-dated the clamant 'Younger Generation,'" only to get "neither cash nor credit for [her] brashness—nothing but a slap on the wrist for being 'naughty, naughty.'" The book hadn't actually assaulted the sexual mores of the time, but its heroine had done fairly well without them, and this was not liked. Paterson also recalled British readers who wished that a zeppelin would drop a bomb on her in payment for *The Shadow Riders*.[26] The reaction is not surprising: Britain was at war, and here was a Canadian author attacking the Empire and extolling the United States, which tried to stay out of the war. The most recent critical judgment of Paterson's early novels, that of Amy Jo Tompkins, finds her work satisfactory in artistic terms and notable for its departures from other Canadian novels of the era. Unlike ordinary Western fiction, it gives serious attention to business and politics; it makes "the human world," not the natural environment, predominate; and it regards the city as the new frontier for men and women to explore. When the great critic H. L. Mencken read *The Shadow Riders*, however, he found in it "a certain readableness, though precious little else." It did show "an occasional mark of respect for the reader's intelligence," in contrast to many other novels, but it would soon be "dead and forgotten" anyway.[27]

Paterson was dissatisfied with her fiction, too. By the mid-1920s, she noticed that she no longer had *The Magpie's Nest* in her library: "Am trying, not very hard, to pick up a copy." In the 1930s, she saw fit to inform her readers that she was glad almost nobody remembered its name. She may have been thinking of the two novels' modest commercial success when she wrote, "The mere fact that a book does not sell is not a guarantee of literary quality."[28] Her good humor and self-criticism went too far. The novels have charm and distinctiveness. They were simply not enough to satisfy her.

In 1916, she said that she wanted to have "some success or to be permanently squelched."[29] But success did not come. By December 1917, she had moved to San Francisco and was again working as a stenographer. She stayed at least until June 1918, living at 1245 Divisidero Street, in a neighborhood of little stores and walk-up apartments. Long afterward she wrote, "What we were doing in San Francisco ever we can't think."[30] She had entered her thirties with no visible plan to do anything but what she felt like doing at the moment.

Her practical options were limited. She was a married woman without a husband and with correspondingly slim prospects of finding another. She was a failed novelist, and the paying jobs that a woman could get around an office would not have brought her much income. But fifteen years later, when she looked back on the America she had seen, she wasn't thinking of hardship or insecurity or the fear of leaving no mark on the world. She was thinking, "How careless this country used to be. Pretty soon it may be all regulated and planned." Like her, most Americans couldn't even "prove that they were born," because there were no official records of the fact; but it wasn't the worst thing in the world to be absent from official records.[31]

The United States was now involved in the world war, and it was during that period, or immediately after it, that Paterson considered going to France with the Red Cross. We know about this only because many years later she happened to remark to a friend that the surgeon who examined her mentioned that she had a chest expansion so large as to be "ridiculous" in a woman of her diminutive stature. Why she wanted to go to France, and why she did not go, are both impossible to discover. The idea seems utterly out of character, especially when one reads her accounts of how the war affected her. Looking back on those days, she would refer to the dreadful goo that was written during wartime about the heroines who went to France. . . . Everybody will now rise and sing, as in wartime: "Jona-vark, Jona-VARK." After which they may look through the pictures of "The First World War," and the day's newspaper headlines of a world made safe for democracy and Hitler and Stalin and Mussolini.[32]

When the war started in 1914 she was so horrified that she had to stay home from work, physically sickened by the prospective loss of life.[33] In *The Shadow Riders*, which concludes with the outbreak of the war, she describes "how sensitive hearts were stunned . . . what an abyss of blackness and terror opened to the imaginative spirit; how the moral vision was darkened by the fume of hatred and frenzied lies which ascended to heaven like the smoke of the pit" (339). She predicted that the war would last four years, because it would be total, like the American Civil War. This was not an optimistic prophecy, but she "had to fix a date . . . to keep from going crazy." She later said that the war gave her "a nervous breakdown. . . . I thought I really would die, only not soon enough. Because naturally all rational thinking stops during war, and to me a world in which no intellectual processes are going on is something like the sub-cellar of hell."[34] This is very much in character, but the nervous breakdown and the idea of witnessing the effects of war at first hand (if that is what she planned to do in the Red Cross) may be symptoms of a psychological turmoil that had more causes than the war.

What is certain is that Paterson regarded the war as an unmitigated disaster. She never forgave any of the responsible parties. For her, President Wilson was a defining image of the modern liberal statesman—a visionary meddler, sacrificing the lives of millions on the altar of his self-conceit. She had no faith in his postwar plans for peace and sympathized with the American public for refusing to support them. But her bitterness toward a public that could accustom itself to war in the first place grew and blossomed. In late life, she was capable of observing that "the primary trouble" about American schools was that "parents care so little about their children, and mainly want to dump 'em anywhere, anyhow—until they are old enough so the boys can be shipped off for slaughter and insurance collected."[35]

Her reaction to the Great War caused some people to call her a Bolshevik. She didn't care whether they did or not. She wasn't a Bolshevik, and she apparently didn't worry about the Bolsheviks, one way or another. Communism became a live issue for her only when she found American intellectuals gravitating to the communist side. At first the Russian Revolution was just a matter of emotionally indifferent speculation for her. Soon after it started, she got into an unfortunate discussion with a nice lady who wondered, "What will they do with the Czar?" Paterson replied, in her confident way, "They will probably shoot him." The nice lady was horrified: "Why do you want to shoot the poor Czar?" It did no good for Paterson to explain that she had just been figuring the odds, and that if the Czar had figured the odds he might have averted the revolution. The lady still looked at her as if she "were summoning the firing squad."[36] This would not be the last time that Paterson's historical theories, however accurate, failed to gain her a sympathetic audience.

Someone who interviewed her after she became a famous author maintained that Paterson moved three times from New York to the Pacific Coast, "but she always returned."[37] That cannot be confirmed. It is clear, however, that experience taught her that she was a stranger and an exile, and she considered this proof that she was a real American. Explaining her sympathy with other immigrants, she wrote,

> But aren't we all? Most of the population of New York should and doubtless does understand. We too are exiles and captives; by the waters of Babylon we have sat down and wept. . . . Haven't we personally been torn from three countries before we grew up? The Michigan woods, the sage and mountains of Utah, and the prairies of the Northwest. Since then we have loved and lost, above all, the north Pacific coast.
> All Americans are in the same situation, even if they have moved much less in space. Time has bereaved them. If they revisit the place where they were born, it is changed beyond recognition.[38]

But she adds, "In a way, we don't want to go back." She never did. By 1920, she was in the East to stay.

That year found her in Stamford, Connecticut, working as a secretarial assistant to Gutzon Borglum, the sculptor of Mount Rushmore. His individualism may have pleased her; hearing that artists should organize, he exclaimed that only "mediocrity has to organize!" While she was working for him, he was designing the Wars of America monument in Newark, New Jersey. She watched him creating that sculpture, and when it was unveiled, she "realized afresh that there is such a thing as genius." And what was that? It was not just "a condition of mind"; it was "the ability to do something superb that nobody else can do." The operative word was "do." Borglum, who could talk "better on art than any one [she] ever knew on anything," discussed "the great Rodin," describing his "extraordinarily thick, stumpy fingers, 'like sausages.'" Yet those fingers could *do* something.[39]

She remembered that idea when, in *The God of the Machine*, she wrote in praise of the sculptors of the American political system, emphasizing the fact that many of them were craftsmen or inventors, and that some were born to "humble occuption[s]." Perhaps they had sausagelike fingers, too, but their hands did the work of genius. Paterson, bred to the humble occupations of diningroom girl and stenographer, was convinced "that there is such a thing as genius"—and that she did "not possess it."[40] But she would have a chance to find out.

In 1922, the *New York Tribune* hired Burton Rascoe as its literary editor. Rascoe, thirty-nine years old, had made a great reputation, as literary editor of the *Chicago Tribune*, by attacking the "genteel tradition" of American literature and the "hypocritical taboos" of American life. He championed a generation of writers who, though hardly examples of flaming youth, were engaged in various species of revolt. His heroes among this pre-Hemingway generation included Theodore Dreiser, James Branch Cabell, Sherwood Anderson, Sinclair Lewis, Ellen Glasgow, Willa Cather, Edna St. Vincent Millay, H. L. Mencken. Conservative and academic critics of the new movements in literature were, in his view, "Ku Kluxers of criticism." He was an irrepressible combatant, and an ingenuous one. Recalling the day when he was finally ousted from the Chicago paper by its editor, Captain Patterson, Rascoe wrote with every appearance of a straight face: "In the first shock of being fired, I had been very bitter toward Patterson, and I had been sunk for hours."[41]

Rascoe came to New York as an editor for *McCall's*. Some time during 1921, a young woman named Alta May Coleman phoned him and asked him to lunch the next day, asserting that they had mutual friends in Chicago. Alta May—Mrs. Pierre Coleman—was the general press representative for the great theatrical producer William A. Brady. She was used to selling colorful commodities to bedazzled strangers. This time, the commodity was Isabel Paterson.[42]

Mrs. Coleman picked Rascoe up in a Rolls-Royce roadster. Sitting in the back was the hitherto-unmentioned Paterson, who, as Rascoe recalled, "had slunk so low in the seat I hadn't noticed her. When I looked back in acknowledgment of the introduction, Mrs. Paterson glowered at me malevolently." Mrs. Paterson was a close friend of Mrs. Coleman, but she had not come on this expedition willingly.

Lunch was a champagne affair at a good restaurant, during which the glowering continued. And there was something worse than glowering.

> [N]early every time I opened my mouth to express an opinion Mrs. Paterson flatly and emphatically expressed a contrary opinion, in a way to imply that I was a little better than an idiot. I took (I think justifiably) a violent dislike to Mrs. Paterson.

After lunch, Mrs. Paterson was dropped off "some place" and Mrs. Coleman revealed the motive of her friendliness by giving Rascoe one of Paterson's short stories to consider for publication. Rascoe disgustedly handed the manuscript (which he "never did read") to the reviewers at *McCall's*, who disgusted him further by recommending that it be published.

Paterson, however, was not disposed of so easily as her story. In 1922, when Rascoe had left *McCall's* and started his job on the *New York Tribune*, he accepted another invitation from Alta May, this time for a drive in the country with his wife and children. Once again, "in the car was the, to me, very much detested Mrs. Paterson." During the drive, Rascoe made the mistake of divulging his need for a secretary.

> Next day Mrs. Paterson came to see me at the office. She said bluntly that she wanted the job I had spoken about yesterday. She had done newspaper as well as secretarial work, she said, and had read her way through the public library; she . . . wanted a chance to work with me. I told her my budget would not allow me to pay what she was worth. She said she would work for whatever I was prepared to pay. I said the pay was forty dollars a week. She said, "I'll work for that."
> I was afraid not to hire her.[43]

Having completed this curious exercise in bargaining, Paterson left Borglum and joined the *Tribune*. Rascoe learned that her rudeness had resulted from her impression that "her short story should sell on its merits," not on those of Alta May's expensive lunch. That was Rascoe's impression, too; and he and Paterson began to get along "famously."[44] He had been looking for a secretary, but he had found an assistant and a fellow-critic. The moment at which he recognized her integrity and intelligence was the turning point of Paterson's career. It assured her place in an enterprise that would soon bring her a national audience, and it demonstrated that character counts, no matter how irritating it may be.

Rascoe would remain Paterson's friend for the rest of his life, one of the few people who could criticize her determinedly and live to tell the tale. He was allowed to inform her that she was both a "persistent" and a "nagging" arguer; that she sometimes focused so closely on minor issues that she not only missed the forest for the trees but came near to destroying both; that she had the "damnable" habit of responding to his own work in a way "especially designed to take the heart out of [him]."[45] He loved her anyway.

Only one episode of their work together on the *Tribune* challenged his high opinion of her. It was her reaction to a certain John Armstrong, a young man whose employment resulted from a government-funded program to train war veterans for civilian occupations. Rascoe didn't have any particular work for him, so Armstrong, who lacked self-motivation, was "trained" mainly to sit around aimlessly. Paterson was not a welcoming presence. She barely recognized Armstrong's existence (to be fair, he seems to have reacted similarly to hers), and she didn't bother to let Rascoe know why. Years later, she explained that there was a "political principle" behind her "getting bored with the sight" of Armstrong. She thought it was absurd to get a government allowance to learn a job:

> One learns to do anything only by taking it on as a real job, positive work which must be done and is done for a living wage; that is the necessary connection. . . . There *wasn't* any job for him there; and if there had been and he had had the ability to do it, the only proper thing would have been to hire him, and for him to be paid by the outfit he worked for.[46]

The political principle was that nothing—certainly not the government—must be allowed to break the "necessary connection" between real work and the individual. This principle, which was as much psychological as political, would provide the necessary connection between Paterson the personality and her libertarian philosophy. A decent social order was not one in which government, or anyone else, tried to make work the secondary thing in life and "welfare" the primary thing. In a decent social order, people in need find productive work in the great "circuit of energy" of the marketplace.[47]

But Rascoe's most important difference from Paterson, at least as he saw it, was literary, not political. In politics, he became as fervently anticollectivist as she was, but he regarded himself as a radical in criticism and her as a critical conservative. She flattered his self-conception by telling him that the *Tribune*, a Republican newspaper, "was nurturing a viper in its bosom by employing [him], just as it had previously nourished such rebels as Margaret Fuller and Karl Marx." He repaid the compliment by making her an assistant editor and reviewer, hoping that her "conservative" views of literature would balance his own antagonism toward the literary Right.[48]

He greatly exaggerated her conservatism. True, she was contemptuous of people who seemed to "believe that life begins with Hemingway." She insisted that William Cullen Bryant and other literary plaster saints be remembered—if only for the sake of disliking them.[49] Yet like Rascoe, she detested the "genteel tradition" in American culture and never tired of lampooning it. She stayed as far away as she could from academic criticism, which in that day was as drearily intent on establishing canons of good literature as it now is determined on destroying them. The first generation of American modernists interested Paterson as it interested Rascoe; and if she could not match his engagement with succeeding generations, it was partly because her taste was rooted in the artistic and psychological problems to which the earlier modernists addressed themselves. With the passing of Yeats (1939) and Woolf (1941), the last exemplars of what she considered great literary technique, her interest in new tendencies in literature evaporated. The place that literature had held in her attention was increasingly devoted to history and philosophy. But this is to get very far ahead of the story.

In 1924, there was "one of those palace revolutions," as Paterson explained it, and Rascoe was fired by the *New York Tribune* as he had been by the *Chicago Tribune*. While he was clearing out, the *Trib* was engaged in swallowing its rival, the *Herald*. To increase the prestige of the new agglomeration, management inaugurated a Sunday literary supplement, *Herald Tribune "Books."* Rascoe had elevated the status of literature in the *Tribune* by treating reviews seriously and attracting the best and most independent reviewers he could find. *Herald Tribune "Books"* was the culmination of his program. But some ironic force decreed that Rascoe's successor, the founding editor of *"Books,"* would be Stuart Pratt Sherman, an academic from Illinois whom Rascoe regarded as the king of the critical "Ku Kluxers."[50]

As Rascoe's friend, Paterson naturally resented the man who had supplanted him; as Rascoe's assistant, she naturally expected that she also would have to go. But her experience with Rascoe, whom she had initially disliked, was repeated by her experience with Sherman:

> I sullenly waited to be fired; I wouldn't spare anyone's feelings by resigning. I was quite ready to hate Stuart, and would hardly speak to him at first. He being as contrary as myself, though milder, rather liked to be treated that way, liked me in spite of my best efforts.[51]

Quite unexpectedly, Sherman was seen to be drifting away from his conservative moorings. Paterson thought he had formulated an austere critical doctrine "first of all as self-discipline, to hold himself to the highest possible standard in his own work." She could understand that, as she could understand his ability to laugh at his own foibles. It was, she thought, a mark of high civilization. Stuart was gentle, easy, unpretentious. She liked him very much.[52] Under his regime, she not only kept her job at *Books* but started her own column, the soon to be famous "Turns With a Bookworm," which appeared in the journal's first issue, September 21, 1924. She signed it with the same initials, "I.M.P.," with which she had signed her eight-week column in the *Vancouver World*.

Two years later, in August 1926, she was stepping from a train in Vermont, where she had gone to teach a class on writing at the Bread Loaf School, when she heard the news: Stuart had suffered a fatal heart attack after a canoe accident in Lake Michigan. "His death was a grief to me," she wrote. It was also a threat. Again, she expected to be fired when a new editor brought in a new staff.[53] But the new editor was Sherman's assistant, Irita Van Doren, and Irita (who will be described in due course) kept things as they were, including I.M.P. and I.M.P.'s column.

"Turns" would last almost a quarter century.[54] It would give Paterson influence and recognition; it would become the vehicle of her wit and humor, her kindness and her indignation. It would end one kind of exile and, eventually, it would bring another.

5

A Matter of Style

The column started as an outlet for literary news and respectable literary gossip, and it fulfilled that function, more or less, throughout its life. Publishers invited Paterson to their parties; they sent her news releases; they wrote, called, and visited her, trying to put the right spin on their products; and they advertised their wares on the pages next to her column. Her business, however, was not to sell their goods; she would give them a fair shake, but it could be a very rough shake.

Writers would be well advised to mind their manners:

"To see an author in a rage," as William Blake almost said, "makes one wish to turn the page."

Some mercy might be offered the young and simple-minded, but they shouldn't presume too far.

[W]hat young writers want most is Encouragement. (A thing we find it difficult to supply).[1]

So much for the authors. The publishers themselves often fared as badly. Paterson loved to draw her audience's attention to the inanities that emerged when they set themselves to solemn meditations on their work. Urgently informed of the momentous problems now being addressed by a publisher's latest offerings, she was capable of replying that she didn't need any more books:

We've got a book.

When the spirit moved her, whole categories of publishing might be dismissed by definition:

Murder mystery yarns, like "Westerns," are formula products. . . . Such books bear no relation to literature.

The main object of a university press seems to be to publish books which one wouldn't be found dead reading.

Psychology [is] a science which tells you what psychologists are like.[2]

Publishing executives were frequently set upon and beaten. Paterson's friend Bennett Cerf of Random House published a book to which she took exception. He defended it, thereby provoking her into giving it, and him, the full treatment. The story is told by the series of little illustrations that adorned her column. The first shows her lecturing the luckless Cerf. The second shows him on his knees, with Paterson choking him. The last shows him lying on the floor with her foot on his stomach, while she continues letting him know exactly what she thinks of his book.[3]

It's clear that Paterson was expressing her convictions when she did this kind of thing, but it's also clear that she knew it was fun for other people to watch. Her literary occupation was to sell herself or, more precisely, to reveal the kind of self that readers would want to buy. Her medium was a weekly column of about 1,800 words. There might also be a substantial book review on another page, and, during some years, book reviews in the daily *Herald Tribune*.[4] But the column was her great work of personality. In it, she defined an individual character that would prove precisely appropriate to the announcement of a radically individualist philosophy.

She began the column with becoming modesty, advancing bland literary judgments, making little jokes about being a "worm," et cetera. Even in the first column, however, the combative Paterson began to show, when she answered an author who had a complaint against the *Herald Tribune* by suggesting that "publicity will soothe" him. The worm gradually became more assertive, aggressively announcing its opinions and annexing whatever territory seemed promising for the growth of more opinions—recent books, books of the distant past, adventures of authors and would-be authors, I.M.P.'s current life and past lives, the lives and fortunes of the friends of I.M.P., arguments with friends, arguments with enemies, arguments with fools (a group not always distinct from either "enemies" or "friends"), historical issues, philosophical issues, politi-

cal issues, economic issues, sexual issues, scientific issues . . . .
The connection was simply the fact that these things were interesting to I.M.P., who could not understand "why more people are not
interested in more things."[5]

I.M.P. was not only interested; she was inspired, outraged, worried, aggrieved, amused, and frequently a bit bemused. She was
anything she needed to be in order to make her point. A master of
the uncompromising assault, she was also a master of the disarm-
ing self-critique. After noticing what she regarded as the pretentiousness of a certain analysis of problems in human history, she
added, "The fact that the majority of people, including you and
me, are none too bright seems to be the one overlooked explanation." She cultivated an attitude of ironic self-toleration, insisting
that her way of writing a column was to

> begin in the middle, as if you'd been talking for hours, and nobody was listening. .
> . . The result, examined coldly in type, will look perfectly idiotic. Proceed then with
> the next sentence on the assumption that you meant to be funny in the first place.[6]

The column justified itself as a work of wit and spontaneous
self-expression, like Heywood Broun's column in the *World*, in
which, as Rascoe said, he "wrote about anything that came into his
head." Wit and humor were the soundest currency of the age, the
age of Mencken and Fitzgerald, Lardner and Cabell and the
Algonquin Round Table, and Paterson had no difficulty exploiting
her own sense of humor. She did it with conviction. "[W]it and
humor," she said, "are the highest forms of intelligence," "the balance wheel or perspective element in the human mind."[7] Where
those qualities were absent, something must be wrong.

Unlike much of the humor of the period, hers was neither sly
nor haughty. She loved the colloquial American language, "the
vulgar tongue of this country" with its "elusive note of poetry."
Her use of that tongue was fully her own. There was no commanding influence on her style. She paid little or no attention to the
doings of the Round Table (unlike Rascoe, who actively disliked
it); its chumminess and forced sophistication meant nothing to
her, although she confessed to a weakness for Robert Benchley,
one of its leading spirits.[8] She had a taste for H. L. Mencken, the
era's greatest exponent of the American language, and undoubtedly its greatest humorist, but she did not try to imitate his ba-

roque improvisations or his zest for gratuitous abuse. Mencken was always ready to announce that some dully respectable citizen was "plainly" a "quack," a "boob," a "fraud," and a "public menace." Paterson enlivened her private conversation with words like that, but in her published writing she restricted their use to the occasional coup de grace. She preferred surprise to shock, and understatement (or plain statement) to overstatement, although her meanings were often shocking enough.

"Only the most accomplished writers," she observed, "possess a sufficiently distinctive style for recognition." No one had the slightest difficulty recognizing Paterson's style. There were influences, of course. She admired the essayist Henry Moore Colby, appreciating both his aphoristic manner and his skeptical approach to politics. She liked his saying that "[r]eformers never seem to understand what an ordinary person is like." But Colby often overdecorates, while Paterson acts on the principle that "practically the whole art of writing consists in getting rid of superfluous words." The necessary words, the words that must be kept, are often homely and ordinary:

> People mostly do as they like, and that would be fine if they'd let other people do the same.
>
> People will believe almost anything that isn't so.
>
> [A]ll the virtues require some one else to practice them upon, which seems to us rather hard on the object.
>
> Nothing that well meaning people might do would surprise us.
>
> [P]ublicity is fairly easy to avoid.
>
> Uniqueness is the secret of art.[9]

Paterson loved the French literature of the Enlightenment, and La Rochefoucauld is a likely influence throughout her work. Another is Finley Peter Dunne, creator of Mr. Dooley, the wry Chicago bartender and analyst of American politics. Like I.M.P., Mr. Dooley knows how to compare supposedly great things to small, and to pose at being small himself, undermining other people's public standing while warding off attacks on his own. Of President McKinley, Mr. Dooley sadly remarked, "I may niver see him. I may go to me grave without gettin' an' eye on th' wan man besides mesilf that don't know what th' furrin' policy iv th' United States is goin' to be."[10] Mr. Dooley also knows how to rouse the conscience. Paterson was right in seeing him as a genuine social critic, a "corrective" of "majority opinion." This, she said, was the distinction between his humor and that of his successors: "The change in tone between Mr. Dooley and Will Rogers is portentous."[11] Paterson had met quite a few men she didn't like.

When she encountered them, in life or in letters, she let them have it, and she never took it back. She was happy to apologize for an error of fact or a dropped credit line, but objections to her judgments would simply lead her to say something worse. In one potentially embarrassing incident, she admitted to having made a remark in her private correspondence that someone had quoted in print, to the effect that the trouble with the famous historian Harry Elmer Barnes was his invincible ignorance. Aware that this comment might cause trouble, she explained that she had written "offhand." Then she added, "But probably a lot of other people had noticed it, anyway." Then she elaborated on the theological and historical significance of the term "invincible ignorance," and on its particular reference to Mr. Barnes.[12]

Some of her rhetorical victories were almost too easy, especially in her column's later years, when her energy was devoted to political criticism and she had developed the ability to spy a jugular at a distance of at least five thousand miles. Recording a literary honor received by Mikhail Sholokhov, the Soviet novelist, she wrote, "A Stalin prize for literature—let it go at that." She liked to quote the pontifical remarks of well-known people, with just enough framing to display their inanity:

> "It is no longer possible to fool ourselves," Freda Kirchwey announces . . . . She is too modest. The editor of "The Nation" should be able to fool herself indefinitely on any subject.[13]

Unmerited fame was easily punished. Hearing that the work of a popular sociologist had been translated into German, she asked, "Why wouldn't it be a popular move to translate it into English?" After watching Bruce Barton's life of Christ, *The Man Nobody Knows*, linger for months on the bestsellers list, she greeted the appearance of his next effort, *The Book Nobody Knows*, with a brief gloss: "Meaning the Bible, which Mr. Barton has just discovered." Pretentious ideas got the same treatment as pretentious works and pretentious people. Few satirists can dispatch a theory as handily as they can dispatch a man or woman, but Paterson always sees exactly where the incision should be made. To point up the strangely fanciful nature of the Freudian theory, she confesses that she "never can guess what is the Freudian interpretation of anything, except by assuming the worst." To dispose of the age-honored idea that one person's profit depends on another person's loss, she asks the innocent question,

> When Americans owned thirty million motor cars, who had "lost" those cars which their owners "gained"?

Erich Maria Remarque expressed one of the most popular sentiments of the twentieth century when he lauded the ability of "democratic man" to retain his "will to live" even after he had lost "home, country, family, money, and most important, freedom." Paterson responded, "Maybe that is what is the matter with 'democratic man.' He will let those things be taken away from him and imagine he can go on living."[14] Remarque's pompous image—"democratic man"—had a lot more potential than he thought it had.

But there were so many kinds of pomposity, and so many delightful ways of punishing them. Frances Newman, an avant-garde novelist, had a style so painfully mannered as virtually to elude description. Paterson pinned it down. Newman, she said, "arrives at her meanings by a process almost as distressing to the sensibilities as the spectacle of a cat being pulled backward by the tail." Winston Churchill called for a different kind of treatment. Disliking his style, which she regarded as oratorical in the bad sense of the term, Paterson laid down the last volume of his *Marlborough* with the comment that "the subject remains interesting; now someone ought to do a good biography of Marlborough." She was perhaps the only person in the Western world who was immune to Churchill's "Blood, Sweat, and Tears" speech. She noted that he had borrowed the salient idea from Garibaldi, and besides,

> All heads of great states are considered great writers while they are in office. It goes with the job. And we mean it goes with the job.[15]

Even great authors were capable of sorry descents; I.M.P. was "never able to accept anything merely because it is in the canon." And authors of the past were no more sacred than modern ones. *The Faerie Queene* and *Prometheus Unbound* showed that "each generation has its favorite method of being bored." Paterson was glad that Pliny's *Natural History* had been preserved, because "[a] man who could classify the seal as a fish has made a strong bid for immortality." Citing the common observation that Benjamin Jowett, Plato's translator, had converted him "into an Anglican Broad Church clergyman," she added that "[i]t's what Plato probably would have been, if he had lived long enough." Classic American authors were also treated frankly. Melville's *Moby–Dick* was "a prodigiously boring book, with a murky streak of genius buried in it." As for that instant classic, Ernest Hemingway, he was "as good as one can be without being a great writer. . . . His characters have no histories and no backs to their heads."[16]

Paterson's column gave some reality to a familiar cliché: it was a republic of letters, vigilantly policed but without any hint of a class system. Every author was assessed as an individual. Paterson made no distinction between ancient and modern, man and woman, poet and novelist, left and right, alive and dead: authors were simply people, the people one knew, or ought to know. She was always being surprised that Garibaldi or Henry George or Robert Owen or the writer of Ecclesiastes had slipped out of the public's memory. How could this be? Surely that person was still living, just a few houses down the literary street. People living in books were as real to her as anyone living in the flesh, and she treated them in the same way, listening to their ideas and responding with appropriate (and usually conclusive) ideas of her own. Reviewing one of Albert Jay Nock's books, she complimented him for having "the art of quotation. In his company one meets Montaigne and Rabelais and Emerson, Marcus Aurelius and Montague Glass . . . each presented with fine courtesy as needing no introduction."[17] It made no practical difference whether the author in question was a useful taxpayer or a drunken alderman; all were members of the community and treated on equally familiar terms. She was willing to let them all have their say, so long as she got to provide the commentary.

In 1936, "a truly amiable correspondent" wrote to the *Herald Tribune* to ask why Isabel Paterson did not "write on politics." "This is a refreshing novelty," she replied. "[O]thers have asked us why don't we shut up about politics."[18] But even after her column became a glorious soapbox for her political ideas, she remained capable of panning books that she might have been expected to like on political grounds[19] and of rendering generous literary judgments on people whose politics she disdained. She found that she could tolerate E. M. Forster's political naiveté and even "inexplicably" like him for it. She was not impressed by Arthur Koestler, or by his performance in political argument with her, but she urged her audience to read his "brilliant" novel *Darkness at Noon*, where "he knew his job, as a fiction writer." She warmly recommended Bertrand Russell's *Freedom Versus Organization*, despite its invidious portrait of the American political and economic institutions she cherished. She appreciated Russell for remembering "the origin of ideas—the fact that they were inevitably colored by the personality, experience and environment of the proponent." Whatever his political views, he remembered the importance of the individual life.[20]

She saw little point in attacking the faults of authors who weren't jostling for the limelight. Like Jonathan Swift, she

> spar'd a hump, or crooked nose,
> Whose owners set not up for beaux.[21]

She said that she had derived "sufficient pleasure" from many books that were not in any way "important," just as she had found many people "good company, although they are quite unknown to fame and no intellectual giants, either." She observed that any reviewer could have continuous fun just by finding fault with the worst books. That would be easy. It was harder to find something of value and to tell readers what it was. Her editor, Irita Van Doren, emphatically agreed with these sentiments. She was known for her habit of encouraging reviewers to be encouraging, a habit that made her very popular in the publishing world.[22]

But Paterson, again like Swift, had "satire in [her] vein,"

> And seem'd determin'd not to starve it,
> Because no age could more deserve it.

She thought that any critic had a duty to demolish the "successful pretensions" of bad authors, and she thought that authors had of late been growing unbearably pretentious. The intellectual, or at least the articulate, members of the community had begun to think of themselves as a class and to feel aggrieved when others failed to sympathize with them, as if they were being deprived of some social entitlement. Yet as far as she was concerned, "what ails the alleged intellectuals . . . is that they aren't." The idea of an intellectual elite was ridiculously un-American. The exalted claims of the intellectuals were based largely on self-mystification, on the implicit assumption that remoteness from common thought and language is evidence of profound ideas. But Paterson didn't "enjoy, for any length of time, a book in which it is impossible to be sure what the author means," and she refused to act as if she did.[23]

In her opinion, the literary jostlers and phonies deserved whatever they got. The mere existence of Gertrude Stein was a standing invitation to ridicule.

> Gertrude Stein, author of "The Autobiography of Alice B. Toklas," is coming over soon for a lecture tour. One of her lecture topics will be "The History of English Literature as I Understand It." That should be a very brief lecture.

The *Autobiography* itself was "a wonderful self-portrait of a perfect egotist. . . . Babies are complete egotists, and they possess a naive charm. If a baby could write a book it would resemble 'The Autobiography of Alice B. Toklas.'"[24]

Paterson also enjoyed a leisurely kill. She recalled that her friend Will Cuppy

> summed up the problem of the writer in one sentence not long ago. He said he would like to write a book (on some subject we have now forgotten), but he couldn't think of the words.
>
> Worse than that, when one sets about writing a book, one thinks of far too many other words. Miss Stein's books appear to us to be composed entirely of those other words.[25]

The muckraking author Upton Sinclair, who through some miracle of literary misapprehension remains assigned reading in America's classrooms, was another favorite target. She started laughing at him in 1927, when he produced an entertainingly goofy book called *Money Writes!* Here he discusses everything that worries him, but chiefly capitalist control of "the printed word." He mentions the conspiracies "of our kept critics." Paterson, who was being kept by the *Herald Tribune*, took it in good part: "Upton

Sinclair must have a lot of boyish fun believing everything is a 'conspiracy'; like Stevenson writing 'Treasure Island,' but with complete conviction." Sinclair wrote a letter of protest, and whatever Paterson said in reply must have been effective, because his response—and Sinclair was a responder, if nothing else—consisted of this note, with its own slightly skewed logic:

> Dear IMP:
>
> When it comes to clever answers, you have me licked before you start.[26]

Two years later, Paterson rejoiced to see Sinclair complimented in the communist press: "The meanest remark in the 'New Masses' is about Upton Sinclair's new book, 'Mountain City.' 'Style and content are one.' We kind of thought so, but felt it would be harsh to say it." Sinclair wrote her another letter of protest, oddly addressed to "Miss Ida M. Purnell" (style and content being one, once more).[27] Alas, it accomplished nothing.

In 1932, Paterson's interest in Sinclair was again aroused. Seven hundred seventy eminent persons had signed a petition demanding that he be awarded the Nobel Prize for Literature. The signers included (such was the power of political sympathies) Laurence Housman, Siegfried Sassoon, and George Bernard Shaw. The committee that put them up to it included John Dewey, Bertrand Russell, and Albert Einstein. Seeing no one else who would "tell these distinguished persons—and such a lot of them—that they are uttering hooey," Paterson told them herself:

> If they feel like giving a prize to Upton Sinclair, we have no objection; but why drag in literature? . . .
>
> How would it strike Professor Einstein or Earl Russell, scientists, if a group of poets rushed in and recommended Henry Ford for the Nobel Physics Prize?[28]

In response to this, she received a "furious epistle" from a reader who demanded that she spend a year reading the opinions of college professors and other "literary" people who expressed "favorable opinions of Upton Sinclair." It struck her as ironic that the supposed literature of rebellion should find its defenders among the "established order." Anyway,

> Why? We can think of lots of better things to do than reading over the same stupidity—even a stupidity of clever people—for a year on end. Fifty thousand Frenchmen can be wrong fifty thousand times.

The year after that, a year that she was not spending on the study of academic opinions of Upton Sinclair, she reported being "in bad" with him "and other horny-handed writers." She then encountered him at a party, and he confessed to her that he had committed thirty years of political mistakes. It was not an act of contrition: "This, oddly enough, convinced him that he is now entirely right."[29]

Self-entitled people had a way of reaching conclusions like that. It was a problem on the intellectual right as well as the intellectual left. Paterson noticed that the right had its hollow authorities too, and its own "spiff" talk—a special language designed to dominate everybody else. In 1930, she weighed in heavily with Rascoe and other advocates of the avant-garde against the New Humanists, a group of literary and philosophical conservatives who succeeded, for a time, in stirring up a popular debate—such, to America's credit, was the power of abstract ideas, the Depression notwithstanding. To the Humanists she preferred even Max Eastman (a writer she detested for his leftwing political views) because he was "the equivalent of a liberal in criticism": he recognized literature as an autonomous realm of interest, not to be subsumed by political or moral preoccupations.[30]

She pictured the disputes of her literary era of critics as a conflict between "the Extreme Right," represented by the New Humanists and their professorial allies, and "the Extreme Left" of experimentalists—Eliot, Joyce, Cummings, Stein, and so forth. She accused both groups of a hare-brained opposition to the skeptical, rational, and practical mentality appropriate to a modern age. The rebels on the left mistakenly assumed that the "poetic values" of life could be restored only by inventing "a new language of their own," thus reducing culture to a private game. The professors on the right, anxious to keep the game in their own hands, cherished the vision of a "static society" and opposed any writer who "criticize[d] social institutions as if they were made for man, not divinely ordained." As a liberal in criticism herself, she asserted that literature has "its own functions and its own laws, like mathematics; and two and two will still make four under any government."[31] She was not referring to a code that all writers must follow; she meant that they must do certain things if they want to communicate with an audience. If they do those things well, literature will result, whatever the writers' politics or social theories may be.

"[S]ince many things are always wrong," the politically radical writer "is quite likely to be right. But his social rightness is not what makes him a good writer. Nor contrariwise."

> Patriotism is not enough; morality is not enough; sociology is not enough; nor timeliness, nor sincerity, nor fervor. These things will not enable a man to write well, no more than they will enable him to play the violin. The Trojan War is no longer news; Milton's theology is outdated, the ethics of many of the great Greek dramas are insanity to us; one may be delighted by Pascal's Provincial Letters without being either Jesuit or Jansenist; the City of Dreadful Night hymns pure despair; and "Come Unto These Yellow Sands" has no meaning except: It's a lovely day, let's dance. But all these belong to literature.[32]

When reading Tolstoy, she was able to "forget all about his tiresome religion, even his sickening morality, in the pleasure of that vast living world he made." But she had no patience with writers who lacked the craft that was necessary to transcend their parochial ideas. She could "never lose sight of [D. H.] Lawrence's hot gospel pulpiteering. He won't let me. . . . his style . . . is a preacher's style—unctuous, fanatical, firstly, secondly, thirdly."[33]

"Style" meant something more to Paterson than tricks with language, and something more than what academics call "formal qualities." At its best, it meant the capacity to project the truth of life in its fullness. She had many ways of projecting truth and fullness in her own writing: wit and humor, the aphorism, the allusion, the skeptical question, the parabolic tale, the demonstration of precisely how "two and two make four," the playful examination of her own identity, the all-out attack on someone else's. She had almost as many ways of evoking her literary principles. Such principles, she thought, could never be frozen into incontestable form, but they might be capable of suggestive definition, and they might be elicited by contrast with ideas that do not happen to work so well.

When she suggested, for example, that "aesthetic values are merely the artistic expression of truth," she stopped short of agreeing with Keats's statement that truth is beauty and beauty, truth. She recognized the necessary tension between the two terms, a tension that could only be signified by keeping "truth" at some distance from "beauty." Expanding her formula to include the idea of audience and communication, she said that "the serious writer" is judged by an ability to "make the essential truth acceptable." "Truth" could be contrasted with naturalism or pure "realism," which she considered as inadequate as pure escapism. Escapist literature is "pleasantly immoral"; its world is "arbitrary, therefore unjust." Yet essential truth is more than truth to fact; it is the meaning of the facts. The ability to develop meaning is an "aesthetic" ability. Facts deprived of meaning lack the mysterious quality that is palpable in good writing, "the persuasive sense of values in life itself."[34] If that's too general, too hard to formulate into a literary code, then so be it: the idea allows for the diversity of life as life is experienced, and for the diversity of literature as well.

Had Paterson wanted to label her literary ideas, she could have called them either eclecticism or catholicism, since she concerned herself with almost every type of literature and felt free to apply any tool of analysis that might illuminate that type. An emphasis on the writer's choice of tools runs throughout her work. She shared Aristotle's assumption that works of literature are *made* things, works of craftsmanship. Certain characters might be enough to "make a novel, but the novel would have to be *made*." Another way of putting that was to say that "[a] carload of bricks doesn't make a mason." Craftsmen have a variety of materials and a variety of means of using them, "and all of them are right so far as they are effective."[35] The job of the literary critic is to identify the specific purpose of a work of art and the means that were used to accomplish it, and then to consider whether those means were sufficient to their end.

Her insistence on the variety of ends and means kept her from critical dogmatism; her insistence on the sufficiency of means to ends kept her from going soft on either the avant-garde or the conservatives. Conservatism, she said, could not entirely be trusted;[36] it was an attitude, not a method. But the methods of advanced modernism tended to be either undersufficient (as in the case of Stein, who was advertising herself to the neglect of any specifically literary effect) or oversufficient (as in the case of Joyce, who was acting as if his rhetorical tools were ends in themselves).[37]

Paterson's critical position was probably most like that of Willa Cather, a first-generation modernist whom she greatly admired. Cather rejected the conservatism of the college professors and the "genteel tradition"; she also rejected naturalism, "realism," and literature as sociology. Having done so, she went her own way, undistracted by the momentary enthusiasms of the avant-garde.

Most of her fiction (like most of Paterson's, as it turned out) was in some way historical, past-centered, not because she was nostalgic for the hard times she described but because she wanted to see what, if anything, would last. For the same reason, she advocated throwing as much "furniture" as one can out of the literary window. It is the bare stage that gives the better view; it is the bare stage that creates perspective.[38] Paterson agreed. She wanted to find the simple terms, the two-plus-two realities, that framed complex problems and provided perspective on them. The best word for her critical approach might, indeed, be "perspectivism."

Despite everything I have said about Paterson's rejecting this and that, her idea was still to see things as they are, not to blind herself to anything that might be a source of pleasure. Even Stein could be enjoyed to the full, once she was seen for what she was, a simple showman. When she met Miss Stein, Paterson said that "sure," she liked her; "[w]e liked Mrs. Billy Sunday." Helen Sunday was the hard-headed manager of her husband's flamboyant evangelistic campaigns.[39] Books should be enjoyed for what they were, too. She was able to praise a good deal of lightly entertaining literature, when it succeeded in its aim of being lightly entertaining. And she was able to separate that kind of work from creations of permanent value.

Here, perspective was important in a somewhat different way. The effect of real art is a transcendence of one's immediate time and place; thus, the gaining of a new perspective. Ordinarily, we are so absorbed in being who we are that "we have no perspective on ourselves. The function of art is to provide that perspective." But it is the play of perspectives that causes problems in assessing a work of lasting significance. Such works have two difficult and challenging qualities. They are "diametrically opposite," but they both contribute to literary value; and they are both

> likely to stand in the way of prompt and full recognition. One is that the author has recorded something of his own times so clearly and simply that it will seem as if "everyone knew that"; therefore its value cannot be perceived until some time has passed. The other is that the author has offered such original ideas or literary forms that they won't be acceptable until people simply get used to them. That is, in both cases, the work must be capable of taking on perspective.[40]

The works in which Paterson found real substance and perspective came from many ages and cultures. She advocated Montaigne's essays, Lady Murasaki's *Tale of Genji*, C. M. Doughty's *Arabia Deserta*, the novels of Jane Austen and Virginia Woolf, the poetry (not the deplorable politics) of William Butler Yeats. She was not ashamed to advocate *Babar the Elephant* (while dismissing *Bambi* as "the life of a deer"). She was especially attentive to work by American authors—such people as Theodore Dreiser, Mary Austin, and Edgar Lee Masters—who made significant "departures and discoveries," even if their art failed to achieve perfect form. She discriminated carefully between different kinds of literary achievement, predicting, for example, that Lewis's books would not survive, but his influence would. His *Main Street* demonstrated that American literature was "completely autonomous, competently self-critical and superior to the opinion of Europe, regardful only of American standards." It signified the end of "the colonial consciousness."[41] It made a change in perspective.

In any event, literary achievements were individual and must always be judged individually. Commenting on the 1933 Pulitzer Prizes, Paterson declared that

[i]t is writing that lasts; the subject never yet made a classic. Well, neither did a prize committee.... [E]ndowments, prizes, academies, scholarships and whatnot produce precisely nothing of value.[42]

Paterson's individualism made her a violent enemy of censorship. It was simply "intolerable" to her for "one adult to take on himself to limit the knowledge or dictate the ideas of another adult." It was an offense both to fair literary judgment and to "American political principles." In opposing censorship, however, she refused to claim that the typical object of censorship had literary merit. She was very irritated by people who made that claim. They obviously had no artistic perspective. Furthermore, they were "working against actual freedom of writing by confusing the issue, refusing to admit that such freedom is bound to include distasteful material." When Kathleen Winsor's novel *Forever Amber* was being pursued by the censors, and its friends sought Paterson's testimony to its artistic worth, she told them that she abhorred all censorship but had no intention of giving her "opinion" to a court; courts had no business judging by such "opinions." Incidentally, the novel was trash.[43]

Paterson knew what obscenity was, and she didn't like it. She also disliked on-stage violence; literature should be "addressed to the mind and the heart, not to the epigastrium." Accused of mere squeamishness, she replied:

> Certainly we are squeamish. The vulture and the hyena are not the highest forms of life; though nobody can say that they are squeamish. And in the writing or enjoyment of horror or brutality for its own sake there is something perilously like the enjoyment of such things in actuality.

Having said that, she made sure to add that she was "unalterably opposed to any degree of censorship." The cost of freedom was a lot of highly visible rubbish, but she was not a utilitarian, always quantifying costs and benefits and trying to manage the results. No, "[f]reedom is worth whatever it costs." Fortunately, however, "the real writers have made a noble use of their liberty by creating American literature in the American language."[44]

Paterson knew the difference between literature and politics, and she insisted on it; but the topics were not unrelated. Her idea of literature as an individual accomplishment was clearly relevant to her advocacy of economic and political individualism. She was a perspectivist about politics as well as literature, believing that real contributions to political thought can be made only by people who speak "clearly and simply," in the language of their own time, but who therefore may not be recognized as having said something fundamental until many years have passed. She also believed that any real contribution to political thought will remain instructive to people who have the perspective to see beyond the hatreds and fears of their age, and its special ways of distrusting original thought. Such ideas often recur in her columns of the 1930s; they were reasons for her continuing to publish her unpopular political views.

During that decade, when she was constantly moving back and forth between literary and political subjects, using each to shed light on the other, someone wrote in to ask what her column was supposed to be, anyhow: "Is it a review of books and authors? Is it a commentary on philosophical problems?" She replied that it was "a clearing house for second thoughts," thoughts that had taken on perspective, regarding books or any issues that books might suggest. "[I]ncidentally" it was a place for "news of authors, books or whatever concerns either."[45] It was I.M.P.'s circus, and it could have as many rings as she wanted it to.

I.M.P.'s purely literary significance was substantial. Her thousands of columns, articles, and reviews—in *Herald Tribune* *"Books,"* in the daily editions of the *Herald Tribune*, and in such other journals as *McNaught's Monthly* and the *Bookman*—are a compendium of the literary life of her period, perhaps its largest compendium. She never attained the brahmin status of certain prominent academic critics, or of certain journalistic devotees of temporarily popular critical isms. She never became a pundit; she was always a working journalist, proud of her status as a "proletarian." She did not appear on the dais at symposiums or confide her thoughts about the world situation to a radio microphone. She was the kind of writer who said that in one of her many employments, she had proofread Marx's *Capital*, "and a dreary job it was." Fittingly, as a "proletarian" writer she was considered as having "more to say than any other critic in New York today as to which books shall be popular."[46]

One reason for her importance was the fact that *Herald Tribune* *"Books"* was a distinguished venue, publishing commentary by virtually everyone of consequence in literature, from Robert Frost to John Steinbeck, Ellen Glasgow to André Maurois, Sinclair Lewis to Virginia Woolf.[47] And unlike most other distinguished journals, it enjoyed a very large circulation, about 500,000 in 1937.[48] It was a nationally circulated publication that had thousands of subscribers outside New York. In the mid-thirties, 30,000 copies of each issue were distributed to bookstores nationwide.[49] And *"Books"* had an audience that actually bought books. Frances Newman, herself a critic and avid student of the literary marketplace, expressed the conventional wisdom when she said that the *Herald Tribune* "reach[ed] more important people than any other review."[50]

The more important reason for I.M.P.'s literary significance was her own distinctive character. People who discussed such matters sometimes considered her the only regular writer for *"Books"* who was worth mentioning, or mentioned the others merely on the way to her column—"the feature most eagerly looked for every Sunday by a large group of readers." As late as 1939, a contemporary source said that her readers "seem to be divided into two camps—those who love her and those who take her as their Sunday morning hair shirt—but everybody reads her!"[51] She was notorious both for her "eccentric" attacks on the books she didn't like and for her merciless insistence that her audience read the books she did like: "She will keep pushing a book years after publication if she likes it enough and feels that it has not received the attention it deserves."[52]

Paterson often identified highly individual talent before other people could quite say what it was. She recognized Thornton Wilder's ability in his first, inconspicuous novel, *The Cabala*, then contributed importantly to the great popular success of his second, *The Bridge of San Luis Rey*. She showed the same generosity to established authors when she feared that their best accomplishments might be overlooked. She asserted the claims of the difficult and demanding, or the currently misunderstood—Swinburne and Kipling, Woolf and Conrad and Yeats—and it was not for nothing that Ford Madox Ford dedicated his novel *The Last Post* to her, with a long Dedicatory Letter in which he called her his "fairy godmother" in America, attributed the writing of his book to her urging, and praised her own "delicate and fierce art."[53]

The fierceness was more famous than the delicacy. Some publishers and authors urged her to notice books that anyone in his right mind could foresee she would attack; but cannier people, like Newman, tried to keep vulnerable books out of her hands. The general opinion was expressed by John O'Hara, writing on the day of publication of his first novel: "I'm very much afraid of Isabel Paterson."[54] A fellow-journalist who had frequent opportunities to observe her in her heyday described the situation in this way:

> Her word carries weight. Publishers kowtow to her; authors look at her wistfully, hoping for the best but fearing the worst. Visiting writers from abroad are always primed before the first handshake at a literary tea: "Now, her name is Isabel Paterson . . ."
> Most of them know it by now.[55]

6

Queen Hatshepsut

In 1924, Paterson told a new acquaintance that she could call her Isabel if she wanted, but "[m]ost people call me Pat."[1] That was how she signed her letters to her friends; that was how virtually all her acquaintances now addressed her.

Perhaps she felt no special emotion about assuming, in this way, the nickname of her long-lost and apparently not much regretted husband. It was, after all, just the latest in a series of names. She had started as Mary Bowler, had decided that Isabel Bowler was more appropriate, and had now become simply "Pat" or "I.M.P." The originally jocular acronym crept into her correspondence and her private notes, even her marginalia. In anyone else, these shifting self-designations might be evidence of an insecure identity. In Paterson, they were evidence of an identity so firm that it could call itself anything it pleased.

The mid-1920s found her "tolerably happy" despite a lack of romance: "[F]lirting is the greatest fun in the world, and when I think that there'll be darned little more for me, I could shriek and yell. And yet I don't know that I mind much." A close friend is certain that Paterson had an affair with a journal editor, later a partner in a prestigious publishing firm, who was famous in the twenties as the most attractive man in publishing; but the men who might have seriously interested her were probably few. As a girl, she had eavesdropped on her oldest sister when she entertained young men, and she had wondered at the "complete absence of rational content" in their conversations. "Rational" doesn't necessarily mean "intellectual," but it does indicate standards of mental soundness that must have put a large part of the male population off-limits for romance. Then there was the question of looks: "This country could do with better looking men. And more of them." As Paterson aged, she lost none of her aesthetic sense. One of her friends at the *Herald Tribune* remembered that on arriving at the paper she usually "marched" into her office and shut the door behind her, but that she opened it gladly when a young, intelligent, good-looking man came to visit: "If you were one of them, you could come and stay all afternoon. But you had to be young, you had to be intelligent, and you had to be good-looking." Informed that she had missed a visit by Ernest Hemingway, she said she was "told a young man had been and gone—that alone distressed us, for we don't want to miss any young men."[2]

If you met Mrs. Paterson, you would see a slight, dark-haired woman, 5' 3" tall, with eyes that other people saw as "dark" or "greenish" or even "malachite" but that she described as a "mild, benevolent blue."[3] She had lost the amazing pompadour that was stylish during her days in Calgary and had adopted the new style of short hair. Her appearance impressed people as "quite charming . . . she had black curly hair and a cute little face." Her way of "looking out at the world" has been likened to that of "a good-natured chipmunk confronted with a strange but rather amusing nut." Her voice was pleasant, without any regional accent.[4] It was what she said that was remarkable.

The poet Elinor Wylie observed that although Paterson looked "precisely like one of Jane Austen's heroines," she was "a woman of singularly pointed and ironical speech." Burton Rascoe, who had many occasions to notice the "devastating thoroughness" of her response to stupidity or pomposity, said that she had a "Thackeray drawing-room air about her—when silent, at ten feet away." Others regarded her as "a drawing-room Tamerlane, whose wit is so searing that no rubber plant ever grows again in a room through which she has trod." There was at least one nice thing about her: unlike most authors, she was "embarrassed by compliments."[5]

Paterson was very near-sighted; her little reading glasses hung on a cord around her neck, but she didn't always use them. Visitors to her office saw her "hunched" over her books like Dr. Johnson, devouring them "greedily," then turning to her typewriter and pounding away "with her face close to the keys." Like almost everyone she knew, she was addicted to cigarettes, but she liked to roll them herself. "He rolls his own" was a favorite expression for the individualism she admired.[6] She was an expert cook, fond of delicate foods and determined to discover the right way to fix them, but quite capable of reverting to wood stoves and beef steaks if the occasion arose. From time to time, she bought some expensive food, called in a hired girl, and gave an elegant little dinner for her friends.

She loved Paris fashions and would pay handsomely for a hat or dress, yet she was an expert seamstress who made most of her own clothes. She liked offbeat styles, wearing bright-colored stockings long before they became fashionable, and hats of her own design. These hats were said to look very much like her own hats.[7] When one of these "famous" but "odd" accessories was mentioned in print, she defended herself by saying that it is "[b]etter to look like a more or less rational person wearing slightly eccentric headgear than a genuine nut mistakenly attempting to conform." She would be satisfied if critical people would just "think it's the hat."[8]

Paterson was not a devoteé of museums or galleries, and she avoided concerts, explaining that she was "tone deaf." She found her music in the sound and rhythm of poetry, which she read with exquisite attention to its musical qualities. When she walked under the elevated tracks, she would recite "some particularly tunable verse," and listen while it went "singing through that thunderous racket." Despite her professed tone deafness, she equipped herself with a good piano and kept it with her until 1959, when she made her last move. The piano was for the use of friends; its owner took music lessons for a year but claimed that she never learned to play the scales right. As late as 1941, she gloried in the fact that she was without a radio. Her chief—sometimes her only—entertainment was books. She read hundreds of them a year ("five or six hundred," she said in the early thirties), and they were not chosen just for professional reasons. She was the unusual author who reads books of virtually all kinds. The worst thing, an acquaintance remarked, was that "[s]he rarely forgets what she reads, which makes her a formidable antagonist in debate."[9] The appalling nature of this fact is evident in "Turns With a Bookworm," where she seldom has any trouble finding the right literary, historical, or economic datum to crush anyone with whom she disagrees.

Paterson avoided motion pictures, a fact that may have something to do with her former employment in the newsreel business. She said that she couldn't "sit just looking at anything."[10] Film presented an "empty, passionless, monstrous, two-dimensional world." Her attendance at the legitimate theatre, once frequent, ceased by the mid-1930s, either because she was unhappy with the bill of fare or because the theatre of history and contemporary events was enough to satisfy her dramatic curiosity. She told an aggrieved playwright (who could not understand what she meant) that she had already "been to the theatre." For diversion, she enjoyed looking around Manhattan's little antique shops and second-hand stores, where she showed a sharp eye for a bargain as well as a connoisseur's understanding of finely made things, especially jewelry and oriental decorative objects. After Rockefeller Center opened, she liked going there to drink tea in the Rainbow Room, at the top of the central tower, where she could look down on the city "with all the appropriate thoughts" and consider the "enormous, unparalleled energy" that had reared the building and lifted her "among the clouds."[11]

Her other means of commanding the landscape was more individual. She was a friend of the Moran Towing and Transportation Company and spent many happy Sundays riding around Manhattan in their tugboats, often entertaining her friends on them. It was an ideal combination—the speed, the powerful machinery, the ever-changing picture of the city, the company of workers who knew their business, the interest of a vessel that was made for business. Paterson's ideal in life was to own either a tugboat or a steam-shovel and be able to use it to her heart's content; that would be "the pinnacle of glory and abiding satisfaction."[12]

About the time when she went to work for the *Tribune*, Paterson moved into an apartment at 508 W. 34th Street, one of a series of narrow old redbrick tenements near the corner of 10th Avenue. She occupied the top floor of the five-story building.[13] The neighborhood was known as Hell's Kitchen, a region of factories, speakeasies, railroad yards, and slaughterhouses. It was famous for its criminal gangs. Her part of Hell's Kitchen was just what the name implies: "[I]t is dirty, noisy, the hall and street are disgusting, there are trains, trucks, a plague of fiendish brats." Her apartment was over a "political club" (i.e., drinking joint). Next door was a factory that caught fire in 1926 and sent firemen climbing up beside her bedroom window. She hurried down to the street, carrying her sacred typewriter; but her apartment escaped the flames. It did not escape the attentions of the "eight hundred small boys" who played ball under her windows, doubtless the same "darling children" who made "rude comments on [her] unpretentious attempts at formal dress."[14] But the apartment was large and cheap, and she could hear the boats on the Hudson. And she had a fireplace. Wherever she lived, she liked to keep a little fire going. In 1931, she thought she should try to escape to better quarters, and she moved across town to another apartment. Within a few months she wanted her old place back, and got it. She lived in Hell's Kitchen until May, 1934.[15]

Often, her windows were bright long after everyone else in the neighborhood had gone to sleep. She sat up until the early morning hours, drinking Chinese tea brewed in the cup, writing letters, and struggling with interminable revisions of novel manuscripts. She functioned best at night and never really adjusted to a normal schedule. Doing things at 8 A.M. was "all right," she said, "if you like staying up so late." Her employment at *"Books"* did not require heroic efforts in this regard. It did give her responsibility for putting the journal to bed on Monday nights, a job that she used as the occasion for an informal salon. Her literary friends gathered and helped her proofread the current issue, going down with her to the composing room, then returning to her office or the cafeteria for more discussions and debates.[16] But her major job was to survey the New York literary scene and write her column.

She made short work of it, once she got started. The column was due on Friday afternoon, nine days before publication date. She arrived at the office every Friday with the intention of sitting down calmly to write so she could leave before 5 P.M. After spending the day searching the premises for books that might distract her from her task, talking to any agreeable persons who happened to drop by, or wandering "eerily" about the office trying to find someone else to chat with, agreeable or otherwise, she discovered that the sun was setting and the column was still unwritten. At this juncture, she asked any conversationalists who might be lingering in her office to excuse her, turned to her typewriter, and banged out the column while they waited. When she was really determined to get the column done, she could write its 1,800 words in forty-five minutes.[17]

In late summer, she abandoned the column and left town for three or four weeks, often repairing to western Canada to visit family and friends. Wherever she traveled, she lugged her typewriter and "a ton of books." She couldn't get along without them. She did very little traveling just to see the sights, and she did practically none to advance her career. Other authors went on lecture tours to advertise their books; Paterson rejected almost all offers to do so. She disliked giving lectures—public lectures, that is—almost as much as she disliked listening to them, maintaining that execution by firing squad should occur only "if the prisoner insists on making a speech." She was willing to be a "special treat" at the summer writers' institute at Bread Loaf, but that was about all.[18]

She spent a great deal of her time frequenting her profession's central social institution, the literary "tea." It was part of her job to mingle with other writers and gather anecdotes and gossip, and she had a good time, too, at least for the first few years. A typical "tea" was organized by a publishing firm to celebrate the achievements, real or imagined, of one of its authors. The point was to corral as many sources of publicity as possible. Free food and drink were sufficient to draw almost everybody who owned a typewriter, but Paterson's presence was indispensable; she was the "pet and terror" of the "teas." No one expected real tea, of course; the drink of choice was alcohol; but Paterson threatened to "scream and throw [her]self on the floor" if she didn't get the advertised infusion, and her hosts were forced to oblige.[19]

She would work her way through the crowd, trying to get as close as possible to the little sandwiches, of which she was very fond, while other people tried to get the nearsighted woman to notice them and felt snubbed when she didn't. Finally she would run up against someone (usually not the guest of honor) who said something that provoked her into conversation. Other people would gather round, and the tea would become a symposium on metaphysics, political economy, the habits of Western wildlife, or whatever else was of interest to her. If she did run into the guest of honor, and recognized that she had, the interview might proceed very briskly: "Tell us, we said, all about your career and be quick about it before we begin telling you ours." Or she might simply ignore him, and everyone else:

Mrs. Paterson always has this elusive quality. Her attention wanders as one speaks to her; her eyes glow with images that have nothing to do with what is being said. She does not always answer. She may amble off, spring a devastating wisecrack, or turn sweet, gentle and kind in her unpredictable way.[20]

Friendly observers considered her "a spontaneous child of nature who believes in doing as she likes." Unfriendly observers had a less idealized impression. Occasionally she encountered an author whom she refused to compliment, or compliment sufficiently to suit his ego, and the situation degenerated until she said something like, "You remind me of the young man in [Browning's] Pippa Passes, who was in love with himself, and in a fair way to prosper with his suit for lack of rivals"—to which the humiliated author would reply, when he figured it out, by saying something like, "You are the most horrible person I ever met."[21]

Understandably, she was often accused of possessing no manners. When fellow journalist Lorine Pruette told her this "in the course of a conversation" (the tone of which can easily be surmised), Paterson made her classic statement on the subject: "All our friends tell us this at frequent intervals, thus giving an example of what manners we ought to have." She added the general principle that good manners are "manners suitable and adequate to the occasion," and exemplified it by suggesting that Pruette tell all the fools she encountered exactly what she thought of their foolish ideas. That would be suitable and adequate to the occasion.[22]

Paterson appreciated the taste and smell of good wine but shunned prohibition beverages. In the mid-twenties, she claimed that she had taken only five or six drinks in as many years.[23] She drank a glass of sauterne at her Christmas party in 1924 and felt so drowsy that she went into the bedroom and fell asleep, leaving her guests to finish the turkey by themselves. She was not exactly the embodiment of the Jazz Age. The hedonists of the era amused her, from a distance, but she had no sympathy for the "lost generation"—naifs who "felt themselves persecuted by 'The Saturday Evening Post.'" "[W]e wish they'd stay lost," she said. "Nobody would go to look for them." She avoided nightclubs and speakeasies; when she went, she was bored by "sitting in a stuffy room crowded with sleepy people half stupefied with bootleg hooch and completely stunned with jazz noises." She predicted that speakeasies would seem romantic in retrospect, but they did not seem ro-

mantic to her at the moment. By 1931 she had paid only one visit
to a nightclub.[24]

She was, however, a frequent guest of Lee Meader, a wealthy
architect who set himself up as a small-time Trimalchio. Paterson
liked him and enjoyed his innocent vulgarities. He maintained a
yacht—the *Thetis*, and when the *Thetis* burned, the *Swan*—where
he entertained select parties of friends. Paterson loved to sail with
him and join the others in swimming from the deck. Meader owned
a penthouse in a midtown skyscraper he had built for the Astor
estate, and he gave elaborate parties in its bizarrely ornamented
rooms. For some reason, he had remodeled his sunroom so as to
exclude all light and air, and he had made the decorations Turkish.
"[I]f I were a germ," Paterson said, "I'd ask no better home—that
is, a color-blind germ." Meader cultivated celebrities (actors, ballet
dancers, boxers) and paid them to perform for the benefit of his
carefully chosen guests. There was singing, dancing, and all that;
and everyone had to wear evening clothes. Paterson arrived at one
in the morning on a New Year's day to find a boxing match in
progress, observed by a "bovine" Gloria Swanson. ("However, she
may be a very nice girl, and kind to her husbands"). I.M.P. was just
in time to get spattered with blood. Eventually she lost track of
Meader. He died (with his fortune intact) in February, 1930, but
she didn't hear about it until two months later.[25] She had left the
roaring twenties with no visible sign of regret.

Her novel of 1934, *The Golden Vanity*, describes America as
harassed by "the blasted reformers" on the one hand and "the earnest immoralists" on the other. Thinking about the kind of people
she saw at Meader's parties, she suggested that they would do better to lead entirely conventional lives, with "a neat house in the
suburbs," "twin beds of maple," and "three children, one of them
called Junior."

> But they've been nagged into believing they've got to drink too much and change
> partners, with the agreement that it doesn't matter as long as they Tell Each Other
> Frankly. . . . If it doesn't matter, then why go to the trouble? You might as well sleep
> at home. Respectability, the domestic virtues, are genuine accomplishments. If you
> want anything more, then it must matter a great deal.

But having thought that, her heroine adds, "It *does* matter."[26]

Paterson felt neither the lure of dissipation nor the obsession of
respectability. "Respectability is a strange thing," she wrote. "The

one virtue for which it has no use is the truth." She probably enjoyed her fame, but she did not rate it very highly: "[F]ame consists in being taken for some one else with a different name, which nobody can quite remember either." It made no difference to her relations with other people. She recognized no class or occupational distinctions in friendship. She was friendly with famous authors and with the women who simply "worked in offices." One of those women was Garreta Busey, a colleague and confidante at the *Herald Tribune* in the 1920s. Garreta wanted to be a novelist but never managed to become one. Her return to her native Urbana, Illinois, where she resigned herself to teaching at the local university, was a serious loss to Paterson, who for several years tried to compensate with long, frequent letters. Garreta was intelligent and good-hearted. She relished Paterson's "wit and brilliance," though she feared the "vehemence" with which she silenced counterarguments. "I never could argue with Pat," she said. "I could only enjoy her."[27]

Of creative people, Paterson had already formed the impression that "[y]ou've got all the best of them in whatever they create." When she was invited to literary dinners, she usually enjoyed herself, particularly if she enjoyed the food, but she was seldom impressed by the other guests. After a dinner with André Maurois and the French ambassador, she asserted that most celebrities looked like Elks or Rotarians. This attitude was not the most practical one for a writer to have. Publishing is the logrolling industry par excellence, and Paterson neglected many opportunities to do herself good with other authors. She was not going to spend any more time than she had to with people who, she thought, were often completely out of touch with reality. She appreciated the grit of the men and women who really kept things going in the publishing world, people like Ruth Raphael, a publicist who, according to Paterson, once spent the morning making arrangements for a visiting author but became "more and more distrait," so distrait that the author finally "asked what was worrying her. She said nervously: 'Well, I was going to get married this morning. . . .'"[28]

Paterson's friends were few but varied. She felt at home with Burton Rascoe and his wife Hazel, and with novelist Louis Bromfield, winner of the Pulitzer Prize for 1926, although she discussed him in a tone of amusement that bordered on some less pleasant emotion. His best-known novel, *The Green Bay Tree* (1924), is a tragedy of small-city America in which the capitalist system appears as the fatal flaw. The heroine is a woman who has inherited money and can therefore spend her life indulging her sensitivity for American socialism and European aristocracy. The novel's depiction of America is a columbarium of clichés, precisely the kind of intellectual guff that Paterson would spend the 1930s attacking. For a long time, however, she was willing to take Bromfield for what he was, a representative American: energetic, hardworking, and adaptable—perhaps too adaptable:

> [H]e is always of the majority opinion and sentiment; he picks up cliches of thought and phrasing as a sheep picks up burrs in its fleece; he takes part in the spectacle of life and yet while going with the crowd he sees how funny it is, and bursts into shouts of mirth. . . . He is just shot with luck to be like that, instead of a natural born minority like ourself.[29]

One of the people she met at Meader's penthouse was Lillian Fischer, a showgirl and model who went to Paris in 1924 to work for the couturier Jean Patou, using the exotic name Dinarzade. In Paris, Lillian became a buyer and stylist, assistant to the editor of *Vogue*, and an editor of *Harper's Bazaar*. She admired Paterson's intellect, and Paterson admired her unusual combination of glamour and ingenuous wit. They wrote to each other for many years. Lillian became Mrs. Frank Farley, vanished in the turmoil of the Second World War, and re-emerged in the 1950s as a widow trying hard to support her aged mother on the income from her job in a Manhattan department store. The correspondence of IMP and Dinarzade is a major source of information about Paterson's life.

Paterson's closest friend, her "unfailing standby," was Alta May Coleman, whom she had met in 1914. Rascoe described Alta May as a lively, talkative person "with the round, cherubic countenance of a Wisconsin dairymaid." She "devoted her life to furthering the interests and careers of her friends, never asking anything for herself." She had a gentle wit and an imperturbably free spirit, and she faced hard times gallantly. Asked why one didn't see the company's emblem on the radiator of her Rolls Royce, which was getting "somewhat venerable," "[s]he said innocently: 'Oh, they're getting so common, don't you think?'"[30]

Another close friend was the humorist Will Cuppy, whom Paterson called "a bright spot in a dismal world." He was born in Auburn, Indiana, in 1884, attended the University of Chicago, and moved to New York City to become a playwright. Here he became acquainted with Isabel Paterson, who, as his biographer explains,

urged Cuppy to give up his efforts at drama. This he would never do, and he continued to fiddle with the Great American Drama until the time of his death, when, after forty-five years of work, several hundred pages of variants on a first draft of Act I were found among his effects.[31]

Cuppy, who lived as a "hermit" on a barrier island off the New York coast, wrote Rascoe an interesting letter, and Rascoe asked him to come to the *Tribune* to see him. Paterson took over from there. Rascoe remembered that she "coaxed and coddled him into writing reviews for us, otherwise we would never have got any work out of him." Without her superintendence, Rascoe thought, Cuppy could not have gone on to success as the writer of humorous articles for the *Saturday Evening Post* and the *New Yorker*. Cuppy dedicated his first popular book, *How to be a Hermit* (which includes two long dialogues between him and Paterson on the subject of "Spinach and the Good Life"), "To Isabel Paterson: than whom there is no—well, than whom there just isn't, that's all." When he dedicated *How to Tell Your Friends from the Apes* to "Isabel Paterson, to whom I always dedicate my books," she said that she had "earned it": "What I've suffered while he was writing that book no one will ever know." In the preface, he attributes whatever is worthwhile in the book to his "frequent debates" with Paterson "about the animals." He confided that some people thought he must be "a figment of Isabel Paterson's imagination," but that was all right: "I know of nobody at all of whose imagination I should feel prouder and more signally honored to be a figment." For him, she was "the incomparable Pat."[32]

She was a sincerely appreciative audience for a man who, she said, "needs all the appreciation he can get." Cuppy's humor consisted of a whimsically realist view of the facts of life. He would spend all day in the New York Public Library, gathering data about fish or fratricide or Frederick the Great and recording it all on note cards. Then he would turn up at Paterson's office, sit down, take the cards out of his pocket, and discuss them, one by one. He was working up his point of view; and it was Paterson's job to trade jokes with him until he thought he had achieved it. That could take a long time. Cuppy was hopelessly addicted to self-pity; he demanded constant reassurance that his stuff was good and that the world was not out to get him—as sometimes, indeed, it appeared to be, especially when provoked by such tactics as his threats to commit suicide in the event that editors failed to accept his articles. If there was a Hate Cuppy Movement, as he suspected, Cuppy was its leader. Aided by Paterson's dogged insistence that her readers notice him and buy his books, he attained a considerable popular success. His work still has a well-deserved following. But in 1933 he reached what he regarded as "the summit of fame." He was walking down the street with Gene Tunney, the famous prizefighter, when a woman shouted from a passing car, "Oh, there's WILL CUPPY!" Characteristically, Cuppy said that "he might as well die to avoid anti-climax."[33]

Some of this was funny, but much of it was hard for Paterson to take. For a while, she would endure Cuppy's demands for assurance and exclusive attention; then she would spurn him, he would cringe his way back into her affections, and Pat and Will would resume their long, late-night conversations in her office, talking hermit to hermit. Will had the proper response to Pat's loneliness. He would say, "I hate to think of you sitting here, without me sitting here pestering you." When he caught her standing in front of a mirror, sighing over her lost youth, he asked her coldly, "Do you want to spend your whole life wallowing in lust?"[34]

Cuppy was homosexual, and Paterson undoubtedly knew that he was. In one of her letters, she describes a small party of friends at her house, with everyone discussing sex, but in the most genteel manner possible. Cuppy brought up the issue of homosexuality and claimed that "anything people did" was "natural." Paterson replied that she did not believe that homosexuals existed, "or that they do anything of the kind. . . . [I]t stands to reason—you have only to think it over; arrangements have been made. . . ." This banter is their only recorded conversation on the topic. She wrote Cuppy into *The Golden Vanity* as Jake Van Buren, a freelance accountant who wants to become a playwright, and she gave him a success that the real Cuppy would never enjoy; his play is a smash at the box office. She added a weird little joke: Jake's best friend, Mysie Brennan, who is the nearest thing to Paterson's self-representation in this novel, makes the astonishing revelation that she and Jake were once man and wife. Not so astonishingly, she observes that the marriage did not survive the honeymoon. "It was so silly; we just liked to talk to each other."[35] That must have given Pat and Will some private amusement that outsiders can only guess at.

Among Cuppy's allusions to Paterson, the character of Queen Hatshepsut, in *The Decline and Fall of Practically Everybody*, is especially worth noticing. "She simply appointed herself King of Egypt," he says, "and that was all there was to it." It became increasingly obvious, however, that the Queen was without social ambitions. She had no desire to shine in the kind of social circles to which her journalistic prominence gave her entrance. She constantly met important people, but she made no effort to ingratiate herself with them. Friends she had, and must have; and she would have liked romantic companionship, if she could have found any man who was compatible with her. But she did not lament her role as social outsider. In an article about Arnold Bennett, a literary outsider who worked hard at becoming a social insider, she remarked that there was "something unconsciously wistful and pathetic about it, like a child at a party who doesn't quite have a good time—more pathetic in a way than the child who does not get to the party at all." Then she added, "One can have a very good time outside."[36]

7

Then or Anywhen

While starting her career as a columnist, Paterson returned to her career as an imaginative writer. Her wide reading and her interest in the variety of human perspectives led her to try her hand at a historical novel. The first novel turned into a series of three—a highly individual series of tales that made her a well-known writer of fiction and marked an important stage in the formulation of her political ideas.

Each of these stories concerns a pair of young lovers whom Paterson regarded as the same pair, appearing in one historical context after another. It is unlikely that she planned the whole series from the start, but when she got to the last book, *The Road of the Gods*, she supplied a brief Foreword in which she suggested that the reader "may recognize a likeness in the young lovers . . . [b]ecause they are the same."[1]

They are bright, ingenuous people, the kind of people Paterson liked; and although their situations are remarkably, even weirdly, different, the theme throughout is youth and energy, always freshly confronting the adventure of life. The three stories are three episodes in the world's illimitable romance. As Paterson's Foreword says, "What else happened to them, 'then or anywhen,' is not certainly known": the tale of youth and energy will never be fully known, because that tale can never be concluded.

The first novel in the series is *The Singing Season: A Romance of Old Spain*. It was published in May, 1924. The title comes from Swinburne's *Ave Atque Vale*:

> Thou sawest, in thine old singing season, brother,
> Secrets and sorrows unbeheld of ours.

The setting is fourteenth-century Castile, during the reign of King Henry II. The young people are Isabella, daughter of the wealthy merchant Sigismund, and Roderigo, an Italian priest who becomes a chaplain in Sigismund's house. Isabella is beautiful, pert, and headstrong; Roderigo is naively and purely pious. He does not realize that he is in love with Isabella, and she with him, until the king allies himself with a wicked cardinal to destroy her father and seize his fortune, a scheme that leads to the young people's destruction as well. Threatened with torture and death, Isabella and Roderigo share a sudden, apocalyptic ecstasy: "time ceased for them altogether; the earth fell away beneath their feet and the heavens were rolled up like a scroll."[2] Their ecstasy is sexual, but wholly innocent: "For surely all the saints approved their love, granting them such great joy of it" (291). It is a romantic testimony to the individual soul's power of transcendence.

All romanticism tries to transcend "the earth"; all historical romanticism tries to transcend the facts of history. But the facts must still be rendered; and in many respects, *The Singing Season* is successful at doing so. It abounds in scenes and images that give a concrete sense of time and place; it successfully evokes the complicated relationships among church and state and commerce that characterized the medieval period, and the relationships among ethnic and religious groups that were important in medieval Spain. Paterson believed in the continuity of human nature; she believed that "medieval people really were very like ourselves." But she did not believe that they were like ourselves "in the obvious sense. They weren't ourselves in fancy dress, conscious of their 'picturesqueness.'" Like the Indians of her youth, "[t]hey had their own reasons for their own ways, just as we have."[3] As a historical novelist, she tried to capture those reasons and avoid the distraction of self-conscious picturesqueness. In *The Singing Season*, she largely succeeded.

She had no intention, however, of trying to write a medieval novel as some non-existent medieval novelist would have written it. She had her own perspective, too. And if her perspective finally predominates, it is because at crucial moments her characters become somewhat too conscious of their author's "reasons" for their "ways." The artistic defect had a considerable intellectual benefit. Long before Paterson became notorious for her controversial views, she announced them in *The Singing Season.* The book leaves no question about where she stood on matters of economics and politics.

Sigismund, the merchant, is the real hero, just as Whittemore was the real hero of *The Shadow Riders.* And this time the hero is wholly good. His aim is to circumvent the power of the state, now in the hands of King Henry, a leeching politician who believes that he has a right to other people's lives and goods. He is as incapable as certain twentieth-century politicians of seeing that the welfare of his realm depends on commerce and hence on freedom.

In their first scene (32-35), the king reproaches the merchant for "scoff[ing] at the knightly spirit which prefers glory to gain," and the merchant replies:

[A] nation unarmed is defenseless against ignoble overthrow; but a nation without commerce is as a man without blood, and falls of its own weakness.

Paterson has plenty of examples to prove the point, and so, therefore, does Sigismund. He provides a list of medieval states that are potent because they cherish commerce or impotent because they don't. The moral, as he indicates, is the necessity of free trade and minimal government:

Keep the roads open, the ports clear; make of Castile a safe haven for the merchants of all nations, and your neighbor states will ask for shelter under your protecting hand. It is better to make than take.

The king, who is as class-conscious as any modern socialist, responds by asking, "Better for whom?" He wants to know whether the merchants or the rulers will stand to gain more. He despises mere profits, but he wants to make sure that he gets any that materialize. As Paterson observes, "Kings and nobles [and modern intellectuals] always speak of money with high disdain, always want it none the less." Sigismund retaliates with the (modern) idea of economic progress. The people who profit from free trade, he argues, will be "[y]our grandson . . . and mine." But now it's the king's turn to play the vulgar utilitarian: "I must deal with today." Well, Sigismund thinks, "Kings take no cognizance of irony."

The topic now turns to taxes, which are the only use that the king thinks he has for merchants. Sigismund tries to make him understand the ironic truth that at some point the more he taxes the less he will get. The king dismisses him with an act of doublethink: "It was hard to look on Sigismund and not believe him; but there too was matter for resentment."

Of course, neither tyranny nor social "resentment"—nor trade, for that matter—is a strictly modern phenomenon. And this is Paterson's point: fundamental relationships endure. No civilization can exist without trade, and every civilization is plagued by people who don't understand how it works. In that way, "medieval people really were very like ourselves." But one can hardly avoid the impression that Sigismund is arguing not with Henry II but with Lenin, Mussolini, and the people who started World War I. The nature of her argument is unusual. She hasn't simply created a spokesman who has all the conventional novelistic virtues—courage, intelligence, compassion—and who happens to be a capitalist; that would not have been strange in an American novel of the period. The peculiar thing is that she uses him to defend capitalism itself, and that she insists on the points at which capitalism was thought to be most vulnerable: competition and the profit motive.

Explicit defenses of capitalism remain extraordinarily rare in the literature of the world's greatest capitalist country. In Paterson's literary era the anti-capitalist mentality was even more entrenched than it is today. The preceding generation of authors had created salient images of voracious industrial octopi; the current generation gave birth to Babbitts in a thousand forms. The idea, in either case, was that competition is wasteful and degrading, and that profit results from base exploitation of other people's needs. A businessman in *Babbitt* sums it up:

> You know, my business isn't distributing roofing—it's principally keeping my competitors from distributing roofing. Same with you. All we do is cut each other's throats and make the public pay for it![4]

The author never explains how cutthroat competition "make[s] the public pay," but he doesn't have to. He can assume that his audience is progressive enough to understand. He can also assume that George Babbitt and his business associates are simply following the logic of capitalism when they use the political process for their economic ends.

Paterson takes the opposite view. *The Singing Season* suggests that commerce is the source of progress because it profits only when it supplies a need, and political power is the source of corruption because it lives by looting and enslaving those who make their living by trade. It is the state, not commerce, that exploits. King Henry adopts the perennial belief that merchants make themselves "ignoble" by "taking advantage of another's necessities," but he is a fool and a hypocrite; the real danger is political power: "Kings, of course, take all advantage as of right" (226). The state creates a world that is "divided by the sword," when it could have been united by trade and "the bonds of interest" (238). According to Sigismund, it is a "lunatic world" where "men whose sole concern was to enrich their kind by exchange of a surplus for a lack, and vice versa, [have] to go about it by stealth or bribed favor" (84-85). There would be peace and progress if rulers only knew the "limits" of their power (85, 151).

Paterson would fight on this ground all the rest of her life. Succeeding events—the Great Depression, the coming of the New Deal, the rise of Hitler, the popularity of communism among her fellow intellectuals—would only deepen her aversion to the coercive state and extend her defense of economic individualism.

For the present, she could rejoice in the commercial success of *The Singing Season*: three large printings sold out within a year.[5] By the end of 1924, she had finished a substantial part of her next historical novel, *The Fourth Queen*, published in 1926.[6] Its subject is the court of Queen Elizabeth, from the coming of the Spanish Armada in 1588 through the aftereffects of Essex's Rebellion in 1601, a period in which Paterson was deeply learned and warmly interested. The lovers in this novel—the pert young woman, the pleasant young man—are both attached to Elizabeth's court, where they function largely as the reader's means of observing its grotesque complications of political intrigue, the game of chess in which, as Paterson says, "[t]he sagest heads in England pored daily over the board, trading pawns."[7]

Paterson's Elizabeth despises the game but finds it necessary; Paterson despises it but believes that Elizabeth's character transcends it. She writes, indeed, of "that profound knowledge of large issues which made Elizabeth a great ruler" (284). Unfortunately, there isn't much in *The Fourth Queen* to substantiate that view. Paterson admired Elizabeth for the same reason she admired other people: "She could make do with whatever means she had."[8] That frontier quality emerges in the book; the grasp of large issues does not. In fact, where Paterson's own political analysis appears, it is not very favorable to Elizabeth. The queen supported herself by granting licenses and monopolies of trade; she was favorable to commerce, but she insisted on having it on her own terms. Her policy meant that merchants had to practice politics to carry on their business, that politicians could make their fortunes by restricting trade, and that corruption and intrigue could increase and prosper (69-70).

This book's chief political message, however, is the importance of peace. If Paterson hadn't gotten over the Great War in 1924, she hadn't gotten over it in 1926, either. Her one big break into political anachronism comes when she has her young hero (who has already killed a host of people in Elizabeth's battles) suddenly decide that he no longer wants to fight: "He had seen enough blood . . . why should some luckless soldier's widow go mourning because of him?" (287). This is romantic in every sense of the term. The very title of the book is an allusion to love as a monarch who can transcend the power of her royal sisters, the fates.

The idea is enacted in the plot. Jack Montagu, the hero, is descended from the chief justice who condemned Sir Thomas More; Jack's sweetheart, Kate, is descended from More himself (189). Their union represents the victory of love and tolerance over political and religious conflict (Jack is a Protestant, and the Mores are still Roman Catholics). Paterson's idea is that love *can* win, so long as individuals act as individuals and not as political pawns, no matter how shrewd the chess master may be.

The Fourth Queen, published by Boni and Liveright in April 1926, achieved a second printing by June, but it was not as successful as *The Singing Season*. In mid-July, Paterson was claiming that she had given up hope of making any money on it. She must have made some money, though not as much as she expected. Soon after the book was published, she had started writing the third novel in the series, *The Road of the Gods*. This book was harder to write and required specialized knowledge that Paterson, for once, had to work up. She finished it around Christmas, 1929, and it was published the following March.[9]

Its extraordinary subject is the lives of central-Germanic tribesmen in the first century B.C. Paterson had never displayed any interest in this uninviting topic, and she never displayed any again. Her interest in the history of Rome would have brought her in due course to the history of the Romans' northern enemies, but if that was the origin of her novel, it is remarkable that the story didn't settle down where it began. Rome itself would have been a much easier subject; maybe that is why she chose the Germans.

She rose to the challenge magnificently. *The Road of the Gods* is the best of her historical novels. Confronting a setting about which even educated readers could be expected to know practically nothing and to feel even less, she must have been tempted to provide a full historical and folkloric treatment. That is exactly what she doesn't do. She offers enough information to keep the book from becoming a guessing game, but she never makes her characters discuss anything they already know, just to fill the reader in. Best of all, she keeps her characters from becoming quaint. Quaintness was, as she knew, the besetting vice of the historical novel.[10] She had generally avoided it in her earlier books; now she avoids it entirely. Her characters never hint that they are on display, that they need to be explained, or that they regard themselves as ancient. They speak in good, spare modern prose, and the narrative is conducted in the same medium.

Paterson might have enlisted a huge cast of characters, depicting the totality of the old Germanic world. Instead, she creates a small group of people and develops them all from the inside, psychologically. The group is even smaller than it looks, because everyone in this novel is, in a sense, Paterson herself, from the high priest who is always "disquieted" by "[n]ews of war and unrest," to the uppity girl who is always demanding, "Why? How do you know?," to the "outcaste" wise woman whose realization of the "wasted knowledge and power within her choked her with bitterness"—a melancholy prophecy of the author's own fate (139, 90, 46). A simple plot is sufficient to energize these characters and to dramatize the issue of cultural integrity and fragility that is the novel's larger theme.

The culture at stake is that of the Cowyth-An, the People of the Holy Wood, a priestly tribe whose function is to conserve the values and mediate the conflicts of the Germanic tribes. Their theology is unsophisticated. Their gods are three stones, three stolid representations of physical entities: sky, sea, and earth. But although their theology is primitive, they are not. Like the Westerners of Paterson's youth, "[t]hey are wise according to their lights" (108). They have reasons for their ways. Even some apparently irrational social arrangements, such as the taboos surrounding the priesthood, have reasons behind them; they provide the balance and limitation of power that are necessary to preserve the People's way of life (143-44).

The leaders of the Cowyth-An do harbor gross intellectual fallacies, but their ideas are no more fallacious than those of many modern people. The high priest is surprised to find that foreign merchants are willing to part with such amazing things as parrots, accepting in exchange such obviously worthless goods as beaver skins. How "childish" these people are! Even an idiot can "trade with them profitably" (18)! He's wrong, of course, and laughably so. But that doesn't mean that he's not intelligent. He has simply fallen for an idea that continued to mislead modern intellectuals, the notion that trade is the means by which one group of people takes advantage of another. True, beaver skins are worthless if you have too many of them, but so are parrots; the purpose of trade is for both sides to exchange what they don't want for what they do want, thus increasing everybody's wealth. And yes, virtually everybody is smart enough to profit, but that is one of the best features of the marketplace.

Paterson emphasizes the idea that the Cowyth-An are poor because they have made themselves that way. They possess an enormous treasure, but they do not use or invest it. They are afraid that knowledge of its existence would destroy their traditional society, which is based not on material wealth but on their status as priests. Their decision makes sense, in its way. "Tradition," Paterson would write, "is not infallible, it may sometimes become outdated; but it always has some relation to experience."[11] The Cowyth-An know what they need to do to maintain their cultural system, although they cannot do it much longer. Paterson captures the frozen culture of the North at the last moment of its independent existence, the moment before it succumbed to the dynamic culture of the Roman South.

If she is sympathetic to one culture or the other, it's to the Cowyth-An. But in a clash of cultures, as she shows, it is the more dynamic culture that brings the greater force to bear. Routes of trade, extending like lines of magnetic force from the great cities of the South, bring the power of the Mediterranean world to the outskirts of the Holy Wood. The ancient sacred way, the Road of the Gods, becomes the circuit of a new form of energy. A band of exiles from the Roman army, losers in the civil wars that turned Caesar's young nephew into the Emperor Augustus, appears in the vicinity. Even these ragged soldiers can project the might of the Mediterranean. When they arrive at their goal, it takes them less than one afternoon to extinguish the Cowyth-An and seize their treasure.

Paterson stages the final clash of cultures and, at the last moment, allows her young couple—Hoath, son of the conservative High Priest, and Greda, granddaughter of a migrant from the sophisticated South—to escape with their lives: "The clasp of their hands tightened. Now they had no one and nothing but each other. With their faces set . . . they ran on." And "what else happened to them, 'then or anywhen,' is not certainly known" (264, 7). Individual people remain alive, transcending all cultures, carrying the essence of youth and energy across the boundaries of space and time. Paterson is on *their* side.

By the time she published *The Road of the Gods*, however, she had embarked on the great work of her life, the identification and defense of a social order from which people do not need to escape. Her thoughts had turned from the politics of "then or anywhen" to the politics of modern America.

8

Never Ask the End

Paterson's direct involvement with American political controversies began in the late 1920s. Her basic political and economic ideas were already in place; *The Singing Season* had shown what they were. But the presidential election of 1928 revealed how strongly she held them.

Her relationship with the Republican Party, which would never be much to brag about, was at that time nonexistent. The fact that the *Herald Tribune* was the nation's leading Republican newspaper made no difference to her own opinions, or to what she said or wrote. She didn't care much for Calvin Coolidge, the Republican incumbent,[1] and she heartily disliked Herbert Hoover, secretary of commerce since 1921 and now the Republican nominee for president. Her reasons can be found in her radical individualism, which now assumed an intensely political form.

Paterson was radically opposed to public interference in the private sphere. It was bad enough, she believed, when private people assumed that they knew enough to run other people's lives. Public-spirited businessmen like Henry Ford, whom the Babbitts of America worshiped as idols of progress, were examples to her of severe moral regress. Ignorant of history, ignorant of government, ignorant of himself, Ford sought public office, engaged in political agitation, and instituted in his factories a system of "petty tyranny over private lives."[2] But what the government could do in this way was a hundred times worse, because it acted with the force of law. That was why Paterson's favorite enemies—the meddlers, snoops, and cranks of this world—always seized on the government as the means of remaking humanity in their own sorry image.

One result was censorship, which nearly all the advanced literati of Paterson's time opposed, and none more than she; it was a subject on which she could not "dwell without a glow of moral indignation." Another issue on which she agreed with the rest of them was prohibition, which was utterly ridiculous and detestable. She took on a tougher issue when she attacked the corruption and inequity of the vice laws, a topic that few of her fellow intellectuals cared to discuss. Why, she asked, intruding her question into the columns of the *Nation*, the oracle of social uplift, were prostitutes arrested while their male customers escaped?[3] It was not just the inequitable enforcement of the law that disturbed her; it was the law itself, and the paternalistic premise behind all such laws.

> Laws based on what people ought to feel, but don't, are nothing new, and conspicuously unsuccessful. We've always been fearful of highbrow reformers; they are useful in opposition only, as a dissenting minority. The passion for doing good to others against their will is an alarming thing.[4]

Long before taking on the vice laws, she had expressed a challenging view of marriage, speculating that it was a spontaneously formed partnership between two people, not a product of laws and rules:

> A couple who live together, whether from affection or expediency or both, for any length of time—it needn't be long—will find themselves married . . . [W]e marry because we discover some fine day that we are married. With those who aren't, the ceremony makes little odds. They do not hold together, not even though necessity constrains them to remain under the same roof for the rest of their lives.

Laws might "attempt to define the *status quo* . . . to protect somebody or everybody from the inherent difficulties of any partnership between imperfect mortals." But that was as far as laws should go. The best thing was for individuals to be left alone to form their own marriage covenants.[5]

A decade after writing her essay for the *Nation*, Paterson boasted to Mark Sullivan, the conservative political journalist, that she had written "the only article ever published in this country against any kind of law to forbid prostitution." It might be shocking to say so, but she was "against all moral legislation affecting adults only." Long before conservatives were provoked by the liberal "reforms" of the 1930s, she had been opposed to any kind of reform "by legislation—social ends by political means." The "American tradition" was very diverse and included many "contradictions," although "the Constitution didn't, except its tacit admission of slavery," which in the very "terms of that admission it left the way open for rectifying." America's continuous "'reform' tradition" was no rectification, however, since it resulted in new restrictions, not the removal of existing ones: "the 'reform' tradition has steadily worked to the aggrandizement of the State," and "the one ultimate monster is the State."[6]

The passion for reforming, fixing, and meddling was the dark shadow of America's belief in progress. It dogged both the Republican and the Democratic parties. The Democrats had been the party of Woodrow Wilson's war for world democracy and William Jennings Bryan's crusade to banish the demons of Wall Street with the magic of "free silver." But the Republicans were currently in power, and their pretensions were even more ridiculous than those of the Democrats. Most of them had supported the war, too; and in the Theodore Roosevelt era they had been leading proponents of "progressive" controls on the economy. They were now upholders of prohibition. But what Paterson chiefly resented was the confidence they had in their ability to provide a New Era of continuously increasing prosperity. That confidence, she thought, could result only from the conviction that certain people were qualified to plan for everyone else's welfare and make everyone else go along with their plans. It was significant that Herbert Hoover was called "the Great Engineer." Engineers plan and run things, and Paterson was strongly averse to having the nation planned and run as if it were one gigantic factory. That was not the American dream.

The great model for "progressive" ideas about social planning and engineering was America's experience in 1917 and 1918, when Secretary of War Newton Baker and other government managers, conspicuously including Herbert Hoover, assumed responsibility for coordinating the nation's business. Although that experiment in state management was popularly considered a success, it merely deepened Paterson's aversion to the paternal state. She regarded America's history since its entry into the Great War as a parable of incompetent good intentions, forcibly applied. In 1932, she summarized it as follows:

[T]he uplifters got their way, the Newton D. Bakers who immediately wished conscription upon us. Then the demand for a "business administration" was heard; and look at the darned thing now. After having boasted how well they could run the country, the bankers and business men are asking the government to rescue them from what they did to it. And meantime the internationalists set about saving the world, and what a swell job they did! And the moral legislators sewed us up in a sack with prohibition. After which the technicians got us—the Great Engineers.[7]

Throughout the twenties, she had been certain that the new and supposedly permanent economic era could not possibly last. She was worried about the lingering effects of the war, and she was very unhappy to discover that other people weren't. "I remember," she said,

telling Stuart Sherman, with sudden exasperation, that Europe would never pay the war debts. He said, politely surprised, why won't they? I could only say, since it was impossible to deliver an explanation that would have had to be as long as Gibbon's Decline and Fall, *Because they won't.*[8]

And if they wouldn't, or couldn't, it was surely not a good sign. The immense economic dislocations of the war-to-end-war had not been remedied by the successive Plans of the Republican administrations, which involved large American loans and guarantees to incompetent European powers. In Paterson's view, the Republicans were fecklessly continuing the Wilson era's delusions about America's ability to control everything for the benefit of everyone.

Herbert Hoover hardly viewed his own efforts in this light, but the "Secretary of Commerce and Undersecretary of all other Departments," as a real undersecretary of the treasury called him, was convinced that astute planners could emerge victorious over economic principles, as commonly understood. By thoughtful and concerted action, government and business could stabilize foreign and domestic economies, arrange the repayment of foreign loans, minimize interest payments on the nation's own debts, promote exports, restrict imports, and maintain high wages. A dispassionate historian has said that

Americans of Hoover's persuasion . . . were eager to expand the agenda of the state. . . . They believed themselves to be on secure ground in calling for a degree of governmental intervention without peacetime precedent in the American economy.[9]

Paterson was not dispassionate. To her, the notion that Hoover and his associates were engineering an economic millennium was nothing short of gruesome, and national confidence in this kind of planned social progress was plainly self-defeating, since it inevitably led to foolhardy investment on a massive scale.

One thing that was slipping out of the administration's control was the rise in stock prices, which danced away from the Federal Reserve system's uncoordinated moves to tackle them. What Burton Rascoe termed "the national dream of perpetual prosperity" led even apparently sensible people (like Rascoe himself) to gamble huge amounts of money on the stock market, as if the New Era had succeeded in abolishing risks.[10] Paterson saw through the illusion. Indeed, she predicted that a crash was coming as early as 1926. Then, acting like a typical American, she kept investing her own money in securities.[11] She stopped far short, however, of investing her faith in the Republicans.

Paterson was a passionate supporter of Al Smith, the Democratic Party's 1928 presidential nominee. She had never met her "hero," whom she finally encountered at a party, a year after the election[12]; but she liked what she knew of him. He was a practical politician with justly limited ideas of his job, not a social engineer or a professional "do-good." He was opposed to prohibition, and this in itself would have won her vote. As a legislator and governor of New York, he had sponsored social legislation (e.g., workmen's compensation, wages and hours laws), acts of political "progressivism" in which he sincerely believed but which he did not envision as part of a social revolution. Paterson didn't like even such relatively mild forms of meddling, but she could happily share the view of one of Smith's biographers, who pronounces him "a social liberal, an economic conservative." Political commentator Walter Lippmann called Smith "a perfectly conservative man about property, American political institutions, and American ideals." He was "the most powerful conservative in urban America." Franklin Roosevelt, campaigning for Smith in 1928, put it this way: "Some of Mr. Hoover's regulatory attempts are undoubtedly for the good of our economic system, but I think the policy of Governor Smith to let businessmen look after business matters is far safer for our country." Smith slashed the state budget and paid the money back in tax cuts, often fighting the Republicans to do so.[13] That was something Paterson could appreciate, although she herself was a very small beneficiary.

She could also appreciate Smith's social background. Born among the tenements of New York's lower east side, he understood that the proper approach to poverty was to get out of it. He was not an intellectual, as Hoover was; but he was an intelligent man, honest in thought, vigorous in argument, and a formidable character in both senses of the term, like Isabel Paterson. In the words of a contemporary journalist, Smith was "a real person."[14] Paterson certainly saw him as such. His connection with the bosses of Tammany Hall did not distress her, so long as Tammany got out the vote for him. In the summer before the election, she published an essay in the *American Mercury* about the death of Tammany chieftain Charles F. Murphy. The essay shows that she was willing to give fair quarter to big-city politicians (Smith as well as Murphy) who really knew their business; whereas personal contact with reformers made her "long to rush out and vote for a prominent racketeer."[15]

In the national Democratic Party, Smith's connections were with leaders who made that party distinctly more conservative (for want of a better term) than the national Republican Party. Besides Al Smith, the "conservative" group included Albert C. Ritchie, governor of Maryland; John W. Davis, the party's presidential nominee in 1924; and John J. Raskob, who ran Smith's campaign and took a leading role in the Association Against the Prohibition Amendment (AAPA), which would do more than any other group to rid the country of prohibition. As Hoover pointed out, the Smith campaign was not free from proposals for government meddling in the economy[16]; but for Paterson it was an easy choice.

The 1928 election was her last opportunity to feel at home with a political party. And the last vote she cast without a qualm was the first vote she cast as a citizen of the United States. She had long regarded herself as an American, but she had waited until September 20, 1928, to be naturalized.[17] By that time, she had already voted in at least one presidential election. In 1920, as she nonchalantly told her readers, she voted for Debs, the Socialist candidate, not because she agreed with his program, but because he was in jail for opposing World War I, and she wanted to salute "integrity regardless of opinions." She romanticized Debs as "a lovely soul" who was happy to endure his time in jail. Anyway, "it seemed better to have one's candidate there before the election

instead of after." Clearly, she thought that being officially naturalized should not be a prerequisite for voting. She probably agreed
with Abraham Lincoln that when foreigners are taxed, "it is but
justice that they should vote."[18]

Naturalization may have seemed a mere formality to a woman
who was used to crossing North America's undefended borders.
But now that she had some money, she was planning a trip to Europe,[19] and she may have thought that she could come and go more
easily if she had a U.S. passport. It is also possible that she timed
her naturalization so that she could vote with proud, though not
strictly required, legality against the Republicans.

She was such an intense partisan of Smith—a "smithereen," as
Garreta Busey called her—that his defeat "nearly killed" her. She
lost a $100 bet, and she lost her composure as well. Visiting the
Trib on election night, she was martyred by the comments of the
"besotted Hooverites"; on the way home, she heard, as if in de-
lirium, a shrill voice proclaiming that "the American people ha[d]
vindicated themselves" by refusing to elect a Catholic president.
Too angry to sleep, she fired off a letter to someone she thought
had voted for Hoover, calling him a "low grade imbecile" and adding that "if he didn't like hearing the fact he could lump it." She
spent the next day cursing Tammany Hall (for not getting out enough
of the vote), the prohibitionists (for obvious reasons), "the solid
ivory South, that broke on a good candidate when it would stick
for a smoked herring like Wilson," and a number of other voting
blocs. She never got over her disgust with Hoover, "the Fat Boy,"[20]
or any of his partisans.

As 1929 began, Paterson was consoling herself with the reflection that prophets of doom were no longer stoned to death, and
with the further reflection that "there was something to be said for
stoning the prophets. Who wants to be told 'Woe, woe' day in and
day out?"[21] The major business of the year was her attempt to finish *The Road of the Gods*, and her long-awaited trip to Europe.
Temporarily abandoning the novel, she collected her old friend from
R. B. Bennett's office, Grace Luckhart, a recent widow in need of
diversion, and left for Europe in the first week of July. She took her
typewriter so that she could do some writing for the *Trib* en route. The
journey would give her a new perspective on America, the start of a
new novel, and some newly complicated emotions.

In Paris, she stayed in Montparnasse at Cayre's Hotel, 4 Boulevard Raspail, a street full of chestnut trees. The delicatessen next door offered "ambrosial" ices. There was drinking (good wine, not the prohibition stuff), dinner at l'Ermitage, and the buying of hats. There was also a gentleman to squire Pat and Grace about—Nat Roberts, an old friend from the states (origin of the relationship unspecified). Roberts was an engineer and businessman, age 49, from Kendallville, Indiana. He had worked from 1924 to 1927 as acting chief engineer of the Nippon Electric Company in Tokyo; now he was technical director of the Bell Telephone Manufacturing Company, a European affiliate of AT&T.[22] In this capacity, and to Paterson's amusement, he had installed a gold telephone in the residence of the Pope.

Nat showed Pat and Grace around Paris and got them agreeably drunk. The three friends then traveled from Paris to Antwerp, where Nat was based, and drove to Louvain, Liege, Brussels, Spa, and the Chateau d'Ardennes. Paterson "saw all the damn battlefields, by accident." She and Grace then crossed the Channel and settled in London at the Park Lane Hotel, which luckily had French cooking. The touristic highlight of England was a side trip to Stratford-on-Avon, with which I.M.P. was immensely pleased.[23] At this point, Grace took ship for North America, and Pat returned to Paris.

At Deux Magots, she conversed with Djuna Barnes and Ford Madox Ford, who "looked very dismal and unshaved and talked of suicide." He asked her to read a book manuscript about New York, "and it was utterly mad. He is mad, anyhow; but during intervals, he certainly can write." She sat in the garden of the Cluny Museum, where medieval statues, half-buried in the earth, suggested worlds of memory that lay, Atlantislike, just beneath one's conscious recognition. And again, before returning to America on the *Caronia* in September, she enjoyed Nat Roberts' company. Her feelings for him are mysterious. He figures in her letters as someone with whom she had "had a grand time" in Paris, "a man I am fond of, I mean a dear friend, not a 'boy friend.'" But the relationship was obviously more important than that.[24]

Roberts knew he was in bad health and in danger of a stroke. He made plans for retirement, two years later. He also planned to visit the States, next spring; and Paterson looked forward to seeing Paris with him once more, next summer. The stroke came too soon. Paterson learned of it on Christmas day, "and it didn't add any cheer to the occasion." Recuperating in Italy, Roberts wrote to "Dear Dear Pat" to tell her that when he returned to America, in June or July, as he meant to do, she was "going to be a much pursued lady. . . . I like to be with you more than with any one else I know and why cant [sic] I try." Then an attendant wrote from a sanatorium in Baden-Baden to say that Mr. Roberts could no longer respond to letters. He still wanted to come home to America; and it was while trying to do so that he died, very quietly, aboard the steamship *Pennland*, two days out of Antwerp. His office called to let her know.[25]

Nat had been one of those simple people who have the knack of creating complexities. After his stroke, he asked Paterson to come to Europe and take him back to America, but the trip was called off, for reasons she had a hard time stating:

> A complicated story—I was going over to visit an old friend, but now his ex-wife has gone ahead of me—this isn't what you think, it probably isn't even what I think—I don't know all the details, having only just heard about the ex-wife from the woman he was engaged to. You'll have to go on with the story from there by yourself. Anyhow, you can see how it would be.[26]

Paterson's feelings about Nat were as complicated as the situation. She liked him for what he was, without cherishing any illusions. She loved him, yet she knew that their story could not have a future, only a past—their brief convergence in Europe, their liking for each other, and their mysterious similarities, which were rooted in a common experience as Americans of a certain age. But that experience of the past was worth understanding. Properly understood, it might even suggest an appropriate attitude toward the future. In any event, it was like those statues at the Cluny, a proof of buried life and energy.

The image of the statues was an inspiration for Paterson's next novel, *Never Ask the End*. She started it immediately after she returned from Europe and finally completed it in June 1932.[27] Writing it was a risky enterprise. Her novels so far had been either autobiographical accounts of the recent North American past or romances about remote ages of European history. *Never Ask the End* would be both personal and historical. It would present the experience of her own generation, but it would also attempt to define their place in history. It would be a story about Americans looking at Europe, and seeing themselves.

Because the issues of the novel were psychological and abstractly historical, the plot would need to be slight, so as not to shift the emphasis onto current, external events. This would be a novel of assessment, not of action. All Paterson needed was a little platform of present time on which her characters could stand while thinking about the experiences that had brought them there.

The current, external events of *Never Ask the End* are these. Marta Brown and Pauline Gardiner, two middle-aged women who have been friends since their youth in the North American West, are traveling in Europe. They visit Paris, Antwerp, and London; and they are entertained by Russ Girard, an American businessman. Marta and Russ have an affair. It is an emotional involvement with no lasting commitments; Russ, as both he and Marta know, has only a short time to live. She has to go back to America, but she promises to visit him next summer, if he has a next summer.

That is the story. "Every character in every novel," Paterson wrote, "had some fragmentary original, sometimes the author himself can't remember who it was; and it doesn't matter." What matters, she says, is the author's literary judgment, not the sources with which she works.[28] That's true; it's a matter of perspective. But in *Never Ask the End*, she is working extremely close to her sources. Marta Brown, the protagonist, resembles Isabel Paterson in virtually every detail that can be checked. Like Paterson, she was one of nine children of a beloved mother and a hated father; she was born in 1886 in the Great Lakes country;[29] she migrated with her family to Utah and then to a more northerly frontier; she left home when she was about eighteen, accepted a job as a hotel waitress for $20 a month, then became a stenographer. She worked for J. K. Hayden, an R. B. Bennett-like attorney and politician. She married in 1910 but soon left her husband, Keith Brown, retaining his last name and using it as the basis of her own nickname, "Brownie." She moved to New York, where she made friends with Alma Kirwin (Alta May Coleman) and frequented a social set like that of Lee Meader. Like Paterson, Marta is a rapid reader; enjoys Yeats's poetry and *The Tale of Genji*; and is disgusted by Mussolini, the international debt situation, all plans for utopias ("paradises for stuffed shirts"), and all Americans who develop a passion for international affairs or believe in "regimentation and suppression." "Americans have become awfully solemn and goofy," Marta says, with something of Paterson's own brand of sarcasm. "Worried about world leadership. They have the mandate for Yap."[30]

Most of the differences between Marta Brown and Isabel Paterson result from the latter's desire to Americanize all the former's biographical associations. Marta's birthplace therefore becomes Sault Ste. Marie, Michigan, not the nearby Tehkummah, Ontario; she spends the crucial years of her youth at Silverton, an otherwise unidentified American town, not Calgary; J. K., her employer, is the governor of an American state, not a future premier of Canada. The geographical adjustments were justified by Paterson's confidence that she herself was a representative American, whatever the transient, surface facts might happen to be.

Her other two representative Americans are also drawn very close to their originals. Russ, of course, is Nat Roberts, and the likeness is so plain that when Nat's niece discovered the book, she immediately realized that it was about her uncle. Afraid that the rest of her family would not understand the novel's intimacy and frankness, she wrote to Paterson secretly to thank her for portraying her beloved uncle as he really was.[31] Grace Luckhart, the model for Pauline, had less reason to congratulate the author. *Never Ask the End* depicts Grace's dead husband as a drunk whom she is happy not to have to see again (211). It depicts Grace herself as a high-strung, emotionally needy, *formerly* beautiful woman, whose witty conversation helps one not to "mind her moods and nerves" (1). Paterson seems to have been oblivious to the idea that this sort of thing might wound her oldest friend. When proofs of the book were ready, she had Grace read them; and when Grace responded with an equivocal statement about not being able to "judge it as a book, because she couldn't get outside it—reading over about the places we wandered through,"[32] that was enough for Paterson; the book was published. Paterson may have felt that only a small circle of friends would know who Pauline was, although she should have realized that friends are the people whose opinions matter most. Or she may simply have been carried away by her subject and thought nothing in particular about Grace's feelings.[33] After Paterson's death, Grace remembered Will Cuppy's asking her how she could forgive Paterson for *Never Ask the End*. Grace didn't know whether she ever had forgiven her.[34]

Paterson seems to have thought that the most autobiographical aspect of *Never Ask the End* was its sense of the difficulty with which modern people come to terms with their autobiographies. No American of her generation, she believed, could write his life story. If he tried, the result would be, not the realization of a whole life growing organically to maturity, but "the pieces of two or three lives" fractured by transitions from one "world" to another. "[R]ecent autobiographies," therefore, "are really travel books. . . . The author is wandering around searching for his own life. He can't quite say what has become of it." If someone had accused Paterson of making *Never Ask the End* into an autobiography, she would probably have replied that she hadn't, because she couldn't. Her life had been fractured by travel across all the "countries" of which time had "bereaved" her—Michigan, Utah, the Alberta frontier, the Pacific Northwest[35] —and there were psychic countries from which she had parted much more painfully. But there was one country from which neither she nor any other American of her generation could ever part. Inside them all was that "strange sunken world," that "real lost Atlantis"; and this is what distinguished Americans from Europeans.[36]

Paterson's alter ego Marta thinks in this way too. In Europe, she says, even the forests have their "decorous limits"; you know that you will "presently come out on the other side." That's not the way it is in America, where freedom and its attendant risk are always features of the landscape. Americans have real "wilderness in [their] blood":

> She thought, we belong to a sunken continent; lost Atlantis, submerged under the westward tide of the peoples of the world. Our little towns are drowned, too. One used to come to the end of a board sidewalk and step off upon virgin sod. . . . After us, nobody will know what it was like. Europeans think Americans are young; we're two thousand years older than they. . . . They've read their history. We've been through it all ourselves. (69)

The freedom of American society permitted "an enormous release of energy, a flowering of talent"; men and women realized that "they *could* escape" the restrictive circumstances of tradition and family. That was how people like Marta and Pauline turned up in Paris; that was how women like Paterson were able to write their books. But freedom was always a psychic challenge. The dissolution of tradition, family, and even the ancient form of the land itself left an emotional residue, "that secret grief, that sense of guilt, as of an undischarged obligation, springing from the inherited moral sentiment of family solidarity, with no fixed duties to acquit it" (190-91). The form and meaning of experience must now be sought by each person individually.

To follow this search, Paterson went as far as she ever went (but that was a considerable distance) down the road of literary modernism. She adopted a technique that she described as similar to that of Virginia Woolf, "but worse." Like Woolf, she traced the stream of her characters' thoughts as they flowed from one "world" of consciousness to another. The "subjective method," as she said, was "[t]he modern method of writing fiction"; but she thought it was especially useful for fiction preoccupied with the past. It gained its interest from the discovery of "a submerged pattern of action in the past lives of its characters." These patterns could be induced to emerge in the "modern type of novel," which "is not built on a story. It is not linear but radial"; it is as various and quick as thoughts raying out from the core of memory, sped by sophisticated feeling. The modern world is too fast for the old kind of story,[37] but it is not too fast for thought. Thought dances at the speed of light across all the strands of sensation and recollection. The novel of sensation and recollection refuses to be reduced to a "message." It cannot be summarized; it demands to be experienced.

In any case, the real subject of *Never Ask the End* is not the past as such but the persistence of individual character, character that continually reasserts itself in its meditations on change. The faster and stranger change comes on, the less likely people are to set their clocks by it, the likelier they are to find true time and space in the half-buried worlds that are most real to their individual consciousness or subconsciousness—their own forms of lost Atlantis, their own versions of the figures in the museum garden, silent witnesses of a connection between past and future. The features of the statues at the Cluny were "blunted, all but effaced"; and yet, Marta thinks, after parting with Russ for the last time, "[i]t is the material substance that is ghostly." The soul still

strives to break through by the keen devices of the intellect, by the intensity of passion, the persuasion of tenderness, even the violence of anger; and falls back on silence at the last. But at parting it cries out, wait, one moment more and I could have told you . . . oh, wait! What we desire is communication. . . . Perhaps, some other where, we achieve it, by a persistence to which even granite must yield. (328)

This novel is not, after all, an exercise in nostalgia, a desire to return to the literal Atlantis of the West and to the mistakes of youth. Paterson derived its title from her friend Elinor Wylie's "strange little poem, 'A Lament from the Breton,'" a work that envisioned life as "a constant and hazardous adventure."[38] The words are a command to accept the risks of life, and live. They are particularly appropriate to a work whose structure insists on the dominance of thought and character over the accidents of time. The sense of personal adventure, the daring, modernist structure, the final vision of the ruins-that-are-not-ruins, give the book the emotional freedom to which its author so strongly aspired. At the conclusion, when Marta parts with Russ at the Gare de Lyon, returning to America with the knowledge both of her love for him and of his approaching death, the energy of life wells up again, and her assessment of life mysteriously completes itself. "We had a good life," Marta thinks. "We would do it all over again, and hope to do better" (332).

Never Ask the End was not for everyone; its meanings eluded readers who were put off by the weak plot and strong method. But enough readers were not put off to make it a best seller. Published in January 1933, it was reprinted at least three times in its first month and was selected as a book club offering by the prestigious Literary Guild. In outward terms, this strangely inward novel was the best thing that happened to Paterson during the 1930s.

While writing it, she had many opportunities to meditate on its themes. She suffered acutely from the crisis of middle life that it unsparingly evokes. The novel manuscript's seemingly perpetual lack of completeness, manifested in repeated revisions of every page,[39] suggested every day that human life was finite. She felt tired and old; she saw graves opening all around her. Nat was dead; her mother was dying[40]; and then, in early spring, 1931, her best friend Alta May Coleman suddenly fell ill. Alta May had gone to Washington as advance agent for a production of Brady's *Street Scene*. While there she suffered a broken pelvic abscess, followed by peritonitis and pneumonia. Paterson took over her newsletter to the *Chicago Tribune*, to help her keep her job; but after five weeks of sickness, Alta May was dead.[41]

It was a terrific blow to Paterson. She had admired Alta May's beauty and elegance; she had relished her wit; she had cared for

her during several alcohol-induced illnesses without, at first, recognizing their cause.[42] For Paterson, who was separated physically
and emotionally from her blood relations, Alta May had been a
"family." She had been "as kind as grass growing. It was like walking on grass to be with her." She had told Paterson that "'People
who can stand you at all get rather fond of you.'... Alta May knew
me better than anyone in the world, and didn't seem to mind."[43]

Death now appeared "restful": "I don't mind the thought of it
for myself, only I wish . . . we could all go at once, and then maybe
we'd have company, and be amused." "[A]fter Alta May died,"
she wrote, "I found it hard to go on."[44] She went out to Alta May's
little place in the country, hoping to discover that her friend's spirit
was still lingering in the house. She thought at first that Alta May
was there, but later decided that she had been mistaken. The house
was empty.[45]

Long afterward, Paterson would tell a friend that it is useless to
try contacting the departed spirit because it is "free of the body's
sensory perceptions" and therefore "free of this world's sense of
time." The spirit is literally in a different world. Yet she was not without supernatural experiences. She did not like to discuss such matters,
knowing that she might easily be misunderstood; but to close friends
she occasionally mentioned them. One thing she said was that when
she sat in her chair at night, sewing, she would sometimes see her
dead mother sitting in the chair across from her, and the sight was
comforting.[46]

Her mother did not die until October 1933. When Paterson visited her in summer of the preceding year, Mrs. Bowler's memory
had failed, and she no longer recognized her daughter. But near
the end, she often called, "Mary!", and when Paterson's sister Zelda
replied, "Do you know who Mary is?", her mother said, "She's
mine." "[A]nd that," Zelda wrote, "was the only clear and decided
reply I had had from her for months."[47]

During this time, the illness of one parent focused Paterson's
mind on the wrongness of the other. Francis Bowler remained as
sinfully ineffectual as ever. For fifteen years he had been largely
supported by his son Mark, and he had wasted the results of Mark's
sacrifice. By late 1931 Paterson had "about given up hope" of her
father's death, but she was anxious that he not commit the concluding irresponsibility of dying intestate. He must leave "the

wretched farm"—a homestead on some drab, flat land just outside Stettler, Alberta, to which the family had at some point removed itself from the ranch at Cardston—to the long-suffering Mark. After years of putting off a task that horrified her so much that she could barely think about it, she decided to intervene.

> I wrote an appalling letter to father, since no other kind would have the least chance of making an effect, practically ordering him to deed the farm to Mark right now. Intimating to him that with one foot in the grave he'd better think about the hereafter and do what is right at the last moment. Do you believe the circumstances justify such an action? . . . Should I have done it?[48]

The letter may have had an effect. After Paterson's father at last died in 1940, at the age of ninety-two, Mark had possession of the land until his own death in 1947. Then Zelda persuaded her siblings to assign the farm to Paterson, in recognition of her financial help to the family. Paterson accepted, but transferred the farm to Zelda, a good soul who had taken much of the responsibility for the family's welfare. Zelda, who was seven years older than her sister, said that the farm gave her an interest in living.[49] Paterson's final experience of her father could only have confirmed her sense that there are two types of people in this world, the responsible and the irresponsible, and that between them there is a great gulf fixed.

Nevertheless, by the time she wrote her appalling letter, she was over the worst of her emotional crisis. She accepted the deaths of Nat and Alta May and the fact that her own life had "radically altered, and entered a new phase," a phase that she thought would be occupied by writing and reflection. She had recovered her habitual attitude toward human existence. Life, she thought, must be accepted "as good for its own sake; in which case all experience, even mistakes and disasters, may be accounted value received, a part of the sum of a full life."[50]

Her new phase of existence would be fuller and richer than she imagined. She may have been resigned to the general conditions of life, but she was not, as she discovered, at all resigned to the conditions of her country's political life. *Never Ask the End* is about a woman who is studying the ruins of the past and trying to make sense of her own history. By the time Paterson finished that book, she was standing in the ruins of the Great Depression and trying to rescue some order and meaning from American history, politics, and economics. On October 24, 1929, a few weeks after her return from Europe, the stock market crashed. "Well," she said, "there's one compensation about the literary life. You don't have money troubles."[51]

9

Let It All Go

Paterson gloated over President Hoover's misfortunes, reminding people that she had warned them not to vote for him. On the whole, however, she was optimistic. In February she told Dinarzade, who was still in France, "[T]here isn't as much gloom or depression as you might imagine; in fact, it's a part of the past already. Americans certainly are resilient."[1]

In mid-1930, after further market shocks, she ruefully remarked:

> The Hoover Prosperity Administration is living up to my specifications beautifully. But for fear it shouldn't, I went and bought some stocks myself. That, between you and me, was what brought on the last market crash. It worked within the week. . . . But what I am down I will not tell you. Everyone says they'll come back. Still, they mightn't find me here when they do. I can't live forever.[2]

Paterson hadn't definitely lost anything in 1929, but in 1930 she lost $700 when she started selling stocks, and by 1940 her known losses amounted to $30,057.43, which works out to something like half a million dollars in today's money. Her 1930-1940 dividends had come to only about a tenth of that.[3] Obviously, literary people can have *some* "money troubles." Her confidence in American resilience had not been very visibly rewarded. Besides her investment losses, she suffered a heavy cut in her pay from the *Herald Tribune*. She had been contributing reviews to the daily editions, but she was no longer assigned to that job, except, apparently, to fill in for other people when they were on vacation. In 1933, the *Trib* paid her just under $5,000, down from a peak of $8,300 in 1930.[4]

Furthermore, her job was precarious. When the *New York World* died in February 1931, the *Herald Tribune* tried to hire its reviewer

Harry Hansen. The impression (which turned out to be wrong) was
that he could draw a lot of advertising to the paper that picked him
up. At any rate, if Hansen was in, Paterson was out. One morning
she called the office and was told that he had been hired. Assuming
the worst, she put on her hat and walked up to the *Trib*, only to be
told that during the interval Hansen had decided to go to the *Telegram* instead. "Between the saddle and the ground," she thought.
But she didn't worry about her job. It wasn't any use to worry
about that.[5]

She saved her worrying for political issues. The depression was
increasingly regarded as a test of American institutions. It was increasingly regarded, indeed, as a judgment on private property,
free enterprise, and limited government, the political hallmarks of
individualism as she defined it. The depression was seen on all
sides as a reason to replace those institutions with a new, purport-
edly "liberal," regime of social planning. An important problem,
therefore, was to identify what had caused the depression, what
kept it going, and what should be done about it. In her letters and
her columns in the *Herald Tribune*, she gave her answers.

Most of the causes, she believed, were evident, but the crucial
thing was to understand that they didn't discredit the capitalist system. Capitalism must be distinguished from popular opinions about
what capitalism should do. As she explained, it simply could not make
everyone's investments pay off, all the time:

> [I]n any economic system by which one can make a couple of million dollars, one
> can LOSE the same amount. The two possibilities, dear children, are equally inher-
> ent. You can't have one without the other, sad as this may seem.[6]

Whatever else it may be, capitalism is not a perpetual motion
machine, endlessly securing higher profits for everyone. If attempts
were made to use it in that way, well, "even an admirable system
can be gummed up or wrecked by folly. Bad driving will strip the
gears of the best car; and even a wheelbarrow can be wrecked."[7]

This, more or less, is the way she thought the wreck had happened. In 1917, the United States had gratuitously involved itself
in a foreign war. It had financed that war by heavy borrowing, and
by lending to foreign powers. After the war, it provided additional
enormous sums to support European economies, but it did not col-
lect its debts. Paterson's "favorite book on the depression"—*A

Bubble that Broke the World (1932), by Garet Garrett, a major financial journalist—emphasized the fact that by the early 1930s interest on debt was as high as 30 percent of the ordinary expenditures of the national government, and much of it involved foreign loans. Meanwhile, private investors, inspired by government and business leaders who promised a New Era of high wages and high profits, lavished billions on stock-market speculations, financed in large part by bank loans. The system of state-encouraged folly finally collapsed. The American stock market crashed, the European financial system once again revealed its nearly fatal weaknesses, and prices for American goods went into a mighty decline, bringing to naught all previous and current efforts to maintain them by means of high tariffs and various kinds of artificial price supports for wages and agricultural products.[8]

Paterson's ideas were prophetic of explanations offered by later libertarian economists and historians, who put much of the blame on attempts by Republican administrations of the 1920s to keep prices steady and incomes up. Paterson, too, held that the government's endeavor to support commodity prices entailed inflation, and that "inflation brought on depression."[9] The general level of prices did stay up during the twenties, despite the natural fall of farm prices after the world war and despite large economies of scale from continued improvements in mass production.

These ideas are precisely opposed to the popular conception, now fully institutionalized in American politics, that the Great Depression resulted from a lack of government involvement in the economy. But they are not just modern libertarian ideas. Lewis Douglas, Franklin Roosevelt's director of the budget, attributed the depression largely to a politically inspired "cheap money policy" that artificially bolstered prices and spread the "pestilence" of "excessive borrowing." Tariffs, he argued, had been another political means of keeping prices and incomes up, with the unfortunate result of subsidizing inefficient businesses and ravaging the world trade and currency system. Stuart Chase, one of the most effective popularizers of leftist economic ideas among Paterson's contemporaries, suggested that prices should have fallen during the 1920s but didn't; inflation was real, though not readily apparent.[10]

Paterson and Chase were acquainted, and she may have been indebted to him for this part of her explanation of what the state had done to the economy. But even President Hoover believed that the Federal Reserve helped bring on the depression by following an easy money policy in the late 1920s, with the goal of propping up European economies by inflating the American money supply. Much of the money went into unusually risky stock market transactions. Hoover, perhaps too late, wanted to put on the brakes; the Federal Reserve was slow to do so. Milton Friedman and Anna Schwartz do not concur with the "many [who] suppose that the United States experienced severe inflation before 1929 and that the Reserve System served as an engine of it." They believe, however, that the System "followed a policy which was too easy to break the speculative boom, yet too tight to promote healthy economic growth."[11] In any case, the lesson, according to Paterson, was that you should not expect too much from the experts' economic manipulations, especially when the experts try to draft their plans on a global scale. Their decisions are not like those of private individuals, who respond to local challenges and whose mistakes have merely local effects. Global plans have global effects.

The origin of the depression was one problem. Its extraordinary persistence was another. Despite government's best efforts, it continued through the 1930s, with a vigorous revival in 1937-1938. Again, Paterson's explanation foreshadowed that of today's libertarians. She believed that the depression persisted because of government's misguided attempts to make it stop. Popular mythology holds that the Hoover administration failed because it tried to do too little; Paterson was certain that it failed because it tried to do too much.

A depression is, of course, a period of falling prices. President Hoover hoped to counter it by continuing the familiar effort to keep prices up. He tried to avert a fall in wages and to support the value of investments in basic financial institutions. He organized business leaders to resist wage and price cuts, and he tried to stimulate the economy by sponsoring large programs of public works at a cost that was greater than direct relief. When this medicine failed to achieve the desired result, he adopted more direct means of managing the economy. In October 1931, he created a bankers' organization, the National Credit Corporation, to bail out commercial banks. In December 1931, he proposed that Congress authorize the creation of the Reconstruction Finance Corporation to guarantee loans to industries and financial institutions. When the RFC started business in January 1932, it was also required to provide large loans to agriculture.[12]

These well-funded organizations prevented immediate loss of much of the capital that had gone into shaky or positively unwise investments, but they preempted new (and probably better) investments. The administration's high-wages policy, so far as it was effectual, kept some people working for what were, indeed, high wages in relation to the declining cost of living, but it made new jobs harder to find for people who were unemployed. The policy of "stabilization" meant that bankers who had invested in overpriced securities and real estate, and farmers who had invested in land that was overpriced by the boom in American agriculture during the Great War, received government support for their attempt to avoid liquidating their investments and taking a loss. Money that might have been invested in profit-making enterprises was thereby diverted to other purposes.

Congress indulged its own desire to manage the economy. In 1930, it went beyond President Hoover's call for higher tariffs and imposed, in the Hawley-Smoot bill, the highest tariffs in American history. In 1931 and 1932, agitation grew on every hand for still vaster economic experiments.[13] But while legislative excitement rose, investment in the economy sank to almost incredible depths. From 1931 through 1935, and again in 1938, net private investment was negative; capital consumption exceeded investment. Money naturally seeks to be invested, and it does get invested during the recovery period of every depression. During the early and mid-thirties, however, the government's many, sudden, and often apparently arbitrary economic interventions did much to foster the kind of insecurity that impedes investment.[14] When Franklin Roosevelt was inaugurated as president in 1933, he faced increasing economic distress and a federal budget mired in debt. Budget Director Douglas jotted a memo to himself to "avoid the fatuity for which the last Administration was notable, of talking soundness and acting looseness."[15]

Many modern liberals, and collectivists such as Stuart Chase, saw the depression as the opportunity to stabilize the political economy in a new way, by engineering a massive collectivization of wealth. President Hoover did not share their view of social progress. For him, the depression was plainly and simply a disaster, not an opportunity to create the New Republic. Always a friend of "true liberalism," as he understood it, he knew that "[f]ree speech does not live many hours after free industry and free commerce die." Nevertheless, he had long favored a more active role for government. He had stated the essence of the new economic ideas of the 1920s when he called for "a widening range of consumption" and stipulated that it could be obtained only by "high wages and low prices." He missed the irony implicit in his phrase: wages themselves have prices. But he did recognize that his views were "a long cry from the conceptions of the old economics." He regarded laissez-faire ideas as a "vicious growth . . . inherited from Europe." According to this curious view, Europe's *dirigiste* economies, with their vast "cartels," "trade restraints," and "price and distribution controls," are features of laissez-faire.[16]

Many of Hoover's political enemies contributed to the carnival-mirror effect by picturing him as the last defender of laissez-faire, which was itself the last remnant of America's superannuated individualism. Those particular enemies did not include Paterson. She insisted that his administration actually favored the *dirigiste* economics to which he believed himself opposed. It favored the type of business interest that was "trying to take over the government, to get the government to run its affairs and save it from the effect of its own insanity of foreign loans," and the insanity of its domestic obligations as well. She noted that J. P. Morgan used the administration's Reconstruction Fund to unload his bankrupt Missouri Pacific bonds and that Vincent Astor, who was "drawing a large inherited income from ground rents, sold slum property which had been exploited till there was no income left in it, to the Federal government." These capitalists wanted to escape the chastening influence of the market by applying for assistance to the public treasury. "Bad debts," as she said, could now "be called 'frozen assets,'" and "credit" could now mean "new loans that cannot possibly be paid."[17]

In late 1931, Paterson was saying that she expected a revolution in England and the destruction of the British Empire, but she thought that the United States would survive the "seismic disturbances" and recover. Getting rid of Hoover at the next election would help.

Still, she confessed to "a slight case of suppressed hysteria; I feel like a person listening for an explosion." A few months later, she was "certain" that

everything our Best Minds and Prominent Men are doing is absolutely wrong—absolutely. That they're making it worse from minute to minute.[18]

Unlike other intellectuals who were disgusted with the Hoover administration, she didn't want more aggressive action; she wanted less. Actually, she wanted none.

In 1932, a cry rose from many quarters for inflationary measures to support wages, prices, and consumption. In response to this proto-Keynesian clamor, Paterson asked why, if such efforts had caused the depression, more of them wouldn't "make it worse?"[19] Beneath her objections to specific measures lay a vast pool of skepticism about the authorities who would implement such policies. People who had guessed wrong in the past should not be allowed to perpetuate their mistakes and inflict them on everybody else. That was the method of a governing class that, she perceived, was steadily extending its power. This class included the politicians and bureaucrats (of course), together with the elements of business that were getting used to collaborating with them. There was another element, too—the "Best Minds."

No matter what the modern liberals thought of him, President Hoover, who had always been distrusted by the conservative wing of his party as a meddling modern intellectual, was not clinging to some remote ideological rock. He was guided by the emerging wisdom of his time, which accorded to government "planning" all the soundness it denied to "laissez-faire." This, or something close to this, is what former Democratic presidential candidate John W. Davis meant when he contended that the administration was relying on "a conception of the government as the universal shepherd and the people as its timid and trusting sheep," and that it was "follow[ing] the road to socialism at a rate never equaled in time of peace by any of its predecessors."[20]

Several generations of government-managed economy have made Davis's charge seem quaint, and this says a great deal about the depth of the country's intellectual transformation during the mid-twentieth century. But a similar judgment could be expressed in more modulated tones. In 1934, Walter Lippmann discerned between the "conservative" President Hoover and his successor, the "liberal" President Roosevelt, "no issue of fundamental principle as to the responsibility of the modern state for the modern economy. . . . Indeed, it may be said that every major move made by Mr. Roosevelt was in principle anticipated by Mr. Hoover." Lippmann appended a long list of Hoover's actions. As to the nation's business leadership, much of it was "moving fast," as an influential modern-liberal historian has shown, "toward ideas of central economic planning."[21]

That is not where Paterson wanted to go. She advocated liquidation of the whole enterprise of planning and managing the economy: "[D]o nothing at all, let nature take her course, let it all go." If this could be allowed to happen, "[t]hen we might pick up the pieces, individually."[22] The remaining assets could be "picked up" by people capable of assessing their value and using them profitably. She compared current economic problems to the depression of the 1890s:

> This country experienced bankruptcy in the nineties. Part of the loss was borne by foreign bondholders. That part of the situation is now reversed. It is a much worse bankruptcy. But that is all it is.[23]

It was a fair comparison. The depression of the 1890s was almost as severe as that of the 1930s, though its outcome was dramatically different. With unemployment over 15 percent, agricultural prices catastrophically low, wages and demand for industrial products plummeting, banks refusing to allow withdrawals or the cashing of any but small checks, even for wealthy depositors, politicians insisting on inflation of the currency, labor leaders demanding that the government provide jobs for all, an apocalyptic railway strike, and armies of angry demonstrators hijacking trains to convey them to Washington to intimidate the government, President Cleveland, a Democrat, resisted all temptations to do much of anything but maintain sound money. He believed, in fact, that previous inflationary schemes had helped to bring on the crisis. His administration made no attempt to institutionalize any recovery mechanisms. It allowed businesses that were going to the wall to go there, as fast as possible. Those businesses were liquidated. It was a painful experience for all concerned. Many people lost their investments, many people were put out of work, and Cleveland was repudiated by his own political party. But a few years after he left office, he received his reward: enormous popular respect for his courage and common sense. Recovery came much more quickly than it would in the 1929 depression. The crash of 1929 was followed by ten years of double-digit unemployment (eight of them during the New Deal recovery program); the crash of 1893 was followed by only six, with a much lower peak. Even before full recovery, lost wages were more than offset by a decline in the cost of living.[24]

Paterson knew all that. She had grown up in the grim nineties; she had entered business in the recovery period. That was one reason why she thought that the gravest danger to national economic health was the government's attempt to "save" everything.[25] She took the same view as Willa Cather, who had also experienced the suffering of the 1890s and had never gotten over it. Writing of the tribulations of her home state, Nebraska, which was the center of populist agitation in the nineties, Cather concluded:

> These years of trial, as everyone now realizes, had a salutary effect on the state. . . . The slack farmer moved on. Superfluous banks failed, and money lenders who drove hard bargains with desperate men came to grief.[26]

Like Paterson, Cather was a "conservative" (i.e., a traditional economic liberal) during the 1930s.

Surveying the Hoover years from the vantage point of March 4, 1933, the day of Franklin Roosevelt's inauguration, Paterson argued that if "the public credit" had not been used to "keep bankrupt banks and businesses afloat . . . then all the unsound, badly managed institutions would long since have been liquidated, the half-wits who brought them to bankruptcy would be out and discredited, and abler men would have taken over."[27] People who are used to stereotypes can call this Social Darwinism if they wish, but there is no evidence of any influence from that source on either Cather or Paterson. Their ideas were as old as the Bible—"whatsoever a man soweth, that shall he also reap"—and as modern as their own experience.[28] Paterson recognized that there was a psychological difference between the hard times of the nineties and the hard times of the thirties. During the intervening forty years, people had grown used to prosperity; when they lost it, they were so frightened that they didn't know what to do.[29] They lacked the courage to "let it all go." They had been misled by political and economic authorities who asserted their own ability to plan for prosperity and fix anything that went wrong with their plans. But that was all. Plans change; economics doesn't. Something might even be done if the authorities would just

> shut up, die, lay off. . . . all the God damned fixers— And they are the men who got us into this. Making the world safe for democracy, and saving Europe, and rescuing the farmers, and finally reconstructing finance, and look at the damn thing now.[30]

As Paterson elaborated her economic ideas, she kept coming back to the concept of what naturally happens when no one tries to "fix" an economy. Eventually, equilibrium will be restored; "nature" will "take her course." Granted, "nature" may take a while, and waiting may be very painful, especially if one's expectations have been inflated by the Best Minds and the Prominent Men. The Best Minds tried to make a quick end of economic problems by restoring the public's "confidence"; they were still trying to do that when the Roosevelt administration began. Paterson agreed with one idea in Roosevelt's inaugural address: "[f]ear was the worst thing." She added, however, that "imbecile optimism" is "the worst kind of fear." She confessed that she was

> tired of being told that "credit depends on confidence." Fudge. Credit depends on real assets, sound money and a clean record. . . . When any one asks us to have confidence we are glad to inform him that the request of itself would shatter any remaining confidence in our mind.[31]

Confidence is merely the natural result of people's paying their debts, just as the gold standard is merely the natural result of people's search for a trustworthy medium of exchange:

> Gold became currency just as leather became shoes; it was a peculiarly suitable material. No government created the gold standard; governments merely recognized it as a fact.[32]

That was true. Gold was a medium of exchange long before there was any such thing as government currency. She could not expect any happy outcome from attempts to ignore or violate such natural principles as the need for sound money. Those principles were the "rules of old, discovered, not devised"—something much more deserving of confidence than anything a government might resolve to do. "Nature," in this case, was not a romantic idealization, as many American versions of that enigmatic concept have shown themselves to be. It was common sense: "[T]wo and two will still make four under any government."[33] Before introducing new ontologies, such as the theory that confidence must be induced and equilibrium must be planned, one should try to understand the old idea of individual, properly self-interested responses to economic fact. The condition of economic progress was a respect for principles that do not "progress."

Some of the Best Minds in the Hoover administration believed that too. Andrew Mellon, the Secretary of the Treasury, recommended a sweeping "liquidation," suggesting, as Paterson did, that "[v]alues will be adjusted, and enterprising people will pick up the wrecks from less competent people." Mellon cited past American experience. Hoover disagreed: the economy was different now. Was it? Hoover had been on both sides of this "progressive" versus "reactionary" argument. Soon after his inauguration, he had warned New York bankers that the stock market might not be sound. He was right, of course; but they responded that "this was a 'New Era,' to which old economic experience did not apply."[34] The response was ironic: the New Era was, in large part, Hoover's own idea. Later, when he rejected Mellon's advice about the lessons of the past, he was resuming his faith in the idea that economic principles could actually evolve, that the old system of laissez-faire could be left where it belonged, in the past.

"Progress" can be defined in many ways, and so can Paterson's own phrase, "let it all go." "Laissez-faire" would be the "reactionary" equivalent. A conservative equivalent, one that was not particularly fashionable in 1930 but would become very much so by 2004, would be "individual responsibility." The liberal equivalent, which never goes out of fashion (though its shades of meaning can vary dramatically), is "individual freedom." For Paterson, who in thinking about the Great Depression was thinking far beyond the immediate, economic realm, those terms were indeed equivalent; each of them evoked the others. America's ideal of individual freedom must entail the practice of laissez-faire capitalism, and a capitalist economic system must entail an ethic of individual responsibility.

Paterson's refusal to separate these ideas defined her as a radical libertarian. She was not preaching the philosophy of the small-town banker; she was interested in freedom from censorship and vice laws as much as she was in freedom from economic regulation. Neither was she preaching the mores of the Lost Generation; its irresponsibility was indicated by the fact that most of its articulate members now showed up as sympathizers of authoritarian political movements. For her, there was no such thing as respect for individual liberty in just one area of life—and it was this attitude that completed her estrangement from the dominant thought of her generation.

On the ship that brought her back from Europe in 1929, she wrote a column about "the real revolution in morals" in the twentieth century. When she wrote it, she was more optimistic about her political era than she would ever be again. She used Tolstoy as an example of the pre-revolutionary attitude, which negated both individual freedom and individual responsibility:

> The way Tolstoy's characters snooped and pried into one another's slightest activities is gruesome. At every turn they demand to know: "Who is that letter from? Where did you go today? Who did you meet there? Did any one call? What are you thinking about?" We should incline to believe that these habits brought on the Bolshevik regime.[35]

Despite the Bolsheviks, she was hopeful that the revolution of privacy would continue. Literary evidence indicated that people were now less inclined to impose on others "their own self-righteous notions of duty." But a month later, still savoring memories of the good wine she had drunk in Europe, she drew a sinister parallel between the "enlightened" despots of Europe's Old Regime and modern Americans who had not surrendered to the revolution of privacy. Peter the Great, she said,

> was a reformer and prohibitionist about everything but liquor; and he did things for your own good. And they were almost always exceedingly unpleasant things. We hope it will be a lesson to us.[36]

The depression began a few days afterward. Paterson was much less concerned about the event itself than about its capacity for reversing the process of privatization. The last thing she wanted was for power to be transferred back to the class of self-righteous governors and meddlers, with the goal of ensuring social stability. "[W]e can imagine no system we should dislike more earnestly," she wrote, "than being governed by the high-brows, the 'best minds,' the self-nominated intellectual aristocracy. We mean it." Mulling things over a bit more, she announced that she would not attend the *New Masses* ball; she was afraid to meet such "lovers of humanity" as the socialist Art Young, the *Masses'* cartoonist. She was very fond of Art, but he was one of those people

who want to make the world a better place to live in. We are not sure we should survive any rigorous application of their program. . . . Art Young is himself a gentle soul, but those are the ones we'd be most worried about as deputies of omnipotence.[37]

The possibility that power might not be entirely safe in the hands of idealistic intellectuals suggested itself much more slowly to many of Paterson's fellow writers. To some of them it required the whole decade of the 1930s to become apparent. In February 1940, after the Hitler-Stalin pact, Malcolm Cowley, a literary leftist who had glossed over Stalin's crimes ("I don't like a lot of things that are happening in Russia, for example in the arts," he wrote in 1938), informed fellow-critic Edmund Wilson that political quarrels in intellectual domains made him "wonder what the world would be like if it were ruled by the intellectuals. . . . [There] would be real murders if the intellectuals controlled the state apparatus. Maybe that is part of the trouble in Russia." Yes, "maybe." Years before, Paterson had described Cowley listening to a discussion of communism's tendency to result in mass murder: "Malcolm wore his usual earnest, innocent expression of hoping for the best."[38]

As an opponent of prohibition, Paterson knew that high-minded attempts to make the world better by political action require the making of laws and the giving of orders. In times of economic crisis, she observed, there was even more competition than usual to get into the "aristocracy" of political command. It would be bad enough if competitors for power were all professional politicians. People like Al Smith might conceivably know what was going on. But now hordes of determinedly naive people, particularly artists and intellectuals, were busy "reforming the world, doing everybody's job but [their] own."[39] The pressure is on the word "job"—on the relationship between the individual and his or her proper work, a relationship that was central to Paterson's life and thought.

She was especially interested in the tendency of literary people not to comprehend the limitations of their jobs. They lost the distinction between people in books, who can be ordered about at will, and real people, who want their own freedom and responsibility. Writers also cherished a confused notion that education is the same as knowledge and that knowledge should be the same as power. They were members of an educated class that ached to make itself a ruling class.

This visceral longing could easily be discovered among communists and other professional believers and boosters, but Paterson found it also among the professional skeptics and debunkers, such as her friend Sinclair Lewis. Returning to Lewis's *Main Street* a decade after its publication, she realized why it had originally "daunted" her. Its protagonist, Carol Kennicott, is a would-be improver of her neighbors; but the vision of a Gopher Prairie, Minnesota, that actually became an American utopia,

> run by Carol, and populated by kindred souls, is too terrible to contemplate—much, much worse than in its untutored condition. It was from that we drew back. A model village with a Doric courthouse and library and amateur productions of Dunsany and Eugene O'Neill and the latest magazines on every table and—and—everything. . . .[40]

Paterson's own ideal village would be democratic in its fraternal willingness to put up with *un*improved humanity:

> It could only consist of the nice people we know and are fond of; and they're all crazy in different ways, just like your friends; and what some of them think of some of the others would make your blood run cold; and those of them who write won't read each other's books, and if forced to do so their mildest remarks are actionable, though they always say we mustn't quote them, but heaven knows we wouldn't dare; and personally, we disapprove of their way of life severally and entirely and wonder how they manage to get along at all because they never take our advice and we fear they will come to no good end. And besides, they wouldn't stay in Gopher Prairie; that's where they came from.[41]

Paterson's utopia (or Atlantis) is a place where people are free to go where they want and be who they are, no matter how mistaken their ideas of themselves may be.

On one level, this is a quarrel of artistic visions. Paterson's views are those of someone used to searching with a novelist's eye for what is various and interesting in the human spectacle, someone with the great literary realists' attitude toward conflict and apparent disorder: laissez-faire, "let it alone" to develop its possibilities, whatever those may be; impose no order that improves away its richness and diversity of meaning. Only an inferior art annihilates its own vitality. But she saw that some artists cannot stop their exercise of power at the appropriate place. For her,

[t]he first, last and continuous duty of a writer is to be interesting. Far too much latitude is allowed to bores in all walks of life. It is assumed that a bore must mean well. Even if he does, what of it? Good intentions are a bad excuse.

Carol Kennicott was a bore, and worse than a bore, because she planned to turn everyone else into a progressive moralist like herself. She was an artist who plotted to ruin her best material—the American experience, which Paterson said was "so various, rich and strange" that no "school of fiction has done it justice or could do so."[42]

Paterson's politics was deeply influenced by this essentially literary vision of America. The vision merged with her political and economic views about the difference between managed and unmanaged societies. She didn't have to turn to literature to locate specimens of good intentions that were a bad excuse. These days, she found them everywhere.

Al Smith had a similar experience. After the election that threw Hoover out, he encountered renewed proposals for the nation to be managed by social-minded engineers: "As for substituting engineers for political leaders in running the country, I cannot refrain from mentioning the fact that we have finished an era of government by engineers in Washington, and that the people of the country did not seem to like it."[43] Or so he hoped. But to the left of Hoover, a modern-liberal consensus was developing that would put economic planning and social engineering at the heart of the American system; and literary people were among its strongest supporters.

They often showed a touching faith in planning. Lincoln Steffens, the great muckraking journalist, raked no muck in Lenin's planned society. Informed by Lenin himself that he, Lenin, had been "all wrong" on the land question, Steffens said, "That is the advantage of a plan. You can go wrong . . . but if you know you are wrong, you can steer back on your course." In 1930, novelist Irving Fineman wrote to Paterson "eloquently advocating that the future of humanity be confided to the engineers."[44] And why not? If the industrial machine had broken down, shouldn't the engineers who built it be called upon to fix it? Engineering offered a vision of power and energy, of capitalist methods of production without the burden of capitalist greed. Industry would be run by college-educated brainworkers like the writers themselves, not by the Babbitts whom they had spent the 1920s satirizing.

This idea fueled the intellectual fad of the day, "technocracy." The technocracy movement was only part of the larger movement for social planning, but it gave Paterson important insights into the fundamental problems of any kind of government management.

The specific origins of technocracy lay in Thorstein Veblen's economic analysis of American history. Veblen, whose work continues to enjoy considerable academic popularity, held that advanced capitalist industry, though controlled by financial "vested interests," was actually run by the engineers. Engineers planned production; vested interests (i.e., owners and investors) "sabotaged" (i.e., limited) it, to keep profits up. Veblen did not see profits as an indication of the market's ability to identify and provide what consumers want; he saw them as unnecessary, ill-gotten gain. He calculated that modern industry could function at many times its current efficiency if the capitalist anarchs were replaced by a "soviet of technicians" that would "take care of the material welfare of the underlying population."[45] Industry could satisfy human needs if its capacity were not limited by the pursuit of private profit.

Some such assumption is basic to virtually any scheme of economic planning, for the obvious reason that there would be no need for planning if the spontaneous transactions of the marketplace were sufficient to supply the people's needs. The Great Depression seemed to indicate that they weren't. Veblen died in 1929, but his book, *The Engineers and the Price System*, was successfully resuscitated and became a best seller. By 1931, his theories were being proclaimed "the customary and slightly worn currency of our thinking." By early 1933, Paterson was complaining that people couldn't move around "without first brushing off a few technocrats." She told her readers that they would have to acquaint themselves with Veblen's book if they wanted to understand current intellectual discussion.[46] Her friend Chase was one of the leading technocrats. He produced a book whose title would not soon be forgotten: *A New Deal* (1932).

Chase was a handsome, athletic man in his forties, who looked much younger. Paterson would retain "fond recollections" of meeting him socially.[47] That may have been one reason why she gave *A New Deal* extraordinarily gentle treatment, considering the fact that it argued against "laissez-faire" and in favor of "collectivism" and "control from the top." Though she was fond of pointing out factual errors in Chase's works and recalling his failed predictions, he remained for her "the artless enthusiast who goes along for the ride. To him everything is really new—it's the first time he's heard it." She wanted to think that his book resulted from a reassuringly American association of progress with a return to basic principles: "[W]hat this country is trying to do is to get home. . . . Stuart Chase may not have realized how significant his title was: 'A New Deal.' Out of the same deck. It's an American phrase."[48]

To Chase, however, "a new deal" meant "the end of the economic system as we have known it—and suffered with it—in the past." He and Paterson had very different ideas about what might constitute a winning or a losing hand. He was against an economic system based on the individual's desire to gain wealth; she was against a political system based on the desire of "benevolent officials" to "Do Us Good." He argued that "political and business government" should be made "essentially one, as in Russia"; she was sure that they were already too firmly connected, like "Laocoon and the python."[49]

A New Deal showed where this zoological experiment could lead. To Chase, the worst thing about a Bolshevik America would be the "technological" disruption that revolutionary violence might occasion; the best thing would be communism's ability to eliminate capitalist ways of making money, "by firing squad if necessary." He advocated the erection of a "planning authority" that could "dig itself so deeply into the economic mechanism" that it could hardly be "dislodged" by electoral processes. The architects of the actual New Deal did not contemplate the use of firing squads, but (to Paterson's disgust) they did devise programs, such as Social Security, that were intended as permanent reconstructions of the economic order.[50]

At least, Paterson thought, Chase was a relief from other writers, because she could tell exactly where she disagreed with him. And he posed a challenge. He said that the modern industrial world demanded "a whole new conception, almost a new philosophy of energy applied in space through time."[51] In *The God of the Machine*, Paterson would offer such a philosophy. Before she did so, however, she needed to think through the issues that the technocrats raised about the economy of the machine.

Certainly the industrial development of America during the past century represented "an enormous release of energy," as she had said in *Never Ask the End*; she agreed with the technocrats on that. And the technocrats agreed with her that the expansion of energy originally resulted from the capitalist application of science to technology. Capitalism, in turn, had been fostered by America's political system: limited government led directly to laissez-faire.[52] Such had been the nature of progress in America. Yet the technocrats, in company with virtually all other "progressives" and "liberals," held that now the conditions of progress had changed; free enterprise, if continued, would no longer produce the same effects. New ways must therefore be found to coordinate the "million delicate gears" of the economic "mechanism."[53] That, of course, would require a new political organization.

Here is where Paterson left the technocrats' company. She had seen no arguments that convinced her of their thesis. Far from it. Progress never resulted from denying the principles that allowed it to happen. "[T]wo and two will still make four under any government"; and when anyone denies that they do, his engineering may turn out to be a little faulty—very faulty, in fact. Progress in America always depended on invention and innovation, on the kinds of human action that cannot be calculated or predicted. But the technocrats had to conceive of human action as calculable and predictable, or they would not be able to make their political plans for the new industrial machine. That was the error of technocratic "science." Living men and women always escape from technocratic measurements; they are not "gears." To treat living organisms as if they were not alive, to treat them as objects instead of subjects, is to deny and ultimately to destroy their ability to generate the energy that runs the machine. It is a "deathward impulse, for the rigidity of forms is the preliminary to their breaking."[54]

Advocates of a planned society assumed that the state, or the soviet of engineers, could find some objective means of making its plans. It would not have to rely on the fluctuating signals of the marketplace to decide what people need, want, value. But what is the nature of economic values? Are they truly objective and predictable? If not, how can an economy be planned and managed for the good of all?

Paterson was sure that economic values are subjective, not objective. "Subjective" need not mean "irrational"; a closer synonym is "relational." People are usually rational in pursuing their economic ends, but the ends are related to them as individuals, not to some common, supposedly objective scale of values. Accordingly, Paterson defined "wealth" as the "goods somebody wants and can use or enjoy. . . . You could put a great deal of energy into producing something nobody wants very much." She added, as a self-reflexive afterthought: "This disconcerting fact is peculiarly noticeable in the production of books."[55]

Her experience as a novelist had taught her a good deal that the technocrats had never learned. They ignored the dynamic subjectivity of "that incalculable animal man" and left "desire, or desirability, out of their reckoning." The author of *Never Ask the End* was incapable of doing that. "[T]hose imponderables," as she knew, "are the real basis of all life, all industry, all production, values, prices." The planners proposed to redistribute "material values" on an egalitarian basis. But there is no such thing as "material values." Material things acquire value when individuals want them, and every individual has his or her own scale of wants: "mere quantitative and objective standards" cannot be applied to them.[56] Demand will always respond unpredictably to individual consumers' desires, and supply will increase or decrease in response to prices generated by consumers' demands.

That is true even of natural resources. In Paterson's day, as in ours, the air was full of warnings about depletion of the world's store of one resource or another. Proven resources of oil were running out in her time, too. But proven resources tend to expand as the demand for them grows and as people develop the skill and enterprise necessary to exploit them. The conception of expanding resources is intimately associated with the idea of America and American individualism:

> The United States was not the "rich" part of the New World. What we now think of as its main resources were not known as such until the way to use them was figured out by pretty hard thinking and hard work—and a continuous zest in the adventure.[57]

Paterson thus affirmed her vision of America as a vast, unpredictable, and therefore risky challenge to thought and action. She also effortlessly allied herself with a revolution in modern thought, the revolution that, unknown even today to the great majority of literary intellectuals, made possible the modern science of economics. John Locke and Adam Smith had derived the value of commodities from the labor required to produce them. Karl Marx had made the theory of these bourgeois predecessors the basis of his own "scientific" theory of social justice, which involved restoring to the laborers the "surplus value" unjustly appropriated by their capitalist employers. The tradition was followed by Veblen and his disciples, who emphasized "work" as the source of value. They had not noticed, or they had not assimilated, the ideas of such late-nineteenth-century economists as William Jevons and Karl Menger, who had shown that values are not inherent in objects or in the processes by which objects are produced but are set by individual consumers' subjective preferences for particular units of commodities.

This is the principle of marginal utility, a foundational concept of modern economics. It is the idea, in Paterson's formulation, that economic value "really depends on what [the consumer] wants and how much he wants it."[58] Only in recent years has the "subjectivist revolution," which began in the 1870s, received anything like the attention it merits from leaders of American opinion outside the professional field of economics. Among conservatives and libertarians, knowledge of its implications was spread by the Austrian economist Ludwig von Mises, who escaped from Europe in 1940, and by his younger colleague Friedrich Hayek. Hayek's seminal work, *The Road to Serfdom* (1944), was welcomed by the right, disparaged by the left, immediately forgotten by the center. Three decades later, Hayek was awarded the Nobel Prize.

Until she read *The Road to Serfdom*, Paterson apparently never heard of the economists who would be linked with her as important influences on the modern libertarian and conservative movements. She had formed her economic theories on her own, years before. Like the continental economists, she had extended the theory of subjective values to nonmaterial goods. She saw that the nonmaterial often takes precedence over the material, though not in a way that can be quantified:

A man may lose money by keeping his word, for instance. His own feeling about himself is worth more than the money to him, but the two factors are incommensurable in any strictly rational terms.[59]

If that was true, then again there was no sense in talking about planning by rational calculation. The illusion of "control" could be established only by means of "suppressions." Some people (Nazis, for example) would be willing to sacrifice their liberty, or their opponents', because it had no value for them. People like Chase, on the other hand, professed to think that all material and spiritual aspirations could be satisfied simultaneously. He predicted that "[i]n a few years" the Soviet Union would "undoubtedly" produce everything that its people needed, presumably including liberty. He also believed that America's technology already enabled it to leave "the economy of scarcity behind"; with proper management, all needs would be met.[60] This was a remarkably narrow vision of human desires and possibilities.

But suppose that social planning *could* be done: who was qualified to do it? Irving Fineman suggested that "it would be better if the engineers could function freely, instead of in the employ of 'unscrupulous business men.'" That was the intellectuals' typical answer to the question. But this, Paterson believed,

> is assuming that engineers never would be unscrupulous—in short, that they aren't human. At present [Fineman] thinks "their power is misused, misdirected, as is the power of slaves." Isn't that in itself a confession of inability? An engineer is a man with a special technique, and presumably special aptitude; but politics, government, also require a technique and an aptitude of quite another sort.[61]

The problem is as old as the question that Socrates asks in the *Republic*: is there some special skill, some *techné*, that is proper to the governors of the state? Like Socrates, Paterson believed that there is. But she did not define that special aptitude as the power to plan and rule. She defined it instead as the power to maintain a regime in which no one rules. She assented to the "Jeffersonian idea that an important part of government consists in letting people alone." Embracing this idea for both economic and political reasons, she indicated that she was willing to return to her proper role as writer, so long as other writers were willing to return to theirs.[62] Naturally, they weren't.

10

Not Mad—But Atlantean

Paterson had announced her "republican-libertarian principles" during the Hoover administration. She announced them again as a greeting for the Roosevelt administration on its first morning in office. It was a good time to remember what she called

the classical American faith in politics and economics . . . the Rights of Man, personal liberty and private property.

She was well aware, she said, "that all those desirable things are damaged at present"; but "they didn't exist at all until they were created and fought for, and they can be restored if people want them."[1]

Paterson called her political philosophy "liberalism" or "classical Americanism,"[2] but it obviously went far beyond the usual associations of those terms. She had assembled the group of ideas and attitudes that are distinctive of the libertarian movement as we know it today: a belief in absolute individual rights and minimal (not just limited) government; advocacy of laissez-faire capitalism and an individualist and "subjective" approach to economic theory; opposition to social planning, victimless crime legislation, and any form of "class" or "status" society.

During the 1930s, a number of other American intellectuals came to share her views, or some of them. A little later, I will examine these interesting people. Libertarianism as a movement, however, was very far in the future. It would be a long time before libertarian ideas pervaded the airwaves and the Internet, a long time before a future president of the United States proclaimed himself a "libertarian."[3] In the 1930s, practically no one but Paterson thought that individualism, let alone radical individualism, had any chance as a political cause. The potent movements were collectivist.

Paterson at first believed that the collectivist movement of the "right," fascism, was more of a danger than the collectivist movement of the "left," communism.[4] A fascist psychology already showed itself in people's tendency to endorse political action without considering its consequences. Prohibition was a good example, but examples came up every day, in all the various action plans to "put America back to work," "share the wealth," make "every man a king," and so forth. These notions did nothing to disturb her conviction that fascism lacked any ideas worth talking about. Neither did the notion that Adolf Hitler was a "political genius." When somebody came into her office and expressed that idea, she began to scream, insisting that

> the mental defects of other people, such as Hitler's followers, do not constitute genius on the part of the leader. Multiply one half-wit by eighteen hundred million half-wits and still the result is not a genius, strange as it may seem.[5]

The fascists derived a political benefit from their paucity of ideas: at least they wouldn't be quarreling with one another about their creed, as the communists were always doing. The communists, the ideological pace-setters in the circles that Paterson frequented, were the ones burdened with ideas and definitions.[6] Nevertheless, she saw the two isms as fruit of the same tree—a hundred years of collectivist social assumptions, rooted in the great nineteenth-century movement for "social welfare" and "social progress," the great nineteenth-century rebellion against the alleged unfairness of competitive capitalism. Fascism was in no sense a "conservative revolution"; it was no more conservative than Bolshevism. They were both "modern totalitarian systems." Fascism ought to be regarded, indeed, as a standing embarrassment to communism, since they were so much the same in their illiberal origins and inhuman results. Paterson enjoyed reminding people that such leftists as George Bernard Shaw often made complimentary comments about fascists.[7]

During the first half of the fascist era, when Mussolini was the movement's principal exponent, American progressives were capable of seeing both him and Lenin as he-man reformers in the dynamically "practical" American mode. Lincoln Steffens represented Mussolini as something like a reform mayor of Cleveland, only of satisfyingly larger dimensions.[8] In those days, even modern-liberal Democrats, such as novelist Grace Zaring Stone, one of Paterson's good friends, could detect worthy qualities in Mussolini. Stone's daughter, Eleanor Perényi, relates a typical confrontation between Paterson and fascism. Stone and her daughter

> had been in Rome to a horse show about 1932; it was in the Borghese gardens, and there was a sun side and a shade side where you could sit. We sat on the shade side, and Mussolini arrived for this event and strode into the sun to be with the people, and I hate to say that we were very much impressed by that, and Isabel quite properly wrote back that he was a disgusting dictator and she wasn't the least impressed by his going to mingle with the hoi polloi and "neither should you be." That was right.[9]

In later years, many Americans tried to plead ignorance of fascist and communist crimes, but the evidence was plain to see. Paterson frequently reminded her audience of Stalin's "executions and exiles" and the "few million" peasants he had happened to starve. Soon after Hitler came to power, she began making sure that her readers understood what he was doing to the Jews. She emphasized Nazism's indebtedness to earlier collectivist movements that had persecuted "class enemies" and other minority groups: "[E]very one who has ever justified the Bolshevik or Fascist methods has thereby helped to make possible the tragedy of the Jews in Germany. Furthermore they are paving the way for the same kind of thing over here."[10]

Fascism's appeal to American progressives is now largely forgotten, as is communism's appeal to middle-class moralism, conformism, and boosterism. The evidence, however, is clear in both cases. Leslie Fiedler has accurately described the "rigid, conventional, hopelessly self-righteous" quality of "the stalinized petty-bourgeois mind." Paterson saw similar features in the "Russia" of the American communist imagination, "a sort of glorified Rotary Land, girls' scout organization, and office conference, in perpetual session," a land chock-full of "Pep and Class Spirit."[11] At the New School for Social Research, where she joined T. S. Eliot in viewing murals by the leftist radical José Orozco, she asked why people raved about such paintings. Eliot explained that they were "the art of the new religion of the masses." Paterson remained unmoved. The pictures looked to her like "precisely the same thing as the old colored Sunday School cards."[12]

Well, maybe not "precisely." But much of the kitschiness and smugness of the old religious attitudes adhered to the new religion of politics. Will Rogers, the maestro of mainstream attitudes, found it all very hard to resist:

> You know those Rascals in Russia along with all their Cuckoo stuff, have got some mighty good ideas. If just part of em work they are going to be hard to get along with. Just think of everybody in a Country going to work. I dont mean just the ones that want to work, but I mean everybody.

That was the sermon, to which was added a confession of sin, inspired, as was now traditional, by the "free land" notion: "We prospered for years on nothing but our natural resources."[13] Paterson didn't care whether this sort of thing was the authentic voice of the people or not; she wanted no part of it. It was Gopher Prairie, hideously "improved." And in Russia, of course, it had the power of the state behind it.

When Theodore Dreiser led a group of leftists to Kentucky for a protest-investigation of the conditions surrounding a miners' strike, Paterson thought it was a "well-meant effort, though probably useless." But when Waldo Frank, a prominent writer on the left, contended that the important point about the Russian communists wasn't their coercive methods but their humanitarian intentions, he was going too far. The methods were "the whole point," Paterson exclaimed.[14]

By spring, 1932, she had grown seriously concerned about

> the way the intellectual writers are going Communist. It's about time that Matushka, Little Grandmother, interviewed some of the children in the woodshed.[15]

Within a few days, Matushka met with further irritation. The John Reed Club confided its intention of working out a complete proletarian theory of literature, with the assistance of Edmund Wilson's articles in *Herald Tribune "Books,"* Paterson's own journal. In response, Paterson provided the *Trib*'s readers with an outline of her own ideology, which was the precise opposite of Marxism.

First, there was the matter of individual freedom:

> Be it understood that we do not object to the airing of Communist opinion. . . . The regimentation of thought and forcible suppression of opinion are the most intolerable aspects of the proposed communistic state, and inseparable from it.[16]

In other words, the communists were a lot safer in Isabel Paterson's world than they would be in their own.

Second, there was the little matter of the truth or falsehood of the communists' views. The basis of their opinions, literary or political, was the materialist interpretation of human action. Wilson had informed Paterson that he no longer respected the Declaration of Independence, the Constitution, or the Bill of Rights, because they resulted from the economic motives of the bourgeois class:

> He believes in economic determinism; people think and act according to their "group interests." . . .
> Which we flatly deny. Jefferson, then, as a landed proprietor, should have been the last person to abolish the laws of entail, which he did. Washington, as a slave owner should have been the last man to set his hand to a declaration of the Rights of Man, which he did.

Such men had consciously designed "a purely political government," intended "to lift the weight of economic considerations from the political balance."[17] That didn't mean that economics and politics were wholly unrelated, only that they were related in quite a different way from that posited by Marx:

> The theory of economic determinism puts the effect before the cause. Economics are created by intelligence; they don't operate automatically, and the skill and knowledge which Russia is now borrowing and hiring from the United States cannot be developed under communism. If they choose political communism—and they have the choice—they will get that, but not the free play of intelligence. They are determining their economics, not being determined by them.[18]

The individual mind not only transcends the social context; it constructs it. There is no objectively necessary social system, and there is no perpetual motion economy.

While this essay was in press, Paterson ran into Wilson at a party, where he confirmed her conclusions about the bad effects of communism on the human intelligence. Standing on the stairs, he told her (drunkenly, one would like to suppose) that "political exterminations—specifically the 'liquidation of the kulaks' in Russia—were right as long as the nonconformist group was completely exterminated." She "could only deduce," she reported, "that he went down to Kentucky to protest about the terrorism in the mining regions because it is not thorough enough. Shoot all the miners and their families and it will be O. K."[19]

Encounters of this kind contributed their share of bitterness to the sense of isolation that grew on Paterson during the 1930s. Looking around her, she found the country "in such a state that it becomes almost funny. . . . I can't imagine whether we'll get through alive or not; and I hope to expire before the Communists get us. For though everything is terrible, I can bear everything except the drabness of being run by our Left Wing Intellectuals." The communists found her as hard to bear as she found them. By the close of the Hoover administration, she was known in leftwing circles for her anti-Marxist "sneers and denunciations," her "misunderstanding and misrepresentation."[20]

Yet it took a long time for her reserves of good humor to seep away. Among her longtime friends was communist novelist and poet Isidor Schneider, who kept favoring her with invitations to communist meetings. When she received his invitation to hear a lecture by Corliss Lamont, the leftwing son of a Morgan banker, she found herself at her wits' end. Why, she asked, should she, a "self-supporting female" with a lot of work to do, "give up an evening to a youthful millionaire Communist with a couple of half-baked books to his credit"? Still, she went along with Schneider's request and printed his announcement of additional communist lectures.[21] That was a great deal more than *The New Masses* would have done for her.

Then she made a good point, one too often neglected amid the diatribes of people arguing about which social system should be imposed by government fiat: if you want to conduct a collectivist social experiment, you have a much better chance to do so in a libertarian society than you have in a collectivist one. In a collectivist society, you have to conform to the Plan. In a libertarian society, you are entirely free to make your own arrangements, so long as you don't try to force anyone else to participate. Paterson had a lifelong fascination with the communal experiments that had flourished in America—New Harmony, the Oneida Community, Nashoba, Brook Farm, and the rest of them. Such endeavors cost money, but the capitalist system allowed individuals to earn that money and spend it as they liked. The results were often peculiar, even repellent to people like Paterson; yet the whole process came under the heading of American individualism:

[P]eople are not all alike, and what will work for a limited group, inspired by a particular prophet, is all right for them and no criterion for a different type of person. It's a good safety valve in the body politic, just as a margin of inconsistency is salutary in one's private life.

This was social libertarianism: "The highest civilization affords the greatest latitude for variations in conduct."[22] A "purely political government" would leave people alone to pay their own costs and reap their own rewards. It would allow for the pursuit of real experiments, experiments that didn't try to decree their own success.

Of course, that wasn't good enough for the Marxists, and neither was it good enough for corporate businessmen who wanted government to rescue them from the effects of their failed financial experiments. In her statement of spring 1932 about the fallacies of the communist intellectuals, Paterson took time to assert that they were not alone in their defection from "political government." Big business and the intellectuals were popularly supposed to be on opposite sides, but they both operated on the principle that government was responsible for the economy, and that the economy must dictate what government would do and be. As a result, they had "already got the political machinery dangerously entangled with the economic system, disrupting both; and they are now demanding that the government should save them from what they've done to it."[23]

Shortly after Hoover's re-nomination in 1932, Paterson recalled that "[a]ll the bankers voted for Hoover" and asked the rhetorical question, "Do you think I care what happens to them? I should like to see them in the breadline." It was the same invitation she extended to the leftist intelligentsia: "I hope to see every damned professor in the breadline yet, before I arrive there myself. It would be worth it."[24] At times, the alleged conservatives seemed even crazier than the communists. Both had gotten the idea that they could *do* things to the economy. If one scheme didn't work, maybe another would; the only course not considered was leaving things alone:

I called on my vice president at the bank the other day, and he informed me that in his opinion the one remedy for the depresssion would be to issue new paper currency in the ratio of five to one, that is, giving everyone now possessed of one dollar in paper money five dollars in paper money. I asked what that would do for those who have not even one dollar, but he was rather vague on that point. He was convinced, however, that the proposed procedure would raise prices without making anything dearer—perfectly clear, isn't it? He thought the government should also take over all gold mines and pay the owners—I don't know what with—and "develop new gold mines." He held the opinion that there were plenty of gold mines lying around waiting to be developed! You think I made that up? You know that one can't. He said too that the five to one multiplication of paper money would raise the price of wheat, thus enabling each farmer to raise twice as much wheat and be prosperous. . . . I asked him, just what would it do for me, reducing the value of my salary to one fifth of what it now is, and he said my salary would be raised proportionately—you can see how that would be, can't you? I felt I had to get this off my chest.[25]

Paterson's ideological vertigo increased, a few weeks after that, when Vincent Sheean, the famous foreign correspondent, accused her of being a "Tory." Presumably he had reached that weighty judgment merely because she was "not a Communist, nor a technocrat." Actually, she replied, "the Communists and technocrats [were] pure Tories," because they held to the ancient idea of the state as the "overlord" that is capable of deciding everything. From her point of view, this obsessive talk of leftists and rightists was useless, anyway. They were all enemies of individualism:

[T]he Left Wing and the extreme Right have marched around in circles until now they are inextricably intertwined, combining the worst features of both.[26]

It was not an inspiring prospect. But the question of how that happened, what it meant, and what it meant in the larger pattern of American life—that was worth writing about. It figures largely in *The Golden Vanity*, the novel that Paterson published in 1934.

This was, perhaps, her best novel, and it was another commercial success. Robust in characterization, dramatic in plot, seamless in its union of private experience and public philosophy, *The Golden Vanity* is one of the few really impressive novels written about the Great Depression—although that was not its original theme. Paterson started writing it before the stock market crash. Its origin predated even *Never Ask the End*, begun in September 1929. One night in September 1932, when that novel was in press, she found herself looking at some "thin" chapters of a manuscript she had set aside and thinking how much she could improve them, using what she had learned while completing the other book. "I know what to do with them," she thought.[27]

In their original form, those "thin" chapters probably contained the framework for a comparative study of three women, each of them representing one variant of the American experience. In the published novel (and, one supposes, in the original draft) the three women are relatives (cousins). Like the majority of Americans of Paterson's generation, they have all been reared in respectably straitened circumstances; but their lives develop in different ways. One of them, Geraldine Wickes, becomes a best-selling novelist. Another, Gina Fuller, marries the heir to a great American fortune. The third, Mysie Brennan, is an actress, when she can get the work. The novel would presumably have investigated the subtle tissue of identity connecting the three women's memories of their common past with their perceptions of the present and their intimations of the future. It would, in short, have been a study of American personalities in their collision with time, something similar to *Never Ask the End*, but without its stream-of-consciousness method. Omniscient narration, with its ability to explore private thoughts while placing them in a firm sequence of external events, would work more easily in a novel that needed to move back and forth among three very different experiments with life.

It is not clear what events would have influenced the plot of *The Golden Vanity* as Paterson originally imagined it. What did happen was the stock market crash. The crash and the ensuing depression became the crucial development in the novel, the development that allowed Paterson to establish a political perspective on her characters' experience. She told Rascoe in 1933 that she hoped to work some of her political and economic views into the text.[28] She succeeded. Although *The Golden Vanity* is in no sense a propaganda novel—Paterson finds numerous ways of conveying her ideas without reducing the book to a set of political propositions—its perspective is thoroughly libertarian.

In one sense, that perspective was easy to establish. If "laissez-faire" means anything, it means allowing individuals to realize their possibilities, whatever those may be. That is her program in *The Golden Vanity*, which allows each character to face the challenge of events in her own way. None of the principal characters appears as either a hero or a villain. Paterson's power as a novelist is shown, not by her ability to maneuver them into one of those categories, but by her ability to present them as real and complex personalities, responsive to their own assumptions and perceptions.

Gina is a good example. Another novelist might have depicted her as that most familiar of female stereotypes, the fortune hunter. Technically speaking, Gina *is* a fortune hunter; she is desperately ambitious for wealth. Yet she is something more interesting than a ruthless adventurer; she is a pure devotee of an American religion, descended, like the "Protestant ethic," from St. Paul's theology:

> Gina's reverence for wealth was mystical, partaking of the quality of veneration of the two extremes of pious minds, the childlike and the erudite. While aware of the physical substance, they conceive it to be transfused by a divine essence, which it imparts inexhaustibly by contact. So its possessors acquire merit, are superior beings, vessels of election. In her yearning toward them, Gina was not a simple mercenary snob, but a novice seeking admission to a difficult way of perfection. She intended to be rich. But she never thought of making money. Salvation was by grace; works would not avail.[29]

Gina has the naiveté of the true believer. When she marries her young heir, Arthur Siddall, it does not occur to her that there is anything wrong about marriage without love. She is soon surprised to discover that her marriage has nothing in it except the decency and courtesy that she and her husband practice toward each other as their social duty. Paterson always thought of Americans as strangely, often untowardly, innocent; that is the good thing and the bad thing about the Siddalls.

Geraldine stands much higher in Paterson's estimation. She exemplifies the American character type in which Paterson invested most of her own faith, the person of practical competence and responsibility. She believed that there are people in every "economic class" who keep society going. These people justify her idea of human energy as spontaneously self-generated, inexplicable in terms of outward circumstances; and they go far toward justifying her libertarian political ideas. They are a minority, but (as she wrote in the *Herald Tribune*) the welfare of everyone

> depends entirely upon a minority being allowed to function. We do not mean a class, but a certain type of mind. It exists in various degrees and forms—business men and farmers and foremen and housewives, the people who will always somehow get things done, get some practicable result from whatever material is at hand and whatever other people they must work with. They are self-starters. And they are seldom conspicuous.
>
> The self-starters are never college professors nor politicians. Neither do we mean inventors, intellectuals, artists or writers—the creative artist [e.g., Paterson herself] is naturally anti-social. The self-starters, of course, use what more original minds discover, and their particular function is to hold everything together. One can't always see how they do it.[30]

Geraldine is one of those self-starters. Admittedly, she is a writer, but she is by no means an "anti-social" intellectual. She is a woman with a husband and children and an apartment to manage. She has a knack for writing stories for a popular audience; that is how she supports her family. So she works at it, with no display of artistic temperament. Again, however, the good and the bad are closely associated. Geraldine's flaw is the defect of her virtues. Her job is to "hold everything together," and to do so, she makes large concessions to her husband. The problem is that Geraldine earns much more money than Leonard, a corporate chemist of distinctly mediocre ability who regards her work as merely "an interesting accomplishment, bringing her pin money. He honestly thought of it that way" (93). What Leonard cares about is social status, not accomplishment. He feels that when he visits Geraldine's wealthy kinfolk "he ought to have a chauffeur" (92). So he speculates in a silly, credulous way on the stock market; and Geraldine, the real head of the family, lets him.

Mysie, the actress, has nothing to "hold together"; she demonstrates the conflicts of the "naturally anti-social" (or at least nonsocial) individualist. *The Golden Vanity* cannot be called autobiographical in the point-by-point manner of *Never Ask the End*; nevertheless, Mysie has a number of Pat-like characteristics: she comes from the Pacific Northwest, she has a close friendship with an eccentric playwright named Jake, a ringer for Will Cuppy (whose nickname was Jake), and she shares Paterson's political ideas. She has none of the social conventionality of Gina or Geraldine. The consequence, however, is that she lacks their external points of reference.

One of her strongest ties to the world is her memory of her first romance, an affair with Michael Busch, her boss when she was a nineteen-year-old working girl. She has never been ashamed of the relationship; she and Michael remain friends. She sees him as a man of integrity, "substantial, dependable," emphatically a self-starter (223). She *almost* loves him (228), but she doesn't, and there is no credible substitute for love. When she is with him, she is reminded of the fact that "every soul" has to be "saved by itself" (251)—another, and more accurate, application of St. Paul's ideas. It's the truth, as Paterson sees it, but it's far from cheery. One can read both the credits and the debits of individualism in Mysie's ledger.

Despite their common origin, Paterson's three major characters differ greatly in their sense of the individual's relationship to the world. The depression draws their stories together again, by confronting them with a common threat to their existence. Mysie survives by doing what she's always been doing, taking care of herself without illusions about her prospects for external success. Geraldine cannot escape so easily; the needs of her family connect her too closely with the world. When her husband's investments dwindle to nothing, he does too; and she suffers a nervous breakdown. Desperately attempting a cure, she escapes on a solitary trip to Cuba, where she, the very essence of responsibility and respectability, finds romance with a gangster. He, at least, has retained his competence.

Gina's story is the most interesting: not because Gina herself is, but because it grows into the story of something more important than Gina. Paterson carefully sets the stage. Gina's husband Arthur is a nice child, attentive, chivalrous, bewildered by a world of conflicts he has not been educated to understand. His wife is in love with her social position and can spare no passion for him. He tries to find some kind of significant work by investing in a little magazine, *The Candle*, which Paterson creates in the image of Vincent Astor's *Today*. The radicals who run the deficit-ridden journal patronize Arthur, while extracting his money. They publish favorable reports on Russia and news about "the art of Stanislas Prezmsyl, a Pole who modeled all his subjects in the likeness of eggs." The editors uniformly oppose machine-age standardization (145, 142-43).

Nothing disgusted Paterson more than Rolls Royce radicalism, but she was too good a novelist to make Arthur a villain. He's just not. He is a man who needs to work and does not understand how to do it. She uses him, however, to suggest the convergence—often the childish, naive convergence—of American wealth with American collectivism. More dangerous examples of this convergence emerge from Arthur's surroundings, in the forms of the "Big Men" who profit from free enterprise while attempting to rule and, therefore, to ruin it. They are, as she later called them, the "Communists" of Big Business.[31]

Arthur's grandmother, the family's ruling authority, makes the definitive discovery of this evil. Her enlightenment is one of the novel's big surprises. At the beginning, Mrs. Siddall appears to be nothing more than the stereotypical old dame with money, a quaint survival of the four hundred socialites for whom Mrs. Astor built her ballroom. Once the pampered heiress of a "great and durable" fortune, now the pampered widow of a Senator, Mrs. Siddall presides over her social world as if nothing had changed since the 1890s (206). She would serve, one would think, as a natural target of satire, but that's not how Paterson uses her. She treats her, instead, as she treats the tribesmen in *The Road of the Gods*, as an example of real, though old-fashioned, values.

Behind the triple draperies that protect Mrs. Siddall from the noise of Fifth Avenue, she honorably maintains the moral and social standards by which her position once legitimized itself. The fact that these values are narrow, unimaginative, and (by most accounts) passé isn't the last word on Mrs. Siddall as a person:

> Though she might have talked nonsense if required to defend her position, she had a genuine practical intelligence, consistent with her experience. Her natural and instinctive morality was so fully accordant with her time, place and circumstances that she had never needed to formulate it. In a complex society there are many moralities. They do not necessarily conflict. (206)

Like the tribesmen, however, Mrs. Siddall is ill equipped to understand any force antagonistic to her values. She is the victim of her own conservatism. She believes so much in solid investment, which she construes as investment in real estate ("great and durable"), that she allows herself to be roped into a scheme to erect a skyscraper. The building that results is solid enough, but the investment isn't. It's a product of the New Era of speculative engineering—something like the new Empire State Building, which Paterson saw every morning on her way to work. Al Smith was the head of that enterprise, but Paterson, the old "Smithereen," knew that the building was in serious financial trouble. It was constructed on the assumption that if you build it, they will come; but they didn't come.

In *The Golden Vanity*, modern financiers fix things up for the Siddall Building in the same way in which Paterson thought they had fixed things up for the country. From the Woodrow Wilson regime to the regimes of Herbert Hoover and Franklin Roosevelt, they had made influence and profit for themselves while saddling their customers with the risks. That was the new "conservatism," the conservatism of the financial planners, who in Paterson's view were simply speculators with other people's resources. In that way they resembled Arthur Siddall's business associates, the new "progressives." Both squandered financial and intellectual wealth on big plans backed by nothing better than promises. It's not surprising that the son of Julius Dickerson, the politically well connected banker who swindles Mrs. Siddall, is the chief ideological officer of *The Candle*, the collectivist journal that is swindling her own son out of his time and money. The banker and the ideologue are both members of the would-be governing class, a class that makes a sorry contrast to Mrs. Siddall and the solid wealth of the old gold-standard businessmen.

Mrs. Siddall is certainly narrow, and she may be wrong; but she is not a contradiction in terms. She is not working to poison the wellsprings of her own life.

> Mrs. Siddall's life was logical and all of a piece, proceeding from the axioms of property, the virtues of which are thrift, tenacity, and faith in the visible world. (206)

Compare the Dickerson family. Young Roger Dickerson, who exists only by virtue of his family's money, has the "most to do" with turning *The Candle* from "a very precious aesthetic publication" into an agent of the war against (other people's) wealth (143). But there is a family interest even here. Arthur wonders why *The Candle* propagandizes for the cancellation of war debts, despite the fact that Roger's father Julius was involved in arranging the debt settlements. What Arthur doesn't understand is the significance of the commissions that Dickerson's father derives from European industrial concessions and loans, loans that may now get paid ahead of the war debts (145-46). Whatever social arrangements the Dickersons engineer, they expect to come out on top of them.

It was Julius who sold Mrs. Siddall a lot of bad investments, then covered them up with financial hypotheses that make perpetual motion seem neat and straightforward. Like his son's political theories, these are presented with the confidence of a priestly caste. Dickerson Senior purports to believe in "business"; Dickerson Junior purports to believe in "social equality"; their real allegiance is simply to power.

> Any morality is posited upon choice and freewill. Confusion arises only in the mind of the individual who professes a morality at variance with his way of life, refusing

to meet the terms. He asks instead that it shall be imposed by force. . . . This is the way of death. (206)

The novel, which at first seems to be so much about wealth, is actually about power. Mrs. Siddall's great moment comes when she finally penetrates the theories of Julius Dickerson and discovers that there is no big idea inside them, nothing but folly and a self-righteous assertion of the ruling caste's right to folly. "Julius said: 'Of course we have all had losses—' 'Have you?'" she asks.

She couldn't see that it was any recommendation of a financial adviser that he had had losses. An incidental suspicion sprang from the question. Julius said deprecatingly: "We could not foresee—" "Why couldn't you foresee?" Mrs. Siddall demanded. "If you can't foresee, what are you paid for?" She marched out, an angry old woman, more formidable in that native character than in her customary complacency of privilege. Even if it wasn't any use to speak her mind, it was a satisfaction; and it gave her the impetus to face the worst. (323)

"An angry old woman": in her wrath, Mrs. Siddall demonstrates that even the rich can transcend their mistakes. It isn't the money that matters, after all; it's the power of individual character. Mrs. Siddall discovers that she is bankrupt, or nearly so, but she is more alive at that moment than she has been in many years. Driving up the Avenue from her interview with Dickerson, who knows only "the way of death," Mrs. Siddall encounters "with fresh force" the "incessant and varied stream of life":

People going about their own affairs, busy, anxious, gay, indifferent. She was carried along with them. Energy flowed into her. (330)

Mrs. Siddall dies before she can complete her plans for dealing with the emergency. Yet she is spiritually triumphant, even in death: "Lying in her coffin, she looked dignified and kind; the last trace of haughtiness was wiped away" (332). No, it was never the money that mattered.

That had always been Mysie's view, and at the end of the novel, it seems to be the view of almost everyone—even Gina and Arthur, who, though bankrupt, somehow keep living (as rich people do) in roughly the same way they always did. In the last chapter, most of the characters assemble for one of those spontaneous gatherings of misfitted personalities that Paterson knew so well. Jake sits at the piano and plays an old ballad:

My love he built a bonny ship and set it on the sea,
And the name of the ship was the Golden Vanitie. . . (367)

The "Golden Vanitie," of course, gets wrecked, like the American economic system; but when Jake starts recalling his own experience of a mishap at sea, "floating in darkness and mist without direction" in a launch whose motor had broken down, disaster turns into jest.

"How were you saved?" Mysie asked.
"By wading ashore," said Jake. . . . "We bumped into a sandbar. . . . We must have been within a few yards of the beach all the time."
Mysie said, "You damn fool!" And shouted with mirth.
And yet, she thinks, "we'll never touch our shore again. That landfall is lost forever, down under" (372).

And that is the end of the book. It concludes with three possible perspectives on the American story: tragic, comic, heroic. Take your pick.

On the tragic side, there is Paterson's withering skepticism: "we'll never touch our shore." On the comic side, there is the interesting idea that, when all is said and done, we are only a few yards from the beach. And on the heroic side, there is Mrs. Siddall, who dies only after she reaches home—which is, as Paterson said, exactly what "this country is trying to do." One also remembers Paterson's myth of Atlantis, the American landfall that is always there, "down under" the troubled surface of events. We were damn fools to lose it, but we can find it again whenever we stand up and stop being fools.

One imagines Paterson's hands poised over the typewriter keys, prepared either to write "The End" immediately after Mysie's shout of mirth or to go on and type in "lost forever. . . ." She chose the tragic alternative—but her book argues more strongly for an optimistic one. It's not just that Mrs. Siddall is so good at illustrating Americans' ability not to be damn fools forever. It's not just that Mysie and her crowd manage to attain a comic perspective on the tragic loss of the "Golden Vanity." It's also that Paterson succeeds in evoking the energy of America, a motor that has never completely broken down.

Describing the traffic on Sixth Avenue, a street she crossed every day on her way to work, Paterson calls it a "spate of power pouring between artificial cliffs" (84). Optimism recurs in Mysie's conversation with a European visitor, who, when asked whether frenetic New York City reminds him of "a madhouse," replies, "Not mad—but Atlantean" (173). In the energy of individual Americans, Atlantis endured. It was ambiguous, risky, even tricky; it was both a "place" and a constant motion and activity. But it endured. Certainly it endured in Isabel Paterson. Whatever doubts she had about other people, she had touched her shore.

11

The Principle of the Lever Remains the Same

By the time Franklin Roosevelt was inaugurated, some of Paterson's readers were begging her to come down off her soapbox, while others were begging her to speak more loudly. It was paradoxical, she confessed, that the battle for individualism had aroused her public spirit. But although she might prefer ("at times") to confine her column to literary subjects, she couldn't do so unless she ignored "practically all current books." She would "much rather talk about Art, Literature, Love or the Language of Flowers, but the new books . . . do not touch on those topics."[1] This, of course, was persiflage. She wanted to talk about politics, so she did.

She had voted for Roosevelt. She didn't like him, but at least he was opposed to prohibition.[2] She made no comment on the fact that his platform favored certain economic policies that she approved, such as a balanced budget and a deep cut in federal spending. Once the New Deal got underway, she reminded people about his unkept campaign pledges; during the election, however, she seems to have taken them no more seriously than he did.[3] As a friendly historian has written, FDR "was the only presidential candidate in either major party who consistently criticized business leadership, who demanded drastic (if unspecified) changes in the economic system, who called for bold experimentation and comprehensive planning."[4] If comprehensive planning and drastic economic change meant anything, they could not mean anything so prosaic as a balanced budget. But Paterson spent election night agreeably, "seeing Hoover get his."[5]

Then, a few weeks after Roosevelt's inauguration, she found herself doing "nothing but curse and swear." The administration was continuing to do "all that our Best Minds have been doing to us for four years and which they keep on doing more and more." For the benefit of her readers she reviewed the economic events of the past fifteen years:

> First the statesmen of all nations must start a war with loud hurrahs, to make the world safe for democracy. Then the financiers must step in and give the impression that war doesn't really cost anything, because you can do it all on loans, and, in fact, everybody will make a nice profit out of commissions on the bonds. . . . Then, mysteriously, the bonds began to fall due. This was never expected.[6]

She turned to Roosevelt's attempts to deal with the results of Republican mismanagement: his new economic programs, his rule by decree during the banking crisis with which his administration began, his rushing of bills through Congress, sometimes with less than an hour for debate. Sarcastically assuming that all of this was just as necessary as the president's supporters believed it was, she said that there had been

> nothing to do but . . . call for a dictator and inaugurate a rain of paper like the ticker tape hurled out of the Wall Street windows on a parade day. Announce that democracy will not work in a crisis, and grab whatever any individual has left. And you have a lovely economics in which nothing need ever be paid, and if you think you have any rights you'll give everybody a big laugh.[7]

The administration's efforts included measures to raise farm prices, guarantee mortgages, and rescue defaulting banks—all extensions of the Hoover programs. But the New Deal centerpiece was the National Recovery Administration, designed to control the industrial life of the country by getting business, government, and labor to collaborate in fixing standards for wages and prices. This was "planning" on a gargantuan scale, and it made all the problems of planning starkly visible.

To create "cooperation" and "coordination," competition must be curtailed. Businessmen must not attempt to rid themselves of bloated inventories by giving their customers a real break on prices; that would be "cut-throat competition." Prices must stay up, and so must wages. But suppose that prices stayed up so far that nobody would pay them? That problem was supposedly solved by the purchasing power of the highly paid workers. They would buy their own products, using inflated wages to pay inflated prices. As the president explained in a Fireside Chat about the NRA, "If all employers will act together to shorten hours and raise wages we can put people back to work. No employer will suffer, because the relative level of competitive cost will advance by the same amount for all."[8]

There were some obvious economic flaws in that argument, but the president brushed them lightly away. "I have no faith in 'cure-alls,'" he said, "but . . . I have no sympathy with the professional economists who insist that things must run their course and that human agencies can have no influence on economic ills." No one had ever denied that such an influence existed; the question was what the influence would be. The success of the president's program depended on the ability of all human agencies to cooperate in making wages keep up with, in fact run faster than, prices. If wages could not be persuaded to work that way, the whole procedure would be counterproductive. No one knew better than the NRA czar, General Hugh Johnson, how chancy it all was. "I have said right along that it is a gamble," he declared; though he added, with a choice of words that merely emphasized the length of the odds, "I think I can put this thing over."[9]

As we have seen, Paterson was skeptical, to say the least, about any effort like this. Even if planning could be carried on in a scientific way, oblivious to the pressure of large interests trying to "stabilize" their current advantages, what scientist could predict the effects of billions of personal economic choices? And what did stabilization have to do with the unpredictable discoveries on which progress depends? "It is perfectly impossible," she concluded, that

> any forecast should be correct. For such correctness, it would be necessary for the prophet to know and understand absolutely all the factors of present and past out of which the future must proceed, and to anticipate inerrantly all the possible new discoveries which may be made. Failing that, the answer is bound, by scientific laws, to be wrong.[10]

No one knew enough; but someone would have to know, if the plan was going to work.

Paterson had charted the rock with which all planned societies have collided, the rock on which the NRA was wrecked (even as viewed by the Roosevelt administration) long before the Supreme Court formally sank it. To appreciate the danger of continuing with such schemes, one can try to imagine what America would look like if its economy had been successfully "stabilized" at some point in the past—perhaps at the point immediately before computers appeared, or the point at which automobiles were still expensive luxury items.[11]

One can also consider the effects on liberty and diversity. The tendency of government management is to favor existing economic interests at the expense of ones that are developing, and large interests at the expense of small. A small business that needs to raise prices in order to employ its workers, or to cut prices in order to reduce its inventory, can easily be ruined by pressure to conform to some general scheme. In this case, as in others, the effort to concert a "plan" is directly destructive of individuality. Paterson, who was the smallest kind of businesswoman, believed that the "necessary diversity of life" was endangered by any variety of "regimentation and bureaucracy." She saw the whole tendency as a personal threat:

> We feel toward Planners as the heroine of the old-time melodrama felt toward the villain. After having pursued her through four acts with threats of a fate worse than death, which he emphasized by shooting at her, setting fire to her home, and tying her to the railroad track just before the down express was expected, he inquired reproachfully, "Nellie, why do you shrink from me?"[12]

To Paterson, one of the most offensive deeds of the new administration was its attack on hard money and, by extension, on the prudent behavior of individuals who, like her, were trying to use their money to achieve some measure of security. The Emergency Banking Bill that Congress rushed into law in eight hours on March 9, 1933, members of the House not having been provided with copies of the bill to read for themselves, authorized the Secretary of the Treasury to confiscate savings in gold and exchange them for paper.[13] A decree was soon issued, demanding that gold be turned in, on pain of fine and imprisonment. Paterson reacted before the decree, finding in the proceedings conclusive evidence of the ruthlessness of the "Big Men" who insisted on "Saving Us":

> The final measure of general assistance was to go down into the family sock and grab any cash that remained to Save it for us. This is a kindness we shall never forget; and we only hope to be able to do something in return some day for our legislators. Maybe election day. It was indeed a most inspiring spectacle to see how unanimously the Big Men went after the unpatriotic widows and orphans who had tried to hold out a nickel. But why only ten years in jail? Oughtn't the hold-outs to be electrocuted?[14]

One afternoon in October 1933, Paterson became a victim of emerging conditions when she tried to remove some belongings (nature unknown) from her safe deposit box. Suspecting an economic crime, bank employees locked her in the vault and let her sit there wondering whether imprisonment would give her time to finish her next novel. Then, having demonstrated the power of the new conformity (and having heard her reminders about the kidnapping law), they allowed her to depart, convinced that "[t]here is practically nothing you can't be put in jail for now."[15]

One of the administration's purposes was to inflate prices by devaluing the dollar and freeing it from the market price of gold. The larger purpose was to put economic values safely in the hands of the government. The administration invalidated the "gold clause," the words written into public and private contracts to stipulate that debts must be paid in gold. FDR then conducted an absurd experiment in raising farm prices by buying gold at inflated levels, thereby depressing the value of the dollar. One morning, when Roosevelt advisor Henry Morgenthau met with the president to set the price of gold, he was startled to hear him decree that it should now go up by twenty-one cents: "'It's a lucky number,' he said with a laugh, 'because it's three times seven.'"[16]

The experiment didn't work, and Roosevelt, to his credit, abandoned it; but at its end, he induced Congress to let him set the value of the gold dollar at 59.06 percent of its last value. Paterson had predicted that the results would lie in this range.[17] The short-term effects were a gush of new fiat money and increased insecurity on the part of private individuals, the kind of insecurity that worked to keep investment at a level too low to produce economic recovery. The long-term effects of government policies can be seen in the fact that 1933 prices have to be multiplied by fifteen or twenty in order to translate them into current dollars.[18]

Friends of the New Deal argued that it had finally freed finance from the traditional domination of the Eastern banks and entrusted it to "the nation."[19] As Paterson saw it, this was a pompous mystification of the actual event, which was simply an enormous concentration of power in the federal government. The government could now do what it wanted, unchecked by the discipline of sound money. The people would have less ability to control their fate than they had ever had: "What is really happening is the economic disfranchisement of the public." The government's currency manipulations amounted to "running the game with a crooked wheel. By that system, we regret to state, the kitty gets it all. And, unfortunately, you've got to play whether you like it or not."[20]

Popular animosity had been aroused against bankers for supposedly adhering to restrictive monetary policies; but the big bankers, stuck with bad investments contracted during Hoover's New Era, generally supported Roosevelt's inflationary policies. Bankers who had made prudent investments, Paterson observed, were now being forced to expend their resources on saving their delinquent brethren.[21] So were all other prudent people—the Mrs. Siddalls and Isabel Patersons of the world.

Whatever the practical effects might be, she found the arrogance of this system infuriating. She was not without arrogance herself. It was so much the occupational disorder of writers that she sometimes reported herself startled to discover a writer who was missing the trait. She accepted it with amusement in private life. She even cheerfully admitted that the tendency "to mind some one else's business" was perfectly "natural," and that she shared it. After all, who asked her to begin her career of advising the republic? But arrogance was intolerable when it was joined with power. She did not admire the president's patrician self-assurance or his willingness to undertake boldly eclectic experiments on the body politic. His boldness, his persuasive charm, his superb talents as an actor and public speaker—those qualities just made the situation worse, because they were the means of dominance. Where other people saw warmth and wit, she saw a man who "behave[d] coyly at press interviews and giggle[d] constantly at his own 'puckishness.'"[22]

She disliked Roosevelt not just for his policies but for what she considered his contagious lack of integrity. According to contemporary reports, Democratic Senator Thomas P. Gore of Oklahoma remarked to Roosevelt that, as president, he could apparently do almost anything he wanted, no matter how illegal it was; and Roosevelt "roared with laughter." Senator Gore probably did not share the president's mirth; Gore had begun his career as a populist but was opposed to the New Deal and particularly to its actions in respect to gold, actions which, he told the president, were nothing but "a government steal."[23] Paterson wasn't laughing either. She thought the incident represented a cynicism that was spreading from Washington throughout the country.

There had been political nonsense in America before, and plenty of it, but now Americans were getting the idea that nonsense would have no consequences:

> It doesn't matter so much that the taxpayer's money should be appropriated to take Mr. Astor's unprofitable slum properties off his hands and give him an addition to his income, as that the taxpayer himself should be doped with the assurance that nobody has to pay for anything.[24]

That certainly wasn't the traditional idea of America.

The president reminded her of Calonne, the charming minister of Louis XVI who spent money in a vain attempt to restore public credit. The parallel extended to the Hoover years; Calonne merely "finished the job, begun by previous spendthrifts." Roosevelt, a man with a secure inherited income, deserved no moral credit for trying to redistribute money that hadn't been so easily acquired: "If this is idealism, it strikes us as almost too idealistic." There was never any question in Paterson's mind about Roosevelt's "saving capitalism," although she noticed that the New Deal had benefited a number of capitalists, such as Vincent Astor and Joseph Kennedy, who weren't worth saving in the first place.[25]

Roosevelt was very far from having the coherent economic program that conservative and libertarian writers have often accused him of having.[26] Paterson never shared their view. The Dickens character who reminded her of FDR wasn't Fagin but Mr. Micawber, who always expects that something will "turn up" to help him. Mrs. Roosevelt, of course, was Mrs. Jellyby, Dickens' empty-headed do-gooder.[27] The Roosevelts' wealth and patroonish social connections completed the picture of a couple whom Paterson did not need to regard as Borgias in order to dislike:

> Personally we do not object to the rich, as long as they know their place. Segregated in Newport and other penal colonies, they do little or no harm. The trouble is they couldn't stand it themselves . . . A lot of them have decided to Help Others. And the results are just about what you'd expect.[28]

Roosevelt surrounded himself with an enormous number of political friends, virtually all of whom Paterson deplored. Some of them were cynical party operatives; others were the allegedly conservative men of business and finance who had given Hoover all the bad advice they could think of and had now turned to Roosevelt; still others—and these were her favorite targets—were feckless idealists, people like Rexford Tugwell, Donald Richberg, Raymond Moley, Henry Wallace, and other bright spirits in and around the so-called Brain Trust. They conformed to a familiar American type; they had "been to Sunday School and college" and had absorbed "the Sayings of Famous After Dinner Speakers. Thus instructed, [they] set out to make the world a better place." Their mental equipment was "a mother's boy economic program with a kind maternal government taking care of everybody out of an inexhaustible income drawn from mysterious sources."[29]

They had no idea of how to generate wealth; their idea was to "distribute" it—distribute it until there was nothing left. "[D]estitution," to be sure, "is easily distributed. It's the one thing political power can insure you." These visionaries who offered to conduct large social experiments on other people were solemnly full of good intentions. Well,

> [s]entimentality is not emotion, and the people who never laugh are prone to "experiment" on others. They aren't going to let any one laugh if they can help it.[30]

Paterson was determined to laugh. It was "a treat" to find that Brain Truster Donald Richberg had published a novel, so she could say, "It's a sad story. The style alone would bring tears to your eyes."[31] An equally convenient target was Eleanor Roosevelt, with her earnestness and obtuseness and her cloying, superior style. When she invited Paterson to visit her, as she invited other women journalists, to charm them and win them over, Paterson did not accept. She did not wish to be charmed.[32] No one could accuse Mrs. Roosevelt's writing of any degree of charm, but it was often instructive. Paterson caught her discussing her travels in the American West, where she saw "houses so far apart" that

> one cannot help but think it requires a different quality to live and be happy where so much of the time must be spent alone. . . . Even the youngsters must have occasions when they know what it is like to see no other human beings anywhere in sight.

Paterson did not need to comment on the writer's oddly redundant syntax; she went right for the social commentary. "Hideous as the prospect appears," she said, it is barely possible that some people could be found who spend five minutes in solitude occasionally. Even children. Should this be allowed to continue? . . . Because otherwise those children may develop the "different quality" which will enable them to support their dire condition; they might find something to do without being told, think their own thoughts, read, or observe nature, or get the notion of becoming independent, instead of planning to grow up and attach themselves forthwith to a government pay roll, where they can be assured of steady supervision and inquisition at intervals into their private lives. . . .[33]

Just as easy to rough up were such exalted journalists as Walter Lippmann, who dismissively suggested, a propos the government's confiscation of gold, that "[a]ny one who does not mind a bad headache can devote himself to figuring out whose gold it is the government is taking." Paterson replied that since "intellectual processes do not give us a headache we will take on the job, and Mr. Lippmann may go home and take an aspirin tablet and devote himself to whatever activity is least injurious to his head. . . . All gold in the U. S. Treasury belonged to whoever had gold certificates." Lippmann had depicted himself, with suddenly assumed bashfulness, as "wandering blindly in a metaphysical swamp" while trying to comprehend the idea of a substance (gold) that actually derived value from its use in commercial exchange. That was, indeed, a weird swamp for him to wade in: "Can he name anything whatever that has any value whatever except for its use?" So much for Lippmann's attempt "to furnish the Administration an alibi for confiscating property in the form of gold."[34]

Paterson's real target, however, wasn't Walter Lippmann or the Brain Trust, or even Franklin and Eleanor Roosevelt. She wasn't running an anti-Roosevelt column; she was running a libertarian column, and whatever fun she made of particular personalities (which was plenty) was in aid of her attack on their ideas. One of those ideas, perhaps the most offensive from a libertarian point of view, was the assumption that some people are qualified by birth, education, idealism, or alleged intelligence to supervise other people's lives. It was the operative assumption of a ruling class. The allied assumption was that social class and economic circumstances are the only things that matter.

This attitude was egregiously personified by Joseph Kennedy, who served as FDR's chairman of the Securities and Exchange Commission, the fox having been put in charge of the henhouse. Kennedy's existence confirmed Paterson's notions about a governing class that subordinated real politics, which in America is the effort to secure individual freedom, to paternalistic social attitudes. He came out with a book called *I'm for Roosevelt*, which had many darkly amusing features. Paterson laughed at its demand for the restoration of "security"—"security naturally being something you can lose—that's why it is so secure." But she bridled at Kennedy's question, "What matters a vote to a hungry man?" That question, she said, would have puzzled "the hungry men at Valley Forge who won Mr. Kennedy's vote for him."[35] It did not puzzle Paterson, who also knew what it meant to go hungry. Having that knowledge, she understood that certain convictions transcend economic circumstances, even in the minds of the working people to whom Kennedy so grossly condescended.

Chief among those convictions was a belief in individual liberty, the right to choose for oneself. Another was individual responsibility, the duty of owning up to one's choices. Throughout the New Deal, Paterson found an astonishing flight from responsibility. A textbook case was Roosevelt's appointment of Hugo Black to the Supreme Court. Black, who became one of the court's leading modern liberals, had been a member of the Ku Klux Klan. From Paterson's perspective, this was an obvious disqualification. But liberal supporters of the administration insisted that Black was relieved of responsibility because he had joined the Klan *only to further his political career*. They maintained that he had no political "alternative" in a state (Alabama) that was dominated by the Klan. They also maintained that opposition to the appointment was merely a means of "discredit[ing] a liberal justice." Well, Paterson wrote, "it just goes to show that conservatives, reactionaries, in fact, any one who doesn't think a Klansman is either a liberal or an ideal choice for the Supreme Court, will stick at nothing." But by the way, Black did have an alternative to joining the Klan: "It was simply to refrain from joining. It is always possible to stick to your principles, if you have any. But there is, of course, the alternative of parading with your head in a pillowcase, in hope of office. It's a matter of taste."[36]

Paterson pursued the Black affair in column after column, year after year, long after he had donned the robes of a Supreme Court justice.[37] In practical terms, her protest was useless. But prophets start where practical people stop, and Paterson was rapidly assuming the role of a prophet. She was not the kind of prophet who thought that her job was to forecast the details of the nation's future. She supposed that that was impossible in any case. What she could try to do was to state the logical consequences of the various choices that people might make. As William Blake wrote, the prophet "utters his opinion both of private and public matters; thus: if you go on so, the result is so."[38] While doing that, she could also try to fulfill the other, still more basic, function of the traditional prophet—to show what had gone wrong with the public's interpretation of its official ideas.

The biblical prophets were outsiders by profession, but they advocated the central religious values of their culture, insisting that the "religion" of their generation was entirely different from what religion ought to be. Similarly, the function of America's prophets has been to demonstrate that something has gone terribly wrong with their fellow citizens' interpretation of essential American ideas. "Thoreau's protest," as Paterson said, "was an act of patriotism, a declaration of true faith and allegiance to his country. . . . Feeling in every fiber of his being the way the world was going he did not mean to go along."[39] Paterson also refused to go along, and she did the prophet's work by getting at the fundamental problems of interpretation.

The really crucial thing was to distinguish America's classical liberal ideas from the "liberalism" that was becoming the creed of the Roosevelt generation. Classical liberalism was associated with decentralized and limited government, modern liberalism with the big-government programs of a centralized welfare state. The formula is overworked, but it may still be helpful: classical liberalism offers "freedom from," the right to be left alone by government; modern liberalism offers "freedom to," the right to do and to have certain things, and to get them from the government if one cannot get them on one's own. What should be on the list of these things is a perpetual subject of debate, but no one doubts that the Great Depression was the moment when a modern-liberal government decisively took charge of the people's economic welfare.

Arthur Schlesinger, Jr., has used the metaphor of convergence to describe the movement of ideas among modern liberals:

The liberal economic thought of the early depression . . . tended to converge on two practical programs. One, stemming from [John Maynard] Keynes, [William T.]

Foster, and [Marriner] Eccles, approached the crisis from the viewpoint of the failure of demand and proposed to revive purchasing power through government spending. The other, stemming from [Thorstein] Veblen and [Simon] Patten, [Adolf] Berle and [Gardiner] Means and [Rexford G.] Tugwell, approached the crisis from the viewpoint of the misworking of the institutional framework and called for economic integration through structural reform. And whether spenders or planners, these men were all pragmatists rather than dogmatists.[40]

But dogmatism would not have kept the planners away from the spenders. As Schlesinger goes on to show, big government planning required big government spending, and vice versa. The two tendencies worked together to produce the New Deal agenda.

Seven years before becoming president, Franklin Roosevelt lamented the fact that both major political parties contained strong conservative and strong progressive elements: "I cannot help feeling that a realignment will come."[41] As president, he became the agent of realignment. In 1932, important factions of his party invoked its historic allegiance to Jeffersonian, small-government principles and attempted to direct its fire against the big-spending, "centralizing" habits of the Hoover administration. After the start of the new administration, these elements reunited under Al Smith to attack the New Deal and try to prevent Roosevelt's renomination.[42] They failed. Roosevelt's landslide in the election of 1936 swept them away, leaving only the impression of a natural and undisputed progress from the liberalism of Jefferson and Jackson to the liberalism of Wilson and Roosevelt.

So complete was the victory of modern liberalism over every other form that after the New Deal period the very existence of the others temporarily vanished from the popular mind. Among intellectuals, the effect was earlier and more intense. In 1933, Granville Hicks, attacking Paterson and other non-Marxist literary figures, goes on from her to a number of critics whom he considers "liberal," "all of whom voted for Norman Thomas in the last election."[43] Thomas was the candidate of the Socialist Party. Back in the Hoover administration, Edmund Wilson, arguing for socialism, had informed Paterson that no one (by this he probably meant no intellectual) believed any longer in America's classical ideas of liberty. He told her that she was "the last surviving person to believe in those quaint old notions on which the republic was founded." She asked, "But is it true?"[44] She meant to find out.

If the answer was yes, that was no reason to change her principles. That was the error of the modern liberals: believers in "progress," they looked at the history of other people's ideas to discover what their own should be. Lincoln Steffens had traveled to Russia soon after the world war and had asked himself the rhetorical question, "How could I, a liberal, grasp the idea of an evolutionary society, which was beginning as a dictatorship to establish a new order. . . . ?" Paterson thought he could at least have grasped the idea that while visiting this new order—of which he said, "I have been over into the future, and it works"—he had been forced to subsist on the canned food that he imported from America. Even more embarrassing was his disillusionment:

> He used to believe in a lot of elegant and noble principles. He couldn't get other people to act according to his principles, to his complete satisfaction, so it appears he has no use for them himself! Evidently they were intended for external application only. If we had any principles, we should assume that it was our business to stick by them whether any one else did or not. That, in fact, is our understanding of the nature of principles. If they won't stand up against defeat, aren't worth more than success, applause or even comfort, then obviously they never were principles, but merely another name for expediency.[45]

That was the difference between a prophet and someone who simply wanted to embrace "the future."

It was very expedient for intellectuals to question whether liberal principles really existed in America—whenever they found that the principles didn't immediately benefit them. Some, for example, denied that America had freedom of the press, because (in Paterson's words) "one cannot invariably get paid for writing what one pleases." This was modern liberalism: the assumption that other people have to give you whatever you think you need. She knew that her own use of "free speech and freedom of the press" was unlikely to be greeted by "applause or even comfort" from her fellow-intellectuals, but that just helped to clarify the distinction between classical liberalism and its modern substitutes.[46]

"Liberalism," she believed, was now a "catch-all term" that stood for anything that anyone might want the government to do. There ought to be a name for people who adhered to that form of liberalism, and Paterson tried to find one. They were "modern liberals," naturally. They were also "pseudo-'liberals,'" "fake 'liberals,'" "phony 'liberals,'" "alleged liberals," "self-labeled liberal[s]," "soi-disant Liberals." But whatever you wanted to call them, they were part of a century-long "reaction against liberty"—the agitation, especially among intellectuals, not to limit the state's power but to increase it to accomplish social ends.[47]

Modern liberals assumed that "conditions have changed," so liberal principles had to change along with them; that was regarded as progress. Paterson insisted that, on the contrary, "[c]onditions do not alter principles and their consequences. . . . the principle of the lever remains the same."[48] What, then, had happened?

Liberalism, she thought, had been a victim of its own success. It had changed the world by limiting government, destroying fixed social classes, and allowing the growth of a dynamic capitalist system. So many benefits flowed from the capitalist industrial machinery that welfare now appeared to depend upon the machine itself, not upon "the free play of intelligence" that had made the machine. Attempting to complete mankind's liberation from economic hardship, "advanced" Europeans used the bounty of the machine to create the first versions of the modern welfare state. Germany, in particular, had been considered "a model in respect of 'social legislation' for a generation past." People who approved of such developments were modern "liberals."[49]

Thus far, Paterson's account differs little from that of modern liberals themselves, except for the part about "the free play of intelligence." She pointed out, however, that the new legislation inevitably created new concentrations of power, which tyrants could use as easily as modern liberals. Germany, the model of social legislation, was now "the totalitarian state"; and social liberalism was everywhere becoming "economic serfdom." That phrase was prophetic in more ways than one. A decade later, the crucial term would reappear in the title of Hayek's *Road to Serfdom*, which made some of the same arguments that Paterson made about state planning and collectivism and the ways in which they enable "the worst" to "get on top."[50] The two authors were independent witnesses to the fact that the principle of the lever remained the same, that classical liberalism had not wholly died, and that it might be revived as a movement.

This was one possible development in the progress of ideas that was not predicted by America's modern-liberal intellectual leadership. In 1934, Lippmann stated with great assurance that practically no one—no one "responsible," that is, no one who could obtain "much of a hearing"—believed that government should abandon the economy to "private initiative":

> The great issues of the contemporary world, as between conservatives and progressives, fascists, communists, and social democrats have to do with the kind of collectivism, how it is to be established, in whose interests, by whom it is to be controlled, and for what ends.[51]

Even the conservatives, in other words, were no longer really conservatives, and traditional liberals had disappeared. There was nothing left but quarrels among collectivists.

In 1950, the situation looked about the same to the influential cultural critic Lionel Trilling, who opined with equal assurance that

> [i]n the United States at this time liberalism [by which he meant modern liberalism, no adjective required] is not only the dominant but even the sole intellectual tradition. For it is the plain fact that nowadays there are no conservative or reactionary ideas in general circulation.

There might be things that looked like ideas, but those were only "irritable mental gestures."[52]

Neither Lippmann nor Trilling thought that modern liberalism was without its flaws; at times, it made both of them very nervous. They were convinced, however, that it had driven its adversaries completely from the field. For academic intellectuals such as Trilling, classical liberalism wasn't even a category of thought. Anything that wasn't modern liberalism was a political nonentity. It is hard to think of a movement in American history more successful in establishing an intellectual monopoly than modern liberalism appeared to be at the end of the Roosevelt era.

Paterson frequently commented on the naiveté of the intellectuals, who assumed that collectivist ideas were daring and advanced and were always being intimidated by anyone advanced enough to appear on their left. "If you go back 150 years," she remarked, "you are a reactionary; but if you go back 1,000 years, you are in the foremost ranks of progress." Opponents of economic and political innovations were continually satirized as "dinosaurs" by the brisk new liberals, and their demise was happily predicted. Paterson returned the compliment. "The Cretaceous dinosaurs are most instructive," she wrote. "They were the early Brain Trust, having

practically none." Her motto was, "If you're going to be a dino-
saur, be one; otherwise you're nothing but a lizard."[53]

A correlative expression was, "People do not realize how important it is to have a good time until it is too late." Paterson was
obviously grieved by the direction that the nation's affairs had taken;
she was outraged; finally she was embittered; yet she was also,
fairly obviously, enjoying her career of jousting with the adversary. No one calls social planning "despotism tempered by imbecility" without feeling a rush of pleasure. When Paterson said in
one of her columns that Rexford Guy Tugwell was "unable to write
even a cliche accurately," she must have smiled her work to see.[54]
But her real pleasure came from acquitting traditional liberalism of
the charge that it was simply a "negative" faith, a retreat from
progress and a perpetual way of saying no. To her, individual freedom was the life of America and its sole source of progress. It was
how Americans get things done.

Reading a book about the Wright brothers' accomplishment, she
said that she particularly liked the episode of Huffman's field:

> The Wrights asked the owner if they could rent it. Mr. Huffman said they could use
> it free; he only requested them incidentally to "drive his cows to a safe place and not
> run over them!" We shall never know whether Mr. Huffman thought anything would
> come of the Wrights' experiments; but that was the American way, too—let them use
> the field, they wouldn't do any harm. Oh, no, no charge. It was private property, so
> there was no red tape. At about the same time another man, the head of an endowed
> institution, with $50,000 of government funds and $20,000 as a special gift, was
> trying to invent a flying machine; and he got nowhere with it. But the two who
> needed nothing whatever except their own brains, their own earnings and their own
> leisure time at their own disposal, performed the feat.
>   That is what we are now urged to be ashamed of, to ignore, to repudiate and deny
> and destroy. That is the United States; that is the capitalist system.[55]

The passage evokes a typically American mode of human action. Its style embodies it. This is not a hesitant or tentative style.
There is a direct dependence of colloquial words on immediate
experience, on what individuals can see and hear for themselves:
"Oh, no, no charge"; watch out for the cows. Yet it modulates easily into the devices of classical rhetoric: the firm and resonant conceptual terms ("private property," "the capitalist system"), the formal
pairs and triads ("their own brains, their own earnings and their
own leisure time at their own disposal"), the noble scorn ("repudi-
ate and deny and destroy"), the urgent pride: "That is the United

States." Across the years, the principles of the rhetorical lever remain the same—but a lever is a versatile tool, always ready for some new task.

People who did not understand the daring and difficulty of the Wrights' accomplishment, which was as much intellectual as practical, or the intellectual challenge of classical liberalism, might mistake all this for routine praise of the American past. For some, material progress appeared so predictable that it no longer seemed to depend on "the free play of intelligence"; everything that needed to be done would be done by some large, machinelike organization. For others, recurrence to first principles was mere nostalgia. Stuart Chase followed the tendency of modern liberal thought when he observed that "George Washington never saw a railroad, let alone a power line," and drew the conclusion that the "old forms" of American social organization were "inadequate" for modern "functions": *too* "loose and flexible." He noted that "[p]olitical scientists have been trying to design improvements to keep pace with the march of the machine."[56]

As far as Paterson was concerned, they could try, but they had not yet succeeded. Indeed, the image of machinery on the march while people bustle along beside it, trying to "keep pace," was a sad reflection on the intellectuals' view of the power of their own intellects. For her, the drama of history was not that of "economic forces"; it was the drama of the "human desires and capacities" that inspired those forces:

> The course of all history resembles the track of a cyclone, a moving point marking the convergence of mysterious energies. . . . It is an imperfect synthesis of innumerable private purposes, individual actions, good and bad intentions, selfish ambitions and disinterested intellectual effort and blind stupidity and sheer physical restlessness.[57]

The cyclone simile was "inadequate," she remarked, because the energy within history "is constructive as well as destructive." Yet the image does capture some of the ideas she was pursuing. A cyclone is a dynamic integration of energy. It is wild and unpredictable, but it is a system; it cannot be controlled, but it can be understood. Better yet, it moves, defying all desires to "stabilize" it. The cyclone image represents one more step in Paterson's motion toward a theory of human action that would satisfy her concern for system and principle as well as her appreciation of spontaneous action, her delight in the wild forces of desire released by liberty.

Those forces can, of course, be destructive. The New Deal had barely begun when she speculated that the final scene of her own drama might be . . . unfortunate. She suggested that her readers turn to II Kings 9:32-33 and see "what happened to an irritating and obstinate woman." The woman was Jezebel, Queen of Israel, who in the finale of a political dispute was ejected from a window, run over by a chariot, and eaten by dogs. Despite all that, Jezebel had a lot more vitality than her foes. Paterson asked readers to "observe the description of the 'two or three'" who threw her to the pavement.[58] They were a gang of palace eunuchs.

12

Spring Day, Too

One afternoon, as Paterson sat writing to a friend about the follies of the national administration, a peculiar noise penetrated her
office.

> Band playing in the street, someone says it's the Internationale. Spring day, too—
> heavens, it must be May Day, communist day. I never thought of that—well, let 'em
> play. Now they're cheering or something, very raucous. I don't know what about.
> One thing no earthly consideration would induce me to do, go to street rallies or
> march in processions, not if it would Save the Country.
> Got to go down and finish in the composing room, it's press day.[1]

Paterson could endure political folly; she could almost enjoy it,
so long as she was still allowed to write about it: "the show is almost worth the money."[2] But somehow it didn't help her feel the
gladness of the May. The workers of the world, so assiduously
assembled in midtown Manhattan, reminded her that there might
be something even worse than Hoover or Roosevelt. They also
reminded her that she had her own work to do.

She rose every Monday through Friday in her flat in Hell's Kitchen
and walked through the clanging city to the *Herald Tribune* building at 230 West 41st Street. She spent the day in a sweltering little
office with a grimy window looking out on nothing. In the late
afternoon, she went to literary parties where drunken people jammed
themselves into other little rooms, shouting, munching their food,
and quarreling with her about their announced ideals. There were
still many people whom she enjoyed meeting, but she had few
close friends. The highlight of her week might be a visit from Will
Cuppy. They would sit with each other sharing jokes and whim-
sies. Later, the jokes—and sometimes the conversation, or some-

thing like it—might turn up in their writing. That was good. But there were other times.

> Cuppy came in for an hour last night, but it was so hot we sat morosely in the dark and I said I didn't care what happened to a nation of halfwits, not if they all starve in breadlines; and he said earnestly: "Now you are talking in a constructive way." So it was too hot to add to that and he went home . . . .[3]

Paterson thought she had to do something to "jolt" herself out of her "mental rut." One way of doing that was to book passage for another trip to Europe: "might as well as long as I have a cent," meaning before the New Deal got it. She left New York in early August 1933, taking her habitual books and typewriter, and arrived a few days later at Lillian Fischer's apartment in Paris. She shopped for clothes and acquired an Empire evening gown that made her feel somewhat like Josephine, "about the time that Napoleon divorced her." She ate, got lost, struggled with French, and finally got sick. Giving up her plan to see Spain, the still unvisited site of her first historical novel, she returned to New York on September 8, never to leave North America again.[4]

A better means of getting herself out of the rut was building a house, her own house, as far away from New York City as possible. It would give her a retreat from an environment that had now grown tiresome; New York had "no relation to the sky and sun." It would also give her a way to invest the money she was earning from *Never Ask the End*. In May 1933, "in a fit of madness," she purchased five acres of rocky land in what was then an underdeveloped part of Stamford, Connecticut, three miles from a station on the line to New York. The land had "a lovely tree on it, a lot of trees but one particular tree which I feel I must have before I die."[5] It was her place on the American landscape.

The sale almost fell through when Roosevelt's bank moratorium confused the seller about what to do with his property, but at last Paterson succeeded. She quickly commissioned a contractor who said "it was his business to build houses," New Deal or not. She told him, "Please build me a house right near that tree. It must contain so many rooms, so you can figure out the size; and build it as high as it ought to be accordingly. Here is all the money [I've] got, and when that is used up you'll have to stop." Then she left him alone.[6]

Once she was notified that the house had attained some kind of shape, she went to take a look at it. She didn't expect it to look like what she'd imagined, but she was surprised that the difference was so great. She had planned something modest, but the place was a good deal more modest than she expected. After thinking it over for a few days (in "suicidal gloom"), she woke her contractor up at night and asked him if the structure could be stretched. "Sure; anything can be done," he said; and within a week he had stretched it to her satisfaction. "It goes to show," she said, "that all is not lost in this country."[7] If she had the money, she could still find people competent to help her spend it to her satisfaction, without the intrusion of higher powers.

Today, her house-stretching adventure would probably require months of paperwork. Even in 1933, there was cause to wonder about her possible betrayal of America's new economic order:

> Possibly we done wrong even to build a house instead of taking the materials out and dumping them in the bay, in order to limit production and stimulate consumption simultaneously, and thus achieve security through experimenting; but we don't care.[8]

Veblen's vision of the vested interests' absurd attempts to limit production in order to maintain prices had now come true, but the vested interests were the government.

The building of the house had taken a large amount of her money, but it gave her a modern, oil-heated building with four bedrooms, two baths, a 23-by-26-foot living room, a fireplace, and a two-car garage. Her neighbors were of two kinds: rich people who couldn't mind their own business and whom she was determined to avoid; and working-class Italians with whom she reached an immediate understanding. She hired them to help her around the place and to drive her to and from the train station in the "flivver" that she bought and never learned to drive.[9] Among them were some of the few friends she retained till death.

Now she could spend her time, as much time as she could wrest from her job at the *Trib*, planting flowers and trees and moving big rocks with a crowbar. The lever was not just a political metaphor; it was an amazing reality. She loved doing things with machines (cars didn't qualify). It was a "point of chronic exasperation" with her that other people resented America for its "ruthless" exploitation of nature. She thought it was an odd conception, this idea that human activity and enjoyment are somehow *un*natural. "Naturally," she wrote, Americans

> have used wood, coal, oil, metals and the like. They have grown crops and eaten them. Why not? Would there be any merit in letting the trees die, fall and rot as they had been doing throughout the ages, or leaving the ore in the ground, or the land unused? . . . The trees the pioneers cut down would have been dead of old age before now. More are growing, and can grow. With those used, Americans built houses, and for the first time in the world's history they made comfortable houses. . . . Americans were not pampered; they worked. They were not wasteful; they made something.[10]

Yet she liked natural objects primarily for what they were, not for what she could do with them. She had no idea of formality in her cultivation of nature; her idea was, this is a good place, plant it here; don't worry about the arrangement. She loved the wildness of nature that could still be seen around her comfortable house. The animals that visited her property, the little stream that ran through it, the weeds and flowers that resisted her best efforts to manage them, all reminded her of the unpredictable, indestructible energies of individual life. "[W]hatever a plant does," she said, "you have to let it."

> And a granite boulder is actually feeble and without effective resistance compared to the apparently delicate and perishable lichen which grows on its surface.[11]

Although she usually did not succeed, she tried to get home early enough to watch her trees in the fading light. Weekends and her vacation in late summer were sacred to reading, napping, writing her next novel, and following the adventures of the wandering deer and her cat, Brainless. Her library began filling up with books about gardening and natural history. She knew what xylobulum was, and she would travel miles to see it bloom. But even a morning glory forced her to rise at dawn to look at it, then stay up for fear that the blossoms would close before she "had looked hard enough."[12]

As the thirties turned into the forties, she saw that property values in Stamford were rising, accompanied by taxes. She decided to make another move; but when she did, she tried to recreate the environment she loved in a new location. In 1942 she moved to a second house—planned, like the house in Stamford, by herself—in semi-rural Ridgefield, Connecticut. On the right, as you entered, was a large living room, running from front to back of the house; on the left, a dining room and behind it a master bedroom and bath. A kitchen stood at the end of the hall, with the kerosene stove that Paterson insisted on having; upstairs: two guest rooms and bath.[13]

Paterson left most of her land undeveloped, so she could have nature right around her. Unlike Stamford, Ridgefield was not on a commuter rail line, so she arranged an abbreviated workweek in order to spend every possible minute there. She slept three or four nights a week in rented accommodations in New York, then she took a late-night bus for home. She didn't mind getting off the bus in the icy darkness and tramping through her miniature wilderness in heavy boots. The door of her house was always unlocked; friends were warmly encouraged to come and stay.[14] But mostly they didn't come. Out of these conditions emerged not just solitary meditations but another novel, *If It Prove Fair Weather*, a book that is about love but that is just as much about being alone.

Paterson's first clear allusion to this book dates to June 1933, when she had not yet completed *The Golden Vanity*. She told Dinarzade, "[A]nother novel has got into my head, and I've had to write some of that immediately because it was insisting upon being written." Immediately after finishing *The Golden Vanity*, she informed the readers of her column that she had begun another novel but would not invite any deadlines from publishers, whom she accused of always "sit[ting] like wolves around a dying campfire[,] waiting."[15] The wolves would have starved. Paterson found *Fair Weather* "more difficult" than her earlier books. Besides, she had the nation's political problems to worry about. The novel was not completed until spring, 1940,[16] a long time after the events that insisted on her starting it.

It is not difficult to guess what those events were. The book is the story of a failed romance. While writing it, she said that she would prefer a husband to novel writing; her letters mention nameless would-be suitors, sometimes two at once;[17] but she was not about to divulge the details of any of her relationships. Although, as a friend has said, she remained irresistibly attractive to certain men, no man survived the intelligence test. She may also have agreed with a sentiment that Jake expresses in *The Golden Vanity*:

Marriage blunts the finer feelings. . . . The very idea of going to bed night after night with someone you're living in the same house with—it's incestuous!

Still, the idea that there might never "be another [man] even mildly interested" sometimes made her "wish [she] was dead."[18]

When *Fair Weather* finally came out, she hinted that it was about her, or at least people like her; other, especially younger, people need not "take it as personal." This story may, indeed, have the closest point of view of any of her novels. Its scope is narrower, and its treatment of its protagonist is accordingly more concentrated, more focused on certain particular aspects of the self. And, as before, her protagonist—Emily Cruger in this case—is very similar to her. Emily is a middle-aged woman who has been married. She is moody, intellectual, jealous of her independence, deeply interested in her friendships, and caustically critical of both her friends and herself. Another way of putting this, perhaps, is to say, with Paterson, that her heroine is "ruined by her sense of humor."[19]

Paterson thought that if the book turned out well, it would be an "unusual, strange book." She was right. The strangest thing about it is the simplicity of its purpose. It is supposed to be about love— not love enduring economic or social or religious conflicts, not love entailing a rivalry of loves, but love, just love. Here love is studied "simply as the way two special people felt about each other, and how it made them behave to each other."[20]

The conflicts are all between and within the lovers, not between them and the world. The novel offers many pungent comments about religion, history, politics, economics, business, and other subjects, but these are pure expressions of the protagonist's personality, not explanations of the plot. Even the man's pre-existing wife is treated more as a peculiar twist in his personality than as an external problem. The real difficulty is that the two central characters can experience complete intimacy only with each other, and that the frankness of their intimacy can only drive them apart. "There was nothing they could not say to each other"—and they say it, with predictable results. That is comedy, and tragedy; and that is romantic love. This novel, according to Paterson, is "the only love story ever written."[21]

"One sees, through a crevice narrow and bright as a sword's edge, life closing against one": the plot is like that—narrow and bright. The various contexts of events are interesting, and deftly developed, but the events themselves are mainly changes of mood, sharpenings of criticism regarding love and the meaning of love.

To make such a novel live is a major literary challenge. Paterson knew that. She knew that success depended on her ability to show that everything in life is important, not just the showy, external conflicts but also the minute internal gestures. While writing *Fair Weather*, she complimented Elizabeth Bowen for having "the rare ability to make one realize that people are alive all the time, not only in high moments or melodramatic situations."[22]

How can this sense of life's energy and wholeness be achieved? That was the problem Paterson faced in writing the story, and also the problem her characters face in living it. Every depth is sounded, every psychological subtlety is appreciated, every insight is expressed; but the conflicts of the beginning remain the conflicts of the end. They are comprehended, but they are unaltered. Love is the novel's whole pursuit, but love proves either too much or not enough for the characters, and perhaps for the novel as well.

One of Paterson's comments in her review of Bowen indicates her own skepticism about love: "After all, who does want another's whole heart? It is a horrifying responsibility; worse than that, it establishes a claim for some equivalent. Or at least, the giver feels so." The novel shows that love does seek the whole, however horrifying the responsibility may be, yet still desires to live alone. The protagonist's long vacillation about love ends in a conversation that she holds with herself at the end of the book: "Not care for him any more? . . . She must love him till the hour of her death. . . . And she wished it were now." This is how love challenges death, and becomes it. Paterson's story is a beautifully realized analysis of intractable conflicts. It must have given its author very little comfort. In *The Golden Vanity*, Mysie had reflected, "You find yourself when you find what belongs to you, your own people."[23] Paterson had never found them; or if she had, they had compounded the problem.

Fair Weather did not sell as well as her immediately preceding novels.[24] It was too responsive to romantic emotions—and therefore, curiously, too intellectual and abstract—to catch the popular mood. A part of her had spoken, and had not been understood.

Meanwhile, the outward Mrs. Paterson remained an intimidating presence in the New York publishing world. Her columns were still the salient feature of *Herald Tribune "Books"*; they still helped or hurt the books she talked about; and, if *Publishers' Weekly* was correct, "everybody" still read her, even though her readership was polarized between love and hatred for what she wrote.[25] Opinions were just as polarized about Paterson the personality. Some people regarded a visit to her office as a privilege; others saw it as a walk through an intellectual minefield. It wasn't that she was pompous or arrogant. No one believed that there was (to use the contemporary expression) any "side" to her. But there was an insidious intentness in her conversation. She knew it; in *The Golden Vanity*, she has Jake comment on Mysie's way with a political conversation:

> I've seen you working on them. They finally get so they can't call their souls their own and say even worse things in their efforts to please.[26]

And she did have a temper; by now she was famous for that. When she was angry, she didn't shout; she didn't gesticulate; she simply spoke her mind, clearly and completely, and that was bad enough. It was her frank refusal to admit any compromise about either ideas or the importance of ideas that intimidated people—or made them feel honored to talk with her.

She was good with young people. One of her young acquaintances in the publishing industry relates a typical experience:

> I met Pat first when I came to Little Brown in 1937 and was very flattered that she always called to me when I entered the Book Dep't, sat me down on a chair beside her, stretched her arms over the typewriter, put her chin on her wrists, & stared me in the eye as she held forth on some subject way over my head. I felt like an "intellectual"![27]

Paterson warned potential conversationalists that "imparting information" was her "weakness."[28] That didn't discourage people who wanted information, but it is probable that nobody ever came to Isabel Paterson strictly to be instructed. They came because—if you were up to the experience—she was fun to talk to. On Monday nights, when it was her job to put *Herald Tribune "Books"* to bed, her office was filled with friends, especially young friends, assisting with the proofs and listening to her incomparable conversation. Yet she now considered herself "a hopeless loss" to social events. "[A]t my age," she said in 1940, "things seem rather unreal, though I know theyre [sic] not. I don't go about, and therefore don't see many people, and when I do, most of what I hear people say seems absurd or crazy, as I suppose I seem to them." She was unable to listen quietly to "the sort of thing everybody says, which is of course invariably idiotic"; she had to get angry. She would rather stay at home, where there were always interesting things to do.[29] Just watching the sky and the sun and the motion of the trees was a full-time job.

13

Implications of Individualism

While watching the trees, she was thinking about a number of subjects besides love and New Deal politics. She was not the kind of person who wants to evolve a complete philosophy simply for the sake of completeness, but she was not the kind of person who thinks along only one or two tracks, either. And she was unlikely to let any territory along her route remain unexplored.

Closely related to her political thought were her opinions about feminism, a subject on which she had a good deal to say during the 1930s. To be sure, some of her statements were reluctantly made. When asked to provide her ideas on the question, she replied that she "never had any, except the original American idea of being free to try anything we had a mind to and take the consequences."[1] This is true, in a way; but it understates the influence that being a woman had on her thoughts about being free.

Her knowledge of women's lives and social roles contributed very significantly to her understanding of the evils of a statist or a status society. The protagonist of *The Shadow Riders* associates her objection to the growth of class society in the West with a parallel objection to women's lack of liberty. Writing in the *Herald Tribune*, Paterson compared the exploitation of women to the exploitation of "the 'lower orders'" by "the governing classes." *The Road of the Gods* is loud with complaints about men's oppression of women. "Men are not brave enough to bear children," admits the high priest. "If [women] had strength to match their courage they would rule the world."[2]

Paterson had mixed feelings, however, about political feminism. Naturally, she was happy to have the vote, although she didn't perceive that her life and property were any more secure after she got it than they had been before. The demands of socially well-placed feminists sometimes appeared to her confused and elitist, the products of a privileged or governing class. She sharply criticized Virginia Woolf's *Three Guineas*, arguing that its demand was not for equal rights for all women but for privileges for some women—"education for the favored jobs in the professions." The rational demand would be for "the abolition of all privilege." Woolf wondered what working-class people thought about men and women of the educated classes who "adopt[ed] the working class cause without sacrificing middle class capital." Paterson said that she knew "what some of them think, and they think right. It's a search for new privilege, and a pain in the neck to the objects of their patronage."[3]

Feminism as a branch of socialism, whether hypocritical or sincere, held no charms for Paterson. She knew that state control of the economy meant control of the economy by a small group of people, and she knew that such groups were unlikely to include many women, at least many women who actually worked. She knew what the New Deal's price-inflation program and its seizure of savings in gold represented for working women like herself. A single image summarized her feelings:

Never shall we forget the line of women we saw turning in their savings, under threat of ten years in jail and ten thousand dollars fine, while the multimillionaire Senator Couzens stood up bravely on the floor of the Senate and promised to "hunt them down" if they tried to hold out a few dollars.[4]

It was strange, she thought, to blame capitalism for women's role as commodities in the sex and marriage market. Before capitalism, women didn't have the opportunity to be anything other than commodities. The rule of history was that "'problems' become problems only when there is some chance of solving them; until then they are accepted as quite natural conditions." It was mere "sentimentality" to use a problem that had been identified only by the progress of the capitalist social system as a judgment against the system itself.[5]

Libertarian ideas had few consistent advocates in Paterson's time, but among those few, women were remarkably important. Indeed, women were more important to the creation of the libertarian movement than they were to the creation of any other political movement not strictly focused on women's rights. Paterson and her friends Rose Wilder Lane and Ayn Rand, whose relationships will be explored in later chapters, have long been recognized as crucial to the formation of American libertarian thought.[6] And these politically engaged libertarians are not the only interesting figures. The fiction of Willa Cather, the greatest of American women novelists, brilliantly embodied classical-liberal ideas; and Gertrude Stein, Paterson's literary bête noire, published a series of manifesto-like utterances defending capitalist ideas about money.[7]

Was there something about libertarian ideas that made them particularly attractive to women? Paterson might say that a question like this can have no answer; the people involved at the start were pitifully few, and besides, individuals make up their minds as individuals, not as "men" or "women." Then, relenting, she might ponder the effects of the individual experience that she was always pondering in her modern novels—her own experience of being on "the edge of things."[8] She started as an outsider, and she remained one; she had to struggle for life, then for identity and recognition. Much the same could be said of Lane, Rand, and Cather. People who were used to doing for themselves might have a larger conception than other people of the things that individuals can and ought to do for themselves.

As for women, Paterson thought that in general they were more practical than men, less addicted to fanciful ideas, and better acquainted with the real conditions of life. Men are generally the ones who are paid to "think," to "theorize," to conduct ever-changing "social experiments." A man in *The Shadow Riders* voices the familiar theory that "the people" are more changeable than "a woman"; and his wife replies, "My dear . . . the whole of civilization depends on the ability of women to stay of one mind all their lives." A woman commits herself to the raising of children, and that's that; she's committed. It's the men "who are always chasing off to the ends of the earth for new scenery and a different kind of work." Men get caught up in abstractions and political schemes; women have more sense about the vital particulars. The "natural female impulse, seeing a lot of great big men just standing in a huddle," is "to tell them to get to work."[9] And on the personal level, that is what the libertarian philosophy comes down to.

In pursuing her own work, Paterson was not about to brook any interference or condescension from men. Informed that a literary gathering was for men only, she immediately decided to go, and the men discovered that they had better let her in. Yet she would not put up with being complimented for thinking "like a man."[10] In her work as a critic, she gave women writers full and fair treatment. Her fairness could be cruel. She mercilessly satirized Gertrude Stein (a literary mountebank), Dorothy Thompson (an establishment dunderhead), and Eleanor Roosevelt (a pathetic fool).[11] But when she saw talent, she welcomed it gladly, whatever its political associations.

She recognized Cather as the great interpreter of American life, but she also recognized Woolf, despite her political vagaries and her often opaque literary experiments, as the great artist of the self's experience in the world of time. She honored women of real though lesser talent, such as Gertrude Atherton and Ellen Glasgow, for breaking with the genteel tradition in women's writing.[12] From the great to the merely interesting or promising, her column lavished attention on women. Her list of women authors was almost bizarrely inclusive. Elinor Wylie, E. M. Delafield, Mabel Dodge Luhan, Naomi Mitchison, Grace Zaring Stone, Angela Thirkell, Ayn Rand, Margaret Mitchell, Lady Murasaki, and countless others deserved to be noticed, and were noticed in Paterson's columns and reviews, often with the kind of insistence and determination that ensured a public hearing.

She had no respect, however, for women's writing in itself. To her, women writers who weren't much good were simply writers who weren't much good; feminist considerations were beside the point. Popular women authors of the nineteenth century were dismissed as yesterday's "red hot mammas of the fiction field." About the literary effects of feminism itself, Paterson was not optimistic. She regretted the priority that some women writers gave it. She said she wasn't "anti-feminist, either; it's just that feminism as a theory is bad for a woman writer in the same way that the he-man attitude is bad for a man writer."[13]

Her attitude toward feminism was (to appropriate one of her own useful terms) detached:

> I suppose I am naturally a feminist, feel perfectly entitled to general equality, and would have obtained it in effect under any system; but I should feel that a world

without men wasn't worth living in, and this not for any specific personal reason—just in general. I admire their accomplishments, and I am inclined to think that women will never equal them in certain fields, for lack of continuous physical energy and detachment (not mental detachment, but women really can't get away from the chores, someone has to mind the baby).

On the other hand, "I may wish to take on what is called men's work; if I succeed, then it becomes woman's work, because I'm doing it."[14] No sense of the outsider in these remarks, whatever their "detachment." In the real world of work, an outsider can get inside.

That shouldn't entail conformity. Paterson's individualism allowed her to emphasize differences of culture and attitude between men and women without feeling that all of them had to be removed: "Women suffered a real injustice when they had to conform to masculine judgments, but they thought what they thought just the same. And if women try to make men over in the same way, they'll get the same results." She was able to appreciate the literary achievements of men whom she considered egregiously oppressive to women. She read *War and Peace* almost once a year, and wished that she had a year just to read it, even though its author "infuriate[d]" her "as a woman. . . . Tolstoy demanded that a woman should be a cow and a doormat. (Quite a difficult combination, you'll admit)."[15]

Paterson summarized many of her habitual views in an essay she contributed to *The more I see of men—*, a collection of papers by nine women, including E. M. Delafield and Rebecca West. Her essay, "Man as Lover," is a fairly genial treatment of the subject. It insists that "women actually like men," despite men's attempts to model themselves on ideals that make women want to laugh. The problem is that men have difficulty trusting in their "individual merits." A related, but more important, problem is that men harbor a "dread of woman as an individual." On individualist grounds, Paterson objects, in roughly the same way in which feminists usually objected, to the law's reduction of woman to "a relative phenomenon" with "no separate legal existence," and to the treatment of women as "classifiable objects," grossly discriminated into the categories of Good Women and Bad Women. Viewed from this perspective, woman becomes a function of her status, which is "determined by her behavior to men."[16] That was an obvious offense to individualism, and one basis of a class or status society.

Good Women, she observes, have been subjected to "the imbecile delicacies of the point of view which regards [them] as only a little lower than the angels." Thus, men have explained that women are

> physically feeble creatures, and therefore must not exert themselves in such arduous ways as would be involved in owning property, holding public office, or even depositing a ballot in a box. Let women stick to such light and genteel occupations as washing clothes, scrubbing floors, or even dragging coal-carts in the mines. They could do a little easy work in the fields if they insisted; and of course there were always the children to take care of, as a pastime.[17]

Bad Women have been treated as objects in another way. They have been denied their rights as individuals, on the premise that they are "not definitely ancillary to some man." They have been exploited by lawyers, cops, and judges, men laboring in the service of a "law which is an expression of the masculine point of view." And this process is only "more revolting superficially" than the "legal definition of 'conjugal rights' in marriage."[18]

Paterson was puzzled, baffled, outraged by men and their political and legal devices. Still, there is no evidence that she ever considered herself a victim of men. Her self-assurance took care of that. In August 1932, she visited Ottawa, dined at the country club, and was escorted back to her lodgings by a justice of the Canadian Supreme Court:

> He was very drunk; and quite an old gentleman. In his intoxicated condition he began pawing me more or less automatically; he was so feeble and fragile I was positively afraid of damaging him, so while I held his wrists firmly and carefully I endeavored to distract his attention, and asked him what kind of robes he wore in court, and did he wear a wig? He said no wig, and described the robes, which I forget now—black silk with a scarlet hood or something. I said, you must look very imposing. He had a queer sudden lucid interval and said in a normal sober tone of voice: "Look like a damn fool." It struck me as extremely funny—the revelation of the uncertainty of the man even when clothed in the majesty of the law![19]

Paterson thought that women were more in control than they looked, even under the false code of "chivalry" that she had known in her younger days:

> Chivalry means that women mustn't smile when the knight falls off his horse. Pick him up and dust him tenderly and if possible lead him around to the stuffed dragon.[20]

She, at any rate, was always emphatically in control. The important thing about sex, as she examined the subject in her letters and columns, and especially in her novels, was that both parties should maintain their dignity. It wasn't a matter of rules that must be enforced in the same way on everyone; today's cult of sexual correctness would have annoyed and amused her as much as the Victorian cult of sexual correctness did. But she was a person for whom the old expression "that's what doors are for" still resonated with meaning.

Her ideas about race and ethnicity were simpler than her ideas about sex and gender, but they crystallized in an equally individualist form. Living in a city and a region that was full of immigrants, and being an immigrant herself, she was used to the melting-pot concept of Americanism. That concept was not the one she preferred. She bridled at Louis Adamic's suggestion that American immigration was a success story of "unity." On the contrary, she thought, it was a success story of "individualism." She observed that people who had once fought over religious questions tolerated one another when they got to America, not because they adopted the same religion but because here religion was left alone by the state. This observation prompted her to a crisply colloquial statement of her political and social beliefs:

> A lot of American principle is contained in the two words: "Just don't." Much of the rest is encompassed by the suggestion of minding one's own business. The whole is summed up in the word "liberty."[21]

If you don't feel like melting, nobody should try to make you melt.

Respect for the individual made American civilization superior to every other. But "all civilizations have had attributes of greatness," and differences of national origin have no effect on individual rights. Everyone has the same rights. Because she was an individualist, Paterson was both an American patriot and a universalist. Praising *Mount Allegro*, a book by the Italian-American writer Jerre Mangione, she said that it was about Italian-Americans but it wasn't about melting pots or immigration problems: immigrants "aren't a problem."[22]

The "scientific" racism of the early twentieth century, and its fad for "eugenics," were plainly "bunk." The "science" had nothing scientific about it. Besides, "a smidge of commonsense," as she said, "tells us that there is no single measure of intrinsic 'superiority' or inferiority" where human beings are at stake. She recognized that many people were superior to her in one way or another. The black woman whom she employed to help out in her apartment on 34th Street was "superior to [her] in her gentle and pleasing manners."[23] That wasn't condescension; it was fact, and she knew it. Race was wholly irrelevant to judgments of worth. Her column was completely colorblind; she discussed black authors such as Richard Wright in the same terms she used for whites, ordinarily not even mentioning the race of the authors involved. On occasion, she would make an issue of it, as when she lauded James Weldon Johnson for saying in his autobiography "that 'if he had a chance to change his race, he would choose to remain a Negro.' This is an honest and profound statement; he has enjoyed life, and realizes that all the values were equal to the odds." She was even willing to praise Arna Bontemps' *Black Thunder*, despite its use of the horrible word "proletariat." During World War II, she was incensed by attacks on the Japanese as Asiatic savages. She pointed out that Europeans were doing the same dastardly things that the Japanese empire was doing; the cause was not their ethnicity but the savage features of unlimited government.[24]

Race was not a complex problem for Paterson. Religion was. She was a skeptic who denied the validity of the Christian creed and all other creeds. But her otherwise pervasive sarcasm seldom, if ever, touched on religion, despite her declaration that she had "little or no religious faculty." In the mid-1930s she confessed:

> If I try to suppose a God, I can never get so far as supposing that God is bothering about me, individually; the most I can do is to imagine a rather ironic scheme in which we are absurd and God finds us amusing. But that is a mere intellectual concept, a fancy, to entertain myself. Not a religious feeling. I find the religious temperament interesting after it has been theologized, but not before.[25]

From her respect for the varieties of individual experience, however, she acquired a respect for the varieties of religious experience. When her friend Hendrik Van Loon, the art historian, approvingly quoted the cliché about religion being the opium of the people, she informed him publicly that the phrase was "shallow and stupid." Religion "is whatever any one is capable of receiving from it." Credulous people will find what they're looking for in religion, but other people will find more. She claimed "full rights for the secular intelligence," but she stipulated that "the first thing intelligence should perceive is that there are many modes of experience."[26]

Paterson's approach to problems of religion began where her approach to problems usually began, with an interest in individuals and a corresponding desire to get beyond any reduction of the meaning of their lives by materialist explanations. She had no trouble accepting the general idea of human evolution, but to her, zoology represented neither human history nor human meaning:

> It is interesting to know that the human frame is composed of this and that, that intelligence—such as it is—is a function of the cerebral cortex; and so forth. I do not deprecate this knowledge. But mightn't it be aside from the big riddle that bothers us—as if one had a flashlight in one's hand, and were studying the object on which the rays fell, while unable to even begin to think what the light itself is.[27]

Reflecting on a book by astronomer Harlow Shapley, she said that she found it "restful to realize our absolute unimportance in the scale of things." But

> then again, how do we know it wasn't all arranged especially for us? There is an idea concealed somewhere on these premises. . . .
> Furthermore, man is so superior a being that he frequently forgets all about the universe to concentrate solely on his own affairs. . . . This we do feel is rather stupendous.[28]

"What do I know?" Paterson, a great reader of Montaigne—fideist and skeptic—rested part of her theology on skepticism about our ability to attain a full understanding of our place in the universe. She harbored the basic skepticism that often produces atheism, but she converted it into a distrust of atheism itself. To skepticism she added a sharp awareness of the difference between material forces—the comet, for example, that cannot do anything but follow its mathematical program—and the movements of human consciousness.[29]

Her final religious position was deism. Though it is not clear when she reached that position, she presumably did so at some time during the 1930s, and her principal reason was the idea that individual intelligence, the power of rational choice, was unaccountable except by reference to a rational creator. Also, as she demonstrated in *The God of the Machine*, published in 1943, she could not conceive either of energy or of equal principles of right and justice, "natural" law, without a divine originator.

In the early days, her deism sometimes succumbed to her skepticism. She could hold off the argument from design by remarking that to us the universe naturally looks like the product of intelligent design because "all our intelligence, such as it is [that phrase again], is derived from contemplation of the universe, and exists within it." That was one of the arguments used by eighteenth-century agnostics to discount the claims of eighteenth-century deists. Of course, it doesn't answer the question of whether our impression of intelligent design might actually result from intelligent design.[30]

Paterson came to regard both agnosticism and an over-specific deism as superficial, lacking in substance. Sir James Jeans' idea of God as a mathematician reminded her of the tribal chief who imagines God as a tribal chief.[31] There must be something more vital, she felt, than the terms in which the argument was usually carried on. Scientistic notions confronted both her suspicion that "there is an idea concealed somewhere on these premises" and her desire to believe in what her atheist friend Ayn Rand would later call a "benevolent universe." In one of her columns, Paterson refers to a feeling that is "perhaps more difficult to define than happiness," a "faith which persists in spite of facts, that the universe is good and that perhaps in the end nothing is lost." She then quotes a passage of poetry:

> They will return, return again, as long as the red earth rolls;
> He never wasted a tree or flower; do you think He would
>   squander souls?[32]

Paterson's ideas about the supernatural were especially complicated and difficult. They were probably never adequately communicated to anyone. She confessed that she was one of those "simp[s]" who enjoy having their fortunes told—and she was amused to tell the story of "a man who showed [her] by his palm lines that he had been dead for years." She recalled participating in (unsuccessful) attempts to levitate a table. In Never Ask the End, Marta toys with the idea of the soul's eternal progress to and from the mortal world and recalls her friend Pauline's clairvoyance when she was a young woman; Pauline somehow remembered details of the lives they lived in seventeenth- or eighteenth-century France.[33] Marta and Pauline are closely modeled on Paterson and Grace Luckhart; the clairvoyant incidents may have happened when they were young women in Calgary.

But here Paterson's constitutional skepticism intervened: "Did not every idle silly woman cherish the belief that she had once been Cleopatra? Nobody remembered being a kitchenmaid." In her columns, she made sarcastic comments about spirit mediums. When she had occasion to mention a book of ghost stories, she wrote, "Now, although we've seen a ghost or two, we don't believe in them. Various members of our family have the knack of seeing ghosts, and maybe that started us off as a skeptic." A few years later, Paterson denied having even so much psychic power "as a tadpole." And she ridiculed Field Marshal Haig for going to seances to solicit military advice.[34]

And yet . . . while commenting ironically about mediums and ghosts, she engaged in her (unsuccessful) attempt to contact Alta May Coleman's spirit. And we have seen that she enjoyed the company of her mother, years after her mother's death. She also let at least one friend know that she sometimes enjoyed what is popularly known as the second sight. She was not inclined to credit General Haig about such matters; but, whatever skeptical remarks she made, she did credit her own experience. The experience may have gained in credibility simply because it managed to survive her habitual skepticism. It also complemented her philosophical speculations about an afterlife. When Mary Austin published a book called *Experiences Facing Death*, Paterson said that Austin's "intimations of immortality" brought "conviction, like a first-hand experience." Death was both "the greatest of all riddles" and (wonderful phrase) "the final sporting chance." In any case, "the soul and the intellect," though nonmaterial, "are realities, because there they are before your eyes."[35]

When science began to concern itself with extrasensory perception, Paterson remarked that the reality of clairvoyance was something that "everybody knows except the professed scientists. . . . It has always been known." It resulted from the "same uncharted faculty" that produced artistic inspiration. Science could not establish its reality because its enabling conditions were not known and could therefore not be reproduced: "The instrument, the human being, is a variable element, and the whole presumable combination of time, place and antecedent conditions is not subject to control." Although "intuition, or clairvoyance, is an observed fact," it could not be depended upon, so "sensible people do not act upon it except so far as it jibes with other evidence or reason."[36]

Out of this complex of speculations and experiences, of skepticism and skepticism about skepticism, Paterson evolved her mature religious view. It was the conception of a universe of personality and purpose—a universe created by God, in which the individual soul, made in the image of God, pursues its way, perhaps forever, with immeasurable spontaneity and energy and the self-determination of belief and action appropriate to a creature made in the image of God. With this view she was content to rest. Paterson's religion, like certain other features of her thought, might seem more at home in the eighteenth than in the twentieth century. If so, her deism was not the complacent determinism of *An Essay on Man*, so easy for subsequent generations to satirize, but the humanism of *The Universal Prayer*, in which the same poet suggests that the deity, while

> binding Nature fast in Fate,
> Left free the human will.[37]

Paterson could agree to that.

Isabel Bowler, fashionably dressed

Isabel and friend

Ready to ride: Isabel and companions in the Young West

November 5, 1912: Harry Bingham Brown and
Isabel Paterson on the day of their flight

Paterson in the modern style

Paterson depicted by Gutzon
Borglum, sculptor of Mt. Rushmore
(author's collection; reproduction
courtesy the Borglum Archives)

IMP in a characteristic attitude

The Bookworm
at the *Trib*, late 1930s

Best friends:
Paterson and Alta May Coleman

"He'd feed her the facts, and she'd make the cracks":
Will Cuppy entertained by IMP

Burton Rascoe, friend of literature, and Stuart
Chase, friend of technocracy, flanking Isabel
Paterson, friend of food; Literary Guild banquet,
Waldorf-Astoria Hotel, January 25, 1933

Buttonwood Farm, early 1940s: IMP, Muriel Welles,
Caroline St. Clair (a Welles family friend), Mabel Welles,
pointer Belle, unidentified cat

The elusive Garet Garrett, captured in
official records (passport photo, by
permission of the Houghton Library,
Harvard University bMS Am 1481
[68])

H. L. Mencken
in a congenial environment
(courtesy Enoch Pratt Free
Library, Baltimore)

Rose Wilder Lane inspecting
the Hetch Hetchy Dam site
(courtesy Herbert Hoover
Presidential Library-Museum)

Paterson's disciple Ayn Rand, with her own disciples at the wedding of
Elayne and Harry Kalberman. From left, Joan Mitchell, artist; Alan
Greenspan, future Chairman of the Federal Reserve Board; Nathaniel
Branden, author and psychotherapist; Barbara Branden, Rand's
biographer; Leonard Peikoff, future head of the Ayn Rand Institute;
Elayne Kalberman, nurse; Harry Kalberman, broker; Rand and her
husband Frank O'Connor; Allan Blumenthal, psychiatrist
(picture courtesy Nathaniel Branden)

14

Others

No one in the 1930s defended individualism more vigorously and consistently than Paterson, but she was not the only radical individualist of her time. To understand her particular contribution to American individualism, one needs to examine her relationship to other people who might be regarded as libertarian pioneers.

Among contemporary libertarians, the dominant opinion about this issue has been defined by economist Murray N. Rothbard and a number of historians who share his views. They suggest that there was a strongly, though imperfectly, libertarian movement in the 1930s that they call, for want of a better term, "the Old Right." They recognize that members of the Old Right differed from one another in many ways. Nevertheless—to quote Sheldon Richman, a particularly able advocate of the Old Right hypothesis—"they knew what they didn't like." They didn't like the New Deal. They didn't like it because it interfered with "individual freedom and initiative," undermined constitutional limitations on government, and pursued an interventionist foreign policy.[1]

The theory of the Old Right has the virtue of directing attention to important figures in American history, some of them unjustly neglected. But disliking the New Deal is not the same as advocating libertarian principles, and it is only by giving his criteria the broadest possible interpretation that Richman finds it possible to name very many members of the Old Right. Paterson makes the list, of course; but so do Herbert Hoover and such veteran enemies of laissez-faire as Senators Hiram Johnson and Burton K. Wheeler. Joining these old-time "progressives" are several "social democrats," such as the historian Charles Beard, popularizer of the "economic interpretation" of the constitution. What all these people have in common is little more than opposition to President Roosevelt's conduct of foreign relations. If we are looking for distinctively libertarian contributions to American ideas, we will find ourselves looking at a much smaller group. As Paterson said when she decided that she had to vote for the Republicans in 1936, "We hate a crowd, anyhow."[2]

Some of the most significant libertarian tendencies in national politics actually existed in Roosevelt's own party, among the people whom Richman aptly calls "Cleveland Democrats."[3] Forty years before, Grover Cleveland had courageously battled imperialism and the first great wave of "progressive" agitation. Al Smith, as I have indicated, continued the limited-government tradition in the Democratic Party. This tendency produced Roosevelt's most dangerous organized opposition, the Liberty League, which Smith, John J. Raskob, and the Du Pont family generated in 1934 from the membership of the Association Against the Prohibition Amendment.

The Association had been strikingly successful; the League was not, despite its effective redeployment of anti-Washington feeling from the battle against prohibition to the battle against the New Deal. Although the League was not in business to take on the larger philosophical and moral issues of individualism, its position papers made good economic arguments against modern liberal ideas. But the League never stood a chance against Roosevelt's popularity or his hold on the party machinery. The League's association with big business also hurt. It allowed Roosevelt to satirize its adherents as the kind of people who just a little while before had been looking for government handouts. Now that the "rugged individualists" were in robust health, he said, "Some of them are even well enough to throw their crutches at the doctor."[4]

Paterson seems to have had no contact with the League. She may have distrusted it for some of the reasons that Roosevelt mentioned. The Du Ponts were all right in her book, because they were not on the government payroll, but she may have associated Raskob with the kind of financial dealings that she deplored in *The Golden Vanity*.[5] Or she may simply have followed her established principle of never joining anything.

The Roosevelt administration was not just attacked from the outside; it had an unprecedented ability to produce angry dissidents from within its own ranks. Among those dissidents, the most effectively libertarian figure was probably Lewis Douglas (1894-1974). Douglas had been strongly influenced by his southwestern upbringing and by the politics of his father, "Rattlesnake Jimmy" Douglas, who called himself an "Andrew Jackson Democrat" and maintained traditional Democratic Party beliefs in "individual liberty, minimal government regulations, equal economic opportunity, states' rights, strict economy, and low tariffs."[6] His son carried these beliefs into the Democratic Party politics of his own generation, where they enabled him to win election to the Arizona legislature and the United States House of Representatives. In 1932, he was attracted to Roosevelt's campaign by the Democratic platform's promise of conservative fiscal policies. Roosevelt, as victor, appointed him the nation's first director of the budget. In that office, Douglas distinguished himself by his charm, warmth, and determined argumentation. He also distinguished himself by his integrity. Disagreeing with New Deal policies, he resigned from the administration in 1934.

Soon afterward, he published a book called *The Liberal Tradition*, an elegantly written critique of the New Deal and of modern liberalism in general, which Douglas strongly associates with "collectivism." He gives very hostile treatment to the favorite project of modern liberalism, government planning and direction of the economy, arguing that it is based on erroneous principles and is certain to produce enormous ills. He sees, as Paterson does, that advocates of planning mistakenly "conceive of the State as something more intelligent, endowed to a greater extent with wisdom, than are the individuals which are but its integral parts." And he believes, as she did, that the progress of planning can be measured by the reduction of individual liberty. Ultimately, "[i]t means, of course, the establishment of a dictatorship."[7]

As an individualist, however, Douglas is by no means as radical as Paterson. He concentrates his analysis on the economic sphere and never extends it to such topics as victimless crime laws. Furthermore, he is a Wilsonian Democrat who believes that the maintenance of free enterprise depends on the state's enforcement of antitrust laws; he even speaks of "compelling competition," a paradox that Paterson would never countenance. He was closer to speaking her language in a manifesto, published in the *New York Times*, in which he attempted to arouse support for traditional capitalism.

Here, Douglas and his co-authors (Leo Wolman, another refugee from the Roosevelt administration, and Newton Baker, Wilson's Secretary of War) decry both the Republican economic plans of the 1920s and the Democratic plans of the 1930s: "two streams from the same source."[8]

Douglas hoped that the manifesto would influence the Republican and Democratic platforms. He even hoped that the Republicans would nominate him for vice president. But with Hoover the Republicans had gotten their permanent fill of intellectuals. Douglas succeeded only in alerting them to the fact that they were really not in favor of laissez-faire. The ubiquitous Walter Lippmann, who had secretly helped to plan the manifesto, wrote in public that although it had taken "the historic position of American liberals . . . there can be no doubt that since the war the country has lost its grip upon these principles." With the slipperiness that assisted him throughout his long career in punditry, Lippmann now suggested that current disgust with the New Deal might *either* mark a revival of liberal principles *or* turn out to be "merely reactionary"; time would tell.[9]

Douglas's subsequent career provides an unfortunate commentary on the fate of traditional liberalism in mid-century America. Realizing that he was getting nowhere politically, he accepted jobs as a corporate director and college administrator. When World War II started, he became a leading advocate of American intervention, often pushing for measures far in advance of Roosevelt's. He beat the drums for universal military service, the least likely application of laissez-faire principles. He became, in fact, one of the primary instigators of the conscription bill that was enacted in 1940 over the astonished protests of such people as Senator Rush Holt of West Virginia, who remembered that Douglas and his friends had lately been fulminating against "regimentation in America."[10] Douglas's blindness to the implications of his liberal ideas facilitated his return to government. President Roosevelt appointed him czar of American merchant shipping. President Truman made him Ambassador to Great Britain. He was a master craftsman of American internationalism as manifested in NATO and the Marshall Plan. Old age found him indulging the pathetic vice of retired statesmen, peddling his counsel and support to one politician after another—Lyndon Johnson, Richard Nixon, Mike Mansfield, Edmund Muskie. . . .

Reviewing Douglas's career, one finds no evidence of conscious change or betrayal of principle; what one finds is evidence of a failure to understand exactly what the principles were about. He advocated stringent limitation of government powers, when that required courage to advocate; but he also advocated the election of Lyndon Johnson, the greatest expander of government power in American history.[11] Douglas was not an outsider, like Paterson; he was a member of America's governing class, and he behaved as such. To Paterson, Douglas was just another wretched ex-New Dealer who was innocently surprised "at the repetitious discovery that two and two make four." He (and some other people she mentions) exemplified the bad side of American optimism, the practice of "getting on to a toboggan for a little ride and then being greatly astonished to find that a toboggan goes down hill."[12]

That wasn't Paterson at her fairest. Her natural affinity was with another type of "Old Rightists," authors and thinkers who were not immediately involved in political action. Like Smith and Douglas, each of these people represents an interesting variant of the American story and America's ideas about itself.

The most influential of them was unquestionably H. L. Mencken (1880-1956), America's most prominent literary critic. Mencken's reflections on American culture set the tone for the intellectual skepticism of the 1920s. Paterson regarded him as "the greatest broadax man we've ever had in American letters," the writer who had done more than anyone else to demolish the "genteel tradition in American publishing and reviewing." She did regret Mencken's tendency to degenerate into "sheer abuse," which "is always rather dull," and she especially regretted his would-be imitators, who reminded her of "a camping trip during which some kerosene got spilled in the grub box." "Yet," she adds, "kerosene is invaluable in its right place." When other intellectuals finally stopped trying to imitate Mencken and became publicly weary of him—when, that is, they finally figured out that they were included in his satires, along with everybody else—she still defended him as her "favorite commentator," a man who could never be "abolished" by a change of fashion.[13] Aspiring writers still try to reproduce Mencken's manner, without success. His style was backed by inexhaustible supplies of reading and experience, fused by the lightning strokes of a unique imagination. Paterson was right. It can't be imitated.

The prestige of Mencken, who was by far the best-known intellectual of his time, strengthened every reader who possessed even a speck of individualism to resist the homogenizing influences of American life. The joyous cruelty of Mencken's attacks on the American political class continues to brighten many a libertarian's dark and troubled night. Mencken, indeed, proclaimed himself "not a liberal, but a libertarian, which is something almost exactly opposite, for liberals are always advocates of more and more laws."[14] He viewed official assaults on human freedom—censorship, prohibition, racial segregation, persecution of political dissidents— with magnificent scorn, a scorn that was hugely influential with American readers.

Yet his libertarianism had serious internal contradictions. In *Men versus the Man*, his early volume of debates with Robert Rives La Monte, a wealthy proponent of socialism, he easily axed his way through a forest of fashionable economic arguments for collectivism. On one point, nevertheless, he found himself in agreement with his adversary—the idea that capitalism is a system of competition by which the strong "exploit" the weak.[15] In this regard, the difference between Mencken and La Monte was that Mencken, inspired by a Nietzschean contempt for losers and a naive Darwinism that could be found at most locations on the early-twentieth-century political spectrum, thought that exploitative competition was both inevitable and good; it led to progress. Few other libertarians would take that view. All classical liberals, from Adam Smith to Friedrich Hayek and Milton Friedman (and, of course, Isabel Paterson) have emphasized the importance of free markets in promoting cooperation between buyers and sellers, not exploitation. All have maintained the importance of the capitalist division of labor in creating a world in which everyone can be a success at something. According to Paterson, the mysterious word "exploitation," once translated into normal language, just means "receiving wages for work."[16]

Mencken's illiberal views persisted. In a salient essay of his mature period, "On Being an American," he treats American prosperity as something made easy by "the lavishness of nature," which creates wealth even for mindless "incompetents," and by a capitalist system that almost automatically multiplies that wealth. This "capitalism" renders the people "pliant slave[s]" while giving them "gaudy ease and plenty of food in return for [their] docility."[17] It's an image that collectivists of the postmodern school would appreciate. Mencken's essays identify the "ideal government" as "one which lets the individual alone" but betray no serious interest in the structure of such a government, except to suggest that the Founding Fathers' concealed purpose was to create an "aristocracy" that could control "the mob." He thinks it unfortunate that "the old landed aristocracy of the colonial era has been engulfed and almost obliterated by the rise of the industrial system, and no new aristocracy has arisen to take its place and discharge its highly necessary functions." Paterson didn't miss the aristocracy. She thought that Mencken was far too prone to miss it. She gave his politics the once-over, and ignored them.[18]

There was a difference of style as well as a difference of ideas. The style of American libertarianism has been a great deal more egalitarian than that of conservatism or modern liberalism. Mencken's style was also egalitarian, in a sense. In *Men versus the Man*, he was very clear on the idea, which was shared by Paterson and all the other founders of libertarianism, that the "class" divisions that really count are defined not by money or by privilege but by intellectual ability.[19] Probably no journal in American history has been more egalitarian in its openness to authorship than Mencken's *American Mercury*, which welcomed submissions from anyone who had anything interesting to say, even clergymen and politicians. In private life, Mencken was as courteous to people of all kinds as Paterson was forthrightly rude. But it was Mencken, not Paterson, who claimed that "[d]ecency, self-restraint, the sense of justice, courage—these virtues belong to a small minority of men," and who characterized America as "the only comic country ever heard of." He pictured American culture "in three layers—the plutocracy on top, a vast mass of undifferentiated human blanks bossed by demagogues at the bottom, and a forlorn *intelligentsia* gasping out a precarious life between."[20] He anticipated no alterations.

Paterson's idea of society was never this schematic, nor this static. She wasted no sympathy on the intelligentsia, which seemed more grasping than forlorn to her. As for the "human blanks," she insisted that "people are not gadgets nor bundles of odds and ends; they have minds and souls of unreckonable potentiality, and the most important thing in the world is for that fact to be recognized, so they won't allow themselves to be packed into containers and labeled for a given use."[21] She saw the American experience as the crucial episode in human progress toward individual freedom and dignity; Mencken saw it as one more episode in the monkeys' attempt to operate the zoo.

A man who kept a solemn distance both from Mencken's position and from Paterson's was Garet Garrett, a financial journalist whose self-reflexive name has appeared in an earlier chapter of this book. Garrett (1878-1954), was a leading writer for the *Saturday Evening Post*, then the nation's principal popular magazine; but he was a magnificently un-*Post*like writer—cranky, iconoclastic, baroquely intelligent, expert in strange tricks of rhetoric and startling shifts of perspective: a writer who wrote to appreciate his own words. In Garrett's writing, spiders do not *spin* their webs—they *cast* them; and the seasons do not change—there is "a rippling of seasons north and south."[22] Garrett was an eloquent commentator on American political history and economic development. As I have noted, his account of the causes of the Great Depression was much to Paterson's taste. In the mid-1930s he argued trenchantly for laissez-faire, attributing America's unexampled economic success to a regime in which "[p]olitical freedom and economic freedom were the two aspects of one thing, inseparable."[23]

But Garrett was a man of strange and unaccountable intellectual perturbations. Some of his ideas smacked strongly of Marx and Veblen, or of a financial journalist who has gotten too close to his topic. He imparted such weird Veblenic wisdom as the notion that there is "[a]n excess of industrial equipment already present in the world," and he credited "free virgin land" with having temporarily provided an "equilibrium" between agriculture and "the wild energy of the machine," of which he often seemed much afraid. He believed that the surplus production of the machine had to be worked off by the stimulation of false desires and by predatory competition for foreign markets, which must result in war. He recurrently fixated on the curious idea that the nations of the world should become economically self-sufficient, so that war will become unnecessary—as if the problem were impersonal economic processes, instead of people's false assumptions about those processes.[24] Paterson never accepted any of this intellectual folklore.

Like her, Garrett always deplored "[t]he advance of government everywhere toward control of the economic life," but his political views were shaped by an intense historical pessimism. American ideas of liberty ordinarily proceed from Enlightenment ideas about the power of reason, chastened by Enlightenment skepticism about people's ability to make dependable use of it. Garrett's skepticism was overwhelming. "The history is this," he wrote.

Never was there a time when people did choose between economic freedom and government administration of the economic affair. They never had a chance to choose; they wouldn't have known how. What happened is clear. At the beginning of the industrial era government did not take its hands off business. Rather, the business on which it kept its hands vanished. In place of it was suddenly and incredibly growing the thing we call modern business, machine, power, industrialism, speed, mass production, modern credit and banking, and no government knew anything about it. Modern business got loose and ran away. It has taken government 150 years to overtake it. That now has happened; and it was inevitable that as soon as government did overtake it the hand of government would be laid upon it. And this, I fear, unless it is undone, which I cannot imagine, will be the end of the world's getting rich.[25]

For Garrett, the sudden growth of the Internet, which now seems to have escaped from the government and run away, at least with the hearts of libertarians, would represent just one more temporary stage in the irrational process of history: "nothing was ever solved by reason . . . never were people sane but in a kind of torpor after a particularly extreme form of madness." "Where is the new base?" Garrett asked in the aftermath of Roosevelt's re-election in 1936. "Where is the fighting position? I haven't any."[26] Garrett understood himself.

The closest thing to a professional individualist among writers of the 1930s was Albert Jay Nock (1870-1945). Raised in Alpena, a northern Michigan town like Paterson's Newberry, Nock became an Episcopal clergyman in Detroit. He married and had children. Then he quitted both his pulpit and his wife and became a writer.[27] He worked as a journalist and associated himself with "progressive" politicians, but gradually drifted away from modern liberalism in its progressive form and became what he called an "anarchist." He edited two journals of radical thought, the *Freeman* (1920-1924) and the *New Freeman* (1930-1931); he wrote essays and collected them; he wrote books about Jefferson, Rabelais, and political and economic theory. Finally he wrote a book about himself.

Nock was an individualist in the most determined way. He was so obsessively secretive that, rumor had it, staff members of the

214   The Woman and the Dynamo

first *Freeman* could reach him only by putting messages under a certain rock in Central Park.[28] Many (indeed most) facts about his life remain obscure. There is a perennial rumor, for instance, that he was the lover and perhaps the husband of Suzanne La Follette, a woman active in radical and later in conservative affairs; no one seems to know whether the rumor is true. But his character and tastes were plain for all to see. He was an old-fashioned humanist and skeptic, fond of a joke and regarding most of human affairs as a joke, inclined in his latter years to believe that most other people were not yet quite fully human (look at the things they do!), yet very much inclined to defend their rights and to deal with them personally as if they were as human as himself.

There is something about Nock's career that appeals both to conservatives and to libertarians, and he has strong admirers in both camps. His writing helped popularize the term "libertarian" in something like its current sense. His own use of the term was generous and free, unconcerned with specific ideology. For him, Rabelais "was one of the world's great libertarians," not because of his political positions but because of his ability to imagine Gargantua's Abbey of Thélème, where the rule is, "Do as thou wilt."[29]

Nock's politics consisted largely of a dogmatic advocacy of the theories of Henry George, the San Francisco printer and economist whose *Progress and Poverty* (1879) became one of the most popular books ever published in America. In 1932, Edmund Wilson "astonished" Paterson by reporting "that he had only lately read Henry George." She wondered "[h]ow any one could have escaped—the works of Henry George were strewn about the West like leaves in Vallombrosa."[30] George was the creator of America's most ingenious economic and political cure-all, the Single Tax. The idea was that the government should support itself solely by a 100 percent tax on the "rental value" of land and natural resources, which were not really private property in the first place. Nock believed that the Single Tax would make land available to everyone, thus destroying the power of economic "monopoly" and of the political state that maintained that monopoly. He was not concerned about any danger that might arise from the political agency that would be empowered to spend the money generated by the Single Tax. He called it a "government," in distinction to a "state," then ceased to worry about it. He therefore saw nothing wrong with describing himself as an "anarchist."[31]

Paterson lavished praise both on Nock's prose style and on his individualism, but she thought she could do without his habit of "looking down on his fellow men," and she politely dissented from his political theories. She considered taxes "a nuisance, but . . . a necessary nuisance," and she put the Single Tax in the familiar Patersonian category of crackpot ideas. As time went on, she got very tired of hearing about George's theories: "The Single Tax is socialism."[32]

She never commented on the strange tendency of Nock's writing in 1930-31, when as collaborator with La Follette on the *New Freeman* he spent many column-inches on what can only be called shameful defenses of the Soviet Union. Nock had adopted a moral equivalency hypothesis, according to which all states are oppressive to approximately the same degree. From this he deduced the idea that American criticism of the Soviet Union was silly and hypocritical.[33] If Paterson read Nock's journal, she would not have cared for it; but there is no evidence that she bothered to read it. Although (as will appear hereafter) Nock had high praise for Paterson's political ideas, his influence on her seems to have been nonexistent.

The same can be said about the influence of Nock's disciple, Frank Chodorov (1887-1966), whom everyone concerned about the Old Right views as one of its most important members. Chodorov, like Paterson, defended the American tradition from a perspective significantly removed from mainstream America. The eleventh child of Jewish immigrants who operated a little restaurant on the lower west side of Manhattan, Chodorov became a high school teacher and later a small businessman. His business was destroyed by the Great Depression, and he picked up some jobs as a salesman. Beginning in the late 1930s, he edited a number of individualist or conservative journals: an obscure Georgeite periodical; his own four-page monthly, *analysis* [sic]; the more prestigious *Human Events*; and in the 1950s yet another *Freeman*.

Chodorov was a man of great courage and integrity. His writing was clear and bold, and it was informed by exceptionally wide reading. No one would call it profound, but it made provocative arguments for such crucial ideas as the "imperviousness of economic law to political law" and the axiom that "state power can grow only at the expense of social power," the power of the people themselves.[34] He influenced a young generation of political activists, most notably William F. Buckley, Jr. Unfortunately, Chodorov and Paterson never converged, though that was not Chodorov's fault. As soon as he started at the *Freeman*, he asked her to contribute; but for reasons that will later develop, she was in a bad humor about his journal, and she did not take up the invitation. She did write to a friend for information about Chodorov; it seems she had never heard of him.[35]

Among the radical individualists of the period, Rose Wilder Lane (1886-1968) probably bears the closest similarity to Paterson. Born in the same year, they were both daughters of the frontier West reared in conditions that taught them the virtue of fending for oneself. They both parted from their husbands soon after marriage and supported themselves in peripheral occupations before becoming successful journalists and novelists. They were both social and economic libertarians, championing laissez-faire capitalism and opposing all governmental attempts at moral uplift. And they were friends. They may have met as early as 1917 or 1918, when they were both living in San Francisco. Lane surfaces a number of times in Paterson's columns, which record both agreements and disputes.[36]

Lane described herself at forty-eight as "a plump, Middle-Western, middle-class, middle-aged woman, with white hair and simple tastes." But she was not a simple person. Attached to the Midwest by ties of love and hatred, she did her best to escape, joining the Lost Generation in Europe in the 1920s. She settled in Europe's least frequented, least fashionable country, Albania, where she made herself a hit with the local population. In 1926, she invited Paterson to visit her new home, and Paterson warned her that she might just do that.[37] But the political situation deteriorated, Lane had trouble with money, and she returned to the United States. Here she struggled to support her parents and the three sons—two American, one Albanian—whom she informally adopted. She helped her mother, Laura Ingalls Wilder, with her novels, the *Little House on the Prairie* series; according to her biographer, William Holtz, the help amounted to ghostwriting. She had some kind of romance with Garet Garrett. She suffered agonizing fits of depression, superbly chronicled in her diaries.[38]

In 1936, she published her first manifesto of radical individualism, "Credo," in the *Saturday Evening Post*. "Credo" is the story of
her conversion from communism—which she once regarded "as
an extension of democracy," the last of several "progressive steps
to freedom"—to a belief in free enterprise and limited government.
The turning point was her realization that "government" always
consists of "a man, or a few men, in power over many men." Any
group of men that tried to control an entire economy would have to
institute "such minute and rigorous supervision of details of individual life as no people will accept without compulsion." A communist state has to be a tyranny. But the real revolution had already
taken place, in America—a revolution that promised "All power to
the individual" and actually delivered on that promise, by cutting
the power of the state "to an irreducible minimum." Absent the
power of the state, there was nothing in America to maintain a rigid
class system: the economy was always too "fluid, changing, and
uncertain" for that. Lane observes that few Americans of the 1930s
would begrudge public assistance to people living as "the majority
of American families" lived in the 1890s, when leftists believed
that capitalism was slowly grinding everyone into poverty. America
is now a place where "hunger marchers do not march but travel in
trucks."[39]

These were basically the same ideas that Paterson had been loudly
advocating for years. She hinted as much while using her column
to advertise "Credo," which was quickly revised and republished
as a book called *Give Me Liberty*. She said she enjoyed the book,
but she asked how Americans could ever have taken liberty "for
granted," as Lane confessed she had.[40] In 1938, Lane published a
finely realistic novel called *Free Land*, a story of western settlement that demonstrated what she and Paterson had always known,
that there was no such thing as free land; any settler had to invest
time, energy, and courage to make the land worth something. Paterson went to a party to celebrate the book's publication, then announced it in her column as a refutation of the fashionable theory
that free land had kept America going in the past but now, because
"that recourse no longer exists, we have to have a totalitarian state."[41]

In 1937, Lane visited Paterson, and the two women stayed up all
night discussing ideas. The next year, at Paterson's urging, Lane
moved to Danbury, Connecticut, "up country a few miles" from

Paterson's house at Ridgefield.[42] The quality of their relationship is indicated by a letter Lane wrote in 1942. It begins: "Look, Isabel, you are a fair person, actually." Then she tells Isabel at length exactly how she thought she was being *un*fair to her. That having been said, Lane ends with a friendly discussion of royalties, human nature, and the irreverent deism they shared: "Whoever arranged the sun, moon and stars and the planets obviously had taste and skill and originality, but for a place to live in I wouldn't have that interior decorator."[43] Within a few years, as I will show, the emotional balance tipped, and the relationship succumbed to the common libertarian assumption that two's a crowd. For a while, however, according to the libertarian journalist John Chamberlain, Paterson and Lane constituted two-thirds of America's cadre of libertarian intellectuals.[44] The third was Ayn Rand, who would enjoy the greatest popular influence of any libertarian author, indeed of any author on the right, and who owed the greatest intellectual debt to Paterson.

Rand (1905-1982) was born Alyssa Rosenbaum in St. Petersburg, Russia. She escaped to America when she was twenty-one and adopted a pen name that she hoped would keep her family from being persecuted by the Soviets when she became a famous writer. For many years she was able to achieve only modest and occasional success: a story sold to a Hollywood studio, never produced; a well-attended Broadway play (*Night of January 16th*, 1935); a commercially disappointing novel about life in Russia (*We the Living*, 1936). Like Paterson, she lived in poverty and struggled to support herself in menial jobs. Her husband, Frank O'Connor, was an unsuccessful actor who represented a romantic ideal but brought her no money or connections. Rand was incomparably intense, astonishingly insightful, and stubbornly one-sided; she was devoid of vanity and full of intellectual pride. There has probably never been an American artist who could equal her devotion to abstract ideas or her skill at dramatizing them. Few, certainly, have equaled her courage in pursuing intellectual ideals.

Rand knew all about Isabel Paterson, a famous literary figure whose political writing Rand enormously admired. That was a great deal more than Paterson could say about her. When *We the Living* appeared, the two authors met at a literary cocktail party. Rand remembered the meeting; Paterson did not.[45] In her column, she confined herself to reproving something in the publicity handouts from Rand's publishers. They reported that Rand, who had suffered great hardship, denied that hardship can have any good effects. Paterson argued gently that bad times can be useful.[46] She then forgot all about Ayn Rand.

It was late 1940 or early 1941 before Rand reminded Paterson of her existence. The occasion was political.[47] Rand, like Paterson, had voted for Roosevelt in 1932, because of the prohibition issue. Later, she suspected that Roosevelt's National Recovery Administration was wrong, but she was conscious of not really knowing why. Concerned about America's increasing collectivism, she started to follow politics more closely in 1936. When the Second World War broke out, she was disturbed by the possibility that America might enter it. She also worried that if Roosevelt was chosen for a third term, there might never be another election. A dictatorship might ensue; the capitalist system might be destroyed. In a world in which one nation after another had turned to authoritarian government, this fear was not as far-fetched as it may seem today.

Rand had reservations about Wendell Willkie, the Republican nominee in 1940, but she threw herself into his campaign, abandoning her writing and consuming her savings to work as a full-time volunteer researcher and public speaker. She stood on the stage of a theatre near Union Square, eulogizing Willkie and sparring with hecklers. Despite her thick Russian accent, she was good at that. When someone shouted, "Who the hell are you to talk about America? You're a foreigner!" she responded, "I *chose* to be an American. What did *you* do, besides having been born?"[48]

The end of the campaign brought defeat and disgust. In Rand's view, Willkie had compromised his ideas, basely squandering the individualist message that would have given his campaign its moral meaning. What was needed, as she now believed, was an organization of intellectuals with a sharply individualist focus. She assumed responsibility for creating such an organization. She conferred with Channing Pollock, a conservative playwright and essayist whom she had met during the campaign.[49] They invited people whom they considered the greatest opponents of modern liberalism (Paterson of course among them) to come to meetings to discuss what to do. The meetings were inconclusive. Rand introduced individualist ideas that she regarded as mild and trite, and was surprised that her colleagues were surprised by them. Nock showed up, because he was a friend of Pollock's, and opined that there was nothing to be done.

Isabel Paterson had not appeared. Wondering why, Rand called her office and arranged a meeting. She discovered that Paterson didn't join anything, and that she was in an even worse mood about Rand's would-be political friends than Rand was. But she was nice enough to Rand, and about two weeks later they met again. Soon Paterson was inviting Rand to spend the weekend at her house in Connecticut. On the first night, they stayed up talking politics until 7 A.M. Many such conversations followed. Rand had finally discovered an intellectual whom she could respect.

Rand's niece, visiting her in New York, believed her aunt was "entranced" by the older woman:

> They'd sit up until four or five in the morning—and Ayn would be sitting at the master's feet. One night, when they were talking, I went to bed, but I could hear the conversation, and it was as if Pat were the guru and teacher—and Ayn *didn't do that*. Ayn would be asking questions, and Pat would be answering. It was very strange.[50]

Rand joined the unpaid assistant proofreaders at Paterson's Monday night gatherings, where, according to Gardner Welles, one of the young friends in attendance, "Ayn used to sit at Pat's feet—he saw it time after time. They would take an issue such as, for instance, the Supreme Court, and discuss it until Ayn had a full understanding."[51]

Paterson read almost everything; Rand was never a wide reader. Much of what she learned came from conversations with trusted friends. She knew the great literature of the nineteenth century, in several languages, and was especially attracted to Hugo, Dostoevsky, and Nietzsche. She received education in history and philosophy, with a modern Russian slant.[52] But she had come only recently and superficially to the study of American history, politics, and political philosophy. Years later, she recalled Carl Snyder's *Capitalism the Creator* (1940) as the first good current book she read on economics.[53] There is no evidence in her published novels, essays, or correspondence of extensive reading in such areas. What she knew about them doubtless came principally from Paterson.

There is evidence, indeed, that Rand's ideas were shifting significantly during the period of their first acquaintance. *We the Living* is an anticommunist novel, but its treatment of alternatives to communism, of political ideas in general, is sketchy, to say the least. It is a novel of psychological individualism. In succeeding years, Rand worked her way from a continental version of individualism influenced by Nietzsche to an American individualism grounded in a political theory of natural and equal rights.[54] In 1942, when she wrote the concluding pages of *The Fountainhead*, the novel that established her fame, she gave her original quasi-Nietzschean ideas a classical-liberal form:

> Men exchange their work by free, mutual consent to mutual advantage when their personal interests agree and they both desire the exchange. If they do not desire it, they are not forced to deal with each other. They seek further. This is the only possible form of relationship between equals. . . .
> The only good which men can do to one another and the only statement of their proper relationship is—Hands off![55]

If there was a crucial, external influence on Rand's political development, Paterson was that influence. The precise extent of her influence could be determined only by someone who overheard their midnight dialogues, but an indication can be found in the inscription that Rand wrote in Paterson's copy of *The Fountainhead*: "You have been the one encounter in my life that can never be repeated."[56]

It was not simply because they agreed on certain things that Paterson liked Ayn Rand. She admired her "unique mental powers, her genius, her heroic effort against deadly odds, and her extraordinary accomplishment."[57] She also enjoyed Rand's little jokes and appreciated her strange ways with English words. She wrote a memo to herself recording two characteristic comments:

> Ayn said there was an ungulfable bridge. She said: "Will you write my autobiography? I can't do myself justice."[58]

Rand, later famous for her candidly exalted opinion of herself, might have meant a number of things by that second remark. Paterson thought it was amusing, whatever it meant. Rand's eccentricities were charming because she had a "natural simplicity of manner." Paterson told readers of her column that Rand was once hit by a taxi and was thenceforth afraid of traffic.

[A]nd the way she shows it is to stand a minute at the crossing, viewing the stream of vehicles with alarm, seize the hand of her escort with a gesture of feminine terror, and then march ahead across the street, hauling her protector after her.[59]

The principal basis of the relationship, however, was not Rand's curious personal charm but the two women's passionate interest in ideas. An apt symbol of the relationship is provided by a little episode that happened during Rand's research for *The Fountainhead*. Much of the novel's action involves a newspaper. To help Rand work up the background, Paterson showed her around the pressroom at the *Herald Tribune*. That bit of local color never made it into the published book; it was one of the many items that Rand omitted as unnecessary.[60] But Paterson's political ideas were not omitted. The important thing wasn't the roar of the presses; it was the quiet conversations in Paterson's office, seven floors up.

15

Attacks and Counterattacks

A very large book could be devoted to describing all the people who *dis*agreed with Isabel Paterson. She had many unpleasant encounters with people of the left, the right, and the emerging New Deal center. In these encounters, neither side was ever likely to declare itself vanquished and converted. No one could deny, however, that Paterson gave as good as she got. And some of the battles helped her to elaborate her ideas—as objectors frequently had cause to regret.

She continually increased her unpopularity with the left, not just by questioning collectivist ideas but by puncturing the pretentiousness of the individuals who mouthed them—a much less forgivable offense. In some cases, virtually all she had to do was to quote their language. In 1935, for instance, she received the pompous Call of the communist-organized American Writers' Congress, which read, in part:

> The capitalist system crumbles so rapidly before our eyes that, whereas ten years ago scarcely more than a handful of writers were sufficiently far-sighted and courageous to take a stand for proletarian revolution, today hundreds of poets, novelists, dramatists, critics, short story writers and journalists recognize the necessity of personally helping to accelerate the destruction of capitalism and the establishment of a workers' government.[1]

Paterson noted that this "appeal to the bandwagon instinct is perhaps not on the highest plane of either art or intellect." There were, to be sure, many prominent names affixed to it. Among the people personally helping to accelerate destruction were Malcolm Cowley, Kenneth Burke, Josephine Herbst, Erskine Caldwell, Horace Gregory, Theodore Dreiser, John Dos Passos, and Lincoln

Steffens, a group that spanned several generations of American literary fame. Some deserved their fame; some didn't. Paterson suggested that the famous Malcolm Cowley had "nothing to worry about, no matter what happens. It takes him twenty years to write one book ('Exile's Return'), and meanwhile world wars, revolutions, booms and depressions roll their appointed course." She obviously didn't like Cowley, but she did have "affectionate respect" for Horace Gregory, who had "a fine and sensitive mind." She even promised to read his poetry, which was of "the T. S. Eliot school," to the next union meeting she might attend. The idea that writers like that were going to produce a new workers' culture was ridiculous: "The grim determination of the working classes NOT to read intellectual proletarian literature has been fairly well proved." So far, American workers weren't suffering from the intellectuals' delusion

> that calling things by different names will save the world. Call your autocrat a dictator instead of a Czar; call your terrorist agency the Ogpu instead of the Okhrana; call your seizure of the peasants' food a quota requisition instead of exploitation and serfdom; call your massacres liquidation; call your bureaucrats commissars; and everything will be lovely. Call the whole thing social justice.[2]

Soon she had a letter from Lincoln Steffens' wife, Ella Winter, who accused her of criticizing the Soviets while ignoring books critical of Nazism. Paterson published the letter, which coyly suggested that she had fascist sympathies, and added the comment that she wouldn't like being liquidated by any totalitarian party. She pointedly referred to a work she had previously recommended, Ignazio Silone's *Fontamara*, an antifascist book by a leftist opponent of Stalinism, and added a list of other antifascist books: "Those who yearn for the totalitarian state under any name will do well to study all these books and ask themselves how they'd enjoy being in the minority if they got what they think they want. Or what makes them so sure they wouldn't be?"[3]

Paterson's remaining leftist friends may have missed the irony in statements like that, because they continued their efforts to salvage her. Isidor Schneider made particular efforts to get her to convert, despite her loud and public protests. Other leftist readers mounted a campaign against her, insisting that she was a paid propagandist for the ruling class. After all, she got a salary from the *Herald Tribune*. She responded by citing the support that leftist authors James Farrell and Josephine Herbst derived from the Guggenheim family. She doubted, however, that this would "do the Guggenheims any good; the net result of a temporary benefaction is to create acute annoyance when it ceases." She summarized her own position by citing an anecdote from her job in the hotel dining room. Her boss accused her of not listening to him and asked her what she thought he paid her for. She answered that if he paid her for listening to him, he wasn't paying her half enough.[4]

A dismal indication of the change from American self-reliance to American self-entitlement was the kind of reader who assumed that society could and must provide a remedy for every ill. These readers harped on the fact that Paterson's political program guaranteed no solution to a variety of problems for which the New Deal, the Townsend Plan, Social Credit, fascism, and communism advertised comprehensive fixes. This was a repetition of the traditional complaint that classical liberalism is a merely negative philosophy, able to show what is wrong with other ideologies but offering no great "positive" program of its own. Paterson was sick of hearing that. She bluntly replied:

> What these correspondents really demand is dope. If we don't believe in their dope, what dope can we suggest in place of it? None whatever. We do not even know a remedy for gullibility.[5]

Leftists who disliked Paterson called her a "snob" and a "hypocrite."[6] In fall 1935, she was attacked in a series of articles that showed how snobbish the left itself could be--not a surprising concept to her, believing as she did that any collectivist system had to be run by a self-aggrandizing elite; naturally, elitists would be attracted to the idea of collectivism. Mary McCarthy, the future bestselling novelist, collaborated with one Margaret Marshall on a series of articles for the *Nation* entitled "Our Critics, Right or Wrong."[7] It was the start of McCarthy's long career as a supplier of superciliousness to the left-liberal intelligentsia, and in the context of the mid-1930s it was an important critical statement. The series reviewed the major groups of American critics and, as one might imagine from its title, put most of them in the "Wrong" category. The opening piece called special attention to the wrong that Paterson and other "big-time critics" had done in praising Paterson's friend Thornton Wilder. Taking their cue from communist writers who were busy disparaging the bourgeois Mr. Wilder, McCarthy and Marshall portray critical approbation of his work as self-evident proof of imbecility.

The second article zeroes in on Paterson and Rascoe and their friends Herschel Brickell and Carl Van Doren, the "group of front-line critics" who wrote for *Herald Tribune "Books."* The "most notable characteristic" of this group is "its militant anti-intellectualism." Paterson's self-affiliation with the Age of Reason is considered a "pathetic masquerade." At best—and that best isn't good enough—Paterson has "the horse sense of the cowpuncher." She is guilty of having predicted that *The Great Gatsby* wouldn't last, of having missed out on the "new philosophy of society" allegedly secreted in *The Magic Mountain*, and of having criticized the plot premise of *The Sun Also Rises*. That wasn't all. She had had the temerity to praise authors like Margaret Kennedy and Louis Bromfield; and she had called Grace Zaring Stone's *The Cold Journey* "the most distinguished novel of 1934." These specifics were real, though not as ludicrous as McCarthy and Marshall assumed they were. Paterson had not risen to the challenge of Hemingway's novel, or Fitzgerald's; but Stone's book (which Paterson generously rated above her own novel of 1934[8]) remains one of the most fully realized works of American historical fiction, while Mann's "new philosophy" is yet to be located.

McCarthy and Marshall notice that Paterson's politics are anti-communist and that, regrettably, her social criticism "has steadily increased both in volume and sharpness." The authors' own politics grow clearer in the third article, which ridicules J. Donald Adams, editor of the *New York Times Book Review*, for his opposition to the Soviet dictatorship. They advise the *Times* to appoint someone like its Moscow correspondent, Walter Duranty, to bring "impartiality" to the *Book Review*. The suggestion shows what Paterson was up against in the American intellectual culture of the 1930s. Duranty, winner of the Pulitzer Prize for his reports on the Soviet Union, is today regarded as one of the most shameful figures in the history of journalism, notorious for having used his official role as impartial reporter to conceal the crimes and practical failures of the Soviet regime. Those were precisely the events that Paterson, with scant applause from anyone, was trying to make her readers understand.

The fourth article takes up Marxist criticism; and although it is written in the same condescending style as the others, its tendency is clearly sympathetic. Marxist critics are said to be burdened with an "inferiority complex" and a "pathetic eagerness to gain converts." But no eyebrows are lifted at Marxism as such, only at certain "sectarian" divisions within the movement. McCarthy and Marshall hope that "the new united front" of communists and liberal "progressives" will "reendow [Marxist authors] with critical and revolutionary dignity."

The series ends with an article that puts the blame for bad (i.e., unduly tolerant) criticism on the profit motive of journals that take advertising (i.e., any journals not fully subsidized by wealthy people). The prevailing kindliness of *Herald Tribune "Books"* is attributed to this pecuniary motivation, with no further notice taken of Paterson's "volume and sharpness." The *New Republic*, the *Nation*, the *New Masses*—the major leftist journals—are praised for their critical vigor and their lack of advertising.

The five-part series was obviously supposed to be a devastating blow to established critics in general and to Paterson in particular. She took time to respond only to the first part. She focused on the authors' ridicule of her liking for Wilder, noticed their misreading of one of the reviews she gave him, and spotlighted the embarrassing language in which her opponents applauded the communist writer Mike Gold, who had mounted a hairy-chested attack on Wilder's preciousness (i.e., homosexuality). "Michael Gold," as Marshall and McCarthy put it, "with a rude proletarian gesture of disgust, put his fist through the pretty pink bubble of Mr. Wilder's world." This sort of thing was plainly disgusting. The only reply Paterson could make was to suggest that

[i]f Miss McCarthy can find a field in which her peculiar—very peculiar—talents are at home, she would be well advised to work in it. It should be as far removed as possible from literature, and require no care for accuracy.

The illustrators of Paterson's column thoughtfully provided a cartoon of McCarthy on her hands and knees, scrubbing a floor.[9]

The odd sequel of the Paterson-McCarthy controversy took place on Christmas day, 1938. McCarthy was in a New York hospital, where she had just given birth to the child of her marriage with Edmund Wilson. Her husband was in Stamford, Connecticut, whiling away the evening with Isabel Paterson. Wilson was visiting the people across the street, and he walked over to Paterson's place and insisted that she join the party. She didn't feel she could refuse. She was certainly not attracted to him, but they were old acquaintances. She had "a pleasant evening . . . he is a well read man and talks interestingly," but she regarded his behavior vis-à-vis his wife as odd, to put it mildly. And she was surprised by his friendliness to herself: "[H]is wife dislikes me—I've never met her at all, but she writes."[10] No need to say more about Mary McCarthy.

A potentially more serious antagonism than McCarthy's surfaced soon after the election of 1936, when Paterson went to lunch with Heywood Broun, a member of the Algonquin Round Table and a reputed wit, and some other literary folk who acted as advisors to the Book-of-the-Month Club. Broun was a big supporter of leftwing causes. He was also the organizer of the American Newspaper Guild, a group that Paterson characterized as "his organization for the benefit of sons-in-law." He tried to convince her to join, informing her that she could object from within if she felt like objecting. She preferred, of course, to object from without—not that she was against labor unions, which she wasn't, but because she did not choose to join one. Broun, whom she had never liked, intimated "delicately" that if she didn't join she would "probably lose [her] job some day." The well-heeled "champion of labor" then got up and departed for his winter vacation in Coral Gables, leaving Paterson in such a bad mood that she was embarrassed by the way she treated the remaining members of the party.[11]

When she reported all this in her column and needled Broun with further reports of his silliness and pomposity, he wrote her a letter that she characterized as a

> rhetorical outburst . . . affirming that "we are standing at Armageddon now," and demanding, "on which side are you going to fight." "Are you going to fight," he asks, "standing beside the Herald Tribune, the Liberty League, and William Randolph Hearst?"

Paterson replied that she would fight on her own side. She also pointed out that "Mr. Broun used to have a job on the H.-T. It didn't seem to worry him until he got another offer." The whole affair was "cheap humbug."[12] But there was a threat in it. If an industrial Armageddon did arrive, or if Broun and his friends could succeed in producing one, Paterson would obviously be first in line for the lake of fire.

At that juncture, she might not get much help from the conservatives who were exerting themselves to outlaw Armageddon. She made no attempt to disguise her dissent from any anti-libertarian idea, whether it came from the left or from the right. Reading through some conservative political literature, she found demands that tolerance be extended only to people who were sincerely in favor of tolerance; radicals were not considered to deserve freedom if they used it for subversive purposes. This suggestion, she said, was "plausible," "deplorably plausible": "In the vernacular, it means: 'I'm for freedom, so you shut up; or I'll put you in jail.'"[13]

Then, to be fair, she turned to the modern liberals, who seemed to agree with their enemies on certain basic ideas:

> The same fallacy may be concealed by various highbrow phrases, as, for instance, this from "The New Republic": "Liberty is a positive purpose, not an absence of restraint." Bosh. Liberty is an absence of restraint. And nothing else whatever. It does not presuppose any purpose, good, bad or indifferent. It is not a means, but an end. . . . We are very well aware that the danger of freedom, including free speech, is that it gives leeway for speech against it; anybody who doesn't know that fact and accept it is not for freedom.

If someone wanted to "take advantage of free institutions to speak against them . . . it must be tolerated." That didn't mean that people have to "run after him and ask him to dinner."[14] This was common sense. It was also a way of making sure that neither side of the political struggle would, as it were, ask I.M.P. to dinner.

If they wouldn't invite her, she could invite herself. In June 1936, she was stirred by "conscience," which informed her that she didn't get around enough, to travel to Philadelphia to attend the Democratic national convention: "What could be more clearly a duty than to go where you're not wanted when you'd rather stay at home?" She made her headquarters at the home of Emily Clark, a well-known literary editor and an old friend of H. L. Mencken. Mencken himself came over for a chat but "didn't dare to stay away from the bars very long, as all the news was in the bars." Paterson got to the convention itself just in time to listen to a speech by party patronage dispenser Jim Farley, Postmaster General of the United States. Twenty minutes of that was sufficient. She returned the next day but was prevented by the loudspeakers from discovering what anyone was saying; she "might just as well have been a delegate." With that, she left. The convention, she told Dinarzade, was

a sickening spectacle. Simply appalling in its meaningles[s]ness. All those dimwits wandering around a huge hall, and someone going blah-blah through a megaphone, and nobody listening.[15]

Even the charm of suspense was absent. Two months before the convention, Mencken had sent a joking offer to let her know "in confidence" who would be nominated. Of course it would be FDR. Paterson predicted that the "permanent nominee" would be on the ticket in 1940, too.[16]

The 1936 Republican convention nominated Alfred Mossman Landon, governor of Kansas. Paterson didn't care much for what she heard of that convention, either. She remained a republican with a small "r," complaining to Rascoe about the "appalling manifestations" at both major-party conventions. Although she insisted that neither of those orgies should make one cynical about the idea of political liberty, she hadn't trusted either party enough to let it make her cynical. Her announcement that she planned to vote Republican came months before the GOP produced its candidate, and the endorsement was plainly no more than a determined protest against the New Deal. She admitted it was

hard on the Grand Old Party—but it's got to put up with our support in times of adversity, whether it likes it or not.[17]

On Election Day, she worked in her garden, then went to the home of some Republican neighbors and told them to prepare for the worst. She was sure that "whatever the majority thinks it will not be what we think," and her opinion was confirmed. "The amiable intention behind the vote," she said, "was to give everybody something for nothing." The result would be more of what the country already had: "bad debts, bad money and bad faith."[18]

After the election, she expressed a view of democracy that had altered since the early thirties, when she described herself as belonging "to that extinct species, the classic American of republican (or democratic) principles." "Republican" now parted ways with "democratic." Paterson's argument was clever and insightful. She maintained that majorities are naturally in the wrong, because they seldom cohere except in times of "stress and doubt," when irrationality can be expected. She was "not arguing against majority rule, because there really cannot be anything else"; everything that happens in politics requires at least the acquiescence of the majority. And of course, "the minority is usually wrong too"; it consists in large part of "cranks." But some people in the minority will be "capable of rational consideration." The best government "that can be hoped for" is one that allows minorities to exist. Intelligent people may not be in control, but that will keep them "from the sin of pride."[19]

Surely it was the intellectuals' pride that made them imagine themselves as social engineers and directors of other people's lives. The correct solution was to keep anyone from having control of that kind, to limit everyone's power. This was her "deep-seated conservative notion of the desirability of limited government." Further, the government can be limited only by "some actual operative instrument" that counteracts the legislative power of the majority. Here she is thinking chiefly of the Supreme Court, with which President Roosevelt was growing increasingly unhappy; three months later, he would unveil his court-packing scheme. Since early 1936, Paterson had been going to the *Federalist* papers for ammunition to defend the principle of judicial review. Now she broadened her discussion to include the issue of the people's legislative power. *The Federalist* was right: "a republic with representative government," the power of the representatives being itself limited, is preferable to "pure democracy."[20]

For the next three years, Paterson said little about the democracy question. When she returned to the subject, in spring 1940, she said a great deal. She stripped "democracy" of the protective adjective "pure" and asserted that "'democracy' contains no other principle than majority rule, which is also tyranny, being absolute." That is why the founding fathers had rejected democracy, choosing liberty and individual rights instead. With another national election looming, she again insisted on the dangers of favoring "democracy" over "representative government." In a column written a few hours before Hitler began his campaign to conquer France, she observed that no democracies currently existed, but that there were more than enough "dictatorships, which were made possible by nonsensical talk about democracy."[21] Hitler, of course, had come to power with the aid of democratic processes.

One striking thing about Paterson's critique of democracy is that it was wholly unnecessary, from the strictly polemical point of view. She didn't need to criticize democracy in order to attack the communists or the fascists, the modern liberals or the New Era conservatives. She had been doing that for a long time. She criticized democracy because she had come to believe that such a critique was the only way of solving the larger problem of liberty and equality. That problem could not be solved just by saying that no class of people should invade the rights and plan the lives of others. It could be solved only by discovering a political structure that could keep that from happening. The structure must provide the means of limiting what any government could gain the power to do. The democratic principle provided no such limitation.

The connection with equality was clear. Individuals could enjoy equal rights and equal opportunity only in a society protected from the overweening power of the majority or (even more to the point) the majority's political managers. Democracy was advocated on egalitarian premises, but its operation always entailed distinctions of power and status. By contrast, "The real idea of the American Revolution," which established a limited government,

> was that any man might be intelligent, or intellectual, regardless of his supposed status. The great distinction of that revolution was that it was made by men of genuine ability, with varied practical productive experience by which they checked their theories—not by the incompetent who wanted to get a political hold on the producers. A printer, a silversmith, a farmer, or for the matter of that a cobbler, had an honest appreciation of the value of liberty and property, and a sound understanding of the necessity of limiting political power so he could get his work done and enjoy what he had earned.[22]

Her interest in the early republic inspired her to take another look at the historical relations between economics and government and to change her emphasis, if not her ideas, on that subject. She had long opposed the "economic interpretation" of American history that had become popular during the Progressive era. She especially disliked the application of this theory (by Charles Beard and others) to the American revolutionary period. She argued that the revolutionaries could not have been impelled by their economic "group interests," because they were individually willing to sacrifice their property, not to mention their lives, for the sake of their political cause.[23] In 1941, she looked at this history from a different angle. She did not concede that economic interests decided the revolution's course, but she explicitly endorsed that part of the economic interpretation which held that the constitution was written to safeguard private property.

This, as she observed, was what modern Americans had been taught to deplore about the constitution. The tendency had gone so far that even Beard, the most effective spokesman for the economic interpretation, was now trying to rescue the document from the charge of enshrining property rights, as if there were something wrong with that. Paterson saw no reason for the rescue attempt. The authors of the constitution had known what they were doing, in both senses of that expression: they had acted freely, not as mere agents of property interests, and they had acted wisely, understanding that property rights are the "only effective basis of all civil rights." With property rights, people can do their work and enjoy what they earn, no matter who wins the next election. That's the idea behind the constitution. People who are startled by it are "capable of being startled by the alphabet."[24]

Startled people often become angry people, at least when "democracy" is at stake. Paterson's opposition to that article of modern American faith was very damaging to her. She started receiving letters warning her that she might wind up in jail if she didn't adjust her attitude. "Isn't that priceless?" she said. She had associated democracy with tyranny, and now she was being told that "we shouldn't say that, or the proponents of democracy will prove that we are right."[25]

Not every leftist or modern liberal thought that Paterson was beyond the pale. To philosopher Sidney Hook, for instance, her words possessed "the unmistakable quality of integrity and moral sensibility."[26] But all popular beliefs have their intellectual enforcers. A man who warmed to the role and performed it in an inimitably self-righteous way was Henry Steele Commager, professor of history at Columbia University. Commager, who would crown his career with a blustering attack on President Reagan's reference to the Soviet Union as an "evil empire"—"the worst presidential speech in American history, and I've read them all"[27]—crept up on Paterson with the nets and springes of ideological entrapment. This was a spectacle.

Professor Commager wrote to her with sarcastic condescension, mentioning her criticism of democracy and "wonder[ing] what particular form of government you do find harmonious with your idea of individual liberty. I am sure your readers would welcome this revelation." He was implying that she must be a supporter of some un-American system; and considering some of the curious statements that he was about to make, he may actually have been politically ignorant enough to think that she might.[28]

What he got, naturally, was a lecture on Paterson's preference for "[t]he American form of government, as originally conceived and instituted. It was called a republic." People like Jefferson, Madison, and Jay had tried to protect liberty against majority rule. This should not come as a shock to people on the left: such progressive stalwarts as Lincoln Steffens had made the founding fathers' opposition to democracy a "cliche."[29]

Commager was determined to keep up the debate, but he was not determined enough to keep his mock civility from becoming simple mockery: "I don't want to impose on you too much"—little lady—"but if you could tell me what a republic is. . . ." I just told you, Paterson replied, by instancing the American republic and its "safeguards for individual liberty against any majority." Commager thanked her for informing him (as if he had never heard of such a ridiculous idea) that "the purpose of the Constitutional Convention and of the constitution was to limit democracy." He, however, thought it was "'to form a more perfect union.'" Well, Paterson recalled, even Eleanor Roosevelt thought that "'the union established was really a republic with a representative form of government and a series of checks and balances to control the various arms of government as well as the people of the country.'" But, Paterson reminded him, she herself had said something slightly different. She hadn't said that the constitution was supposed to limit democracy (or control the people). She had said that "the purpose was to avoid democracy and to limit government." This was not just a verbal distinction.[30]

By his third letter, Commager was dithering: "The fact is that neither you nor I know what a republic is, nor does any one else for that matter. But at least I do know enough to know that I don't know." Another thing about which he was triumphantly ignorant was why Paterson thought democracy and liberty were at odds, "while republicanism and liberty are buddies." She restated her views, adding that she hoped he would not "feel impelled to write and tell us that he doesn't know what liberty is either. He doesn't need to."[31] And he didn't.

The skirmish had ended, with Paterson in possession of the field— something that, in practical terms, was worth very little. Commager wasn't shaken. According to his respectful biographer, he was wont to "discomfort . . . even his supporters" by his slapdash methods, but no such discomfort impeded his career in political punditry. He went on to achieve "forty-three honorary degrees and the Gold Medal of the American Academy of Arts and Letters." It is not specified whether these awards were given for his "impatien[ce] with philosophical precision," for his impatience with minority views, or simply for his remarkable smugness.[32] In any event, he was more than some little woman in a dingy office on 41st Street; he was a member of the intellectual establishment.

As both he and Paterson knew, however, their debate was about something greater than intellectual pretensions, or textbook definitions; it was about incompatible visions of America and incompatible ideas about who had the authority to project a vision. She, at any rate, was happy to keep it there. During the second Roosevelt administration, she ordinarily withheld comment on political issues that did not directly illuminate the clash of visions. At the end of her last column of the second term, she took notice of Bernard de Voto's celebration of democracy's "success" and mentioned, in summary: "Fifty billions in debt and diving deeper; millions on relief; the great success story of democracy." It was true: unemployment was 14.6 percent in 1940; federal expenditures and federal debt had nearly doubled since 1933, while long-term corporate debt had declined by 8 percent, the sign of a severe lack of investor confidence. The federal budget had not been balanced since 1930, despite the fact that intake from individual and corporate income taxes had much more than doubled since 1934. But Paterson infrequently mentioned Roosevelt himself, and still less frequently by name.[33] Perhaps this indicates her lack of respect for him, even in his role as villain. Certainly it illustrates her conviction that the country was being ruined not by one man but by a whole class of intellectual spendthrifts and bankrupts.

She was, indeed, becoming embattled against virtually everyone. Her process of intellectual self-definition, which would result in alienation even from most of her libertarian would-be allies, was already well advanced. She continued giving good literary notices to authors with whom she disagreed; she sometimes gave warm recognition to their political works, if they were well researched or well written;[34] but she no longer wanted to call those people friends.

It was part of a larger withdrawal from the world around her, and a corresponding intensification of her inner life. Time had always been an enemy; now it was visibly winning. Quoting Will Cuppy, she said that "[w]e have only one life to live, if that"; and she added, "it's not enough." She also said, "It takes the best part of a lifetime to find out what you don't want."[35] She didn't want to waste any more time than necessary on ideas that she considered palpably false, or with people who insisted on believing them. So she spent less and less time mingling with acquaintances in New York, and as much time as she possibly could at her home in Connecticut, where the trees and the animals and the books that she loved, not merely tolerated, were always full of life and energy.

Another large distance was opening between outward and inward. On the outside, Isabel Paterson was the increasingly difficult and cantankerous I.M.P. On the inside, she was an adventurer, pursuing a quest. She had her political opinions, which she announced. But there was more she wanted to know. She was trying, through study and silent thought, to understand the nature of the world's energy and the vital connection between it and the individual self. To understand that was to understand America, and the modern world. Her withdrawal was partly a result of her passionate contempt for her contemporaries and partly a strategic retreat, an attempt to focus on the problems that were most important to her. She diagnosed her own condition:

> [A]chievement depending on prolonged, concentrated effort is so hard that any one who is intent upon it will unconsciously contrive an environment which provides a reinforcement of external compulsion and repels distracting influences. . . . It's quite unnecessary for any one else to make life hard for them; they'll do that only too thoroughly themselves.[36]

By the time she presented her theory of America and its energy in *The God of the Machine*, she had done that very thoroughly indeed—and no more thoroughly than in her opposition to the disaster of energy in its cruelest form, the Second World War.

16

War and the Intellectuals

Paterson tried to discount the danger of another war. She believed that Germany's internal weakness might keep it from running the "fearful risk" of starting a conflict: "No country is really strong when the government must maintain itself by force and terror." She wrote that in 1934. Three years later, she was still trying to believe that war would be averted. If the dictators started a war, she thought, "they couldn't carry it on." Resources would be lacking: "the forces men have begun to tap cannot be managed by any dictator."[1]

True; dictatorships have an excellent chance of being crippled or destroyed by their own misorganization. But that can take a long time to happen, and the world's dictators were not as good as Paterson at understanding the risks they ran if they started the process. In the conjunction of these facts lies the intellectual strength and the practical difficulty of her ideas on foreign policy. She knew that, too: "No despotism can maintain independently and indefinitely a machine economy or a mechanized army. But until the batteries are completely exhausted, a despotism can do enormous damage." In that case, "a commensurate counter-attack is called for."[2]

One of her strongest points of agreement with other intellectuals of her generation was a concern that America would be drawn into a war by its weakness for minding other people's business.[3] The precedent was the Great War. Like most of the others, she took that war as a benchmark of criminal stupidity; like many of them, she became an isolationist, of a certain kind, because she did not want to repeat the experience. Yet when asked to sign one of the pacifist pledges that were popular in the mid-thirties, she rejected the invitation, saying (truly enough) that she had no talent for passive resistance. Pacifism was "not a new idea," but she considered it an intellectually dishonest idea. It wasn't hard to see its logic, but neither was it hard to imagine "circumstances in which defensive war would appear . . . right and proper—that is, if those who must fight it also felt so." The issue, after all, was the defense of *freedom.*[4]

The pledge "to refuse to engage in any war" was so "sweeping" as to remind her of "the regimentation of war itself." There were "many cases" in which she would prefer to "fight, and, if necessary, die, than submit." She was on the lookout for antiwar books to recommend to her audience, but she was skeptical about the usefulness of much of the antiwar material she saw: "Fury about war is too much like the militant spirit itself." Antiwar literature should show that war is ugly, uncomfortable, stupid, and boring, "that there's nothing in it, not even excitement, at least for the common soldier." Her literary judgment was that "[t]his is the view of war which may, in the long run, end it."[5]

The antiwar book she liked best was H. M. Tomlinson's *Mars His Idiot*, which preached her own doctrine: war is horror and degradation; it is made possible by unquestioning obedience to the state, "the new idol"; and it is instigated by public men who would be imprisoned for lunacy if they resorted to similar expedients in private life. The difference between public and private behavior is crucial. People are very seldom murderous as individuals; they become murderous when they become gullible followers of that monster, the state. "Their great fault," she says, echoing Tomlinson, "is not being sufficiently individualistic."[6]

She never denied the right of people to defend themselves, even if that entailed foreign combat. She had nothing to say against Jefferson because he "smacked down" the Barbary pirates.[7] She could support war so long as it was "defensive" and so long as people who did not support it were not forced to fight in it. The great political principle was limitation of state power. In the domestic arena, that meant laissez-faire; in the arena of foreign relations, it meant opposition to military engagement for any purpose except self-defense. Despite her continual attacks on fascism and communism, she advocated intervention against neither Germany nor Russia. She probably regarded the conflict that erupted between them in June 1941 in the way in which Jefferson regarded a war between Russia and Turkey: "Whichever destroys the other, leaves a destroyer the less for the world."[8] Her isolationism, however, was not based on *realpolitik*; it was not a covert interventionism. At times she could even go so far as to maintain that the political mistakes of the Russians were their own business. In any event, "Good fences make good neighbors," as Robert Frost had written.[9]

With anti-interventionism went a mild anti-imperialism. Despite her Canadian grievances against the British Empire, she respected it to the degree that it promoted peaceful commerce among peoples. Believing, in fact, that a real, enduring empire derived its power from money, she thought that empires needed for their own sake to maintain property rights and personal liberty. If they did so, that would be an achievement worth noticing. Still, she saluted Jawaharlal Nehru, the rebel against the British Empire; and she agreed with Arnold Toynbee that imperialism in the usual sense of the term was antithetical to the development of a civilization, the source of which was individual freedom and variety. The United States hadn't been "set up" with any "intention of being an empire or colonial power," and that was all to the good.[10] She now saw that the problem with the British Empire was the problem with the modern world in general, which had lost freedom "by mistaking force for power, regimentation for discipline." She thought one could see that mistake in the "unexpected moments" when the great poet of empire, Rudyard Kipling, "goes off key."[11]

The idea that America must plan for its own supposedly global mission filled her with trepidation. If no one could know enough to plan America's future, it was certain that no American could know enough to plan the future of the world. She had lived through one bout of internationalism in World War I, and she hoped she would never have to repeat the experience. She understood the objection that "the United States used to be isolated, but is so no longer, and must now develop the international mind," if only for its own protection. But people who argued from history in this way ought to know

> that when it was founded the United States had Europe in the back yard and on both sides—French sovereignty in Louisiana, Spain to the South, and British troops garrisoned in Canada. It had had one European war fought on American soil—the French and Indian war, and George Washington fought in it. He couldn't have felt nearly so "isolated" as he would have wished.[12]

These facts have rarely been noticed in modern debates about foreign entanglements, perhaps because the debaters have rarely thought as much about history as Paterson did.

The Munich crisis occurred in late September 1938, and from that point on, isolationism was put to an increasingly serious test. After that, Paterson's attitudes and reactions tell the story of a well-informed American's struggle to understand a course of events to which the passage of time has given a false appearance of clarity. In retrospect, only one sequence of horrors is visible, but Paterson could envision many alternative sequences, some of them even more horrible.

During the crisis, she shut herself off from newspapers and went to work moving rocks around in her garden, trying to relish what might be her "last days of enjoyment." The emergency ended with the apparently ignominious appeasement of Germany by France and Britain. Writing to her friend in France, Dinarzade, Paterson confessed to being "glad the war has been at least postponed."

> Though I don't want any war whatever, now or later, I will say that if Germany, Russia and Italy should want to chew one another up, I'd care least about that. . . . Well, let's hope for a slow emergence of sanity everywhere. . . . The fact is that modern war is ruin, win or lose or draw. We had enough saps here earnestly trying to steer us in—as if that wouldn't simply blot out the last hope for the world, instead of doing any good whatever.[13]

But after Munich, Paterson returned to her column with only an expression of nauseated disgust at people's tendency to follow such "human pests" as the spellbinding dictators.[14]

Ten months later, Stalin concluded the pact with Hitler that allowed both of them to make war on their neighbors. Paterson at first said nothing to her audience about the pact, even though it dramatically discredited the American communists and vindicated her thesis that all forms of totalitarianism are basically the same. She waited until several months afterward to signify her relief at the cessation of pro-Russian books from former fellow-travelers.[15] Then, responding to American Stalinists' acquiescence in the "Communazi" pact, she gave renewed publicity to books by repentant or partially repentant communists.[16] She seems to have felt that the communists' intellectual disgrace spoke for itself; but she may also have wanted to disassociate her kind of isolationism from the kind they were now fervently preaching.

From her perspective, the isolationists and the interventionists must often have appeared very similar. The interventionists who thought that fascist totalitarianism was on the verge of world conquest, the communists (whether interventionists or isolationists, depending on the season) whose respect for totalitarianism never wavered, the conservative isolationists (some of them) who, like Anne Morrow Lindbergh, regarded collectivism as "the wave of the future," a form of progress, repulsive but inevitable, to which America would have to adjust itself[17] —all these people assumed that radical collectivism somehow actually *worked*. To Paterson, this was a wildly eccentric notion, and reason enough not to ally herself with anyone who held it.

Her sympathy, she said, was "wholly engaged by the rational people" who now had to shelter themselves from bombing raids, "because the world is being run by the people who are now running it."[18] She was convinced, however, that direct American intervention was unnecessary, unlikely to accomplish strictly humanitarian ends, and dangerous to the survival of America's remnants of limited government, which were the only hope of averting tyranny. Contrary to popular belief, she argued, the stronger the government, the weaker its armed forces will eventually be found; military power is inversely related to the power of the state. She warned America against locking itself into the chains of conscription and militarization.[19]

Her published remarks about the war tended to assume the war's own temperature. By early spring 1940, the time of the "phony war," she was practically ignoring the subject. Later in that season, however, she made three vigorous and well-timed attacks on interventionism. The first was probably written three days after Hitler's invasion of Denmark and Norway, the second a few hours before his invasion of the low countries, aiming at France, and the third just one week later, while the outcome remained in doubt.[20] She was attacking intervention just when it started to seem like a good idea; and that, presumably, is why she did it.

On May 10, Lane wrote in her diary: "I.M.P. phoned at midnight. . . . Germans attacked Holland, Belgium, France at 1 a m European time." Lane and her close friends Ruth and Isaac Don Levine had planned to drive over to Paterson's place that day, to see the blooming of her enormous shadbush. (Paterson claimed

that "[p]eople go to foreign countries to see less wonderful sights.")
But now the Levines, whom Lane had regarded as politically sympathetic, startled her by declaring that America should get into the
war. She took a taxi to Paterson's without them and witnessed the
shadbush. She found Paterson deep in speculations:

> I.M.P. says, *How* can U.S.A. enter the war? Japan will not attack our navy. If
> England, and France lose, are Americans to declare a new war and reconquer all
> Europe? . . .
>   She says, The British Empire is ended by industry. It was essentially a *commer-
> cial* empire. Germany commits suicide. The cause is sense of inferiority because
> historically Germany is *behind* and can not see why. Our age, our civilization, is new,
> the *power* era. Its essential base is liberty and private property: it can not exist
> without that base. . . . Germany *can* not live, combining Power Age with the State.[21]

By May 28, King Leopold had surrendered the Belgian army,
leaving his allies in the lurch and, as Lane noted, "virtually giving"
Dunkirk to the Germans. When Lane talked with Paterson the next
day, I.M.P. denounced Leopold, pungently declaring that the form
of "suicide now prevalent is the saving of life." She thought his
troops must hate him for his act. Lane demurred: "I think they're
damn glad to be out of it." On June 15, with the Germans in Paris,
the French government in flight, and the Russians entering Lithuania,
Paterson warned Lane against believing predictions about the future shape of Europe that merely reflected what Germany wanted
people to believe. As for the Allies, she maintained that they had
not really fought the Nazis, as Europe had not really fought Napoleon; they were "rotten with collectivism, false by the Marxian lie,
which Germany revolted against and went to despotism. Which is
also, she says, a lie, a poison." Two days later, Marshal Pétain surrendered France, asking Germany for an armistice. I.M.P. was "stag-
gered." She denounced the incompetence of the world's
"paper-minded" rulers who don't know "how to *do* anything."[22]
The loss of France was what she had most feared from a European
war. She had wanted "to see a few remnants of civilization preserved, and the French are civilized."[23]

In mid-summer, she held out the hope of an ultimate deliver-
ance, confiding mysteriously to her audience that "[t]he machines
are going to break up the German army"—an allusion to her theories about the machine age, or "power age," and its incompatibility
with collectivism. For the next year and a half, there is little spe-

cific discussion of isolationism in her columns. She was now aware of her inability to make anything other than general and imperfect comments on the course of the European war itself, and she may have come to regard intervention as virtually inevitable, no matter what might be said in opposition. And the second war, like the first one, disturbed her so profoundly that she could hardly bear to think about it.[24]

The issue that preoccupied her, because it was an issue that, unlike the war, she believed she might do something about, was the survival of freedom in America. War invigorated the spirit of collectivism, a spirit that throve especially among intellectuals. She had long been uncomfortable with their practice of organizing themselves into groups and pledging their agreement to political programs. She refused to join any isolationist group, or any other group, for that matter, even if it supposedly agreed with her. She said that she wanted to avoid being "thrown out as soon as we get down to cases." Besides, as she declared, "authors should not indulge in deliberate organized propaganda for the best cause under heaven," because in doing so they "destroy all faith and credit in the written word." She refused to telegraph her advice to Congress when requested to do so by proponents of political causes, and she noticed that the requests always seemed to come from people who had helped to create the situations they now wanted her to protest against.[25]

One of the things that bothered her about the mid-thirties pacifist pledges was the fact that many of the "eminent names" who subscribed to them had been "equally prominent in advocating a previous war while it was still popular." The phenomenon was now repeating itself. And even before "Comrade Hitler," as she called him, surprised Comrade Stalin with an invasion of Russia, at which point Stalin's diehard friends in the United States decided that war might be a good thing after all, she observed that pro-war arguments came increasingly from people who thought "it is necessary to fight in order to retain the power to make ourselves over into the very form of society which we are supposed to be fighting against."[26]

Toward the beginning of August 1940, she ran into Freda Utley, a writer who had lived in the Soviet Union but who now wanted to assure her that she had never supported "terrorism." Utley had, indeed, become severely disillusioned with the Soviets, who had sent her husband to a prison camp. Paterson offered sympathy and said that she was looking forward to reading Utley's next book. Utley's change of heart, however, gave Paterson an opportunity to warn her readers that people who had recently found themselves mistaken about the Soviet experiment had no business urging other people to new political crusades. Such people should be told, "The fact that you have lately given up work on your perpetual-motion machine is no strong recommendation of your new project for squaring the circle." She followed her own advice. When pro-communists of the 1930s came over to her side and became anti-communists, she (unlike other leading "conservatives") emphatically rejected their claims to leadership. As for pro-communists who had grown disgusted with Stalin and had become modern liberals, she believed that they had "changed their labels but not their minds." They had embraced collectivism "just because it was fashionable," but it had shaped their mentality and they could not give it up. They were now trying to defend a free society with such authoritarian means as conscription.[27]

In February 1941, she received a "nice letter" from James Boyd, a novelist she liked. He invited her to help with an organization called The Free Company. The Company, which boasted such supporters as Archibald MacLeish and Robert Sherwood, was intended to unite "America's greatest writers" to propagandize for "the basic civil rights of a democracy." Paterson was one "greatest writer" who did not consider herself honored by the invitation. The very name of the group struck her as ridiculously oxymoronic, and she was startled to find that the "spontaneous" movement had been hatched in meetings at the Department of Justice and approved by the solicitor general and attorney general of the United States. The Free Company included a number of famous people who were "versatile opinion changer[s]," not to mention a nice quota of "government jobholders." But whoever its agents of influence might be, the state had no business involving itself in voluntary organizations. Government propaganda could never serve American freedom, since "the American principle of freedom consists wholly in the limitation of government."[28]

As fashionable writers, once so self-consciously radical, worked to solidify their ties to Washington, Paterson appeared to be working night and day to sever her ties to them. It didn't take much. She had only to turn down one of their "unopened prize packages" of ideas:

> The general implication is that if, for instance, Mr. Archibald MacLeish says he is for home and mother, you must either stand behind Mr. MacLeish and cheer his utterances or kick mother in the face and set fire to the ancestral roof-tree.[29]

In refusing fashionable fellowship, of course, Paterson did more than politely demur. She was aggressive, obnoxious, offensive— and courageous. She pictured her fellow intellectuals as "incurable stooges" who would

> join practically any group whatever which begins by denouncing Fascism or Nazism. On such premises the joiner will soon find himself committed to "leadership" demanding—we quote Miss Dorothy Thompson—"for President Roosevelt the power and the authority completely to organize the economic and moral strength of this country" on "a total war footing." What more did Hitler ever ask? What more is there to ask? Nothing.

She thus heaped scorn on the interventionists, while doing nothing to endear herself to those isolationists who were still sympathetic to the Communist Party, to modern liberalism, or to the pacifist movements of the thirties.[30]

The election of 1940 had considerable personal significance for Paterson. She was well acquainted with Willkie, the Republican candidate. He enjoyed Paterson's writing and attended at least one of the Monday night gatherings at her office. She told her readers that she was going to vote for him "no matter what," the announced explanation of the "what" being his unfulfilled promise to buy her a drink.[31] But there was a good deal that she did not choose to announce. Behind her bland endorsement lay not only her considerable reservations about Willkie's ideas but also her attendance at the curious drama of his private life.

Willkie, a son of small-town Indiana, had risen to national prominence as a lawyer and utilities-company executive who fought against New Deal encroachments on industry. A reader of books who longed for intellectual and literary stimulation, he became acquainted with Paterson's editor, Irita Van Doren, and saw in her the embodiment of the sophisticated culture he sought. If nothing else, she had the cultural patina that comes from knowing books and authors, and she was, by the testimony of everyone who knew her, a very charming person. Mencken describes her as "a small, slight, dark woman whose bushy hair had now turned iron gray, and there were few pleasanter companions for a dinner party."[32] Willkie, too, was a person of great charm and—though this is not evoked by surviving photographs—magnetic sex appeal.[33] He was a big, rumpled, tousled man, a man whose warmth and friendliness made him easy to love.

He and Irita became lovers. She had been divorced from her husband, but Willkie was still married. Those times were more innocent or more cynical than our own; the relationship never became public knowledge, despite the fact that it was intimately known to everyone at the *Herald Tribune*. Irita gave Wendell books, introduced him to fashionable authors, revised his prose, and made him feel like an intellectual. She also counseled his political ambitions. The Republican Party, plagued with weak presidential candidates, was desperate to find someone who could mobilize the broad middle range of voters. Willkie, a lifelong Democrat, decided to try for the nomination; and, after a lightning campaign, he got it. He was one of the great dark horses of American political history.

The leaders of the party were, by and large, isolationist, but Willkie wanted strong measures in aid of Britain. He waffled and hedged, but he supported conscription, the transfer of American warships to Britain, and most of FDR's other war-related policies. In addition, he supported such New Deal programs as social security (in some form), slum clearance, government-sponsored collective bargaining, and "the principle of federal supervision over industrial activities."[34] He was a perfect example of the characteristically modern convergence of "moderate" big businessmen, cosmopolitan media, and self-consciously modern intellectuals. He was, that is to say, a perfect example of the withering of older styles of liberalism, including his native Wilsonian variety, and their replacement by the New Deal brand.

Willkie's politics were not to Paterson's taste, yet she supported him, she and Rand and millions of other people who feared Roosevelt's precedent-shattering drive for a third term. Willkie's various positions on the war were beside this particular point. The view that Paterson took of the third term question was similar to that of Roosevelt's former assistant Lewis Douglas. Although Douglas, the arch-interventionist, had little more reason to trust Willkie than she had, he nevertheless believed that

[n]o matter how grave the National Emergency the continuation in authority for three terms of this political machine—clothed as it is with tremendous public power—is a still graver menace to America.[35]

All this helps explain Paterson's "no matter what" declaration for Willkie. The declaration, which waited until the last column she wrote before Election Day, constituted her only public discussion of his candidacy.[36] Henceforth, she would make no such political concessions. Big business, the middle-of-the-road, and the intellectually prostituted Republican Party would get the back of her hand, no matter what.

On Election Day, she voted, then proceeded to Lane's house in Danbury, where she spent the night. It was not a happy evening. The returns came in; Roosevelt had been reelected. Lane said, "It's the crowd, the mass. Loss of liberty ends the industrial revolution." Paterson replied, "The power will explode. In war." They argued about the dependence of "the crowd" on government. Paterson maintained that political states that catered to the crowd would destroy themselves, and the crowd along with them. Lane suggested that tyranny could continue indefinitely: look at the continuance of "starving" Russia. On that issue, of course, Paterson was right and Lane was wrong, though the final evidence would not appear until many years after their deaths.[37]

Paterson also showed herself somewhat less inclined to moralize than Lane, at least in any conventional way. Lane contended that Americans were losing freedom because they lacked "morals," by which she meant "respect for human rights, equality." But Paterson emphasized the idea that good things can have bad effects, including bad effects on themselves: "loss of morals was inevitable" in a capitalist society, a society in which people can make a "profit on recklessness. Under such strains, morality crumbles"—"morality" meaning the old-fashioned sense that there is something intrinsically good about saving and something intrinsically bad about "gambling." Politics and economics are not simply a function of morals, narrowly considered. But even a broader sense of morality, such as we invoke when we speak of "a good person," can produce unfavorable results. Indeed, "all the harm is done by 'good' people. Because a majority of any species is good, in the sense of well-meaning toward fellows."[38] But that was the reason for having a limited government, such as she and Lane were trying to preserve—to keep the force of anyone, including the majority, under restraint. Good government cannot be dependent on good intentions or morals. It must have a properly limiting structure.

The unfortunate Willkie was the last candidate whom Paterson publicly endorsed. In the first column she wrote after the 1940 election, she mourned the weakness, amounting to nonentity, of his campaign: "Incurably obstinate, we still think it would have been a good idea to have had a Republican party. Fact is, we could use one now." Fourteen years later, she wrote, "[A]s a real republican, at present I have no party; there is none."[39] After 1940, she never voted again.

During most of 1941, America was at war, de facto, with the Axis powers. On December 7, Japan attacked Pearl Harbor, and America's war formally began. Paterson's next column says nothing directly about the event. She was not a pacifist; she would not protest against a war that had become defensive. A "commensurate counter-attack" was "called for." And she was not a politician, so she did not have to pretend that all would now be well, so long as everybody pulled together. She concluded her column with a simple, solemn valedictory: "Well, come what may, we have lived in the best country the world has ever known."[40]

She followed the war closely, but she made little attempt to advise her audience about its progress. As a friend suggests, she may have thought that "once she got started she would go too far" and end up losing her job. Also, she disclaimed any expertise on military strategy.[41] She was, however, deeply upset by the loss of life, much of which she attributed to strategies that she considered foolish, such as "island hopping" in the Pacific and the long, messy invasion of southern Italy: "She thought they should have gone right into Rome."[42] On at least one occasion, she attempted to save lives. Horrified by Allied "obliteration" bombing, she tried to enlist the power of the *Time-Life* empire to stop it. Her target was Whittaker Chambers, then a back-of-the-book editor at *Time* and not yet famous for his dramatic exposé of communist infiltration of the federal government. He and Paterson had mutual friends, and she sent one of them to suggest that he might raise questions about the bombing in *Time*, using as his journalistic hook a recent news item about the Pope's disapproval. Her efforts were unsuccessful.[43]

Naturally, the war's political conduct was shrouded in secrecy; in that sense, there was less to criticize about it than there had been about the New Deal. As a writer, however, Paterson kept up a fire of criticism against wartime censorship and propaganda:

> As for official propaganda, of any kind, it can only confuse the issue, if that issue is freedom. . . . The information that should be obtained from official sources is another matter—it concerns official action—and half the time we don't get that, except by rumor or indirection or favor.[44]

When she wrote things like that, she was almost "going too far." She was certainly not increasing her popularity. But she could not resist going farther and renewing her attack on conscription, a very dangerous idol to touch at a time when victory was popularly associated with universal mobilization. In World War I, critiques of conscription had sent their authors to jail. To Paterson, however, conscription was not just morally wrong but practically dangerous. Forcing millions of men to march against millions of other men was the greatest waste that could be imagined; it was the folly of the totalitarian states, which were throwbacks to barbarism. Using the theories she was developing for *The God of the Machine*, she argued that the range and speed of a nation's military forces depended on the type of economic "energy system" that supported them. Conscription took men out of the system that produces such efficient and powerful weapons as airplanes and turned them into such weak and vulnerable weapons as infantrymen.[45]

She clearly did not expect to be heeded on that issue. Her reason for taking the risk of expressing her view was to get her readers to remember what the war was about. It was about defending the idea of America, or it was about nothing. That was why she reminded them that America's current ally, the Soviet Union, had originally been Hitler's ally, and was now "keeping on good terms with Japan," while accepting massive aid from the United States. And that was why she insisted on analyzing President Roosevelt's statement of war aims, "the Four Freedoms," as a serious intellectual document. The Four Freedoms were freedom of speech, freedom of worship, freedom from want, and freedom from fear. The first two, she believed, were indeed crucial, but they could exist only where state power was limited by the people's freedom to own private property (which had not made the list). But to talk of freedom from want and freedom from fear was dangerously wrong. Human "needs" are endless; no government can guarantee to supply them, and only "courage or rigor mortis" can eliminate fear. If people tried to use government to obtain these new rights, they would get only "freedom from soap, freedom from shoes, freedom from food."[46]

As long as America maintained its basic institutions of liberty and private property, she had no doubt that it would continue to participate in the "vast amelioration of human living" that has resulted from them, and them alone.[47] And she had no doubt that America would succeed in defending itself. She had utter contempt for the Nazis and believed that both they and the Japanese imperialists would collapse soon after they had used up all they had acquired "from the Western production circuit." In the short term, until "the batteries [were] completely exhausted," despotism could do its "enormous damage"; but the batteries could not hold out for long. She was confident that Hitler, who was foolishly regarded in many circles as a "great soldier," would bring "his country to complete destruction."[48] He could not maintain himself by running a modern economy with slave labor, as he planned to do. Japan could not maintain itself by exploiting the Chinese in that way, either. Paterson's knowledge of Japanese history led her to believe that once American troops landed on the home islands, Japan would surrender.[49]

She may have been right, though the atomic bomb ended any possibility of knowing for sure. When it fell, she was "stun[ned]" by the "terrifying possibilities" and disgusted by the men whose great scientific discovery had been a way "to fry Japanese babies in atomic radiation." She was happy, for everyone's sake, that President Truman concluded peace without demanding the removal of the Japanese emperor. There was no point in continuing the war until Japan was beaten into total submission. Enough was enough.[50] As always, the important thing for her was the ability of individual people to survive and create a freer life for themselves.

All this having been said, her chief public notice of the war was the attention she paid to individual soldiers. They were always welcome in her column, and she delighted to discover the evidence, in their correspondence, that Americans were still a book-reading people, and not shy about expressing their ideas. She bragged about soldiers who wrote to criticize her views on such apparently trivial, merely intellectual issues as the meaning of Virginia Woolf's novels.[51] And when one of her soldiers reviewed his experience in the war and asked, "can any one understand if I say that I was happy?", Paterson used his remark to express her own view of war and life. "Why not?" she said.

> Nobody of military age made this war, or wished for it. It was just their tough luck. But we have to live in this world, if at all, as we find it; and make what we can of it. If in the face of chance and danger and a hard task, a soldier got some happiness out of experience, which is the stuff of life, we can't think of any one who would have a better right. We have an earnest dislike of artificial "optimism," and the attitude that "things will turn out all right" regardless; they won't; but if it is looked at as a job to be done and a life to be lived, that's a promising prospect.[52]

She hoped, above all, that the courage and energy of youth would not be expended in another war or, still worse, enslaved by ignorance and tyranny.

Her own best contribution to life "in this world" had already been made. In 1943 she had published *The God of the Machine*, her account of America's past, her challenge to America's future, and her explanation of how America works and ought to work.

17

The Grand Perspective

The God of the Machine begins with a literary symbol that is also a historical fact. In the fourth century B.C., a Greek navigator named Pytheas sailed from what is now Mediterranean France, through the Pillars of Hercules, and into the Atlantic Ocean. He was not the first sailor to attempt that journey; the Carthaginians had traded in the Atlantic for many years, but they killed anyone else who tried to do so. To put this in modern terms, they maintained a planned and managed economy, with appropriate penalties for regulatory violations. Pytheas broke their chains:

> He appears to the imagination, a solitary figure framed in light, as if a gate had swung open between the Pillars of Hercules toward the western world.

Paterson adds, "He could not know that he was looking toward America."[1]

The ancient Mediterranean myth of Atlantis and the later European myth of the Blessed Isles pointed the way toward a West that held the hope of happiness and of "the prerequisite of happiness," liberty (53). Pytheas' voyage was one step toward the discovery of America, a place where people like Pytheas would be able to pursue happiness in their own way.

The pursuit has never been easy. It has always involved serious risks. It is very appropriate, therefore, that Pytheas' voyage was the journey of a "merchant adventurer" flouting an "official barrier of the utmost rigor to try the chances of the unknown" (13, 14). The Carthaginians (and where are they now?) tried to eliminate economic risks; that was the perennial idea of the Old World: security. The American conception is different. The American idea is that progress results from accepting risks and daring to make innovations. Pytheas seems to have anticipated that conception. He did more. By breaking the Carthaginians' blockade of the Straits, he helped to extend the "long circuit of energy" that would become the central economic feature of the modern world.

What does Paterson mean by the "long circuit"?

The idea is challenging but simple. It starts from the most basic kind of economic reasoning. Suppose I have something that you want, and you have something that I want. If we exchange these goods, both of us will obtain something more valuable to us than the something we surrendered. The exchange will increase our wealth. We can increase our wealth still more if we extend the circuit of our commercial relations and trade with more people, people who can give us access to more kinds of goods. By buying their goods, we encourage them to use their energy to enlarge their production and to specialize in what they are best at producing. They have a reciprocal influence on us. Mutual desire for what each party regards as wealth induces energy to flow ever more strongly and efficiently along the circuit of production and distribution.

What permits the circuit to be extended in space and time is money. Money is the long-range signal that lets producers know what consumers most desire. Money allows people to transmit their desires to distant parts of the world and to coordinate economic processes that continue far into the future. Money enables local circuits of exchange to grow together into the long circuit of "self-sustaining, self-augmenting, and self-renewing" energy (269). The circuit of production and distribution expands wherever men and women are free to expand it. All along that circuit, operating "by the inductive pull of distribution by free exchange," inventions are made, new products and industries develop, skills diversify, and the value of goods continues to increase (194). When we think in this way, we are thinking, at the simplest but also at the highest level of abstraction, about the economic structure of the modern world. We have gone from the stone age of local production and consumption of bartered goods to the constantly self-revolutionizing global markets of the machine age.

The long circuit was not the product of physical circumstances. It did not develop because certain "natural resources" accidentally became available. It was the circuit itself that made natural objects available for use and turned them into "resources." Within the economic process there is something that has the same function as a generating plant in the electrical power system: it converts pre-existing matter and energy into a new, more useful energy form. But the crucial element in the economy is not some piece of machinery. It is you and I. It is anyone who generates energy by making individual, creative choices: "the dynamo . . . is in the individual" (130).

"Individual" is the salient term. The still-evolving long circuit of energy is not the effect of centralized planning by any body of experts; it is the effect of individual, self-interested actions:

> In free enterprise, the jobs are spontaneously created by the productive system. The person who wants to work is hired directly by the person who wants work done, each being free to seek the other; each is interested personally in the benefit. . . . Throughout the longest series of exchanges, every person has a direct interest in getting the goods through, or producing them; so that the general sequence creates the long circuit of energy, by an unbroken transmission. (194)

To use the vocabulary of Friedrich Hayek and his followers, the long circuit is an artifact of "spontaneous order." The phrase may seem a contradiction in terms. Economic and social order has traditionally been associated with the idea of a government to decree that order. It is an idea endemic to pre-enlightenment Europe, an idea naturally formed by people who were unacquainted with the kind of dynamic society and economy that developed in America with minimal supervision by the state. America showed that the circuit of energy attains its highest potential when it is freest of government interference.

To be sure, governments can develop their own economic enterprises, but they can do so only by expropriating resources that might otherwise have been invested by private individuals in producing things that other people would want enough to purchase freely: "The government certainly can 'make jobs,' but there is no connection of supply and demand, no induction on the flow of energy" (87, 197). Government, in fact, has been the primary means of short-circuiting the energy flow. Extension of the energy circuit requires individual initiative, something that Old World governments were always good at prohibiting, preempting, or taxing into oblivion. When other methods failed, they disrupted the system by manipulating the value of money, thus confusing the signal that stimulates and rewards creation of goods. Any such action is an invasion of liberty and responsibility. It is also a violation of basic engineering principles. As Paterson argues, the operating ideas of a free economy

> are not sentimental considerations; they constitute the mechanism of production and therefore of power. Personal liberty is the pre-condition of the release of energy. Private property is the inductor which initiates the flow. Real money is the transmission line; and the payment of debts comprises half the circuit. . . . The possibility of a short circuit, ensuing leakage and breakdown or explosion, occurs in the hook-up of the political organization to the productive process. This is not a figure of speech or analogy, but a specific physical description of what happens. (62)

The idea of the long circuit and its dynamo, the individual mind, allows Paterson to unite several great themes of her writing: the nature of historical progress, the diverse structures of societies and civilizations, the difference between spontaneous action and social planning, the central importance of the individual experience, and the mysterious and astonishing energy that exists in this world, and especially in America. It is not clear when the energy theory of history first occurred to her. She may have started thinking along these lines when she read Stuart Chase's theories of technocracy. Chase was thinking in a more constricted context. When he wrote about a "new conception, almost a new philosophy of energy applied in space through time," he was speculating about techniques of scientific management. Paterson saw more possibilities in the idea.[2]

Soon after, in *The Golden Vanity*, she offered a number of pungent observations about machines and individuals, about the "spate of power pouring between [Manhattan's] artificial cliffs," and about "the planes, the motors" that "operate by mechanical laws" but

> are driven by a force in the men who invented and built them. They won't go of themselves. And you can't gear everybody to the machines for efficiency; nothing would get done.[3]

By 1934, machines and energy were a major, though still an evolving, component of her thought.

When, in 1936, novelist Harvey Fergusson urged her to produce a "think-book," she replied that philosophy was both too easy and too hard: "it's either what your grandmother knew or what nobody knows."[4] During the next few years, publishers repeatedly suggested that she "should write a book on politics or economics," but she said that she wasn't "ready to do so, had not thought through the material and ideas."[5] Nevertheless, essays preparatory to *The God of the Machine* were appearing in her columns. On July 16, 1939, for example, she describes the difference between American and European civilizations as a difference between "dynamic" and "static" systems, between two different approaches to the release of human energy. In her column of December 15, 1940, she defines "the condition of the machine age" as "the increased extension of individual liberty, the strict limitation of government itself, according to the original American principle." In a column of early 1941, she says that she intends to write a book about the problems of "industrial affairs." Finally, toward the end of that year, she reports herself encumbered with an unfinished book.[6]

Four months thereafter, we find her soliciting the advice of her friend Thomas T. Read, an engineering professor at Columbia University. If she was going to talk about the handling of energy, she wanted the advice of a real engineer, not a "social" engineer.[7] In May 1942, her agent was showing a version of the book to publishers. Late in that year, Paterson consulted Robert Selph Henry, an historian and an executive of the Association of American Railroads, telling him, "I have long been working on a book about what I call the long circuit of energy in production, and the political organization it calls for. That's as much as to say, about our own country, what is it and how come." On March 17, 1943, her publishers, G. P. Putnam's, presented Colonel Henry with page proofs of the completed work, *The God of the Machine*.[8] It was published on May 14, 1943.

In the first chapter, Paterson delights in the fact that her hero Pytheas was a scientist and intellectual as well as an explorer and trader. It was a long intellectual voyage for Pytheas and his successors, from the gates of the Atlantic to the American republic, from the daring act of one individual to the almost unimaginably complex organization of the machine age. Paterson completed her part of that voyage by pursuing a set of principles that she regarded as universally applicable to the problem of energy, its generation and its use. The result was an extraordinarily complex book, a book that has something to say about nearly everything related to "energy"—which means that it has something to say about nearly everything.

One of Paterson's many avenues of approach to her central topic is provided by her emphasis on the role of the individual mind in history, a theme immediately suggested by Pytheas' role as intellectual. No social or environmental condition forced him into the Atlantic. No external condition simply determined the actions and choices that have made modern civilization possible. Ideas were the vital influence. Mind works with its "social environment" and "conditions," as it works with "natural resources"; but it remains the preponderant historical force. "An abstraction," she had written, "will move a mountain; nothing can withstand an idea."[9]

The ideas do not have to be vast Hegelian abstractions. They are, more often, ideas of immediate application to problems of work and life, the kind of ideas that manifest themselves directly in economic choices. They are ideas nonetheless; and America is full of pungent examples of their leverage on history. Paterson had long ago rejected the "frontier" or "free land" theory that made American culture seem almost like an accident of natural history. In *The God of the Machine*, she recalls what she learned in her Western youth, that the frontier was only a thought away from the economic mainline. "The solitary frontier trapper," she says, "was an advance guard capitalist"; his significance came from the fact that he decided to risk his time and money on an enterprise in which he thought he could make a profit (167). Transactions don't just happen; they are willed. And out of such transactions, not out of the land itself, grew the American political institutions that guarantee the continued freedom of such choices.

Of course, many theories were available to explain America's history, most of them based on an examination of social or environmental contexts of human action, not on the nature of human action itself. Marxism was the classic example of the inability of such theories to explain the processes by which new ways of generating and transmitting energy were developed. At most, it could try to describe what happens when people compete for political control of energy already generated. Its picture of the world resembled nothing so much as the blueprints of a perpetual motion machine: the economic machinery keeps itself going, somehow, without any infusions of the peculiar energy derived from individual choice and enterprise. Marxism could not even explain the existence of people like Marx, who taught that the motions of the social machine were predetermined, then tried to change them anyway (97, 152, 146).

Racial and national theories contributed still less, if less be possible, to historical explanation. Race—"to the extent it exists"—was of no significance in itself. Races, like nations, can be merged or divided by ideas, and nations themselves really "are" ideas (53). Arnold Toynbee's theory of history, which treated civilizations as units whose progress was either advanced or retarded by contact with their environments, was attracting a great deal of attention, but Paterson found it banal. You could talk about civilizations in that way, but it was just a general and external summary; it didn't account for their sources of action.[10]

Equally useless to her were historical theories based on *realpolitik* or military power, such as Admiral Mahan's seminal *Influence of Sea-Power Upon History*. Paterson thought that Mahan "might as well have called his book the influence of history upon sea-power" (7). He should have asked what historical events created power in the first place. Carthage, she observes, had sea power and used it unsparingly against innovators like Pytheas who endangered its monopoly of trade. By doing so, however, it let itself be drawn into conflict with the upstart power of Rome. The Roman republic originally had no sea power, but it had the initiative to create it and to finance it with loans, not confiscations. Energy was released much more freely in Rome than in Carthage; and in a conflict of civilizations, the margin of victory goes to the side whose institutional structure permits energy to be exploited more effectively:

> Nations are not powerful because they possess wide lands, safe ports, large navies, huge armies, fortifications, stores, money, and credit. They acquire those advantages because they are powerful, having devised on correct principles the political structure which allows the flow of energy to take its proper course. (13)

An American historical conception that bears a superficial resemblance to Paterson's is the "dynamic" theory of Henry Adams, which has been popular among American intellectuals since the publication of Adams' celebrated autobiography (1918). Paterson had studied his work. Like her, Adams uses the language of engineering ("energy," "sequence," "resistance"). He describes the immense increase in energy or "force" during the nineteenth century and marvels at the industrial "dynamo" which radiated that force. In his theory, however, the dynamo is not "in the individual"; the dynamo is a mechanical object, and its force, like the other great forces in the world, exerts an irresistible influence. Adams assumes, indeed, that "the forces of nature capture man," that even the scientific revolution "seemed voluntary, but in fact was as mechanical as the fall of a feather. Man created nothing." Unlike Paterson, he believes that energy expands in a roughly predictable way. He offers no analysis of human, let alone individual, choice and invention; he assigns no particular importance to political or economic structures, or to anyone's role in devising them. The closest he gets to "structure" is to suggest that there is a "law of acceleration" in the extension of energy.[11] His image of the world is related to Paterson's as a negative is related to its positive.

Paterson's emphasis on "structure" distinguishes her both from Adams and from the historical theorist she most admired, Lord Acton. Like Acton, "[t]he most profound scholar of the past century" (291), she saw the history of freedom as the history of an idea, not the history of social accommodations to environmental factors. But she was not just interested in ideas as such. First as a literary artist, later as a political theorist, she was interested in ideas as embodied in specific forms. This interest allowed her to give full weight to partial and gradual applications of ideas, applications discovered by private individuals, contested by political processes, reinforced by economic events, and lastingly expressed by social customs. Her liberalism was as inflexible as Acton's, but she was more concerned than he was to put the history of liberty in the context of changes in social and economic structures.

Here, in Paterson's interest in "structure," is another avenue of approach to the system of *The God of the Machine*, one that would prove attractive to conservative as well as classical-liberal readers. It helps to account for the influence that her book exerted among intellectuals of both parties. "Structure" gave Paterson a strong conceptual link between the social-historical and the individual levels of human action. It also enabled her to demonstrate the difference between ideas that work and ideas that don't.

The democratic ideals of ancient Greece might seem more favorable to the release of individual energy than Rome's quirky, tradition-bound republicanism; but, as Paterson explains, Roman institutions allowed energy to be transmitted in ways that the Greek democracies never could have allowed. In those freewheeling states, there was nothing to prevent laws from becoming as tyrannous and arbitrary, hence as unstable, as the majority wished them to be; and individual enterprise suffered accordingly. The Romans were often revoltingly cruel, but their republic at least preserved institutional limitations on government's ability to abuse its power. The limitations included offices of restricted power and duration, often arranged in mutually frustrating pairs; a veto power exercised by tribunes on behalf of the people; and, best of all, the institution of objective law. "[T]he political structure of the Roman republic was the strongest that has yet been put together," not because the Roman republic was the most efficient at coercing its citizens, but because it provided the firmest guarantee of their freedom of action, the machinery best able to protect the transmission of energy by putting a brake on arbitrary force (29).

As the conquering republic transformed itself into an empire, it betrayed the types of structural weakness that illustrate the importance of structure. From everywhere in the empire, riches flowed toward Rome, unbalancing the old republican institutions. The "intake of energy" had become "centripetal," and the central structures were overwhelmed by it (38). At first, resistance from the empire's outlying regions helped regulate the system. The emperors, who were often nobodies, could also fulfill a useful purpose, just because they were incompetent nobodies. When there was a serious overload in the redistributing mechanism, the central element, the emperor, could always be removed. In Paterson's ingenious image, he was "a crude fuse plug, which may blow out" (32).

But "[w]hen finally the provincials regarded themselves as Romans, and could not imagine themselves reverting to a separate nationality, the empire was done for. In effect, it blew the cylinder head" (39). The state extorted more and more funds to satisfy more and more wants; wealth leaked out of the transmission lines into unprofitable state enterprises; the empire began to consume more than it produced; the state imposed wage and price controls and other regulations designed to force people to work in agreement with the central plan; and the machine collapsed. Rome's material achievements vanished with its political structure. Yet its intellectual achievement remained—the republican idea of impersonal law, of an order that was not simply decreed by officials or majorities. This was the kind of law that "affirmed a moral order in the universe," the kind of law to which even St. Paul, "a poor street preacher, of the working class, under arrest, and with enemies in high places," could appeal (24, 27).

Meanwhile, two other great ideas were discovered that defined the place of individual human beings in the universal order. These ideas are also avenues into the central meaning of *The God of the Machine*.

One was the idea espoused by that poor street preacher, "the Christian doctrine of the individual soul, born to immortality, with the faculty of free will," exalted by its nature above its material circumstances (69-70). This doctrine waited a long time for political expression in a structure of government that could ensure full freedom of individual choice. The other idea was a Greek invention: the concept of objective scientific inquiry. Science is a rational process and, in that sense, an individual one. It may be either protected or prevented by the state, but it is not the result of any collective enactment. The potential of science failed to be realized in the ancient world; again, the political system was not up to it. As Paterson suggests, "[t]he application of science to production requires assured protection of private property, free labor, and time enough to return benefits for the effort and capital expended" (17). The turbulent democracies of ancient Greece certainly could not provide that protection. Hellenistic Greeks invented the steam engine, but they never developed it for industrial purposes; the protective social structure still did not exist. Only in America was the "dynamo," the creative mind, finally "withdrawn from political interference by a formal reservation, along with the means and material by which it can organize the great world circuit of energy" (28, 130).

The physical machinery of the modern world was born in the great Atlantean movement known as the American revolution. The principles of that revolution were individual liberty within an objective order: "We hold these truths to be self-evident, that all men are created equal, that they are endowed by their creator with certain inalienable rights. . . ." The structure of the American government, which was devised "to secure these rights," conformed to the axioms by which God had engineered (if you will) the nature of men. The political structure, once in place, allowed individuals to act as engineers in their own right, spontaneously organizing "the great world circuit" of the machine age. This was not social engineering but the "reservation" of the engineering power to individuals by the proper use of political institutions.

By following the avenue of Paterson's thoughts on "engineering," we approach the mystery of her title. *The God of the Machine* is a superbly evocative phrase, suggestive of many possible meanings. It puzzled Paterson's friends, but they were reluctant to request an explanation, fearing that she would consider them stupid for asking.[12] Some saw the title as an inversion of the socialist idea that the machine is the commanding force in modern society, the force to which everything else must submit. In Paterson's youth, American socialists had summoned workers to "bow to the command of the industrial Jehovah."[13] They, and many modern liberals, regarded the machine as the virtual dictator of social arrangements. Marx had taught that it decreed even people's conceptions of their own nature. Such ideas, according to Paterson, were what truly "made [human beings] subject to mechanized industry" (155). The machine had been created by human minds, and "if it is to run, it must be by the will and intelligence of man. *A machine economy cannot run on a mechanistic philosophy*" (156). Interpreted in this light, the God of the Machine is the individual human intelligence.

Another interpretation becomes available when one gives full weight to Paterson's religious ideas. This interpretation does not work by oppositions and reversals; according to it, the God of the Machine is, straightforwardly, God, the original "Source of energy" for the human dynamo and the guarantor of the principles from which human liberty proceeds:

> Let anyone who does not recognize the connection of these principles try to rewrite the Declaration of Independence without reference to a divine source of human rights. It cannot be done; the axiom is missing. (152, 70)

Both interpretations of Paterson's title allow for an allusion to the familiar expression *deus ex machina*, which originally referred to the actor, impersonating a god, who in the ancient theatre was lowered onto the stage by machinery so that plays could be provided with resolutions that could not happen in any other way. The irony of the allusion emphasizes Paterson's very different idea of divinity. Her God is not a function of the machinery; he is its engineer. Yet he allows the drama to develop spontaneously. He refuses to resolve its tensions with an exercise in Planning. He leaves "free the human will."

Neither of the two interpretations precludes a third, incorporating both. In Paterson's world, there is both a God who created human beings and a godlike creative spirit within human beings. The Machine is the world, the invention of God, but it is also all those human inventions, those human structures, that provide for the generation and transmission of energies originally divine.

The Machine includes the material features of modern industrial capitalism—railways, airplanes, power plants, factories, banks. More fundamental, however, are the political arrangements that allow capitalism to exist. Paterson had become so sensitive to the charge of anarchism that she devoted an entire chapter of *The God of the Machine* to an argument against it. True, she wrote, government is merely "an end appliance"; it uses energy, but it does not produce it (82). As her historical novels had shown, societies can be constructed in many ways. Some have had no need for government. In those societies, people exchange goods from hand to hand, without the use of money. For them, the energy circuit is limited in time and space, and attempts to disrupt it can be punished immediately, by the simple withholding of goods. But for the energy circuit to extend itself more fully, government is necessary. Extension depends on the keeping of long-range promises. It depends on my keeping my word to pay you a certain amount at a certain time, perhaps far in the future, and perhaps from a far distant place, for goods that you give me here and now. It depends, that is, on making, fulfilling, and enforcing contracts. An economy "which consists of production and exchanges in a sequence extending through time and space" demands the creation of "an agency to witness long-term contracts and see that they are fulfilled in the absence of either of the parties, or to enforce an agreed penalty in case of default" (85). That agency is government. To maintain a high-energy economy, you must have a governmental structure.

Paterson's radicalism comes out in her refusal to allow any role for government in the direction of the economy, and hence of society. *The God of the Machine* extends the arguments she had made against the technocrats. The "social organization," cannot run without its "dynamo," which is the individual human being, and a human being is not like any other kind of mechanism: "it is not possible to measure and predict what will cause him to start, stop, turn, or accelerate" (82). If this is true, then any engineer who tried to redesign the long circuit in accordance with his own, inevitably inaccurate predictions would simply betray his ignorance, because no one can know enough to plan a vital and complex human economy. Anyone who purported to know how to do it would end up having to apply his prescriptions by force, against the inclinations that lead other individuals to invest their energy in ways more profitable to themselves.

Would it work? Could a machine economy be run by force? Consider the results of the Soviet Union's famous Plans, so impressive to Paterson's fellow intellectuals, so pathetic to us, so contemptible to her. Or simply ask yourself, as she asks, Can any skilled work, the kind of work required by the machine age, be done by compulsion? If railroad engineers were made to substitute someone else's judgment for their own,

> [t]here would not be a railroad in operation within six weeks. For the very reason that the action of inanimate machinery is predetermined, the men who use it must be free. (283)

Nineteenth-century socialists described the ideal workforce of the machine age as an "industrial army"; twentieth-century socialists longed for Thorstein Veblen's "soviet of technicians." When there was an actual soviet directing an actual industrial army, the economic system existed in a perpetual state of collapse, kept alive by periodic applications of state-controlled "capitalism." Finally it imploded, just as Paterson expected (283). The long circuit has to function by contract, not by command.

The idea of contract is fundamental both to Paterson's economics and to her politics and sociology. She derives from Sir Henry Maine, the nineteenth-century historian, a basic distinction between "contract" societies and "status" societies (41). A contract society is constituted by a web of agreements among individuals, each of whom has an equal right to make his or her own economic choices. When government intervenes, it preempts or countermands these choices, ordinarily with the purpose of ensuring some special advantage to one group or another. It thereby fosters a status or class society, in which individuals are treated primarily as members of groups and in which groups tend to be frozen in place and separated from one another by their privileges or disabilities.

A status society necessarily lacks the dynamism of a contract society, since it restricts the energies of some people in order to give advantages to others. The economic difficulties of authoritarian states—e.g., the Soviet Union, whose civilian economy remained stuck in a pre-computer, even pre-photocopy mode—confirm the idea that a status society is "obliged to restrict production to the energy potential it can accommodate" (48). This is one of Paterson's several formulations of a concept she shared with such free-market economists as Ludwig von Mises and Frank Knight—the idea that only a static society can make any show at "planning."[14] Economic futility and activist government belong together.

Their relationship, as Paterson shows, has had a long history. The late Roman Empire tried to stabilize its economy by binding farmers to their land and artisans to their occupations. It failed. The antebellum South tried to maintain a competitive economy while denying a large part of its populace, the slaves, the ability to make their own way. It also failed. In such reactionary societies, the maintenance of status conditions was mistakenly preferred to the risks of unrestricted enterprise. To one degree or another, the same could be said about the restrictive status traditionally accorded to women, the restrictions of Jewish enterprise in medieval Europe, the restriction of modern Russian peasants to collective farms, the supposedly progressive American practice of restricting competition under the pretense of controlling "monopoly," and virtually all the other contemporary schemes designed to ensure economic stability or "fairness."

Societies that try to secure economic advantages (real or imagined) to certain groups can do so only by inhibiting economic development. Security of this kind is not what Paterson regards as structure. Structure accommodates the flow of energy; it does not block it except when the flow imperils itself, as in the conduct of business by force or fraud. A structure ideally consists of self-balancing forces, forces that do not require adjustment by revolution or dictatorship and that permit energy to be applied with the greatest possible efficiency. In particular, a structure incorporates strong institutional resistances to the power of the state, which is generally the instrument of "status."

Several types of resistance are available. One of them, the most ancient, is the "elective principle." Paterson did not accept the common idea, held also by many libertarians, such as Nock, that government originates in conquest. No government, she believed, could ever exist simply by force or intimidation; there must always be an element of consent. When the people elect to withdraw their consent (by refusing to work, for example), government is finished. In some societies, the process is regularized by voting, and a vote of No on an issue or a set of candidates leads to a change of government. This is the function of the elective principle—the power to stop something. In a society of any size, no amount of voting can effectively direct the government in its normal business; to believe that voting can or should do so is a superstition of democracy. But voting can throw the government out.

Other checks can be placed on government. In the Roman empire, the power of the central government was checked by regional interests in the provinces, aversion to taxes, and conflicting centers of power in the armed forces and the civilian authorities. When all else fails, even the threat of assassination can have a healthy effect. But for long-term safety of the individual, the great thing is possession of property. It is no use talking about freedom unless one has a place to be free. A state may promise, and tyrannical states commonly do promise, such rights as freedom of speech and freedom of religion, but in the absence of private property, the promise is always found to be meaningless:

> How can a man speak freely if there is no spot on which he and his audience have the right to stand? How can he practice his religion if he has no right to own a religious edifice, or to his own person? How is a free press to exist if the materials are not in private ownership? With state ownership, *nothing can be done except by command or permission.* (184)

Like John Locke, the most important early exponent of liberal theory, Paterson grounds all rights in the right to property, which is ultimately the right to property in one's "own person." She dispenses with Locke's cumbersome speculations about the origins of property in material objects.[15] She doesn't need them. What she needs is the observation that if a person has no right to property and to "the first benefit of property, which is standing ground," then there is "no place on earth where he ha[s] a right to be; which is to say, *he ha[s] no right to be*" (178). If you believe in any individual rights at all, you have to believe in the property right. As Paterson points out, every machine needs a "base." The system of industrial enterprise, the long circuit of energy, cannot exist without an adequate base in private property, in things that individuals hold as their own, against and in reserve from government. Only a firm base can counterbalance the government's thrusts and kicks.

The problem for friends of the long circuit is how to protect the base—and the problem is greatly exacerbated by the circuit's own immense energy, energy that can be channeled in destructive as well as constructive ways. Voting, for example, can be used either to cut off energy from a malfunctioning part of the political mechanism or to devastate parts that are working well. When voters choose officials who impose taxes on business in order to set up collectivist institutions that will, in turn, devise further impositions and restrictions on business, they are directing energy against the system that generated it. When they choose officials who restrict personal liberty—something that can be done very handily with the aid of modern technology—they are directing energy against the dynamo itself.

This is a problem that has many moral implications, but it is not essentially a moral problem. Continuing her argument with Lane in 1940, Paterson stipulates that

> [m]ost of the harm in the world is done by good people, and not by accident, lapse, or omission. It is the result of their deliberate actions, long persevered in, which they hold to be motivated by high ideals toward virtuous ends. (235)

There are never enough wicked people to destroy the system, but we good people are another matter. The world must be protected from us. In general terms:

> Nothing is more essential to the welfare of a nation than the countercheck on government, by legitimate means. A mechanism without a brake, a motor without a cut-off, is built for self-destruction. (23).

To prevent self-destruction, some kind of brake must be provided on the things that even good people long to do with government. This is a structural problem. It is a problem for intellectual (as opposed to social) engineers.

The three great libertarian ideas—scientific rationality, impersonal law, and the sanctity of the individual soul—provide a guiding inspiration, but they are obviously not enough in themselves to maintain a system of limited government. They had been current for many centuries before a libertarian polity emerged. Paterson agreed with James Madison that when people have both the impulse and the means to commit some oppressive act, noble concepts may not compete very well with the possibility of immediate self-gratification. As Madison put it, "neither moral nor religious motives can be relied on as an adequate control."[16] To construct an adequate control, a reliable brake on government, something more is needed than the suspicion that a brake would be useful. Someone needs to know how to construct a brake.

Neither Paterson nor Madison believed that democracy was the solution. The unconstrained rule of the majority was no structure at all; it was only the movements of "dislocated mass," which can never provide the stability that political organization requires (122, 124). The mass has all the energy that individuals can give to it, but energy without structure is simply blind force. Again, every machine needs a base. A political organization must have a "fixed base" to which its "agencies of action" are attached, a base that can keep any particularly vigorous movement of the machine from transforming those agencies into the means of self-destruction.

In the construction of the American constitutional system, a firm base was discovered in the right to property and, further, in the division of the electorate into separate geographical regions with "delimited local sovereignty" (124-25). "Mass" was provided by the elective principle, the principle of popular suffrage; but local powers and interests kept the mass from shifting all at once and carrying the rest of the structure with it. Additional stays against destructive political movements were secured by the principle of representative (as opposed to popular) legislative action; and by a division of powers among the presidency, the courts, and the two houses of Congress. The Senate, whose members were originally elected by state legislatures, expressed the "regional bases" of the machine, while the House of Representatives, with members elected in proportion to population, expressed the "mass veto function" that Paterson admired in the Roman republic and in popular resistance to government in all eras (124).

Like an inspecting engineer, Paterson pried into every part of the American constitutional structure, noticing features that other people might not perceive. Everyone knows that the constitution's second amendment mentions "a well-regulated militia" and guarantees "the right of the people to keep and bear arms." Paterson sees in the constitution's arms provisions an important braking action of one part of the machine on another. The amendment, she says, reserves to individuals "the primary right to bear arms and form militia companies," but it is balanced by other parts of the constitution, which give state and federal authorities "inhibitory power" where matters of actual war are at stake (133-34). Such provisions allow both for political stability and for freedom of personal action; or rather, they provide exactly the kind of stability that protects individual freedom. The constitutional structure "was established on [an] enduring base, without pinning men down under the foundation" (130).

All of this demonstrates the architectural ingenuity of the men aptly known as the "framers" of America's political machine. Nine years before, Paterson had noted that some people believe "there never was an Age of Reason; just a reasonable person now and then." "Yes," she replied, "but sometimes there were as many as four or five at once; that is what was called the Age of Reason."[17] Now she was more delighted than ever by the framers' instinct for rational procedure, for the idea of *how* to get things done. She mentions Washington, the surveyor; Franklin, the craftsman and scientist; Jefferson, the architect; and Roger Sherman, cobbler and mathematician, who instigated the dual system of representation in the House and Senate:

> Once he was invited to speak on the occasion of opening a new bridge. "He walked critically over the structure," and delivered his oration in one sentence: "I don't see but it stands steady."

Sherman's "structural sense" was equally sound when he calculated the stresses of the constitutional system: "he hit on both the regional bases and the mass veto function at once. He knew what would stand steady" (123-24).

The framers knew their engineering principles, and they knew their objective, the preservation of individual liberty; but they could not know exactly what structure they needed to build until they had worked their way through the problems:

In like case, it could not have been said that a keystone must be designed to complete the form of the arch, or a zero sign for the use of position in numbers, until these devices had been found. (118)

Like the long circuit of energy, the constitution was the cumulative effect of many discoveries. The final discoveries were made in America, by particular American minds; but there was nothing merely personal, accidental, or exceptionally American about the principles involved. With appropriately varied applications to local terrain, a structure of mutual resistances could be built by anyone who wanted to preserve or enhance individual liberty. The constitution was a distinctively American document, resulting from a sequence of historical events that had long been "looking toward America," yet it was no parochial document; its axioms were universal. The same can be said about *The God of the Machine*. Paterson writes as an American, assessing American institutions; but her principles know no nationality.

Judged by those principles, there was obviously one great flaw in the framers' structure—the sanction it gave to slavery, a preexisting institution that stood in absolute contradiction to the individualist and libertarian axioms on which the structure as a whole was erected. Political defects followed directly from the moral defect: the nation was divided into slave states and free states, and the division rendered the bases of the structure "unequal." The constitution's fugitive-slave provisions allowed the South to make "an uncompensated cross-thrust" against the North, while the North, unburdened by slavery, dynamically extended its energy circuit into the territories, further unbalancing the structure (139-41). The result was the Civil War and an era in which the victorious central government received major additions to its power to shape the nation's development, additions that created other kinds of imbalance.

Paterson makes especially interesting comments on two of these additions. Both concern the development of the West. The right way to go about it, she argues, was to allow the long circuit to extend itself in a spontaneous and self-liquidating manner. Experience showed that pioneers who made profitable investments in land or transportation soon hooked up to the nation's main circuit of production and consumption, while those who made poor or premature investments simply lost them, without wasting anyone else's energy or placing any new burdens on the political structure (167).

Profitable settlements in the West quickly evolved their own stabilizing political structures and became regional bases of the national structure.

But as the nineteenth century went on, and the federal government acquired an increasingly directive influence, territories were hurried into statehood "before they had time to develop true regional interests and political entities." They were "creatures of the Federal government," creatures that were inclined to keep seeking its favors (170).[18] Here was one unbalanced addition of federal power. An even more significant imbalance resulted from federal subsidies to the great agents of modern industrial power, the railroads.

Rails extended themselves readily wherever there were markets to be reached. But rather than waiting for this to happen, government procured their extension into areas where they were not yet able to pay their way.[19] Of course, wherever such subsidized enterprises went, they killed both present and prospective competition. Settlers who moved in after the railroads often felt themselves helpless against them, and sometimes they were. Western people, as Paterson acutely observed, loved railroads but resented their power and the corruption that resulted from their relationship to government. "Robber barons" were well named, when their robbery was licensed by the state.

Unfortunately, Westerners tended to believe that the solution to such problems was yet more intervention by government. They demanded that government fix prices and manipulate the currency; they demanded that all successful businesses be regulated or even outlawed when they grew "too big." These demands were a major tributary of "progressive" American thought:

> Now the sole remedy for the abuse of political power is to limit it; but when politics corrupt business, modern reformers invariably demand the enlargement of the political power. (171)

The "progressive" tendency was in fact reactionary; it was a throwback to the political axioms of Europe. Much of it was an indulgence in "administrative law," which had once been abandoned nearly everywhere in Europe, though it was, at the moment, staging a mighty comeback there (175).

Many "progressive" innovations were old-fashioned "status" enactments, penalizing or rewarding people not as individuals but as economic instruments. The same action—a raising of prices, for instance, or perhaps a lowering of prices—might be legal for a "small" businessman but illegal for a "big" one, according to the edict of a government official who had been given the power to decide such matters. Notoriously, status legislation often worked in favor of people who were already wealthy; it discouraged vigorous ("cut-throat") competition and rewarded established figures who had the money and influence to win concessions from the state. It invited the kind of corruption and manipulation that Paterson described in *The Shadow Riders* and favored the kind of business people whom she satirized in *The Golden Vanity*.

Industrial legislation was based on the false assumption that the state, and only the state, can handle a high-energy economy. Social welfare legislation (an idea borrowed directly from Europe) was based on the false assumption that social relationships need to be managed in the same way. The result, as Paterson saw it, was anything but a surge of energy on the part of the supposed beneficiaries. Welfare kept them in the static role of dependence on government—which is another way of saying dependence on the will of government officials. What people really wanted wasn't welfare at all; it was a real job, a profitable place on the energy circuit. And that was precisely what the government could not assure them, no matter how emphatically it asserted their "right" to a job: "It is idle to demand it as a right, for they have not the least power to enforce such a demand." In a welfare system, people have to *"ask for everything"* (195-96).

For Paterson, who was well acquainted with poverty, the welfare issue was of special importance. Her experience convinced her that needy people "shrink from relief, and hate the very word." Permanent welfare meant being "cut off from the living springs of self-renewing energy." That was why people "who perform works of charity under a true vocation do their best to keep it marginal" and temporary (249). Welfare schemes designed to secure "freedom from want" or "need" could not bring an end to need itself; they merely transferred to government the power to decide what constituted need and to stabilize the needy population at some low level of existence (219-20).

To finance its burgeoning welfare legislation (as well as its frequent military involvements), the central government relied on the income tax, which Paterson describes as a "fatal" addition to the federal system (157). By means of this tax, boundless energy flowed toward Washington, where it was transformed into federal power and redirected against the producers of energy, coercing some, awarding unfair advantage to others, and tempting even some of its critics to demand that the tax be increased to repair some of the damage it was constantly doing. Originally, the most social-democratic supporters of the income tax saw it as a tool for leveling incomes, for taking money away from the rich and giving it to the poor; some still see it that way. Paterson noticed, however, that such taxes never stop with the rich, or put the generality of wealthy people at a relative disadvantage. The tax, she said, was "bound to cause an increase in all taxation, reaching down inchmeal." She was right. "[O]ne tax," she continues,

> tends to increase all other taxes . . . because tax expenditure goes into things which require upkeep and yield no return (public buildings and political jobs). Kinetic energy has been converted into static forms, which then necessitate the diversion of more kinetic energy to carry the dead-load. (161)

Paterson's engineering language allows modern political history to be described in at least two ways—as a steadily increasing diversion of productive energy and as a steadily increasing overload on the upper reaches of the state's facade. Both images have an obvious relevance to the stupendous growth of the federal government during the twentieth century. There is now no area of American life that the governing class neglects to govern, with the conspicuous exception of the (still untaxed) Internet, whose expansion presents the most obvious contemporary product and analogue of Paterson's long circuit of energy. By means of such inventions, the circuit continues to extend its spontaneous order wherever individual minds find profit in extending it. An index of the power of private enterprise is its ability to continue bearing the increasingly astonishing load of taxes and regulations. An engineer recently described the process as that of "inventing things faster than the government can regulate them." The mind has a way of evading regulation; without that tendency, the history of America would be inexplicable, from the voyage of Pytheas to the million uses of the microchip.

But mind is the creator of dangers as well as opportunities. Beneath modern America's economic and political problems, Paterson saw clear evidence of faulty, perhaps "fatal," choices of ideas. One of the most important was a misunderstanding of the machine as something that lacked a spiritual dimension, of material progress as something irrelevant or antagonistic to intellectual and spiritual progress. On this issue, Paterson was closer to the Marxists than she was to anyone else; at least they saw the machine as an agent of both kinds of advancement. Conservative intellectual opinion, such as that of Allen Tate and his fellow Agrarian fugitives from industrial capitalism, tended strongly toward suspicion of the machine.[20] Many years would pass before a conservative political party would gain power in Washington by advocating positions formerly advocated by such radicals as Paterson. The modern-liberal or mainstream cliché was that the machine was good or bad insofar as society (or, more candidly, the state) could "tame" it.

The tone of much intellectual opinion about the spiritual status of the machine had been set by Henry Adams, who inquired into the relationship between the industrial "dynamo" and a psychological and spiritual entity that he called the "virgin." Paterson said that Adams was asking the right question. Indeed, she characterized his essentially determinist theory of historical "forces" in the most charitable way she could, describing his "virgin" as "an unconstrained element, grace or mercy, which implies free will in man." Adams' failure, she suggested, was his inability to see that the dynamo was the complement and product of the virgin, not its opposite. He "failed to realize that it is by freedom of personal volition that man is capable of pursuing his intellectual inquiries and making his inventions. This is the genesis of the dynamo" (156).

Thus Paterson established herself as a believer in progress in both senses—and thus she demonstrated her need to emphasize the fallacies of rival versions of progressivism. It was an especially sticky problem, because American "progressives" almost always believed they were fighting for the rights and well-being of the individual. Their political program, ordinarily involving massive use of government power, didn't look like individualism to her. It wasn't just a question of rival positions on public policy. There were spiritual as well as political issues at stake, extending to rival positions about the basic requirements of thought.

That was why Paterson took up the matter of "progressive education" and made it the subject of one of the strongest chapters of *The God of the Machine*. The ideal of the progressive educators was individual self-expression; their weakness, as she regarded it, was the emphasis they placed on expression of feeling rather than knowledge of facts and use of reason. Self-expression of that kind might look like individualism, but it wasn't. Only facts and reason allow individuals to reach an independent position and hold onto it, whether anyone else agrees with them or not. Facts and reason are the tools of individualism. The concrete effect of "progressive" education is to deny the ability to use these tools to the young people who need them:

> It is difficult to bring one to any conclusion, when detached from the group. They will say, "Well, I just don't think so," as if there could be no facts or connected mental processes, which should lead to one opinion rather than another, or distinguish a conviction from a taste. They have an impression that "everything is different now" from anything that may have been in the past; though they have no idea how or why. Do not two and two make four? Does not a lever operate on exactly the same principle today as it did for Archimedes? They do not quite know. They may say, "Oh, I don't agree with you," but they can give no reason for dissent. They are "not quite convinced," but they can offer no argument in rebuttal. That is to say, when called upon to think, they cannot, because they have been trained to accept the class, the group, or the "social trend," as the sole authority. (254)

Paterson's analysis anticipated today's conservative critique of public education, although it is today's libertarians who appear to be in the direct line of descent. One of the distinguishing characteristics of the American libertarian movement is its close identification of individualism with reason. One can easily imagine an individualist movement that did not make that identification. Paterson, indeed, was one of the few individualists of her generation who emphasized the supremacy of reason. Even Ayn Rand, who would become America's most devoted rationalist and the largest single influence on American libertarianism, came to that emphasis only in mid-career, and Paterson may have had been an influence in that regard.[21] In any event, today's largest-selling libertarian journal is *Reason*, not *Feeling*, *Custom*, *Tradition*, or *Pure Self-Expression*. From Paterson's time to this, libertarians have focused on a rational accounting of the individual's relationship both to ideas and to political institutions.

The irony is that Paterson was far from being a rationalist in the usual sense of the term. She spent many years criticizing the kind of rationalism that manifests itself in dogmatic scientific and religious ideas, in social planning and prediction, and in an unsophisticated confidence in technical expertise. She distrusted any use of reason that denied the claims of individual experience. There was always Montaigne's question, "What do I know?" Nevertheless, one thing she knew was that certain things—many things—*could* be known: "Does not a lever operate on exactly the same principle today as it did for Archimedes?"

That kind of rationalism distinguished her firmly from Marx, on the left, and Adams, on the right, both of whom pictured the machine, with its millions of wheels and levers, as the manufacturer of its own changing principles. "Mind," in Adams' description, is "the subtlest of all known forces," but it doesn't stand a chance against the mechanical forces that have assumed the role of educators of the modern world. History, wrote Adams, the professional historian, has "few lessons . . . that would be useful in the future," except the lesson that the mind can do nothing more than react to history. He sympathized with the efforts of Theodore Roosevelt to control the "mechanical power" of business, but he doubted that any mere man could perform that miracle. "Progress" happened by means of forces: "[T]he forces would continue to educate, and the mind would continue to react." The role of the intellectual was to teach the mind this principle of "reaction."[22]

To Paterson, that seemed a bizarre short-circuiting of thought. To maintain that history shows us nothing more than that history shows us practically nothing is to use reason against reason, experience against experience. It is also to short-circuit productive action. A businessman who thinks that business is actually just a "mechanical power" and who therefore allows his business to progress in its own way will not keep his business very long. Ridiculous? Yes. But would that be very different from some contemporary American ideas of political and intellectual progress? Paterson saw that there was a fatalist or determinist view of history abroad in the land, a radically anti-intellectual view, no matter how many intellectuals expounded it; and she thought that it posed a threat to the survival of America.

The Wave of the Future (1940), Anne Morrow Lindbergh's popular book, summed it all up. Comparatively few people agreed with her specific argument—a plea, directed from the right, for America to come to terms with the collectivist world of "the future." But nothing was more common than agreement with her motivating assumption, the idea that America's destiny was controlled by "social and economic forces" emanating from the machine.[23]

This way of thinking was a prescription for intellectual and moral paralysis. For Paterson, it was the greatest enemy, since it reacted against the very basis of independent thought. After all, she had more reason than most people to believe that nothing could be done about emerging "conditions." A decade earlier, she had started one of her political columns by saying, "Ophelia will now stick a few more straws in her hair and go through her weekly mad scene."[24] Every year, she seemed to see herself growing more isolated, and the world drifting farther and farther away from liberal ideals— Europe a charnel house, its best people either slaughtered or in flight; America gradually accepting false and futile European principles, under the assumption that historical progression made that course inevitable. But it wasn't:

> There is no "wave of the future"; humanity shapes its future by moral purpose and the use of reason. . . .
> Everything can be done for a living future, if men take the long view by which the long circuit of energy is created. (291)

She was not willing to predict whether they would do so or not. Her own theory ruled out the possibility of detailed prediction; its central emphasis was on the imponderable nature of the dynamo, the individual mind, the potential of which could never be measured or predicted. No one could know how much productive energy it might supply, or how far it might go in making up for the increasing loss of energy to government, or in halting that loss.

Principles, however, do not depend on prediction. The discoveries of Pytheas remained discoveries; they may not have been immediately followed up, but they could be rediscovered, and they were. The principles of human action can certainly be ignored, if people decide to ignore them; but they are rational nonetheless, and they can be found by people who want to find them. Even if America should turn against itself, the political principles discovered by Americans will survive, like the principle of the lever, to be rediscovered by other rational and individual minds:

> Progress is always possible, but it depends upon the unpredictable use of intelligence. From the known record, it does not appear that men have ever wholly lost any important body of knowledge once attained. . . . [T]he principles involved are universals. They do not change with "history." Whenever and wherever they are understood and applied they will work, always in the same way. (290-91)

This is "the long view," and the final, most severely intellectual, perspective on the vast complex of ideas that make up *The God of the Machine*. To understand the machine, Paterson looked beyond it, to the principles that made it work; to understand the alleged inevitabilities of the moment, she looked beyond the moment, to the diverse possibilities of human action; to understand America, she looked beyond America, to the universals that anyone could identify and put to use.

It was a great imaginative achievement, this lofty, yet concretely exemplified, view of history. Paterson honored the experience of the past while allowing for the spontaneous developments of the future. She showed how to combine a conservative reverence for proven principle with a traditionally liberal enthusiasm for discovery and progress. Most important, she showed her readers how to find their own place on an intellectual circuit of energy that is longer than the longest circuit of material production and exchange, a circuit that extends from Pytheas, framed in light at the gates of the Atlantic, to the mind of every other solitary figure who, like herself, could imagine a new Atlantis, free and unconstrained.

18

The Libertarians of '43

Paterson and her publisher thought that the book's "best chance was for a long, slow sale." Reviews differed widely. The *Library Journal*, which was capable of selling a lot of books, certified *The God of the Machine* as a "serious work . . . for all readers who will exercise their minds." The *New Yorker*, which had contracted the dotty idea that Paterson was arguing for "free enterprise, in a Hamiltonian republic," considered her supposed position "not very novel"; nevertheless, it suggested that the book offered "interesting observations" and was "well written, too." *The Atlantic* agreed on that—"[t]he style is uncommonly pungent, lively, and witty"—and it actually got the argument right: "Where some timid souls . . . would settle for a mixed economy, Mrs. Paterson will be content with nothing short of complete freedom in economic relations."[1]

Other, less favorable notices came in. The *New Republic*'s reviewer was sociologist C. Wright Mills, later to become a major fixture on the intellectual left. Mills offers 500 words of sarcasm about Paterson's "muddied [sic] pages." He is scandalized to find her calling Marx a "fool," and he is sure that his readers will also be scandalized. *Saturday Review* recognized the importance of *The God of the Machine* by making it the subject of a lead review, along with a new book by Harold Laski, an English Marxist who was one of the century's most effective exponents of collectivism. The results of this attempt to stimulate controversy were not as interesting as might have been anticipated. Laski emerges from the notice as a "wise counsellor" and a "[m]agnificent" writer. According to the reviewer, his sweeping schemes for postwar planning and irreversible state ownership may not be perfect, but something must obviously be done along such lines, and done right away. Paterson is also a good writer, but her book is no match for Laski's. It is simultaneously "a cold, passionless piece of reasoning" and "startling in its implications." The reviewer might have been less startled if he had read the whole book, which there are indications he had not.[2]

One of the worst notices appeared in the *New York Times Book Review*. "Most of us are already acquainted with Mrs. Paterson's brilliant Olympianisms on current questions," the reviewer acknowledges. In *The God of the Machine*, however, she "does irreparable damage to her own thinking and seriously compromises the possibility of understanding" by her "bad temper" and "intolerance." Example: what she says about Marx. Paterson is also at fault for her unprogressive belief that reason is "a finality. Reason is not today what it once was. . . ." Paterson's general view of human action is "valuable and stimulating" and allows her to make "devastating criticisms" of opposing views. But her lack of "discipline" allows her to advance sheerly "perverse" ideas, such as "the inadvisability of conscription." Imagine that.[3]

The review in Paterson's own paper was given, undoubtedly at her suggestion, to an editor of the journal *Machinery*, a person who knew about engineering. His own opinions are mildly modern liberal, but he finds "exhilaration" in Paterson's fighting spirit. He states her ideas fairly, reserving judgment about whether her engineering "analogy" is "valid and fundamental." The most important favorable notice was John Chamberlain's review in the daily *New York Times*. During the 1930s, Chamberlain remarks, the literature of political economy was dominated by collectivists; but Paterson's book is a sign that "individualist liberals are beginning to recover their poise." It is a "brilliant, searching and closely reasoned" work. Chamberlain is not ready to go all the way with Paterson's suggestions about privatizing the economy, but his own suggestions about the form and meaning of *The God of the Machine* are penetrating. The book is difficult to summarize, he observes, because of its brilliant concision and its reach into many subjects:

> [S]ince Mrs. Paterson's concern is with the freedom of all the powers of the individual, she cannot stop with either a philosophy of history or a discussion of how human energy circuits are set up or smashed. The sections of the book ray out from a central concept like the spokes of a great wheel.[4]

Chamberlain gets to the heart of the supposed contradiction between liberty and security, as Paterson understands it. In his adept paraphrase, "there can be no real security in a society which is operated under administrative law, for such a society is at the mercy of the administrators." He warns his readers not to misinterpret the work "as an apology for the 'rugged individualism' which resulted in the depression of the Thirties." This kind of "individualism," as Paterson believes, "dug its own grave by invoking political power in its own behalf." He represents the publication of *The God of the Machine* as a defining moment of liberation for authentic liberalism.

If Paterson's publishers had cared to advance the book's sales, they might have seized on the dramatic differences among its reviews and advertised the fact that it was sparking debate. They might have tried to pour some gasoline on the fire. They did not. By 1949 Paterson was getting letters indicating that stores could not obtain the book for people who wanted it. The "gentleman's agreement" that her publisher had made to keep it available was not being kept, "possibly for lack of gentlemen."[5] *The God of the Machine* was left to make its own way among the scattered individualists whom Albert Jay Nock called, in Old Testament language, the Remnant, the few who had not bowed the knee to the Baal of the modern state.[6]

Nineteen forty-three was an important year for the Remnant and the nascent libertarian movement. It saw the publication of four major books by prophets of radical individualism. One of them was *The God of the Machine*. Another was Nock's *Memoirs of a Superfluous Man*, his final, most famous, and most peculiar book. The work has to be classified as an autobiography; its subject, even to a tiresome degree, is Albert Jay Nock. Yet it conveys remarkably little concrete knowledge of his life. Nock's strategy of omission is, perhaps, the best means of self-revelation he could have chosen. He emerges in his book as he really was—secretive, elusive, minutely conscientious in his literary art, pure in devotion to libertarian ideals, pessimistic about anyone else's ability to measure up to them.

Paterson liked Nock's book, and defended it against (plausible) charges of arrogance, because of its high literary quality. Its author had "a genuine prose style." He didn't write down to "the Common Man"—he knew that was "wholly unnecessary"—but he did maintain an "attitude of respect for literature and for intellectual matters." If that was arrogance, make the most of it. She found in Nock's style the features of her own: "[c]lear as a running spring, it sparkles with wit and humor." Nock considers himself "superfluous" to America, but she does not consider him so, any more than she considers herself so. She pays no attention to his self-conscious "superfluousness," or to the faintly sublimated elitism that it represents. It's beneath her.[7]

Memoirs of a Superfluous Man continues to be respected among libertarians and conservatives (especially the latter). They see in it what Paterson saw, an individual embodiment of high cultural values, the kind of values that she and Nock associated with a less pretentious but more genuinely cultivated past. What Nock saw in Paterson was something more important in a political sense. He pronounced *The God of the Machine* and Rose Wilder Lane's *The Discovery of Freedom* "the only intelligible books on the philosophy of individualism that have been written in America this century." He said that "Rose and old Isabel [she was sixteen years younger than he was] have shown the male world of this period how to think *fundamentally*. They make all of us male writers look like Confederate money."[8] Nock was not used to paying compliments of this kind. They rise like giant palms from the suavely modulated desert of his final writings.

It made sense for Nock to group *The God of the Machine* with Lane's *Discovery of Freedom*, the third important libertarian book of 1943. Both works are meditations on "energy" and outlines of world history from an individualist point of view; both espouse the principles of the early Republic; and both argue for continuing America's revolutionary career by "decreasing the uses of force which individuals permit to Government."[9] The style and method of each book, however, is unmistakably that of its author.

Lane delighted in colorful exaggerations, and her book is full of them. Preaching against nationalism, she says that the European nations have no inner reality; they are simply frontiers maintained by force. Preaching against oppressive social conditions, she claims that Europeans are "working harder and getting little more than their ancestors did in the feudal system." She also claims that medieval Islam was "the first scientific civilization" (a distinction that on the next page she awards to the Minoans).[10] Paterson would never dream of saying things like that.

Paterson was constitutionally a skeptic; Lane was constitutionally an enthusiast. She cultivated a lyrical style, similar in its dramatic transitions and ellipses to that of her friend Garet Garrett, and she enforced her arguments with the strongest images she could find. Her book is light on analysis and heavy with insights, many of them true. Like Paterson, she knows the principal economic reason why state-run economies will not work, which is that they lack reference to the price-setting mechanisms of the free market and therefore *"have no means of knowing real costs."* And like Paterson, she has the frontier woman's unshakable grip on the concrete meanings of economic theory:

> Anyone who says that economic security is a human right, has been too much babied. . . .
>
> Let him get out on the front lines. Let him bring one slow freight through a snowstorm in the Rockies; let him drive one rivet to hold his apartment roof over his head. Let him keep his own electric light burning through one quiet, cosy winter evening when mist is freezing to the wires. Let him make, from seed to table, just one slice of bread, and we will hear no more from him about the human right to security.[11]

But despite similarities in their view of life, Lane's book and Paterson's are quite distinct in argument. Lane begins by picturing "a planet, whirling in sunlit space." "This planet," she says, "is energy." Indeed, "[l]ife is energy," and every "human being is a dynamo, generating energy." The "dynamo" sounds like Paterson; the rest is somewhat hazy. From this roughly Patersonian starting point, however, Lane quickly arrives at the idea she herself regards as central, which is that human beings are free by nature to control their own energies and that social and economic problems can be solved when people realize that fact and stop submitting superstitiously to external authorities. The rest of the book consists largely of picturesque historical exemplifications of the thesis. There is little hint of Paterson's concern with the specific structures through which energy exerts itself. At the start of the work, Lane emphasizes the idea that control of people's "combined energies" is the primary social problem, but this remains an undeveloped theme. *Discovery of Freedom* has none of the intellectual complexity of *The God of the Machine*.[12] It is not surprising that libertarian readers have generally turned to Lane for emotional satisfaction and to Paterson for intellectual challenge.

Some of the similarities between *The God of the Machine* and *The Discovery of Freedom*, such as the shared emphasis on "energy," may have resulted from coincidence.[13] But Lane's preceding political work, "Credo" (1936), gives the concept of energy no special emphasis. (It does mention the energies "released" by American individualism.[14]) In a 1939 article, Lane includes one brief paragraph about "the sum of free individual energies in action."[15] Paterson, by contrast, had been emphasizing the concept of energy and its political and economic implications since at least 1932.[16] Her column of July 16, 1939 presents much of the "energy" argument that she would use in *The God of the Machine*. It explains that America's limited government "released undreamed-of energies," including "the inventive power of free minds. It ushered in the dynamic age." She argues that "static political framework[s]" cannot contain "expanding energy": "Admit that power to such a political structure, and it must burst it in fragments; it can only operate with reasonable safety under minimum government, where it originated." Four years later, in *Discovery of Freedom*, Lane also refers to "minimum" government, nineteenth-century inventiveness, dynamic versus static political ideas and frameworks, and social explosions resulting from the restriction of energy.[17] And that is just about all she does with the concept.

Paterson was elaborating her ideas during the period when she and Lane were neighbors and talkative friends.[18] Wherever comparison can be made, Lane presents the ideas in reduced and simplified form, while Paterson develops them enormously. It is possible that Lane derived many of her key concepts from her all-night conversations with Paterson. If so, she derived what people normally derive from conversations—certain general ideas, without their heavier analytical supports. "Energy" for Paterson always led to "structure," the structure of dynamos and circuits and brakes, the irreducibly complicated structure of the system of limited government. "Energy" for Lane was a good deal simpler.

She, however, proved to have a much happier political disposition than Paterson. Paterson's interest in politics left her embittered at the world's refusal to accept her ideas, while Lane's political interests freed her from her crippling depressions and her chronic sense of futility. In 1943, she was on her way to doing some of her best work (and very good work it is, by any standard), her essays for the *Economic Council Review of Books*, which she edited from 1945 to 1950. She corresponded widely, charmingly, and persuasively, making her version of libertarianism attractive and accessible to anyone who wanted to know. She was friendly with Herbert Hoover; she was friendly with Du Pont executives; she was friendly with counter-cultural activists of the 1960s.[19] She led community tax protests in Danbury, got herself investigated by the FBI and received excellent publicity as a result, taught at Robert LeFevre's libertarian Freedom School in Colorado, where she was worshiped as a god, and was sent to Vietnam as a war correspondent for *Woman's Day*. She died in 1968, a reasonably happy woman.[20]

Paterson, who usually trumpeted any ideas, including Lane's, that could possibly be regarded as libertarian, mentioned *The Discovery of Freedom* only once in her column: "Rose Wilder Lane, author of 'The Discovery of Freedom,' says she'd like to live indefinitely to see how things work out."[21] Thus she satisfied the duties of friendship without committing herself to an exposition of her friend's work. When Lane angrily complained of her failure to recommend it, Paterson said she would tell her what was wrong with the book, if she insisted. Lane didn't. Paterson declined to take the book seriously; perhaps, also, she was embarrassed by its inaccuracies. Lane, however, took *The God of the Machine* very seriously indeed. In the week it was published, she wrote to Hoover: "I try to restrain my enthusiasm, but it seems to me a book ranking with the best of Paine and Madison." In the *Economic Council Review*, she praised Paterson's book as "the first approach ever made to a scientific study" of the relationship between political structure and productive energy.[22]

She thus helped to keep Paterson's ideas alive among the small though intense circle of next-generation libertarians and individualist conservatives. But the most important intellectual conjunction, and collision, among the radical individualists of 1943 happened between Paterson and Ayn Rand. Rand's breakthrough novel, *The Fountainhead*, published a few days before *The God of the Machine*, was by far the most popular of the big individualist books of 1943.

Paterson's influence on this book, like her influence on *The Discovery of Freedom*, is impossible to describe completely, notwithstanding Rand's reference to "the one encounter in my life that can never be repeated." We know that Rand showed the speeches in her novel to Paterson, and that Paterson gave her "one of the most valuable pieces of advice [she] ever got in regard to writing," which was to leave out all contemporary political names and terms, so as to focus on the problem of "collectivism—any past, present, or future form of it."[23] Some of the literary concepts that Rand would later emphasize as essential to her method had longstanding precedents in Paterson. One was the idea that "romanticism" (Rand considered herself a "romantic realist") was a matter of volition, choice, and reason, not pure emotion. Similarly, Paterson had written in 1935 that "the great romantic effort of humanity" was "the effort to think." Another central concept was the importance of artistic "integration." Paterson had long held that a novel has to have a "a definite integrating factor, a backbone. . . . You have to write toward or around a given point in a novel—everything must have a reference, remote or direct, to the idea, theme or plot." She seems to have been particularly interested in aesthetic "integration" during the time when she and Rand were first acquainted.[24]

Paterson's largest influence, however, was unquestionably political. *The Fountainhead*, as everyone knows, is the story of Howard Roark, an architect who fights a heroically individualist battle to establish himself in his profession. Rand wrote the first third of the novel before taking time off for the Willkie campaign, and before meeting Paterson. In that part of the book, and in most of the rest of it, political and economic issues are by no means prominent. Roark's opponents are cultural authorities. Only in the book's last section, which Rand wrote in 1942 after many months of intense discussions with Paterson about political theory and American history and institutions, does she develop the political meaning of Roark's experience. In the long speech that forms the novel's intellectual climax, Roark argues eloquently for Paterson's idea of America:

> [O]bserve the results of a society built on the principle of individualism. This, our country. The noblest country in the history of men. The country of greatest achievement, greatest prosperity, greatest freedom. . . [25]

Rand's praise of *The God of the Machine* was unrestrained. She called it "the best and most complete statement of the basic principles of our side, and the greatest defense of capitalism I have ever read. It does for capitalism what *Das Kapital* did for the Reds." In another formulation: "*The God of the Machine* does for capitalism what the Bible did for Christianity." *The God of the Machine* was "the greatest book written in the last three hundred years," "the first complete statement of the philosophy of individualism as a political and economic system," "the basic document of capitalism." It would "live forever," and it "could literally save the world."[26]

Sales of Rand's own book started slowly. Its publisher had little faith in it, and reviews were generally disappointing. But by the fall of 1943, sales in the hinterland were picking up, and *The Fountainhead* was on its way to becoming the perennial bestseller that it is today. She was able to sell the film rights to Warner Brothers for an amazing $50,000. She had no taste for luxury or ostentation; after decades of poverty, she thought only about saving as much money as she could. But Paterson and Rand's husband Frank insisted that she buy a mink coat. The coat was duly bought, and she went up to Paterson's office to show it to her. Paterson wasn't there, so Rand, shyly proud, enjoyed herself by getting the other women in the office to try it on—an appropriate gesture toward the little world that had given her friendship.[27] The Warner Brothers contract called for her to write a *Fountainhead* film script. In late 1943, she and Frank took the train for Hollywood, ending an important phase of her life, and of Paterson's.

On November 30, 1943, Paterson had one of those encounters that must have impressed her anew with the unpredictability of American life. She lunched by invitation with her old target of abuse, former President Hoover, in his apartment at the Waldorf-Astoria Towers.[28] The appointment was presumably arranged by Lane, who as a young hack writer had written a biography of Hoover and who had so warmly recommended *The God of the Machine* to him. Paterson arrived with small expectation of intellectual profit, or of help in publicizing her book, and she was not disappointed in her expectation.

Hoover amused her by leaving the door open while they talked, allegedly because he wished to smoke. Really, she thought, he was afraid that some compromising situation might erupt while he conferred with the fifty-seven-year-old author. The former president applauded the contribution that her book had made, and he urged her to write more on the same theme, although he did not know what to reply when she asked him who would print what she wrote. They tussled over what she meant by the engineering principles of a free society: he thought it was a metaphor; she insisted it wasn't. But then, to her surprise, he agreed with her emphatically—he who had tried to end the depression by government intervention—on the idea that a mixed economy could not work, that it was an engineering mistake to interfere at one point or another in the economy, thereby causing breakage somewhere down the line. So he read her "metaphors" literally after all.

Most of his conversation, however, consisted of complaints that his own books were neglected, except by his enemies, who kept stealing his ideas. Paterson was wondering what ideas he had in mind. It was the kind of afternoon that authors often pass in one another's company. Even Lane, who was so much better at ingratiating herself than Paterson, got little more than cordial letters out of Hoover, and Paterson got nothing except the lunch.

But she was in this war for the duration. She didn't expect her book to change the world overnight. She had expressed her conviction in *The God of the Machine* that useful discoveries were never lost; they were there to be found whenever people were interested. And some people were interested. Furthermore, people who were interested tended to remain that way.

One such person was Robert Selph Henry. Colonel Henry, who corresponded voluminously with Paterson until her death, and elicited some of her most interesting ideas, demonstrated that intelligent business people might not be wholly immune to radical individualist ideas. He was one of the few people with whom she never quarreled.

John Chamberlain was an especially important and interesting disciple. In the 1930s, he was a prominent leftwing journalist. He was also one of those handsome, intelligent young men with whom Paterson enjoyed spending her afternoons. Intellectual men habitually condescended to intellectual women; Chamberlain was one of the few who never tried it with her.[29] They argued for years about politics, their arguments often resulting in sheer bafflement with each other. At one point, she said, Chamberlain informed her that "the trouble" with her was that she "expect[ed] people to be intelligent"; she replied that she didn't know "how he gained this impression." In 1939, she was still lecturing him against claiming to be a friend of limited government while wanting government to reduce social inequalities by redistributing property. She did note that he was the only "liberal" she knew who opposed the shockingly illiberal policy of conscription. That was something.[30] Meanwhile, however, he was labeling her—accusing her, as she thought—of being a "philosophical anarchist."[31] That was how far even the best-disposed intellectuals had drifted from an understanding of limited government.

When *The God of the Machine* came out, Paterson's explanation of capitalism struck Chamberlain as agreeing with everything he had learned as a financial journalist. Her theory hit him "like a ton of bricks."[32] It was a crucial influence in completing his conversion to libertarianism. For the rest of his long life, he occupied a universally respected position on the American right. He used that position to keep Paterson's work before his audience.

Another admirer was the distinguished scientist Pierre Lecomte du Noüy, student of the Curies, director of the Sorbonne's Ecole des Hautes Etudes, deducer of the three dimensions of the molecule, and author of many other discoveries about living and nonliving things. During the Second World War he fled the German occupation of France and came to America. He was referred to Paterson as someone who might be useful to him. She welcomed him as a sympathetic friend and helped him make the connections necessary to publish his big book, *Human Destiny* (1947).

Written from an evolutionary perspective, *Human Destiny* might be expected to offer a materialist view of its subject. Instead, it provides an argument for the ability of human beings to transcend their circumstances through the power of reason and moral choice. Humans, it maintains, cannot be studied scientifically unless their power of choice is recognized. The process of evolution has made them free individuals, not determined units; and their future evolution depends upon their coming to terms with the fact of the "real independence" that God, the master of evolution, willed them to possess.[33]

Lecomte du Noüy's thinking was clearly parallel to Paterson's. Although she never liked to invoke the shadow of omnipotence—

and although, for that matter, she had no particular interest in physical evolution—she was clear on the idea that the world was created by an intelligence that willed the free development of other intelligences. Lecomte du Noüy's deductions about social and political questions were also similar to hers. "We must," he says,

> not blindfold [people] under the pretext that society will lead them by the hand and guide them. Nobody has the right to substitute his own conscience for that of another, for progress depends on *personal effort*, and to suppress this effort constitutes a crime.

On the issue of liberty, Lecomte du Noüy proclaimed himself "in perfect agreement with a very remarkable and amazingly intelligent book, *The God of the Machine*, which deals with all the problems man has to face today."[34] Paterson and Lecomte du Noüy remained friends until his death, and she maintained a friendship with his widow.

Other admirers, including some who would attain positions of great influence on the right, were not so lucky. One of them, Russell Kirk, was among the young soldiers who wrote to Paterson during World War II. Kirk was soon to become a powerful—perhaps the most powerful—exponent of the conservative intellectual tradition in America. The Kirk-Paterson correspondence continued for several years. In July 1948, when he was teaching, running a bookstore, and planning a book on Edmund Burke, I.M.P. quoted him at length on the misunderstanding of science that led people to believe that they ought to take "nature" as their moral exemplar. Morality, she added, is equivalent neither to "nature" nor to "legal enactment"; it arises from the individual mind's engagement with the conditions of life: "The highest success . . . is obtained from the highest moral code; but it is quite impossible for human beings to exist with no moral code at all."[35] The Paterson-Kirk correspondence was fruitful on both sides, but it could not withstand Paterson's ability to find fault with friends as well as enemies. Kirk "happened to mention that we ought not to suppose that most people are persuaded by pure reason." Mercilessly over-reading, Paterson "answered angrily that she wouldn't waste her time corresponding with someone who didn't believe in rationality." Kirk "did not trouble her thereafter."[36]

Other hopeful relationships turned out badly too. In 1946, Leonard E. Read, who had been the manager of the Los Angeles Chamber of Commerce, created America's first libertarian institution, the Foundation for Economic Education in Irvington-on-Hudson, New York. Read was a clear (though hardly a profound) writer and a charismatic personality who could convert total strangers into libertarians during only a few minutes of conversation. Read appears to have sought Paterson out in early 1944, after reading *The God of the Machine*. He was impressed by her; she was impressed by him "as a really exceptional individual, and I am not often impressed in that way, unfortunately." She disputed amicably with him about the meaning of *The God of the Machine*, and she tried to connect him with friends who might do him some good. She gave Chamberlain an introduction to him, and when they met, they "agreed that Isabel Paterson was a phenomenon." Later she took issue with Read's "pious platitudes" in public speeches and his raising of money for people whom she did not regard as friends of private enterprise.[37] In correspondence, he tried her patience by telling her ideas she already knew, and she tried his patience by lecturing him about his failure to understand her own ideas.[38] Correspondence ceased. Following her death, Read said, "Isabel and I were good friends and I was one of the first to read [*The God of the Machine*] when it was originally published." In the Foundation's journal he printed a fine tribute to her by Chamberlain.[39] She was easier to deal with after her death.

Perhaps the saddest example of Paterson's inability to work with people was her ruptured relationship with H. M. Griffith, executive of a prominent New York public relations firm. Griffith, who was brilliantly well-informed about all the issues that mattered to Paterson, read *The God of the Machine* and pronounced it "one of the great books of the world." He became a fervent disciple and submitted to her a variety of plans to make her ideas more widely known. The well-connected Mr. Griffith even wondered "whether there might not be a bare possibility of having you as a professor or lecturer in a college of which I am one of the trustees." Then he had the temerity to dissent from her in a purely academic dispute over the nature and historical importance of Calvin's thought. There was a violent reaction; Paterson would never countenance disagreement on any point touching the idea of free will. Reluctantly breaking off the relationship, Griffith assured her of his lasting indebtedness to her work; and he said a wise thing:

> Some minds work better in the give and take of discussion, others unilaterally. The first are not necessarily to be commended, nor the second to be blamed. . . . The least and sometimes the most anyone can do is to respect the constitution of another. . . .[40]

Paterson's constitutional intransigence was the determined enemy of her attempt to make an impact on American culture. But there is a passage in *The Fountainhead* that applies to her. It indicates that despite Howard Roark's intransigence about the purity of his artistic ideas and his consequent inability to get along with would-be clients, he still finds individuals who want him to build for them. It is as if there were "an underground stream flow[ing] through the country and [breaking] out in sudden springs that shot to the surface at random, in unpredictable places."[41]

For Paterson, one of those places was the United States House of Representatives, where Nebraska congressman Howard Buffett, a very independent Republican, warmly welcomed her intellectual leadership. Another was Southern California, where the redoubtable R. C. Hoiles established the headquarters of his newspaper chain, the Freedom Newspapers. Hoiles thought so highly of *The God of the Machine* that he bought a hundred copies. It was "a wonderful book," he thought; it made him think that perhaps women will "have to lead us out of the wilderness." He went east to talk to Paterson, and bought a new suit for the occasion. His wife "teased" him, saying that "Paterson could get him to do what she could not."[42] Paterson's relationship with Hoiles was not without disputes, but he retained his respect for her and for *The God of the Machine*, which he was "very anxious" to have reprinted. Long after his death, the Freedom Newspapers continued paying tribute to Paterson.[43]

Besides her following among libertarian and conservative intellectuals, Paterson possessed a large nonintellectual following, now more political than literary, that manifested itself in all sorts of unlikely places. These people might not be as important as, say, Herbert Hoover, but they were much more lovable. One was Mr. Roberts of the Roberts Seed Company (Texico, New Mexico), who wrote to Rose Wilder Lane to ask if her friend Isabel Paterson could possibly hop a TWA flight for Amarillo and come out to meet his family and friends:

I am having my vacation starting August 16th, and I am going to the mountains of Red River, New Mexico where they have a nice Summer resort hotel, with plenty of steaks. If Miss Patterson [sic] could come around the 15th of August, I would be glad for her to go with myself and family. It will be a pleasure to entertain her.

Paterson wrote Mr. Roberts a nice letter about politics and said that she regretted not being able to visit him.[44] She threw out a lot of letters from important people, but his letter was one she saved.

19

The Mustard Seed

Paterson had reacted badly when Herbert Hoover encouraged her to elaborate the insights of *The God of the Machine* in other publications; but, consciously or unconsciously, she took his advice. She kept writing in the *Herald Tribune*, of course, and in 1947 she wrote an article that was eagerly accepted by John Wade, editor of the fledgling *Georgia Review*. The essay is called "Has the World Grown Smaller?"[1]

Paterson's answer is No. People believe that the world has grown smaller because they believe that one can travel to its remotest parts in only a few days, and that one can traverse it by means of television in only a few minutes. But "can you?" she asks. You can't if some government refuses to let you. Since the beginning of the Great War, which has "not yet ended," enormous areas of the world have been effectively closed to visitation from abroad. Try bringing television to bear on the Soviet Union.

Taking the broadest historical view, she observes that for thousands of years, up until the nineteenth century, the maximum velocity of transportation remained about three miles per hour. Why? "The problem that had to be solved . . . was the problem of government," government that "claimed authority to bind men to the soil, to prescribe and limit their work, to prevent exchange of goods, and to put them to forced labor—in brief, to stop productive enterprise." In England and America, however, there evolved the "necessary institutions for the fullest exercise of freedom: freehold land, contract law, and limited government." In 1707, the largest free trade area in Europe was the little kingdom of England. Then, suddenly, the energy circuit expanded, the circuit whose "transcendent power" was finally expressed in the speed of the airplane and the radio. Yielding to the power of commerce, every nation except Russia and Turkey opened its borders to passportless trade.

Now, the progressive tendency had been neatly reversed. Almost every border was guarded by passport, most were guarded by guns, and many had become completely impenetrable by normal human beings. The world had grown larger, slower, and very much more dangerous. Capitalism was not responsible, and neither was technology or physical machinery; what must be blamed was the state: "The long circuit . . . was formed during the period in which government diminished; it has collapsed as government has increased." Those who seek a smaller world should not seek it in dreams of world government but in the reduction of government in the world. That is the prerequisite for "high energy" and "high velocity."

While thinking about the shape of the human world and the fate of strictly human applications of energy, Paterson was meditating on a larger theme, which she developed in letters and working papers and inquiries to scientists and engineers during the decades following *The God of the Machine*. Two months before that book was published, she received a review copy of Sir James Jeans' *Physics and Philosophy*. She studied it with close attention, taking sharp notice of what she considered its fallacious arguments for determinism. She responded with one form of a concept that current science writers call the ACP, the Anthropic Cosmological Principle: "[T]he universe must be such that our minds can do such and such with and in it"—the things that our minds actually do.[2] Any satisfactory account of the universe must allow for the functioning of the human mind as we know it.

Very well. The important questions are these (in Jeans' wording): "Are we . . . automata, or are we free agents capable of influencing the course of events by our volitions? Is the world material or mental in its ultimate nature? Or is it both?"[3] Paterson underlined the passage. We know her answer to its first question: We do make decisions, and our decisions do influence the course of events. As for the second and third questions, her answer is: Both; the world is both material and mental.

Then she asks her own question: Is the material universe "closed" or "open"? Her answer is: Neither; those expressions imply the existence of some other universe, one that this universe is either closed or open to. But clearly, there are two "orders" in the universe. There is a measurable, physical order, and there is a non-dimensional order of judgments and decisions that, as we know, is capable of affecting the other order. Now, the dimensional order must be "calculable mathematically in its own terms, else the 'interference' from the other Order would be ineffective." "[N]o doubt," Paterson wrote, anticipating the objections of people who wish to equate the mind with the physical brain, "the physical (electronic) process which occurs in the brain while thinking is quantitative" and measurable. "Thought itself," however, "is not quantitative." When a person decides to move a lever to the left, he may use the same amount of energy he uses when he decides to move it to the right; but the important thing, in relation to his effect on the physical universe, is the decision itself; and that is not quantifiable, even if the decision initiates a process that transforms the world. The physical effects are measurable; the mental event is not. Mathematically based sciences are insufficient to describe the universe we actually inhabit.[4]

According to the Second Law of Thermodynamics, the physical universe is continually losing its energy, "running down," as entropy tends toward its maximum. Life, however, creates at least local resistances to this process, and Paterson posited the existence of a simultaneous "up" process in which energy tends constantly toward its own maximum. One problem is that we "cannot *detect* the 'up' process *in general* but only in odd glimpses which *seem unrelated*." She thought that we see the "down" process, rather than the "up" process, "as a continuum" because *"our sensory apparatus* is framed or made to or for *use on the 'down' side*[;] it is functional to the phenomena of the 'down' side, because it is on the down side that we do our material, practical work."[5]

For a number of reasons Paterson found it inconceivable that the universe would ever run "down" into an end state of total inertness. (Would gravity cease to operate, and is gravity unrelated to energy?) Likewise, she found it inconceivable that the universe could ever run all the way "up," attaining a state of pure energy. She believed, instead, that the "up" and "down" processes work together to create a "constant and total kinetic equilibrium."[6]

If there is constant equilibrium in the universe, however, there must be "constant disequilibrium" at "every given time and point in space." The alternative, a universal equilibrium created by an equilibrium at every time and point in space, would be contrary to observed fact: we observe the lack of equilibrium in our surroundings. And, as Paterson notes, one doesn't knock the sun out of the sky whenever one decides to walk across the room, as one might do if equilibrium had to be maintained throughout time and space. The existence of the actual conditions—one kind of equilibrium and one kind of disequilibrim—is what allows mind to affect the physical universe in the way it does. Physical laws are determined and dependable, but changes of direction can still be made through local interventions. It's a fact that one easily takes for granted, but for Paterson it's the humble gateway to a cosmic speculation:

> If your motor car really had its *own* unalterable *direction* you couldn't use it, could you? But because it *hasn't*, one could deduce rationally that it is and must have been made for use; and the word use there implies "use by a *mind* with a purpose"—a being of the rational order.

Like the car, the entire "physical universe answers to any reasonable description of a mechanism designed for *use*."[7]

As Paterson sees it, the "whole secret of freedom" lies in the ability, which we know we have, to initiate changes of direction in the universe without altering its physical laws. The creator of the universe would have the same freedom, on a larger scale: "the nature of the physical universe is such that a super-power of the same order could work *all through it*, command it wholly, yet without destroying or really *disturbing* it."[8]

On one side, Paterson's theory of equilibrium is common sense and assured intuition; on the other side (or sides, because there is more to the theory than I can fairly represent in this place) it extends to the end-state physics of imploded stars and the theological problems of a creator working within his own natural laws. And on that side it reaches to the ultimate problem of God's collaborator, the self—the problem of mortality. Thinking of time as working "on the 'down' side," but "equated on the 'up' side in some way we probably can't understand," Paterson says,

> I think we go through or under it (metaphors, not a scientific statement), like a diver duck under a wave, and come up again where we want to. (Hence death).[9]

At once homely and startling, this image of the living creature, emerging and re-emerging into its native light, is uniquely the product of Paterson's mind. Whatever else it may be, her theory is a poetic achievement, the discovery of a perspective from which the motion of the individual mind and the beam from the farthest star can be seen at once, and as one, harmonious as the duck and the wave, in a universe instinct with life and choice.

Besides speculating on this cosmic scale, Paterson was continuing to pursue purely American and political applications of her theories. In 1948, she took up "a question that the Civil War didn't settle," the question of liberty's relationship to voting. Her article on this problem, a second contribution to the *Georgia Review*, focuses on one of the most notorious episodes in the history of the Supreme Court, Chief Justice Taney's opinion in the Dred Scott case (1857).[10]

Taney argued that neither slaves nor their descendants could ever be citizens; the founding fathers had never intended their notions about inalienable rights to apply to blacks. One could scarcely imagine a more soulless or illiberal position for an American to take; Paterson considered it also "absurd." But there is a riddle here. Taney was a learned man who had grown up in the eighteenth century; he knew very well that it was hardly the "fixed and universal" opinion of that century's intellectuals that blacks were "beings of an inferior order . . . so far inferior that they had no rights which a white man was bound to respect." As a jurist, Taney was distinguished by his technical proficiency; yet the Dred Scott decision was a tissue of absurdities.[11]

Paterson thought that Taney found justification in the great nineteenth-century movement for unqualified manhood suffrage. This manifestation of democracy gave ammunition to the foes of emancipation, who spread the fear that if slaves ever became free citizens, they would achieve the right to vote and destroy republican government. Taney's decision reveals his own fear that free black people, if considered citizens, would avail themselves of the constitution's "privileges and immunities" clause to secure all kinds of liberties, everywhere in the country.[12] He may have been particularly concerned about voting, as Paterson argues, because he was one of the nation's leading Jacksonian democrats, a leading participant in the campaign to give full effect to the will of the people as manifested at the ballot box.

For their part, northern friends of democracy scrambled to deny that former slaves would vote, and actually prohibited them from voting in some northern states. That was their form of racism. According to Paterson, however, both sides had missed the point. The purpose of republican government is not to encourage voting or to allow majorities to do whatever they want; it is "to preserve individual liberty." Racial qualifications for voting were no means of doing that; it could be done only by limiting the scope of government. Voters, whoever they may be, can accomplish that purpose by cutting off the government's supplies of property, in the form of taxes. Property holders have a natural interest in doing that. The true qualification for suffrage, therefore, is possession of property. Anyone, white or black, can meet that qualification, and there is nothing to be feared from it.

Unlimited suffrage, on the other hand, promotes unlimited government, because its justification is the simple idea that the majority should prevail, no matter what. The idea is absurd, yet widely held. Fear of its consequences blinded white southerners and led to such absurdities as the Dred Scott decision. Unfortunately, the issue was of more than antiquarian interest. The majoritarian assumption continued to blind the world to the real question, the question of individual liberty; and it continued to be used as an apology for every kind of ruthless political experiment. "It was Taney's worst luck," Paterson concludes, "that he had a majority with him; and he has it to this day, in a world enslaved."

Nineteen forty-eight saw the Soviets advancing briskly across Eastern Europe, and the approach of what Paterson regarded as a very drab presidential election in America. She was bitterly out of sympathy with both major parties. Adding to her bitterness were personal disappointments, one of which was the disastrous course of her friendship with Ayn Rand.

Their relationship had been evolving, and devolving, in interesting ways. *The Fountainhead* remained a tremendous commercial success. In 1945, Paterson ungrudgingly compared its sales to those of *The God of the Machine* and said it was like the relationship of "a grain of mustard seed to a mountain."[13] Meanwhile, Rand was outlining a new novel. Her inspiration came from a phone conversation with Paterson in 1943, before *The Fountainhead* started to sell. Paterson urged Rand to produce a nonfiction book embodying her philosophy. Rand demurred; if people didn't buy *The Fountainhead*, that was it. "What if I went on strike?" she demanded. "What if *all* the creative minds of the world went on strike?" Where would that leave everybody else? Then it occurred to her that the idea "would make a good novel."[14] She started to plan a short book called *The Strike*. Fourteen years later, it was published as *Atlas Shrugged*, the immense summation of her worldview. Like *The Fountainhead*, it would become a perennial bestseller and a perennial focus of radical libertarian enthusiasm and debate.

Paterson had doubts about various features of *Atlas*, but in many ways it is an eminently Patersonian novel, a 1,146-page exposition of her argument that the real America is not an accident of material conditions but a continuous invention of the human mind. The novel's great example of the truth of this idea is the American railway system. Railroads created the industrial features of America as we know it, but they were themselves created, and need constantly to be maintained, by individual minds at work in a capitalist network of exchange. The railroad was Paterson's great example, too: "[R]ailroads don't just happen." Nothing illustrates "the high potential long circuit of energy" better than a railroad.[15]

A railroad needs energy, and a means of producing it. Paterson identified the individual mind as the dynamo of American history; in *Atlas*, Rand embodies that idea in John Galt, the individualist inventor of a new way of generating motive power. The villains in *Atlas* are social planners, economic regulators, and political fixers and demagogues, exactly the people one would expect to find as villains in a Patersonian novel. They preach a moral code that Rand associates with Robin Hood, that fabled redistributor of wealth by force. Paterson had told her readers that the redistributionists "go on believing in Robin Hood," not noticing that "Robin Hood's name is Hitler."[16] Whatever hold Rand's villains have on her heroes comes from the sense of duty that the heroes feel about doing their jobs and keeping things running. This is also Patersonian: "how else can a man suffer," she had written, "except through what is best in him?"[17]

Established in a beautiful, ultramodern house in the San Fernando Valley, Rand outlined *Atlas Shrugged*, wrote film scripts, cultivated movie stars and local conservatives, acquired disciples of her own, and enjoyed a success that in some ways went far beyond Paterson's. The two women remained friends. Letters and calls went back and forth, and Rand was happy to visit Paterson when she came east. The many surviving letters show Paterson in a very bad temper about current political events and about the failure of businessmen to understand capitalism or give it effectual support, but overwhelmingly loving and encouraging to Rand, "my dear," "my child," "my little sister"—with Rand responding in kind. There were periods in 1944 and 1945 in which Rand did not write, because, as she claimed, she was intimidated by her desire to get everything exactly right in her letters.[18] Later, there were some sharp philosophical conflicts. But the correspondence survived even Paterson's repeated demand that Rand stop taking the "dope" that her doctor said wouldn't hurt her: "Stop taking that benzedrine, you idiot. I don't care what excuse you have—stop it."[19] Rand discussed Paterson's work with her own friends,[20] praised *The God of the Machine* to all and sundry, and included an homage to Paterson in one of her scripts. In *Love Letters* (1945), Joseph Cotten picks up a model of a sailing ship and exclaims, "'The Golden Vanity!'"

The Rand whom Paterson knew in the 1940s was not the grim little demigod of her later reputation. There was still something fresh and spontaneous, almost girlish, about her, at least when ideological issues were not at stake. Paterson still considered her "very important (but not self-important)" and tried to introduce her to people who could be useful to her. When Rand wanted railway background for *Atlas*, Paterson contacted Colonel Henry and arranged for her to be given the royal tour of the Twentieth Century Limited, en route from New York to Chicago. In Indiana, Rand even got to drive the train—an experience that, she told Paterson, "completely ruined" her as a mere passenger.[21]

But when Rand called Paterson "the one encounter in my life that can never be repeated," she may have been revealing more than she consciously intended. The words are a quotation from *The Fountainhead*, where they are spoken by Howard Roark, the incorruptible creative genius, to Gail Wynand, the would-be creator who compromises himself by trying to force other people to obey his will.[22] That, very likely, was Rand's obscurely developing vision of her relationship with Paterson. Rand was the struggling, ultimately victorious genius; Paterson was the stifling would-be dictator.

Rand had looked all her life for a great intellectual friendship, and she wanted to believe she had found it in Paterson. It was her misfortune that she could not conceive of a friendship that transcended intellectual disagreements. She was disturbed by Paterson's divergent attitudes, including attitudes that Rand merely interpreted as divergent. Both she and Paterson had fiery tempers and enjoyed consigning ideological enemies to hell. Rand, however, saw herself as calm and even-tempered, while discerning the "malice" in Paterson.[23] Paterson's sense of humor was robust and irrepressible, while Rand's was often difficult to locate outside the satirical portions of her novels.[24] She took Paterson's words seriously and literally and tended to give them the significance they would have had if she herself had used them. This could easily lead to trouble.[25]

One matter about which Rand very definitely did not have a sense of humor was the value of her own writing. Her respect for Paterson—and perhaps her fear of her—is indicated by the fact that she managed to endure her literary critiques, a courtesy she would never extend to anyone else. She knew, for example, that Paterson disliked her little novel *Anthem* (1938) "because," as Rand recalled, "she felt the characters weren't characterized enough, whatever that means."[26] Any author knows what that means, except when somebody says it about the author's own characters. What Rand did not know was that Paterson took her copy of *The Fountainhead* and inscribed it with scores of editorial corrections. Rand's biographer remarks that if Rand had known about that, those would have been the last annotations Paterson ever made.[27]

The most important source of disagreement was religion. The earliest dogma to which Rand attached herself was atheism. In her girlhood she decided she was an atheist, and that was that: "Since the concept of God is rationally untenable and degrading to man, I'm against it."[28] Paterson's religious conceptions were of the least dogmatic kind, but they were deeply offensive to Rand, who considered every form of religion an affront to reason, and every affront to reason an affront to human dignity. Paterson suggested that reason itself could define the questions it was incapable of answering—a classic philosophical position that baffled Rand. She pestered Paterson to explain herself, and Paterson (who was probably baffled by Rand's bafflement) never did so, at least to the questioner's satisfaction. Rand was appalled by Paterson's very traditional belief in a soul that could not be reduced to anything that people thought or did or made: what could such an object be? To make matters worse, Paterson was candid enough to share with Rand some of her speculations about reincarnation and some intimations she felt of her own past lives. Then it was Rand's turn to refuse to discuss an issue. About two years into the relationship, Paterson stopped mentioning any "mystical" intuitions.[29]

Rand was a scientific atheist of a familiar nineteenth-century kind. Paterson had known people like that all her life. She was probably bored with the thinness of Rand's cosmos, although she also probably enjoyed provoking Rand from time to time with dissenting views. She could put up with Rand's metaphysics, although Rand obviously had trouble putting up with hers. But when they came to the place where metaphysics verges on ethics, or Rand thought it did, a strange thing happened. Rand resented Paterson for refusing to accept her views, but she also resented her for accepting them without giving her full credit.

In speculative moments, Paterson said that she thought the Christian morality would ultimately be superseded by something else, but she didn't know what that was; in any event, the Christian morality was the best that anyone had yet discovered. She had written that the "harshness" of life "can be mitigated only by personal decency, a sense of obligation of human beings to help one another personally in times of stress." This was the morality of her early story "A Question of Values," with a strong relationship to the morality of Jesus' story of the Good Samaritan. The gospel tells us that the Samaritan paid for the injured stranger's convalescence; it does not say that he supported him for the rest of his life or lobbied Congress for passage of a healthcare bill. That distinction was by no means good enough for Rand, who based her ethical theory on the firmest possible contrast between the virtue of "selfishness" and the evil of "altruism." "Man's first duty is to himself," she writes in The Fountainhead, and she pictures that duty as permeating all human relationships.[30] The distinction between "first" and "only" has a way of disappearing in Rand's work, as it seldom does in Paterson's.

Rand told her friends that the older woman's absurd Christianity prevented her from sympathizing with the revolutionary attitudes of The Fountainhead.[31] Yet decades after publication of The Foun-

tainhead and *The God of the Machine*, Rand remembered being dismayed to discover that Paterson's book included her ethical theory but failed to mention her as its source.[32]

The genesis of this dismay is murky. In 1946, Rand wrote a letter bearing on the subject to Leonard Read, who had obligingly sent her some correspondence in which Paterson said something dismissive about *Anthem*. Rand angrily responded with the following propositions: "Pat read *Anthem* in 1942" and "did not like it. . . Much later, after long abstract discussions with me and after she read *The Fountainhead* (do you know that she doesn't like *The Fountainhead*, either?), Pat understood and evaluated my theory of the proper ethics of individualism, and told me that it was 'the greatest ethical discovery since Christianity.' (These are her exact words.)" But "[e]verything" that Rand said in *The Fountainhead* she had said in *Anthem*. Now Paterson was dismissing *Anthem*, despite the fact that she had "learned" its ideas from Rand. The moral? Paterson read *Anthem* but "miss[ed] its idea," so she is not really "interested in ideas" after all.[33]

Notice that Rand remembered Paterson's using the phrase, "the greatest ethical discovery *since* Christianity," which allows for the idea that Christianity still has something to say about ethics. Notice also that Rand's authorial ego was more easily bruised in 1946 than it was in 1942, but that in 1946 she is still not saying that *The God of the Machine* owed anything to her own great idea. She claims that Paterson understood the idea only "after she read *The Fountainhead*," presumably as a whole. Rand wrote the bulk of *The Fountainhead* in 1942, and Paterson was not given the chance to read it through until the novel was published, almost simultaneously with *The God of the Machine*.[34] In any case, Rand told Read that Paterson first understood her ideas "much later" than 1942.

Paterson was by no means averse to crediting other people with the origin of any ideas that were helpful to her. In *The God of the Machine* as well as in her columns, she goes out of her way to welcome intellectual collaborators, sometimes in response to relatively slight contributions.[35] But there is no evidence in her columns or correspondence of any change in views that might be attributed to Rand's ethical theory; more to the point, there is no such evidence in *The God of the Machine*.

Certainly, the book is opposed to a kind of altruism. Paterson had always regarded professional altruists as meddlers, cranks, and spiritual incompetents who are incapable of doing even the strange kinds of "good" they want to do. One of her most frequent themes was their political and moral destructiveness. She said that "[t]he most trying people are altruists; they are the reformers who want to dragoon the world into virtue."[36] Like Rand, she contrasted altruists with egoists, to the advantage of the latter; and she used the contrast to make roughly the same political point that Rand made in *The Fountainhead*: "It is not the robust and genuine ego but the half ego which seeks external power."[37]

Rand could have read this, and other discussions of altruists and do-gooders, in the *Herald Tribune* columns that she considered so brilliant. She would have agreed with them, but there was nothing distinctively Randian about them. Unlike Rand, Paterson always stopped short of identifying "ego" with any very wide range of good qualities. She remarked that altruists and egotists are often hard to tell apart, because both of them can have trouble "meeting any real obligation." Followers of the ego, she allowed, "are not necessarily unamiable, and are frequently very interesting," but that was a backhanded compliment. Its immediate object was Gertrude Stein, whom Paterson regarded with cordial contempt. But for her, this was not a foundational topic. At a climactic moment in *The Fountainhead*, Howard Roark says that "[t]he world is perishing from an orgy of self-sacrificing." At the climax of her first essay in the *Georgia Review*, five years after *The Fountainhead* appeared, Paterson says, "The world is perishing from too much government."[38] The difference is clear.

How, then, did Rand come to think, at some point, that Paterson had adopted her ideas in *The God of the Machine*? The chapter that she believed was obviously indebted to her is "The Humanitarian with the Guillotine,"[39] which vigorously attacks the "do-goods" in Paterson's usual manner, while barely glancing at the issue of altruism per se. In fact, the chapter's complaisant discussion of the charities of the medieval church demonstrates that Paterson was far from adopting Rand's moral philosophy. Rand regarded virtually all charity as a culpable form of altruism, but Paterson thought there was nothing morally wrong with charity so long as it remained intelligent and uncoerced:

There are millions of genuinely kindly people who do actual good without ever thinking about it in that light, by unforced sympathy and giving at need the product of their own efforts; but they don't ask to have any "power" or position for it. They don't expect some third party to foot the bill.[40]

That passage appeared in one of Paterson's columns a year before she published *The God of the Machine*, and neither the book nor anything else she wrote retracts the opinion there expressed. Her closest approach to Rand's concept of altruism appears in the following sentence from "The Humanitarian with the Guillotine":

The philanthropist, the politician, and the pimp are inevitably found in alliance because they have the same motives, they seek the same ends, to exist for, through, and by others.

Compare *The Fountainhead*:

The parasite lives second-hand. He needs others. Others become his prime motive. . . .
    Rulers of men are not egotists. They create nothing. They exist entirely through the persons of others. Their goal is in their subjects, in the activity of enslaving. They are as dependent as the beggar, the social worker and the bandit.

Anyone can assess the extent of dependence or convergence that is manifested here, and its significance for one's final view of the writers involved. Almost twenty years before, Paterson had written that those whom the world calls "egoists" actually "cannot live without the attention and approval of their fellow beings."[41]

Another type of "dependence" appears in Paterson's argument that humanitarians can't give things away unless someone has already produced them. She says that benevolence must be "*secondary to production*." Rand puts it this way: "Men have been taught that the highest virtue is not to achieve, but to give. Yet one cannot give that which has not been created. Creation comes before distribution—or there will be nothing to distribute."[42] This is an important idea, but it is not exactly new. It is prominent in the Bible (see, for example, Ephesians 4:28), and it has appeared in virtually every satire of social softheadedness since the French Revolution. Paterson had been using the idea for years, without claiming that she invented it.

The idea always had a good deal to do with her concept of social classes; and here again, there are similarities to Rand, but no indebtedness to her. The two classes of people in *The Fountainhead*— the "creators" and the "second handers"—are in economic terms the same two classes that Paterson had been describing ever since *The Singing Season*: "The industrious, the provident and the honest . . . pay continuously for all that the politicians, the borrowers and wasters destroy." Long before the protagonist of *The Fountainhead* warned that collectivism and parasitism had "swallowed most of Europe" and were now "engulfing our country," Paterson had warned her readers about the

> "collectivist" revolution and disaster in which the world is now crashing down . . . a revolt of the non-productive, of the parasitical temperament.
>
> Naturally it takes refuge under a "working class" label, but none of the leaders ever did a lick of work . . . none of them ever did a hand's turn toward producing anything but paper schemes to exploit somebody else by power they hoped to usurp by lies and force.[43]

To make her universal indictment of "altruism" stick, Rand argued that people who want to wield power over others are actually the psychological slaves of the people they rule. Paterson sometimes wanted to believe that, too; though more often, she regretted their pigheaded pride in their own ideas. At any rate, she had been discussing the concept for a long time:

> [T]he demagogue is afraid of missing a vote or a place. He has to count noses before he knows what he "thinks." Or what he will do or stand for. And the private citizen is Caspar Milquetoast in person. When he gets stepped on he apologizes for being in the way.[44]

This doesn't mean that Paterson agreed with Rand on the idea that "altruism," as Rand defined it, is the basic problem. That is where the lines were drawn: Paterson saw nothing particularly wrong with the conventional social virtues and the duties they imply (which did not include a duty to let oneself be stepped on), so long as the exercise of those virtues and duties was neither coerced nor forcibly subsidized by "third parties." Rand did see something wrong with them. Paterson did not believe that one's primary duty to help oneself cancels all duties to help other people; Rand identified individualism with "selfishness."[45] And she thought that Paterson agreed with her.

She eventually concluded that Paterson's agreement with and indebtedness to her were proved by two conversations they had while she was writing *The Fountainhead* and Paterson was writing *The God of the Machine*. The discussion began with the episode in

Boswell's *Life of Johnson* in which Dr. Johnson is pestered by his biographer to say what he would do if he were imprisoned in a castle with a newborn child.[46] Rand argued that even a parent's duty to a child is secondary to his duty to himself, since he can hardly keep the child alive if he fails to keep himself alive; and Paterson acquiesced. Rand recounted the episode as evidence that Paterson had accepted her whole moral system and had then used it without attribution in *The God of the Machine*.

In fact, there was no substantial indebtedness of Paterson to Rand, but at some point Rand began to resent Paterson's failure to acknowledge the significance of her ideas and their supposed influence on Paterson's work. In early 1948, she told Paterson, "It was from my theory of ethics that you learned why the morality of altruism and sacrifice is evil." Paterson wrote back and denied it ("No, my dear"), recalling the Dr. Johnson conversations and saying that Rand had indeed taught her something, which she should have figured out for herself, about the comparatively small moral problem of the "enlightened *self*-interest" of parents.[47]

Rand, however, was also storing up grievances of a more practical kind. She had expected Paterson to do more than she did to publicize *The Fountainhead*, and she finally convinced herself that Paterson had done next to nothing. She had talked about Rand in her column, but her references were not intellectual enough. Rand liked only one of them: a discussion of various types of heroes in literature, in which Paterson wrote:

> The only strictly American hero appeared mostly in popular fiction of the last fifty or sixty years. Yet he marked a genuine change in human history; he was the man who built, made, invented, produced. He did something, instead of striking an attitude. He is presented (on the grand scale) in only one recent novel, "The Fountainhead."[48]

Paterson provided that little advertisement almost a year after *The Fountainhead* was published; but she had begun giving Rand publicity before the book came out, and she continued giving it for years afterward.[49] She also let Rand have her own say. On June 20, 1943, she mentioned the Wright brothers' "originality and independence," then quoted Rand at length on the ideological meaning of her book and the inability of reviewers to understand it. At that time, *The Fountainhead* had experienced no surge of popularity, and Rand had received no $50,000 check for its movie rights. Her publisher was providing "only the most perfunctory advertising support."[50] Paterson's eight advertisements of Rand in 1943 alone make *The Fountainhead*'s supposedly mysterious breakthrough into national popularity seem somewhat less mysterious, especially when one reflects on the reach of *Herald Tribune "Books"* into mid-America, where the surge of popularity began. Rand ignored all that. As she grew more successful, she became more devoted to the theory that nobody had ever helped her to become that way.[51]

These were some of the thunderheads darkening the horizon when, in late May 1948, Isabel Paterson flew to Los Angeles to visit Ayn Rand. She came at Rand's invitation and at Rand's expense. Rand was generous, but Paterson was clearly not looking forward to the trip. To Colonel Henry she wrote, "[H]ave to make a trip during my vacation, rather long and tedious, so I don't know where I'll be all the time. I'm leaving this weekend. . . . I had meant to spend the month [of June] just sitting and watching the grass grow, but it was not to be."[52] According to Rand, Paterson suddenly decided to accept her invitation to visit so she could meet Rand's conservative friends and raise money to start a journal (ultimately entitled the *Freeman* and involving such people as Chamberlain and Chodorov) to advance free-enterprise ideas.[53]

Whatever the purpose may have been, Paterson's journey was not a pleasant one. She couldn't follow the scenery as well as she had been able to from her precarious position on the wing of Harry Bingham Brown's little biplane, thirty-six years before, and she regarded the trip as "tedious" to begin with.[54] She must have been in a very unhappy mood by the time she got to Los Angeles. We have only Rand's account of what happened next.[55] She, too, was unhappy. She was trying to finish the film script of *The Fountainhead*, and she had to drop her work to entertain Paterson. She had been nursing injured feelings for several years, and Paterson now inflamed them by remarking (correctly enough) that Rand was not the source of her belief in the moral principle that people are entitled to act for their own benefit. The two women disputed the point, inconclusively. The issue of reason, what it could and couldn't do, also came up; of course, that was not settled either. Then there was the issue of what Paterson did or didn't do to advance the cause of *The Fountainhead*. She let Rand know that she had turned down the opportunity to write a formal review of the book for the

Herald Tribune—a courageous admission to make, since Rand, the atheist, had once told Paterson that not reviewing the book was an affront to the deity. Rand was so upset that she forgot precisely what Paterson said in extenuation; she thought she said something about not agreeing with everything in the book but not wanting to hurt her friend. This principled position had no appeal to Rand; she felt that she should "throw [Paterson] out."

Nevertheless, Rand pursued the public purpose of the visit, inviting friends from Hollywood and the Los Angeles business community to meet "the great conservative." The meetings began well, but there was an altercation following the visit of playwright Morrie Ryskind (Gershwin's collaborator) and his wife Mary. Paterson was displeased for some reason, and when she was alone with Rand she dismissed Rand's friends with a tasteless remark: "I don't like Jewish intellectuals." This was almost undoubtedly intended as the kind of absurd joke (tasteless as it was) that is meant to sidetrack any seriously contentious conversation. Paterson was the very rare author of her generation whose public and private writings and remembered conversations are innocent of derogatory ethnic and religious references. And the audience of her remark, Rand herself, was a Jewish intellectual, as Paterson well knew. Rand quickly reminded Paterson of that, and Paterson laughed. She hadn't meant it "that way." Indeed she hadn't, but she should have known how Rand, who was notorious for not understanding other people's jokes, would take her sorry attempt at humor.

The round of social events continued. There was a party given by actress Janet Gaynor and her husband and attended, it seems, by gossip columnist Hedda Hopper. Here Paterson manifested more ill humor. Ten years later, reflecting with discouragement on her habitual lack of "tact," she recalled Gaynor's saying that she "ought to be kept out of sight and produced only on special occasions." Paterson's comment was, "She's a very smart woman and I know what she meant!"[56] Finally Rand's friends gathered to discuss the *Freeman* project. One of them was Bill Mullendore, president of Consolidated Edison and a particular friend of Rand. When it was suggested that a dummy issue of the magazine be constructed, with articles by Paterson, she heatedly launched into her usual complaint that businessmen did nothing to defend free enterprise, leaving it all for her to do. This was true in general, but the specific application was dead wrong. Her listeners were certainly trying to help the cause.

Rand was understandably embarrassed by Paterson's "tirade," and after the guests had departed, there was another fight. According to Rand, Paterson would not accept criticism, and "[f]inally she said, 'If that's the way you feel, I'll leave tomorrow.'" Rand agreed; and although Paterson tried to make enough literary small talk to let Rand change her mind, that was it. At the airport, Paterson said she would always wish Rand the greatest success. Rand said, "I hope you'll be happier than you are"—a comment that showed much insight. Then Paterson got on the plane.

In relating these events, thirteen years later, Rand's voice lost its wonted self-complacency; it became exasperated, weary, sad. She remembered that Paterson wrote to her sometime afterwards and asked her to use her influence about a matter of who should be hired for the *Freeman*'s staff; then she sent Rand a long, familiar letter, which Rand didn't answer.[57]

Paterson never discussed the disastrous conclusion of her friendship with Rand,[58] and Rand was not much more communicative. Each continued to admire the other's genius, regret the other's failings, and lament the difficulty of finding people whom one could really talk with. Libertarians are a combative lot, and Rand and Paterson personified that combativeness. Rand, indeed, would disavow the very name of "libertarian," so angry did she become with libertarians who resisted her own interpretation of individualism. Her break with Paterson provided the basic script for the personal disputes that would plague her throughout her life and that would continue to plague the individualist movement, disputes in which principles and temperaments became inextricably confused and the only solution was a "break."

The effect of this particular break was to deprive Paterson of the audience that might have come to her from a continued association with Rand, and to deprive Rand of Paterson's deep learning and persistent, though embattled, common sense. It was a disaster, all right.

20

The Committee of One Will Now Adjourn

One Monday night in the 1940s when Paterson was staying late at the office to put *Herald Tribune "Books"* to bed, she and a young visitor went down to the employees' cafeteria, and there they saw Irita Van Doren, her editor, sitting at one of the other tables. With her was Helen Reid, the owner's wife. Paterson whispered, "Look who's over there—I wonder what kept the two ladies so late?" The "two ladies," thought her friend, "seemed incongruous in that dingy place."[1] She was viewing the intersection of three oddly representative stories of American life in the twentieth century.

Helen Rogers Reid was reared in Appleton, Wisconsin, the last of a family of eleven children. Her father died when she was three years old, and his survivors worked hard to support themselves in what has been described as "genteel poverty."[2] After graduation from Barnard College, Helen got a job as secretary to the fabulously wealthy Elisabeth Mills Reid. Mrs. Reid's father, who had struck it rich as a provisioner and banker in the California gold rush, left a fortune amounting to one billion dollars in today's money, a fortune of about the same size as the one commanded by the imaginary Mrs. Siddall. Elisabeth married Whitelaw Reid, the not-nearly-so-wealthy proprietor of the *New York Tribune*; thereafter, the Reid family's money financed the paper, which the Reids regarded more as "a public duty" than as "a profit-making opportunity." After several years as secretary to Mrs. Reid, Helen Rogers succeeded in marrying her son Ogden, an indifferent manager who gradually surrendered more and more control of the paper to his wife.

> We love little Helen
> Her heart is so warm,
> And if you don't cross her,
> She'll do you no harm.

Thus the designated "poet" of Helen's graduating class at Barnard.[3]

Carving out a career at the conservative *Tribune*, she tried to make her own kind of friends and give effect to her own kind of principles. She was no political thinker, but she preserved what has been favorably termed "the liberal and reformist instincts of her youth," instinctual attractions to causes as discordant, from Paterson's point of view, as women's suffrage, the League of Nations, and prohibition. She liked people with "background" and "cultivation."[4] Where she found such people, such as Lewis Gannett, Paterson's longtime colleague in the *Herald Tribune* book review business, she often disregarded such small matters as leftist or communist sympathies.[5] The staff of the *Herald Tribune* became a peculiar melange of conservatives and leftists, with Helen Reid drifting somewhere off to the left of center.

Like Helen Reid—and Isabel Paterson—Irita Van Doren was reared in a backwater of North America. In Irita's case, it was Tallahassee, Florida. Her father, a mill owner, was murdered by a discharged employee; her mother kept things going by selling preserves and music lessons. Irita's relentless ascent of the social ladder began with her graduation from Florida State College for Women. She then migrated to Columbia University, where she pursued doctoral studies in literature. One of her fellow students was Carl Van Doren, who became literary editor of the *Nation* in 1919 and thereafter wrote many influential books on literature and history. He and Irita were married in 1912. By 1920, she too was working for the *Nation*, on the advertising side; but when Carl vacated his job as editor, Irita took it over. Then Stuart Sherman, one of her husband's friends, brought her to *Herald Tribune* "*Books*" as his assistant editor. He also fell in love with her. After his death, as we have seen, she took his job.[6]

But her true literary ladyhood was yet to come. Paterson saw the *Herald Tribune* as a place where she could write and work; Van Doren grasped its social significance. She understood how important she could become, both to the authors who reviewed for her and to the authors who were reviewed; and she understood how to

use her widening circles of friends to make herself a literary celeb-
rity. She had no literary or intellectual gift, but she had charm, and
she worked well with Mrs. Reid to enhance the paper's social prestige. The Book and Author luncheons that she began staging in
the Astor ballroom in 1938 were important public occasions,
worthy even of radio broadcast. Her literary and political salons
had long attracted important guests, and she had ensconced herself
in such remarkable places (for someone who had done no original literary work) as the board of *The American Scholar*, where
"gallant older men . . . attended her like Castiglione's court-
iers." Author and editor Hiram Haydn, who supplied this account of her success, added (admiringly), "Irita comes close to
defying description."[7]

She had climbed from nowhere to make herself the embodiment
of mainstream intellectual culture. That culture, as Haydn's memoir makes abundantly clear, was axiomatically leftist. In the early
1930s, Pat and Irita were friends and colleagues; by the 1940s,
they had taken citizenship in different countries. As early as 1936,
Irita's doings had become opaque to Paterson and the other mere
workers at *"Books."*[8] By 1940, when *If It Prove Fair Weather* was
published, Paterson and Van Doren were quarreling over the unusually long time that *"Books"* took to review it. The quarrel, which
was embarrassing to both, took place by letter.[9]

But *"Books"* was no longer Irita's central concern. In 1938, Mrs.
Reid introduced her to Wendell Willkie; in 1940, Irita was running
him for president. Although his campaign was unsuccessful, her
role in getting him nominated was sufficient evidence that she had
finally become part of the American governing class. She left many
of the day-to-day operations of *"Books"* to her assistant Belle
Rosenbaum, who was a social as well as a business friend (though
by no means a friend of Paterson).[10] After Willkie's defeat, Irita
continued to act as his advisor and literary collaborator. Willkie
himself continued to exert some influence on the public. In 1942,
he embarked on a world tour, sponsored by President Roosevelt.
He visited Stalin, Chiang Kai-Shek, and other generalissimos. On
his return, he settled down to write in Irita's apartment and with her
help produced a book about his views and experiences: *One World*.
It was published in April 1943, one month before *The God of the
Machine*. With strong support from the Republican journals *Time*
and *Life*, it became an enormous bestseller.[11]

The moral content of *One World* is an unstable mixture of idealism and cynicism. Willkie is capable of saying, in a matter-of-fact way, that "practically the whole upper and middle classes of Russia have been completely exterminated," while adding, with equal matter-of-factness, "But I had not gone to Russia to remember the past . . . . [T]he Soviet Union, whether we like it or not, exists." This bold statement somehow leads to the conclusion that "we must work with Russia after the war." Warming to that theme, which he does very readily, Willkie declares that "there can be no enduring peace, no economic stability, unless the two work together." In interviews, he grew even warmer, saying such things as, "I tell you that if a man is not, deep in his belly, in favor of the closest possible relations with Britain and Russia [peculiar pair], then it does not matter what else he is."[12]

Willkie's electoral opponents had derided him as "the barefoot boy from Wall Street." Now he was writing himself into the final scene of *Animal Farm*:

> Once I was telling [Stalin] of the Soviet schools and libraries I had seen—how good they seemed to me. And I added, "But if you continue to educate the Russian people, Mr. Stalin, the first thing you know you'll educate yourself out of a job."
> He threw his head back and laughed and laughed. Nothing I said to him, or heard anyone else say to him, through two long evenings, seemed to amuse him as much.
> Strange as it may seem, Stalin dresses in light pastel shades. . . .[13]

Paterson had read that kind of thing before. What must have especially irritated her, in light of her analysis in *The God of the Machine*, was the fact that Willkie, a businessman, betrayed no suspicion about the ability of the Soviet political economy to function without individual freedom: "Russia is an effective society. It works." He said this while littering his text with references to the Russians' dependence on tools from Sheffield and Cincinnati and their desperate desire for more help from capitalist countries.[14]

Willkie's attempt to bother the Republican Party into steering by his increasingly leftward star ended in disastrous defeat in the 1944 Wisconsin presidential primary. He died soon after. But he deserves his reputation as one of the Republican "moderates" who helped to create the "nonideological" or "me-too" party of the postwar era. From Paterson's point of view, his influence could only have been malign—and whatever could be said of Wendell Willkie's political commitments could undoubtedly be said of Irita Van Doren's. She had adopted an ideological role, her ideology was radically opposed to Paterson's, and she was Paterson's boss.

Probably Irita never tried straightforwardly to censor her.[15] In the mid-1930s, Paterson wrote two columns in response to readers (one of whom called *Herald Tribune "Books"* "as red as a log in a pokeberry patch") who wanted to know whether censorship happened at the *Herald Tribune*. Paterson ridiculed the idea.[16] But by the 1940s, "the administration" (Irita and Mrs. Reid) certainly disliked her politics, and she was well aware of her growing unpopularity with them.[17] There was a sense of forces massing against her.

Paterson's persistent attacks on the Soviet Union, at a time when America and the Soviets were partners in arms, were not considered especially endearing. When she brought up the Soviets' erstwhile alliance with Hitler, the *Herald Tribune* got mail—some typed on Wall Street letterhead—charging that she was "com[ing] pretty near treason." She suspected that communists and their sympathizers were working to get her and anyone like her fired, but communists and fellow-travelers were not the only members of the public looking critically in her direction. After she took issue with Quentin Reynolds' absurd manifestations of friendship toward the Soviets in his book *Only the Stars are Neutral*, her old acquaintance Bennett Cerf, a political naif, decided it was his turn to chastise her for regarding Russia as America's enemy. Paterson spiritedly defended herself, reminding him that the Russians had apparently mistaken their enemy, too, since they maintained a neutrality treaty with Japan.[18]

"To be in the literary world . . . and not to be friendly" to communist sympathizers "was an excessively disagreeable job."[19] There was a Communist club among *Herald Tribune* employees, and an acknowledged Soviet sympathizer was editor of the paper's foreign dispatches.[20] More people, some influential, formed a penumbra of sympathizers with the far left, and Paterson must have been very disagreeable to them. It may have been as a result of their good offices that Tass, the Soviet news agency, requested an advance copy of *The God of the Machine*, even before the publisher's pre-season catalogue was put together. Who tipped them off? she wondered.[21] Then there was the long campaign, conducted in part by communists, for unionization of the *Trib*. Paterson resisted the idea that someone whom she had not asked to do so should presume to "represent" her. As we have seen, she made an issue of it in her column. This in itself would be viewed as treason by many people on the left, and it does not appear to have made her many friends in management, either. Resisting unionization is ordinarily a thankless job.

Paterson was used to the reactions that her outspokenness produced. Many of them she greeted with amused toleration. When, in 1934, she heard that Clifton Fadiman, book editor of the *New Yorker* and a potent figure in the publishing world, had attacked her as "malicious," she claimed that attacking people one hardly knows can be "an admirable safety valve. . . . Many a man might go home and beat his wife or kick the cat if he couldn't localize his general annoyance on some public figure or passing stranger." Anyway, she had never been so deluded as to believe she was "universally beloved." As for "Fellow Travelers" and other "Pinks," she wrote in 1941, she knew that they attacked her, but she just didn't care. In 1944, however, she was startled by a woman who walked up to her at a literary party and said, "How are you—I thought your head would be rolling in the dust by now."[22]

And Paterson was growing old. About a year after *The God of the Machine* was published, she had a dream that she was fifty-eight years old, and she woke up depressed. Then she realized that she really was fifty-eight years old. And obviously, she was not fighting a winning war at the *Herald Tribune*. It did not help when in 1948 conservative columnist Westbrook Pegler attacked the paper as "the Uptown Daily Worker."[23] The charges, though greatly overstated, were distressing to Mrs. Reid, who feared that she might lose her paper's conservative audience. Conservative members of the staff were worried about the extent of leftwing influence, and Mrs. Reid had been hearing complaints about it for years from outside the paper. But she met complaints with painfully naive defensiveness:

> It has been my experience that there are always people who rush into designating as a communist or fellow traveler any one who believes in being informed [!] on Russia or who considers that the future security of the world is dependent on the United States and the Soviet Union being friends.[24]

One need not be a McCarthyite to sense the peculiarity of this anti-anticommunism.

Eventually, stung by Pegler and other critics, Helen's son Ogden Rogers Reid started a journalistic campaign against communist subversion—without going so far as actually to remove any communists from the paper itself.[25] Paterson was in much more danger than the communists. She may have seen the attack on her by Henry Steele Commager in December 1940 as related to her bosses' political hostility. Commager had been one of Irita's "discoveries" in the late 1920s and had reviewed 234 books for her in the first decade of their association.[26] It would be naive to think that he started his crusade against Paterson, Van Doren's assistant, without securing at least the tacit consent of Van Doren. At some point, Mrs. Reid joined the fray, issuing a "threat" of some kind over what Paterson called a "silly book" by liberal journalist Wallace Carroll.[27]

The book may have been either *We're in This with Russia* (1942) or *Persuade or Perish* (1948). The second is more likely, since it was published when Paterson's relations with Mrs. Reid had had six more years to deteriorate. *We're in This with Russia* goes far beyond the license of wartime books to be silly. Carroll, a prominent foreign correspondent, is not a communist sympathizer; he simply justifies Paterson's view that there are people who "ought to be Communists, if they had brains enough." *Persuade or Perish* witnesses Carroll's disillusionment with the Soviets, though not with himself. It is a long-winded account of World War II propaganda, in which Carroll had been professionally engaged. It concludes with bitter remarks about the Soviets' role in starting the Cold War, but it argues for a managed peacetime economy, with continued application of wage and price controls, and it makes the bizarre suggestion that food rationing should have been maintained in America so that people overseas could feel as much "in common" with Americans as with "the hungry people of Russia." This is precisely the kind of book that Paterson would dismiss with a sneer, and that many other intellectuals would welcome as a contribution to international understanding. Paterson may have made an inopportune effort to review it. The published review in *"Books"* is by Arthur M. Schlesinger, Jr., and is unreservedly favorable.[28]

Paterson's well-placed coworkers were not inclined to "tangle" with her in person,[29] but they did not view her as an asset, and she knew it. She felt that her sole protector was the elder Ogden Reid. He was a political conservative of a conventional kind, with whom she had had her disagreements. He supported conscription; she violently opposed it. Yet she thought she had his sympathy. They would meet in passing, and he would acknowledge her in a way that she thought she understood.[30] Ogden Reid died on January 3, 1947. In January 1949, Paterson was told that she was being "retired."

The *Trib* was in one of its recurring periods of financial difficulty; for several years during the late 1940s, management went about trying to get rid of employees.[31] Paterson's firing may have been prompted, in the immediate sense, by motives of economy, though neither Helen Reid nor Irita Van Doren seems to have explained it that way. The political and personal tension offers explanation enough. Paterson herself never doubted that explanation. No playwright would accept any other. The symbolism was exactly right. It was the kind of conflict that is always taking place "on the west side of town" in an Ibsen play, the conflict between fractious individualism and the defensive gentility of "the compact majority." But even Ibsen might not have grasped the inwardness of this particular conflict, because he was not an American. He could not know the obscure channels through which American desires are channeled toward either respectability or rebellion. Yet . . . put it on the stage, and any American would understand.

Only one element of the drama was missing: the heroine's climactic speech. Paterson's response was silence. At her last Monday Night, January 24, 1949, she told the few people in attendance that the column now being printed was her final column, that she had been fired. She offered neither explanation nor protest. On the same day, she wrote to Colonel Henry, "Thought I had better tell you I have just been fired." And that was that.[32] Her last column makes no attempt at farewell. It simply ends.

Paterson's friends were surprised that the great protester never publicly protested her firing and never explained why she didn't.[33] A decade later, she wrote a kind of explanation in notes for an article or memoir:

Must sa[y] in favor of H. T. — no feud with them — it is my considered conviction that if I had got on any other paper by chance (I got on the H. T. by chance) I think I would have been fired years before, and furthermore, that I would not have been allowed to get in print one quarter of what the H. T. printed of mine. They did keep me employed for many years, though they didn't pay me very well . . . not half of what the leftish gentry got — still, it is obvious no other newspaper desired to print what I wrote.

That was the market, and you didn't always win by it. Paterson took it on those terms.

Far from having any special animus against the H. T., I bear the above truth in mind. Screwball outfit, of course — if they were going to print such-and-such they *ought* to have fired me, to be honest, and I told them so. But as they did not, certainly I should not be the one to complain.[34]

When startled readers wrote to Irita Van Doren, demanding to know what had happened to their favorite columnist, she replied in a friendly way that Paterson "was retired" or had "been retired" and was now enjoying her garden.[35] When people got through to Paterson herself, she told them a different story: she hadn't left her job voluntarily; she had been removed.

But she left without complaint. She was tired. She had been tired for years. She conveyed the news with great simplicity to her friends, and that was the end, for her, of the *Herald Tribune*. In the last line of her columns, she had often said things like, "The committee of one will now adjourn."[36] It would have been a good line for her final exit.

21

Completing the Circuit

Paterson planned her future. The *Herald Tribune* paid her a pension of $1,980 a year, which after a few years was reduced to $918 in recognition of her eligibility for Social Security benefits of $1,062. But she had no intention of accepting those benefits. She would starve rather than do that. Her Social Security card remained in an envelope marked "'Social Security' Swindle." Besides the $918, she had some savings, and she owned her home in Ridgefield—though she could see that the neighborhood was bound to become suburban, with all the annoyances and, in particular, all the taxes that suburbia entailed. She was completely on her own, and she feared that she would live to be ninety.

> "Now what you need," said the power-saw salesman, "is a generator." (Can you imagine?) "What I need," I said coldly, "is money."[1]

Paterson thought she could support herself if she managed her investments carefully. Real estate appealed to her; she liked houses and land. In 1949 she purchased a run-down hundred-acre farm on Canal Road near Rocky Hill, New Jersey, close to Princeton and just up the road from one of Washington's headquarters in the Revolutionary War. There were two barns, one of them in ruins; fields; a brook; and an old frame house. There were tenants. She rented out the house until 1952, when she took advantage of rising property values, sold her home in Ridgefield, and moved to Rocky Hill. She rented the fields to nearby farmers, and she rented half the house to a young family, the Sanners: mother, father, daughters. In 1956, she bought a nice modern-Tudor house (mortgaged) on two acres of land in Greenwich, Connecticut, and leased it "for a comfortable sum." She knew she could sell the house for a good price when she felt like it. She also invested in an unimproved lot in Greenwich and sold it in 1958. She offered the property at Rocky Hill for sale but was content to stay there until she got the price she wanted. That took several years.[2]

The Canal Road farm was the dilapidated outpost of a dilapidated village, but it completed a circuit. Rocky Hill seemed "home-like" to her, because, as she said, "it went to seed about the time I was born, and therefore in its period or style it fits into my early memories." One of her friends made a typically American response: looking at Rocky Hill, he said, made you feel like going to work and "improv[ing] it all to hell." At this, Paterson "laughed like anything." To keep her new home running, if not precisely to improve it, she chopped wood, planted roses, crusaded against tent caterpillars, climbed down in her well and up on her roof, making sure she knew what needed to be fixed. She was cheerful about the scrimping she had to do to make sure she would remain independent. She told the story of a wealthy woman who "was vexed because her house-maid had given notice." Paterson added, "Mine can't." She was not discontented: "I enjoy my elegant leisure and exclusiveness because, like the Wife of Bath, 'I have had my world as in my time.'"[3]

Now she could spend the night reading without worrying about having to get up in the morning. When, at length, she did get up, she sat by the fire, drank "Johnsonian quantities of tea," and read some more. A great advantage of Rocky Hill was its proximity to the Princeton University Library and its thousands of aids to reflection.[4] She followed modern novels only in a half-hearted way, complaining that they had "[n]o feelings" in them; the books that aroused her own feelings were works of history and philosophy. As shown by the plentiful annotations in her books, she had certainly lost none of her vigor, especially when confronted by laxity, absurdity, or what she called a "smarty style." Neither had she lost her ability to recognize ideas she could use, even when they came from an angle different from her own. Among the authors she read with close attention was the Roman Catholic philosopher Etienne Gilson, in whom she was pleased to find a fellow refugee from materialism.[5]

It had seemed that *The God of the Machine* might be her last book, but by early 1948 she had begun writing another, a ninth novel. She took her time. As usual, her work was like needlepoint:

careful and slow.[6] In 1956, she describes the project as her "eternal novel." The next year, it is "my Book of Job," and she is working in her "coral-insect way" on the final chapter. Not until February 1958 can she report that the book is "*done*, fair copied, etc." She called it *Joyous Gard*—in legend, the castle to which Launcelot and Guinevere retire amid the sundering of Arthur's kingdom; and, as Paterson herself once summarized the story, the place where Isolt and Tristram "enjoyed a brief interlude of bliss" before Tristram was surprised and slain by King Mark. The novel was conceived as a refuge and escape, a timeless place where Paterson and her readers (if any) could contemplate the mysteries of time.[7]

The novel's treatment of time is itself mysterious and dislocating, and is probably meant to be. References to current events are curiously absent. Nothing happens in *Joyous Gard* that could not happen in the 1950s, when it was written; and some of its atmosphere seems clearly to derive from that era—its casual attitude, for instance, toward air travel and air conditioning. But if one gathers the clues that Paterson stitched into the narrative at various points, one finds that the action would have to take place in about 1935. Truly, as Paterson said, "[t]he people in this novel . . . are characters out of their time."[8] The sense that one is slipping constantly from one world into another, or that one is slipping steadily into exile from any time-bound world at all, is increased by the central characters' preoccupation with a lost past. The heroine, Louise Maclane, is forced to think back to the ruinous decision that she made, soon after World War I, to marry a man she did not love. Her stepmother and alter ego, Mrs. Herne, imagines the era of her own youth as a lost world, a world "[b]efore the Flood" (273).

Atlantis again—and that world was not well lost. What replaced it was the present "world of standardized mediocrity" (241). *Joyous Gard* is not a social or political novel, but the contrast of worlds is suggested by many means, including social and political commentary. Most of that commentary emerges in a subplot centered on Louise's half-sister Kate. Kate has married Marvin Kimball, a man who lost money (not a good sign in a Paterson novel) that he had inherited (an even worse sign), and who is currently functioning as a corporate executive (what more can be said?). Marvin's big idea is public relations; he exemplifies what Paterson termed the communism of the modern big businessmen[9]:

The keynote was interdependence and service. We have got to sell our industrial leaders to the public, on the human side. . . . Marvin was just thinking out loud. You have an idea and you bat it around, get the other fellow's angle, let him contribute, work the bugs out of it. Swing one man and the next one is easier, and so on; they fall into line. . . .

Presumably Marvin and his industrial leaders yearned for an apotheosis of themselves and their job, like the medical profession. Men in white, selfless and dedicated; little tin gods on wheels. (248)

Marvin is a case study in modern "capitalist" collectivism.

His boss, Jared Croft, is a different and better kind of businessman. He dismisses Marvin's ideas about public-relations capitalism: "I don't relish begging the public to excuse me for living" (315). Jared is a businessman of the older generation, a fact that reflects well on him, in Paterson's eyes; but this fact also makes him responsible for having propagated the new generation of Marvin Kimballs. It wasn't the floods of ocean that intervened between the old world and the new; it was a failure of intellect on the part of Jared Croft and his compeers. The good thing about Jared is that he, unlike most of them, realizes (somewhat obscurely) that it's up to him to accept his share of responsibility for the modern "loss of energy."

Why does it happen? He hadn't got the answer, though it was his business to know. Foresight was what he was paid for, and he hadn't earned his pay. (315)

Paterson had often argued that American big businessmen didn't know their primary business, which was the intelligent defense of the capitalist system. Her portrayal of Jared Croft continues that favorite argument. Yet the portrayal is sympathetic. He may not have taken sufficient responsibility in the past, but he has sufficient integrity to admit it now. And he has sufficient integrity both to show respect for independent thought and to show contempt for the prevailing "professional" group-think.

People are not, after all, simply historical or social artifacts, condemned to be creatures of their times. To enforce this point, Paterson arranges for Kate to leave Marvin, her contemporary, for Jared, the best representative of the preceding generation. Kate is not trying to make a political statement. She dislikes Marvin's ideas, which are conditioned by modern political trends; but the issue for her is that Marvin is the kind of person who is capable of being conditioned in this way, and Jared is not. As Mysie remarked in *The*

Golden Vanity, "[y]ou find yourself when you find what belongs to you, your own people."[10]

The protagonist, Louise Maclane, is certainly one of Paterson's own people. She shares her tastes, her reading, her intense privacy; she even likes to spend time at an old farmhouse in New Jersey that resembles Paterson's place on Canal Road.[11] One similarity is startling. Like Paterson, Louise married suddenly and unwisely; she has not seen her husband in many years; and she has never been divorced. The novel begins with her discovery that her husband, George Maclane, is stalking her. He watches her house. He appears at the subway entrance across from her place of work. He insists on trying to convince her to return to him. He has some hypocritical notion of helping her, of doing good to her, even if the good is done against her will. She has no intention of letting that happen. To her, George is immature and "ineffectual." She is "ashamed of him," and "[t]hat is the one irrevocable feeling" (156-57).

Why, then, did she neglect to obtain a divorce? Why had she "shrunk from and postponed" it? The motive was her desire to avoid "the surrender of privacy, the plea and interrogation required for relief by law" (156-57). Besides, she has found no other man she wants to marry: "If it had made any difference, I'd have found a way out. I didn't want to be bothered, as long as he let me alone" (193). No one knows—though everyone can guess—how closely this reflects Paterson's attitude toward her own marriage. Literature can seem strangely separate from life, as separate as the world before the flood: none of the friends who read Paterson's manuscript seems to have questioned her about the relationship between her life and her story. Some of them would have been afraid to question her, but others became too engrossed in the novel to recognize the suggestive parallels.[12] One can only speculate about whether Kenneth Paterson ever appeared outside one of Isabel Paterson's doors, or whether she spent forty years wondering about the possibility that he might do that some day. Probably he was too "ineffectual."

Joyous Gard is not, however, a roman à clef. It is not a story about Paterson's personal disclosures and concealments. It's a story—actually a group of three related stories—about the issues of life that Paterson considered essential. It's a series of fables, if you will, about those essential things. The mythological title, the odd treatment of time, and the unlikely events provide the distance that a fable needs for its focus on what is basic.

One story is a fable of identity. That was why Louise married George: she wanted an identity. After her father died, she accidentally discovered that she was his daughter by an illicit union, and that her supposed mother was actually her stepmother, a woman with an identity alien to her own. She recoiled from the shock of being motherless as well as fatherless. She ran away from home and learned to support herself, hoping to "make for herself a place where she had a right to be, an identity defined by independence" (105).

There is, certainly, a personal connection here. Paterson had no stepmother, but (like Jay Gatsby, that other representative American) she had never fully accepted her father as her own. Her attainment of full identity required the attainment of independence. Louise leaves home at 17, about when Mary Bowler did. At this point, however, the fable diverges significantly from the life. The young Mary Bowler was, in Paterson's words, "a happy cat";[13] the young Louise Maclane still feels like a refugee with "no right to be anywhere" or "to be let alone." Fearing that she will be legally compelled to return to her stepmother's home, she agrees to marry George, an older man who offers to protect her and asks "no privilege beyond" (128-29). No one should infer from this evidence that Isabel Paterson had a sexless, as well as a foolish, marriage; we are dealing with symbols of identity and independence, and symbols of entrapment by other people's ineffectual lives.

To escape the trap, Louise leaves George and returns to her stepmother, who, as she learns, loves her deeply and respects both her identity and her independence. Mrs. Herne isn't alien at all; she is just like Louise. In the riches of human diversity, there is always the chance of a saving irony: this is the story of a *good* stepmother. The two women live quietly together for the next seventeen years. In one sense, their old house in New York and their old farm in the countryside are a modern Joyous Gard, a place whose inhabitants possess what Paterson speaks so much about in *The God of the Machine*: "standing ground," the "right to be."[14]

But that's not the end of the story. George's return is still to come. The fable of identity lost and identity regained is surrounded by a fable of something larger, a fable of substantiality. George Maclane is nothing, and his return, which is the return of "nobody" (197), awakens Louise to the idea that her own life still lacks substance.

[S]he had finally arrived at a conviction of negative wrongdoing. Fearing she might commit herself to a second failure, she had passively withdrawn from the risk and responsibility. "I've been happy; perhaps I've been too happy." (130)

She travels to Reno and returns with an annulment of her "marriage." She is still a virgin, with the virgin's mythical freedom from anything but her own identity. She is free, but she is "[f]ree for what?" (254).

The answer materializes in the form of Victor de Saussure, a quiet, self-assured, brilliantly competent young engineer. Victor is more than a decade younger than Louise, but he has an antediluvian integrity and capacity. "[H]e isn't merely going to be successful, make money," Louise believes, "he will be . . . something more." In the past, there were men who "made a world. If you thought of them, it was with the light on their faces." Victor is one of them (301). It is the light, the connection with the larger system, with the world, that reveals both identity and substance and transcends the tensions of time that otherwise mean so much in this novel. In the language of *The God of the Machine*, energy completes a circuit.

Victor is a youth; Louise is a mature woman; but they are the same age in character. Victor courts her passionately and tenderly; she refuses—then suddenly consents. They are married secretly and go to live in a cottage by the ocean. This is an appropriate place for a myth of romance to end; but Paterson does not want to suggest that independence is the same as total isolation. She makes sure that the cottage is not mistaken for Arcadia. It is modest, even primitive, and modestly remote; yet it is close enough to the city to allow Victor and Louise to continue working. And they do; they understand—as Hope Fielding understood when she returned to work in the strange last act of *The Magpie's Nest*, so many years before—that the price of life is full engagement.

A conventional honeymoon, love in idleness, would have been happy enough; but this was better to begin with, having the rich texture of full reality. Their delight was mixed with and pressed from the actual terms of life. (331)

This is substantial happiness, a higher and better Joyous Gard.

Still, the fable of substantiality is not complete; it is surrounded and resolved by a third fable, a fable of meaning. Louise has made her life substantial by accepting the terms of life, but the full meaning of those terms awaits the novel's final episode. George reappears and accosts Louise. At last he does something effectual, at least in his own terms: he takes out a gun and shoots her She lingers a while, and then she dies.

This is a very strange thing to happen in one of Paterson's modern novels, where violence is otherwise virtually nonexistent. Why does she permit it? There are two reasons. On the one hand, it gives her a chance to control her romantic idealization of the central characters by insisting with new emphasis on their engagement with the actual terms of life: Louise has made mistakes (George is one of them) and mistakes have consequences. On the other hand, it allows Paterson to open her story to a wider perspective, a more intense idea, a fuller vision of life—a vision that Louise attains only when life itself is leaving her.

She wakes in the night in her hospital room and remembers

> a black night shot through with crystalline light, as if in solution; and she knew that next spring's flowers, their colors and sweet odors, and the running streams, and grassy meadows, were implicit in the vast forces of the storm and the icy cold. . . . She saw that the universe was a work of intellect; how else could it be intelligible?

She turns to the flowers beside her bed.

> The yellow roses had been cut half-blown; they were still uncurling, expending in pure grace the ultimate power of sunlight traversing interstellar space. (347)

Here, in the sun ray, is the final Joyous Gard, the perception, conception, and intellect of the universe, working from whole to part, from small to great, in ever-renewing cycles. The circuit closes; the final terms, as Paterson envisioned them, are fully known. They are the terms of life and power. With this knowledge and this power, Louise de Saussure can die. The vision is her final exile, and her final home.

During 1958 and 1959, Paterson submitted *Joyous Gard* to numerous publishers, all of whom rejected it. They considered it too old-fashioned. It remains unpublished.[15]

22

Friends

Paterson's intellectual life flourished amid her increasing isolation from other people. "At my age, in the course of nature," she said, "one cannot expect to have many friends; and the world being what it is, and me being what I am, perhaps I really can't expect to have *any*."[1] That expectation nearly came true.

She retained some of the friends she had among the proficient, responsible, nonintellectual people who, she thought, made things run, no matter what the intellectuals tried to do. Patsy Orrico, a neighbor who had worked for her at Stamford, remained a good friend, as did Frank Spinelli, an old associate from the pressroom at the *Herald Tribune*. In 1946, when Frankie and his wife Marian and their daughter Andrea were for some reason threatened with homelessness, Paterson immediately invited them to move in with her. They lived happily together for several months, until the family found a new place. When Andrea was three years old, Paterson taught her to read.[2] Paterson and the Spinellis would always be affectionate friends and allies. They understood one another.

Most of Paterson's friends in the literary world had died or drifted away or fought with her about politics. Grace Zaring Stone, who as a supporter of FDR had had many disputes with Paterson, wrote to her after she left the *Herald Tribune* to say that she was still "immensely fond" of her, despite their disagreements; and Paterson made a stinging, hurtful response.[3] Louis Bromfield had embarked on a second career as a gentleman farmer and writer about agriculture and life-in-general, but Paterson had no respect left for him. "One thing we can say for him," she announced in an attack on one of his books, "not a cliché escaped his grasp." Her correspondence with Garreta Busey, formerly a favorite, concluded with lectures against Garreta's activism in a modern-liberal cause; Paterson's later attempt to revive it came to nothing.[4] Burton Rascoe, a fervent anticommunist who disliked the people Paterson disliked, always retained her respect; he wrote to her with the old familiarity and light-heartedness, but they did not visit each other.[5]

Paterson's friendship with Will Cuppy had a tragic end. For years, he had been exhausting her with his hypochondria, his demands for emotional support, his absurdly uninformed questions about politics, and his assumption that she should be available at all times to discuss his work. She, in turn, had exhausted him with her "political tirades." Sometime in the late 1940s, she made a final break in the relationship. Gone were the days when he would come to her office to discuss his latest research on flora and fauna, while she made the kind of jokes he could use in writing it up. "He'd feed her the facts, and she'd make the cracks"; but now it was over.[6] So was Cuppy's life.

In 1949 he was sixty-five years old. He was still being published, but he had quarreled with his best publisher, the *New Yorker*, and he submitted nothing more to it. Cuppy, who "hated noise in all forms," had for two decades occupied an apartment in Greenwich Village where he was continually harassed by the sounds of a neighboring playground; but when the owner developed new plans for the building and threatened him with eviction, Cuppy ended his life with an overdose of sleeping pills. The *Herald Tribune* accidentally illustrated his obituary with someone else's photo. Paterson said, "very matter-of-factly, 'He committed suicide, you know.'" But she had missed him after their break, and she would always miss him.[7]

Ayn Rand was permanently alienated. She remained in California, working on *Atlas Shrugged* and conversing with disciples. One of them, Nathaniel Branden, became acquainted with her in 1950 after writing her a fan letter and receiving a letter back in which she berated him for his "appalling ignorance of Capitalism" and advised him to read *The God of the Machine*.[8] Branden and his wife Barbara, whom he married in 1953, became Rand's closest friends and assistants during the 1950s and 1960s. When, in 1951, Nathaniel and Barbara moved to New York, Rand and her husband followed them.

There she completed *Atlas Shrugged* and, in 1958, collaborated with Nathaniel in starting the Nathaniel Branden Institute, which used modern educational and marketing methods to disseminate her system of ideas, Objectivism. In Paterson's view, "Ayn was limiting her talents and taking herself out of the mainstream by that Objectivism philosophy,"[9] and that was something to say, considering her own skill at extricating herself from the mainstream. Rand insisted more and more on her originality, shedding all acquaintances who disagreed with her. Ultimately, she shed even the Brandens. She continued to recommend that her disciples read *The God of the Machine*, but she sought no contact with its author.

Other people who should have been Paterson's political friends were no longer her friends in any way. The causes were often light and transient. Rose Wilder Lane is one example, according to her account of her break with Paterson, sometime around 1946. "What do you reply," Lane wrote,

> when you get—in substance, in various forms—the retort that Isabel Paterson always made to "the brotherhood of man": "Stalin is no brother of *mine*."?? (After about a year of hearing that, one day I said to her, "Nobody agrees with you more heartily than Stalin." Thus ended our conversations and what had been called friendship. Isabel cried aloud that she can no longer BEAR my intolerable *lying*— As if I knew anything about what Stalin would or would not agree with, when (she said) I never even saw the man. —I did in fact meet him in Tiflis in 1922, but she doesn't know that, I happened never to mention it. And it is true that I did not ask him whether he agreed with Isabel that he was not her brother. Isn't it wonderful that we are always so superbly comical? always something to laugh about?)[10]

Why would Paterson charge Lane with *lying* about Stalin? One possibility is that Paterson thought that Stalin held an official, though hypocritical, belief in human brotherhood, and that Lane was perversely denying this aspect of Soviet Marxism. What is obvious, however, is that Paterson and Lane had grown very, very tired of each other.

One of Paterson's best chances to participate in a good cause perished in the wreckage of John Chamberlain's attempt to unite the libertarian right in a common journalistic endeavor, the *Freeman*, which began publication in 1950. When she first heard of the project, in 1945 or before, she was very hopeful. She met with some of the planners[11] and gave Chamberlain plentiful advice, urging him particularly to conduct the journal as a profit-making enterprise. A magazine that advocated capitalism should practice what it preached; besides, no one respected anything that was undervalued by its own publishers. *"Ends cannot be divorced from means."*[12]

But commercial methods were not pursued. Subsidies were repeatedly sought from wealthy donors; advertising was neglected; responsibility was diffused among a number of editors and business associates, and these people naturally had trouble getting along. Money ran out. Chamberlain and the other principal editors resigned in January 1953. In the next year, the journal was taken over by Read's Foundation for Economic Education and became literally free—outreach literature sent to anyone who wanted it.[13]

During his editorship, Chamberlain had wanted Paterson to write for the *Freeman*, but she was so angry with him for not taking her advice that he was afraid to ask. When he did ask, he got nowhere. Her anger was kindled indeed when he used the *Freeman* to pay her homage. In an article about her and four other women on the right (Lane, Rand, Vivian Kellems, and Taylor Caldwell), Chamberlain gave Paterson the highest praise. He called *The God of the Machine* "a brilliantly original and sound exposition of the moral, intellectual, theological and psychological justifications" of capitalism and limited government, "a basic book on the American system." He criticized the capitalist press for not sufficiently exploiting Paterson, its great defender and exponent. But then, in an obvious effort to disarm knowledgeable criticism, he admitted that Paterson was "intransigent and therefore 'difficult'"—although she was well worth publishing, nonetheless.[14]

Paterson, of course, focused on the word "difficult" and immediately demonstrated how accurate it was. She wrote Chamberlain a bitter missive denying that she was difficult, at least on the job. She also challenged him to hire her himself, if he was so upset about other people's failure to do so. That was a good point. She may also have been right in suggesting that his use of the term "difficult" was not the best way to advertise her; it would probably do her damage with any would-be employer who did come to light.[15] But whenever she complained in this way about personal affronts, she made it less likely for anyone to dare writing anything about her, for fear of repercussions.

Additional correspondence followed between Paterson and Chamberlain, whom she now considered "an unmitigated chump." Even before the offensive article appeared, the two had been engaged in a full-scale raking-over of the history of the *Freeman*, its motivating ideas, its financing, its editorial policies, and its editors.

Chamberlain insisted that he was merely one of several more or less co-equal editors and could not always have things his own way; furthermore, his way was not *always* Paterson's way, and there was no reason why it should be. He challenged her to put her complaint about his article in writing so that he could publish that, at least. She didn't. He asked her, "Why don't you see that your friends are your friends??"[16] She couldn't. The letters stopped, and another old relationship was broken.

Involved in the *Freeman* follies was a man who was never Paterson's friend but who nonetheless became a target of angry analysis, a man called Jasper Crane. The possessor of that marvelously Joycean name was a top executive for the Du Pont Corporation. He was, quite possibly, a distant model for Jared Croft in *Joyous Gard*. In Paterson's opinion, however, he was not so good as Croft at living up to his initials.

Crane was a man of placid though firm libertarian principles, much cultivated by Rose Wilder Lane. He was a crucial financial supporter of the *Freeman* and the motivator of many of its decisions. When *The God of the Machine* came out, he bought up "quite a few copies" and sent them around. He also made a pilgrimage to Paterson's office, prompting her to say that he seemed "to have some brains, if they could be excavated from the layers of secretaries and 'important' affairs on which our top men have so long been engaged with such brilliant results as we now see."[17]

This was not, as it happened, a favorable beginning. Crane suggested that *The God of the Machine* be given out, apparently at his expense, to a variety of institutions. Paterson objected that the plan sounded like charity, not capitalism. Then Crane submitted the book to a panel of supposed experts, who said that they liked it but that it wouldn't go over with people in general—at which Paterson, of course, exploded. She demanded to know whether the real reason for the consultants' view wasn't their fear of offending humanitarians, schoolteachers, and other persons whose oxen the book had gored. Soon she was horrified to discover that Du Pont had sponsored an idiotically simplified radio drama in praise of American capitalism, thus implementing an idea that she had found too embarrassing even to discuss when Crane had broached it to her.[18] Crane was now firmly in the ranks of the intellectual incompetents.

For several years thereafter, Paterson seems to have given him up for dead; but in 1950, 1951, and 1952, as her concern about the *Freeman* mounted, declined, and remounted, she visited, called, and wrote him and his associates repeatedly with suggestions about what ought to be done with it. The burden of this advice was, make it a journal that supports itself by advertising. She got along well with a man who was trying to deal with the advertising question (but who did not succeed in altering the journal's focus); she got nowhere with anybody else. In 1954, she wrote yet another lecture to Crane. Her excuse was that the new editor of the journal, Frank Chodorov, had asked her to write for it, whereas she was sure that Crane wanted her not to.[19] This approach was also going nowhere, and it was no longer clear where it was supposed to go. She didn't send the letter.

Paterson's failure with Crane—who will cross our path again—can serve as an example of her several failures to influence men of wealth and position. The Crane-Paterson relationship was a long-running comedy in which each character was constantly baffled by the other's inability to mind his own business. Paterson must have seemed to Crane an embarrassing radical, a cranky sage who could not be content with intellectual deference but insisted that she knew how everybody else should conduct himself. She wouldn't just analyze the capitalist system; she had to run it. Crane seemed to Paterson the typical capitalist who had no idea of the measures necessary to maintain the capitalist system; he was an incompetent masquerading as a corporate leader, and the awful thing was that he was the best of the bunch. It was a sad sort of comedy, on the whole. When she stepped back from such conflicts and viewed them from a distance, she was willing to say that she was, "*socially*, just a queer, frequently disagreeable, old woman; which is to say, I am in a category of quite tiresome people, unattractive, and best out of the way."[20] It is not clear whether Crane ever stepped back from himself.

One group of friends, however, was not content to leave Paterson "out of the way," and it attained a unique importance in her life. It was a family that, like her, was still close to America's pioneer roots.

The Welles family arrived from England during the colonial period and turned up around 1805 on the frontier of settlement in western New York.[21] By 1859, they had reached Red Wing, Minnesota, where Edward Randolph Welles, an Episcopal priest, built a little church. In 1874, Edward was consecrated Episcopal bishop of Wisconsin. His episcopate was strong on devotion, weak on grandeur. He cared nothing about money or social position. His son Samuel Gardner Welles, who followed him into the priesthood, felt the same way. He also found a frontier: Oklahoma Territory, where he went as a missionary in 1903. There he met Mabel De Geer, a teacher in a sod schoolhouse; they married in 1905 and thereafter maintained the Welles family tradition of a life rich in responsibility and poor in funds.

A chain of church jobs culminated in Samuel's appointment as Canon of the Episcopal diocese of New Jersey. He was the bishop's assistant for social welfare issues and institutions. In *The God of the Machine*, Paterson remembered that there was once a time when the people in charge of charitable enterprises were sincere enough not to insist on being well paid for their services.[22] Canon Welles was such a person. When his five children grew up, they knew that they would all have to work. That was the family tradition.

One of them, Mary, found a job as a secretary in the book section of the *Herald Tribune*, working in the "bull pen" next to Paterson's office. A lively, intelligent young woman, Mary charmed the writers who stopped by the office, and she charmed Paterson, too. Mary's ambition was to travel around the world. She saved her money, and in 1936 she departed, with a list of the things she wanted to see—Victoria Falls, the Taj Mahal, the Great Wall of China. . . . [23] It was the kind of trip that Paterson had always wanted to take.

Meanwhile, Paterson had become interested in the other members of the family. She liked and respected Mary's mother, whom she regarded as a western woman like herself—competent, commonsensical, and sharing "a certain attitude toward the effete easterners."[24] Paterson corresponded extensively with Mrs. Welles, sent her the kind of books that she thought a clergyman's wife would like, solicited her advice about gardening, and visited her and Canon Welles at their house in Trenton and later at Buttonwood Farm, a primitive homestead they bought near Crosswicks, New Jersey, about 1941.

Paterson grew especially close to Welles's son Samuel Gardner, Jr. ("Sam"), a writer and intellectual who became an editor for *Time*.

Sam visited Paterson frequently in her office and was a regular at her Monday Nights. Devoutly religious, like his parents, but skeptical, as they were not, about the New Deal and the course of modern liberalism, Sam became more and more sympathetic to Paterson's libertarian ideas. "Not many thinkers in human history," he said, "have evolved a new system of political theory," but she had, and he considered it sound. When *The God of the Machine* was published, Sam did his best to promote it, going so far as to produce a 22,000-word condensation that he tried, unsuccessfully, to get the *Reader's Digest* to publish.[25]

But it was Muriel, the youngest child of the family, who become the most important person in the Paterson-Welles relationship. She was an attractive woman with a mind of her own, the kind of woman Paterson liked. Along with her independent mind came an emotional temperature that could rival Paterson's own, and would qualify her to deal with it. Muriel met Paterson in 1937, when the Welles family stopped in Stamford to visit her on their return from the Wellesley College graduation of Muriel's sister Mabel. Paterson needed to get to New York to go to work, so the Welleses offered her a ride to the train station. Paterson climbed into the front seat, took a cigarette from her pocket, and casually began to smoke. Muriel was impressed: "It just looked so glamorous to me." Paterson thought that Muriel was a "mighty nice girl . . . and extremely pretty."[26]

In later years, Muriel saw Paterson periodically when she visited the Welles family at Trenton. She was there when Paterson encountered another family friend, Whittaker Chambers, former communist spy and future nemesis of Alger Hiss. Sam met Chambers in 1939, when he came out of the underground and went to work for *Time*. Sam, his office-mate, gradually gained his confidence and heard his early warnings about Hiss, who was steadily climbing his way up in the national administration. When Chambers became a Christian, Sam arranged for his baptism in the Episcopal church. Chambers tried to keep a low profile, hoping not to be liquidated by his former associates in the communist movement; and he was always welcome to "lay low," if he liked, at the Welles's place. In 1941 or 1942, Muriel was a silent and astonished witness to an argument between Chambers and Paterson about *where* a revolution in America would likely take place. The idea that such a revolution *might* take place had never occurred to Muriel. About this time, Paterson also amazed Mab and Muriel by suggesting that public schools should be abolished. Paterson thought it was funny to see their faces when she said that.[27]

After her graduation from the New Jersey College for Women (now Douglass College), Muriel took a job in *Time*'s research department. While working there, she served as intermediary in Paterson's attempt to get Chambers to raise the moral issue of obliteration bombing. The article that Paterson had in mind never appeared, although Muriel got the chance to hear Chambers' view of Paterson's intellectual arrogance: "You know, the trouble with Isabel Paterson is, she thinks she is the only one who has all these thoughts."[28] He would have more to say on that subject in the future.

Muriel hung out in Paterson's office in the evenings, talking with her and Cuppy even after they had made it courteously apparent that it was time for young folks to go home. At the end of the European war, Muriel was admitted to post-graduate study at Oxford, her admission having been facilitated by Paterson's influence with Lord Bennett. During her year in England, she married a sailor in the American merchant marine, Edward Matson (Ted) Hall. Ted, as it happened, was also a member of the Welles family—Muriel's second cousin—and he was an aspiring journalist. When they returned to America, he worked as a reporter and reviewer for the *Newark News*, later becoming an editor. A daughter, Rebecca, was born in 1947; a son, Thomas, in 1956.

After Rebecca's birth, Muriel started work as a researcher for *Life*. She was present for Paterson's last Monday Night, and made sure to keep in touch with her afterwards. Paterson and Ted also became good friends; he shared her political ideas, and she thought highly of his writing. Muriel and Ted helped Paterson find her land in New Jersey; their home in Montclair was about thirty-five miles away, and they could easily visit one another when she moved there. Ted went down to Canal Road and sawed wood for Paterson's fireplace; Muriel drove her to Arlington, Virginia, for pleasant chats with Colonel Henry, and to Wilmington, Delaware, for an uncomfortable interview with Jasper Crane.[29]

In 1954, Paterson accompanied Muriel, Rebecca, and Muriel's teenage second cousins John and Mary McLaren on a trip to

Gettysburg, then to Virginia and North Carolina. Ted received post-cards: "Keep off the Skyline Drive. *This means you.*" "Avoid Asheville. You all hurry away." In Jefferson's bedroom at Monticello, Paterson took vengeance on behalf of all knowledge-able visitors who have ever been subjected to guided tours: she halted the guide in the midst of her panegyric to Jefferson's univer-sal genius and insisted that (as was true) "he died a bankrupt!" At restaurants, Muriel contrived to supplement Paterson's tips, which were always a previously munificent ten cents. The next year, Muriel drove her to Newport, Rhode Island; the excuse was their desire to see the house where Bishop Berkeley lived during his sojourn in America. The house was closed, so they contented themselves with peering through the windows; then they made an unsentimental inspection of the giant "cottages" erected by Newport's Victorian magnates.[30]

Paterson, Muriel discovered, could still view life gaily from her perspective as the knowing outsider. But outsiders, in America, are often not so far outside as they think. No sooner had Paterson and her ideas been "forgotten" than they started being remembered again.

23

The Heart and Soul

The crucial event in the formation of the modern conservative movement took place in 1955, with the start of *National Review*, a journal of "fact and opinion." The young publisher, William F. Buckley, Jr., was unencumbered by the sectarian quarrels of the past and determined that divisions on the right should not deter a full-scale attack on the left. He welcomed writers representing all three of the tendencies that would jell, more or less, into modern conservatism: anti-communism; traditionalist, usually religious, conservatism; and libertarianism.

Exponents of these tendencies weren't always prepared to get along with one another—far from it. Some of their premises were sharply opposed. Russell Kirk, who was emerging as the most distinguished advocate of traditionalist views, detested the "fusionism" promoted by one of Buckley's other friends, the libertarian Frank Meyer. Libertarianism, as both Kirk and Paterson knew, was a radical form of conservatism's ancient enemy, classical liberalism; it was often explicitly nonreligious or anti-religious, and it insisted on the economic freedom and individualism that had dissolved much of traditional "organic" society. It was sometimes open to the conservatives' charge of simple-minded rationalism and economism. Yet both conservatives and libertarians recognized their greatest enemy as the modern state—enormous, inhuman, ignorant, and cruel. Kirk emphatically denied that there "was anything *liberal* about" his own ideas; he also said that he had been strongly influenced by Paterson's "individualism."[1]

The sixties generation of libertarian thinkers, with whom Paterson would have felt a contentious kinship, did their best to distance themselves from conservative "authoritarianism" in the social sphere. But libertarians, like conservatives, wanted to conserve the American tradition of limited government; and they were just as insistent as the conservatives, or as Paterson, on the idea that the economic order of capitalism was justified by moral as well as utilitarian concerns.[2]

American intellectual life has changed a great deal since 1950, when Lionel Trilling declared intellectual conservatism extinct. The change started when conservatism became conscious of itself as a system of ideas that could hold their own as explanations of the contemporary world. The new conservatism was not just a way of moving more slowly toward the welfare state; it offered an intellectual alternative. To provide this alternative, it could not rely on romantic ideas of a pre-capitalist past. It had to incorporate the classical-liberal defense of capitalism and of individualism in general. The defense came from European emigré economists such as Mises and Hayek, and from such American exponents of libertarianism as Paterson. Conservatism and classical liberalism became so hard for people to distinguish that Hayek felt the need to write an essay called "Why I Am Not a Conservative."[3]

By 1975, future President Ronald Reagan was telling the libertarian magazine *Reason*, "I believe the very heart and soul of conservatism is libertarianism." Paterson would have seized the opportunity to identify every rotten, non-libertarian plank in Governor Reagan's platform. Nevertheless, it is inconceivable that conservatism could have modernized itself and, by the 1980s, have become a dominant force in American politics had it not incorporated a specifically libertarian understanding of social engineering and the welfare state—and if it had not developed a sense of humor and a sense of life as it is lived outside the church and the country club. *National Review* showed how these adjustments could be made.[4]

While he was planning the magazine, Buckley did his best to get Paterson's help, telling her that "[n]eedless to say," he had thought of her "immediately as a possible contributor. . . . I am anxious for you to know that the columns of the magazine are open to you on a regular basis, and that to be known as a publisher of your regular output will greatly enhance the magazine's chances of success." Paterson was cranky about the *Freeman* experience, and she was always suspicious about rich people (Buckley came from a wealthy family) who wanted to *found* things. But she was curious. She had written for information to Gertrude Vogt, who formerly worked as an assistant at *Herald Tribune "Books"* and who now worked as Buckley's secretary; and she had been willing to signal her interest.[5]

She and Buckley conferred. A year after their first contact, however, he found himself still waiting for her to accept his offer. This time he wrote her in imperative terms:

> I admire you. . . .
>   I know all about your reservations, your conditions, your prejudices, your rights, your pride, and the rest of it, and I still want you to write for the magazine and am willing to pay the top rate for your copy, which is nine cents per word. . . .
>   And then, too, I must tell you that *in addition* to solid expositions of and elaborations on your Weltanschauung, I must have from you critiques of the Liberals and their position, and, to use a phrase I disapprove of, textual analyses of some of their mushiest statements. This last you do so superbly—and don't come back at me by telling me you don't enjoy doing it; transparently you do.[6]

That was true enough. His following suggestion was also true:

> You may sniff that to ask you to do this kind of thing is akin to asking a virtuoso to play chopsticks, to which I could only reply that when chopsticks sound like that, they *ought* to be played by virtuosos.

"Madame," he concluded, "I have had a very tough time among our pygmies. Please don't come back at me with a thousand conditions and qualifications. . . ."

If rhetoric meant anything—and good rhetoric did mean something to Paterson—she had met someone more impressive than anyone she had run across in a long time. She replied with a good deal of advice, which Buckley said was wise, and a recommendation that the title of *National Review* be changed, which he said was too late. But he agreed to handle all of Paterson's copy personally.[7] The first issue of the journal had yet to appear, but she was clearly on board, if only as a potential mutineer.

By November 1955 she had submitted her first contribution. She was still complaining about pay, but Buckley was more convinced than ever that he should keep her working for him. He tried to stop her haggling for more money per word by inviting her to join the staff and accept a monthly salary. It wasn't a bad deal, and he sweetened it by telling her that Willmoore Kendall, his teacher at Yale, said she was "as great a craftsman as Katherine Anne Porter, his heroine."[8] She wasn't buying. She evidently wanted her attachment to the journal to remain tenuous. She was retired, she didn't want to be tied down by anything, and she may have thought that if she kept Buckley begging for more, she could get him to accept virtually anything she chose to write. Little of her copy consisted of the disparaging "textual analyses" that he had said he wanted. It had a good deal more variety.

Her first *National Review* article, "The Southern Breakthrough," was an ingenious application of the historical theories of *The God of the Machine* to the history of the North-South relationship.[9] Unlike many traditionalist conservatives, Paterson had no illusions about the old "feudal" South. Both the North and the South had capitalist economies; the difference was that "[t]he North relied chiefly on the profit margin from trade and transport to bring in money," while "[t]he South raised cash crops." Slavery was "a hopeless anomaly" even in the South. It could not be squared with either the political principles or the economic realities of America. Nineteenth-century inventions, such as the cotton gin, deluded Southerners into believing that a machine economy could be run with slave labor. It couldn't. Southern production fell dramatically below Northern production; energy flowed westward, not southward, and the South became "more and more isolated from the national economy as a whole." The Republican Party, which represented the interests of industry and finance capital, was the "kinetic" factor in politics. It won the Civil War.

A century later, capital was flowing southward again, toward what we now call the Sun Belt; and political parties must once again come to terms with the substantial interests they were supposed to represent. It was a time of "torsion," a time when old parties must dissolve or realign themselves. Although the Republican leadership was oblivious to the fact, "the old Republican regional interest is ready to slide South," toward the position of the Southern Democrats. She stipulated that "[p]rediction of short run and particular events is impossible from the relations of major forces and long run causes and effects." Still, she was right in looking for a realignment of parties, roughly the kind of realignment that we have seen. She was nowhere more prescient than in her final warning:

The ultimate question is whether real political parties can continue to exist at all under a vast bureaucracy. . . . That is a very grave question, a prospect of paralysis.

The question is still undecided; the bureaucracy at Washington, with all its ideological associations, continues to command more power than any political party or movement.

Paterson might have pursued a number of political themes connected to her topic: states' rights, which she considered essential to the constitutional system; race relations, which she did not consider a proper field for government intervention, whether to force blacks and whites to associate or to hinder them from associating;[10] and the electoral antics of the Republicans, who had won the election of 1952 "chiefly by the seat of their candidate's pants and an appeal by the vice candidate's pup on television" (Richard Nixon's "Checkers" speech). These issues were interesting, but she left them for others to explore. It was not her job to develop a party line or to move legislation.

Even the issue of communist infiltration failed to entice her into writing at length on the subject. Despite her strong feelings about her own victimization by communists and fellow travelers, her attention was not much engaged by the politics of anticommunist investigations. She was wholly unmoved by the alleged romance and mystery of the communist underground and the revelations of former communists. If these people, so prominent in rightwing circles, had been fooled by their supposedly humanitarian ideal, that was because they were fools to start with; and fools were not, after all, very interesting. When she read the report of the committee that investigated the security clearance of J. Robert Oppenheimer, principal creator of the atomic bomb, she was primarily interested in the evidence it unearthed about America's class system. It was not a system of economic classes, as the communists imagined, but a system in which an official class indulged its follies at the expense of everyone else. This is the subject of her May 23, 1956, contribution to *National Review*, "The Oracles are Dumb"—the oracles, in this case, being the official class of scientists.[11]

She had always looked askance at them. She was disgusted by their search for bigger and bigger bombs, she surmised that atomic energy would not be of "practical use for industrial power" (all it would do is "poison the earth"), and she was determinedly skeptical about the Russians' ability to compete in an atomic arms race.[12]

Her apprehensions about the bomb's destructive power were balanced by the reflection that "[i]f an atom bomb ever does hit New York, it will be a good idea." She vigorously dissented from the common rightwing idea that many of the atom scientists were communists. One or two of them were, she believed, but the rest were "vague, muddled, sometimes 'leftish' in a vague muddled way . . . very like Oppenheimer for the most part." Wading through the testimony presented to Oppenheimer's investigators, she found it "extravagantly funny."[13]

She supposed that Oppenheimer's comments were sincere. She was convinced by his testimony, and that of others, that many members of the scientific community lacked discretion about even the most obvious and important matters. They were incapable of seeing what anyone of normal intelligence should be able to see. Equally ludicrous was the reasoning used to shelter them from criticism. A person identified as the "'top security officer' for the atom bomb project" blamed the "atmosphere" of the 1940s, claiming that virtually all scientists were "on at least one list of an association which was later determined to be subversive or to have leaned that way." But, Paterson noted, "nobody explained why scientists and professors are to be specially excused for succumbing to an 'atmosphere' instead of forming rational judgments." The scientific brass condescendingly explained that their colleagues were curious "about facts, about systems, about life," that they had a "willingness to explore other areas of human activity"—to which Paterson responded, "How that agrees with an obstinate ignorance of the visible realities of Communism is not apparent."[14] Bullseye.

Another early-1956 contribution to *National Review* takes a very different approach to science. It is ostensibly a review of Mary Lecomte du Noüy's biography of her husband Pierre; in reality, it is an exposition of Paterson's religious views.[15] It begins with an appreciation of Lecomte du Noüy's life and accomplishments, an account from which Paterson modestly omits all reference to the help she gave him, then expands into a consideration of Darwinian thought. Lecomte du Noüy rejected scientific materialism and atheism, because his own investigations indicated "that God exists and *acts* in a rational universe." The emphasis is Paterson's, and it is not the emphasis we expect from a deist. Deists are popularly supposed to believe in a "watchmaker God" who made the world, then vanished. Paterson was entertaining other views; something at least godlike is active in the world.

Lecomte du Noüy had expounded a theory of guided evolution. Paterson does not announce in favor of that theory, but she denies that Darwinian evolution could work on its own, in the way in which Darwinians think it did. The crucial thing about Darwin's theory is the idea that organisms that survive and reproduce are those "best adapted to the environment." But, she argues, this cannot explain "the human species," which survived by adapting the environment to itself. Its motive wasn't, and couldn't have been, the desire to satisfy "bare needs"; it aimed at something higher. Only desires that transcended mere survival could produce the "technology" necessary for mere survival. Humanity could not have survived if it had not striven to fulfill some kind of moral law; that is what "the material technology of survival requires for its use."

To Paterson, humanity's desire and power to shape its world is the "most conspicuous" fact about humanity, and it is ignored at humanity's peril. Darwinians imagine a machine that runs by itself, by accident or determinism, and they exclude any "conception of the universe *as an instrument of value*." A mechanistic view of nature is then available to legitimize mechanistic and deterministic views of society. Paterson mentions Marxist communism, the notorious example. She also finds fault with a familiar religious answer to the threat of mechanistic science, the idea that "scientists really don't know what they are talking about anyhow; and we may validate religion by our emotions toward the universe, and by personal religious experience." This, to Paterson, is simply throwing away the real basis of the religious conception, which is a rational belief in a rational universe. It is throwing away the evidence that we live in a universe in which there is "a tendency toward organization" at every level. And who knows? The conception of a rational, creative, value-laden universe might even lead to "hope for a rational society."

Paterson's last piece for *National Review* was an article about a supremely rational endeavor—teaching children how to read. She had a longstanding theory that reading is "as natural as speech."[16] In the article she decries professional educators' contorted theories and methods and argues that children are much smarter, and reading is much easier, than the educationists think. She recurs to her experience as a ten-year-old who taught three younger siblings to read. "The sad aspect of this juvenile episode," she says, "is that I didn't get a 'thrill' out of it; whereas 'progressive' teachers are 'thrilled' if a child recognizes a word." Paterson shows how the phonetic method can be used to teach very young children, and to teach them at home, thus preempting the professionals.

Her ideas on this subject were a characteristic combination of frontier common sense and radical individualism. Friends were surprised that Paterson, the childless intellectual, cranky and impatient with adults, should enjoy the company of children; but she saw in a child what she looked for, "a pure intellectual being," occupied in almost Wordsworthian fashion in the "contemplation" of the universe. After watching Thomas Hall at play, she matter-of-factly reported that "today he discovered the cantilever."[17] Children, she writes in her *National Review* article, begin with "nothing," yet they learn everything. Our mental powers would startle us, if we could only remember how we first discovered them. Taking another crack at Darwinism, she remarks that this "power of conscious knowledge does not belong to a creature which exists by adapting itself to its environment; it connotes a being who lives by adapting its environment to itself."

The learning-to-read article, which was strongly prophetic of today's home school movement, became a very popular *National Review* reprint.[18] Buckley had always regarded Paterson as one of his most valuable contributors, and he always made sure that she knew it. "[Y]our faith in the venture," he wrote, "has become just about indispensable to me. And boy how we need you!" This wasn't just strategic flattery; in private, he called her "a genius." When pressed, he reminded her that she was "paid considerably more than anyone else."[19]

His intentions were certainly generous. He offered her help with her mortgage. He offered her a weekly book column. He tried to engage her to teach his four-year-old son to read. Meanwhile, she found countless ways of demonstrating her independence. He signed his letters "Bill"; she addressed hers to "Mr. Buckley." She threatened to sever relations when he cut the length of the Oppenheimer article. She wrote him letters that he found "full of acid and ill humor—and brilliance and wisdom." She called and visited his office to deliver free lectures, and she needed to be placated when he was too busy to listen.[20]

She liked him,[21] and she enjoyed needling him. He liked her and found her maddeningly ill mannered. She gratuitously snubbed the venerable Suzanne La Follette—who had been Nock's editorial associate, and Chamberlain's, and now was Buckley's—when La Follette had the effrontery to enter Buckley's office while Paterson was talking to him. La Follette was, after all, a disciple of Henry George, and George's theories were "socialism."[22] Buckley found Paterson amusing, even when she didn't mean to be; and he hoped to amuse her, too. There were things about their relationship that he simply couldn't take seriously.

One of them was her defense of *Atlas Shrugged*. To review Rand's novel, he commissioned Whittaker Chambers, who was certain to hate it. Chambers' long review, "Big Sister Is Watching You," accused Rand of unconscious totalitarianism. Publication of this review was a signal that her atheism and ethical egoism were not to be included in *National Review*'s (hence modern conservatism's) one big tent. Rand took it as such and spent the rest of her life detesting conservatives. Paterson took it as potentially actionable.

She wrote Gertrude Vogt to advise her that the review could be taken as the basis for a libel suit and that it was worthless anyway. *Atlas Shrugged* could certainly be criticized, but Chambers (who had been a communist) was not the man to do it. She told Muriel Hall that the review was "the dirtiest job imaginable. . . If I ever see Mr. Chambers again I won't speak to him."[23]

Buckley wrote immediately to tell Paterson that although he wasn't worried about the legal angle, he was "startled" by her letter. He assured her that he liked Rand personally—he had just written her a postcard to tell her so—but he did not take her entirely at her own estimation as a philosopher. He suggested that Paterson must have seen something that "was *not* there" in Chambers' review, probably (as he theorized, with heavy jocularity) because Paterson was a woman.[24]

That must have gone over as badly as it deserved to go,[25] but the final test of the relationship came with another disputed review, this time a review by Paterson herself. Crawford H. Greenewalt, president of E. I. Du Pont de Nemours, a man with whom she had corresponded during her quarrels with his associate Jasper Crane, had now written a book—"a mild little book," Paterson called it—

entitled *The Uncommon Man*.[26] In it, he recorded various platitudes about America and American corporations. Among his un-
lucky phrases appeared the contention that "the modern corporation
is a slice of society in microcosm." Paterson's opinion was, naturally,
rather different. If such an "erroneous notion prevails," she wrote,
"corporations will be expected to do numerous things [for society]
that are none of their business" (which, of course, is what has happened). She assumed the responsibility of telling Greenewalt and other
corporate readers of *National Review* what she had told Jasper Crane:
they had left their real business, the understanding and defense of
free enterprise.

Her review of Greenewalt's book was enlivened by accounts of
her failure to convert capitalists like him to her own point of view.
Now he was writing a "plaint . . . on behalf of big business men."
But "[b]efore he undertakes their defence," she advised, "he might
take a long, close, thoughtful look at them." Even the most pro-
capitalist among them, such as Greenewalt's friend, Mr. Crane, were
too stupid or supine to act in their own best interest. Consider what
Crane had said to her when she suggested that businessmen pull
their advertising from leftwing publications. "Oh, we couldn't do
that," he replied. By reducing his own influence to "nullity," a man
like that "*shuts out of the market* the writers who would be on his
side." Just where was the support of capitalists when she was defending capitalism in the *Herald Tribune* and *The God of the Machine*?

The review was long, funny, and completely unembarrassed.
Her bitterness was clear; so was the fecklessness of the businessmen
she was discussing. What she wrote was brutal, and she knew it.

> If at this point the reader sympathizes with Mr. Crane, that's all right with me. He is
> a very nice man. So are they all, most amiable men. And their feelings are hurt. Will
> Cuppy once asked me reproachfully, didn't I want to be America's sweetheart? The
> answer—I'll bet you've guessed it—is No. That is not my job.

Her job was to pry capitalism apart from the leading capitalists.

And Buckley's job was to figure out what to do with a brilliant
piece of writing that, he felt, made a jackass out of a man who had
contributed significantly to the free-market cause and who, in any
event, was not the subject of the review. He "did not feel *National
Review* should be the instrument through which Mrs. Paterson, *en*

esprit d'escalier, got back at Jasper Crane."[27] So he edited the piece, turning "Mr. Crane" into "the Du Pont executive." The response was a predictable and emphatic No.

When he received Paterson's manuscript, he had telegraphed her, "I think your piece is brilliant, amusing, readable and uncharitable and that we should publish it. . . . I will suggest a few minor changes aimed at disappating [sic] the impression that you are pursuing a vendetta." She would not see the logic of this proposal; in fact, she would not discuss it. She replied in the words of a Civil War general: "'I tole you twicet, Goddamit, NO.' (Nathan Bedford Forrest) And me *IMP*." Buckley's appeal "to think about the piece, rather than about our respective prides" did nothing to mollify her own pride.[28] So that was the end of her association with *National Review*.

She had already alienated such important conservatives as Russell Kirk. Others, such as Whittaker Chambers, viewed her as a disruptive influence. "I am not 'sound' on Mrs. Paterson," he wrote to Buckley.

> Unlike many others, I go by the general rule that almost anything she says is likely to be wrong. My observation is that she is capable of brilliant insights which merely confuse things the more because they play upon a corpus of notions, which are neither bad nor undesirable: by and large. I think they have almost no relation to reality as it is. She grew up, as she once told me, in an age when men were men. She seems to me to overlook completely the fact that it was those men who prepared our age when pygmies are pygmies.

Chambers objected to Paterson as he objected to Hayek: "These people are admirable heads, good characters, good critics, handsome appreciators—but that was in another country, and the wench is dying."[29]

The quarrel, as always, was about two different perspectives on America. Paterson focused on understanding and restoring the principles of the early republic; Chambers focused on saving the current republic by restoring the Republican Party. If the Party failed to win the election of 1960, he believed, "[a]ll else is lost for about a decade." The future lay not with "the Republican Right" but with "the Republican Left," with Theodore Roosevelt-style progressivism:

> The Republican Party will win the masses, or history will find for it a quiet, uncrowded spot in the potter's field; the grass will grow greenly because no mourning

foot will ever tread it down. Besides, people will dread the spot because of the banshee screams, heard there even at noonday—Isabel Paterson, of course.[30]

An interesting divergence of historical judgments. The Republicans did lose the election of 1960, and all else was, indeed, lost for them, for even longer than a decade. But the masses were eventually won for the Republican Party by the right, not by the left, and it was a right that could not have put itself over without an appeal to free-enterprise individualism and the ideal of the early republic, as understood by Paterson and a few other "banshees."

24

Rays of Light

By now, however, Paterson thought of herself as "an aged tree stump in the landscape, which nobody minds." Mentally, she had not changed, but physically, the old age that she had always feared was upon her. She took some enjoyment in being frank. "I think I look rather like an old witch drawn by Chas Addams (New Yorker). A dumpy little old woman with no teeth!" She did hate old age, but she consoled herself with Mme. de Sévigné's saying that "the only way to avoid that is to die young."[1]

Of course, she was still quite capable of taking care of her own affairs. In May 1959, years of waiting to sell the farm at Rocky Hill finally paid off; she found a couple who wanted to buy. "The young wife," she told Muriel, "'loves an old house.' She has certainly got something to love." Paterson was so happy to get rid of the charming old place that she gave little thought to the next problem— where was she going to live? Eventually, she would go to her house in Greenwich, but the tenants had a lease, and October was the deadline for her to move out of Rocky Hill. Muriel and Ted were eager for her to move in with them, but as late as late August, she was refusing. Finally she agreed. She would stay with the Halls until her own house was ready, but she insisted on paying rent. After all, she was demonstrating that people weren't doomed to exist as paupers just because they lacked an income from Social Security.[2]

Her place in the Halls' comfortable old three-story house at 101 S. Mountain Avenue in Montclair, New Jersey, was a large corner bedroom, second floor, left front. By this time, the household consisted of Muriel; Ted; their children Rebecca and Thomas; John and Mary McLaren, whom the Halls had informally adopted after the death of their mother; and a crotchety Finnish housekeeper, Hilda. Hilda disliked Paterson, viewing her as a person who sat in the living room and read all day, pausing at Christmas to sit in the kitchen and argue about the creeds.[3]

To Ted and Muriel, Pat was the gold in the treasury. They loved and honored her, and they had no difficulty forgiving her fits of temper, which Muriel found easiest to handle by saying, "Oh, Pat!", and going to bed. The rest was sheer profit. It was, Muriel said,

> so much fun, you know. It was just laugh, laugh, laugh. You know, she had that Irish wit. . . . There's no college education that could be anywhere close to what it was like to be with Pat.[4]

In their dialogues with Paterson, the Halls were on the lookout for her to make some slip in her account of the facts; and they were impishly triumphant when she did. But the facts were almost always on her side, and the Halls had the pleasure of being on that side, too. They enjoyed watching pompous visitors airing their theories while she sat calmly watching, "like a lion waiting to spring." She was an education, like it or not. She was especially good with the children, giving Rebecca a refresher course in reading and starting Thomas's education with simple lessons and stories from Uncle Remus. To the little boy, the old philosopher was clever "Br'er Fox."[5]

She arose in the late morning, ate her habitual breakfast of toast and tea and orange juice, then sat by the fire and read. Some afternoons were devoted to experiments with organic gardening in the Halls' back yard, "with spectacular results," according to Muriel. Regarding television as, basically, a purveyor of trash, Paterson confined her viewing to the network news and the party conventions of 1960, which she watched with mordant interest. Kennedy had no attraction for her, and her degree of sympathy for Nixon is indicated by her comments about the mob attack on him during his visit to Venezuela in 1958: she referred to "the Goodwill Mission of our International Boy Scout," remembered "Wilson's messiahship in Europe," and suggested that it would be better for such people to get "chucked out on [their] ear officially."[6]

Her serious thoughts had turned increasingly to old times and old friends. She had formed the intention of writing the story of her life, of the world she had seen.[7] She spent some time looking through her disordered collections of papers and photographs. There was a lot to see: a girl on horseback, a stylish young lady in a business office, an adventurous woman smiling from the wing of a biplane, an aging author sitting at a desk. They were all, somehow, the same person; they all captured light from the same star. The connections would be interesting to develop. She was already trying to recover some of them by reviving relationships with other people.

Through much of the 1950s she had been out of touch with her family, but in 1959 she reestablished communication with her oldest sister, Zelda, who had always been her favorite. The esteem was mutual. Zelda regarded "Mary" as "a person who would only happen once in a hundred years. There were nine of us and she was the only one with any brains." Zelda was running the family farm, which Paterson had secured for her, and she wanted to keep running it, despite her age: "the little farm and the cows are of great interest to me." She was eighty-one years old, but she didn't "give a damn." She looked forward to a visit from her sister.[8]

In early 1959, Paterson wrote to John Chamberlain for the first time in years. He responded with his old kindness and humor, saying that he didn't miss Mary Heaton Vorse (an ancient and unctuous leftwing writer) but he did miss Isabel Paterson. In 1956 she had shared reminiscences with her teacher from the little school on Willow Creek, W. Everard Edmonds. The next year, she surprised Grace Luckhart with a letter and found Lillian Fischer again, after losing her during the world war.[9] And in February 1959 she decided to phone Ayn Rand.

The reason, or the excuse, was *Joyous Gard*. Paterson asked Rand if she would recommend the novel for publication, and Rand agreed to read it. Although Paterson could be bitter and resentful, she obviously suffered from no false pride. She expected Rand not to like her novel, but she would go to see her anyway. On the phone, however, she caught an echo of the old conflict about God, and an echo of Rand's own pride:

Talking to her, I realized how impossible it has become to communicate with her at all. (If she read this sentence she would have a fit!) . . . It's the darnedest thing, but professed atheists (one of whom she is which) are really more bigoted than any adherents of any religion, except perhaps Whirling Dervishes. . . . I fancy she'd spin at 1200 rpm if I mentioned that atheism isn't news to an American; that we've always had a few atheists around, and nobody minds. . . . Oh, I should have mentioned that

it would seem she has decided, or is on the verge of coming to the conclusion, that I
am not rational. That worries me a lot.[10]

So, one afternoon in the early spring, Paterson visited Rand in
her apartment in Manhattan.[11] It was a small, modest place, far
removed from the architectural theories that Rand had celebrated
in *The Fountainhead*; she made as little attempt as Paterson to im-
press anyone with external things. The two women got down to
business. Rand told Paterson that *Joyous Gard* had little prospect
of success; it was too old-fashioned. Paterson countered by suggesting that it might appeal to old-fashioned people, and Rand
thought she detected an aristocratic tone in that remark. Responding to specific questions, Rand tried to praise what she thought she
could praise in the novel, and Paterson responded with pleasure.
But Rand did not resist the temptation to ask what Paterson thought
of *The Fountainhead*, which she still felt Paterson had neglected.
Paterson responded vaguely, deflecting the topic.

Rand then pressed her to say what she thought of *Atlas Shrugged*.
Paterson said that the book had not dealt adequately with the nature of man. She turned to her own theory, not of course comprehended in *Atlas Shrugged*, about man's transcendence of natural
law, as commonly understood. The energy that man derived from
the external world did not correspond to the energy he himself
generated. . . . They were circling around the question of God.
Rand wasn't interested in theories of physics (certainly not any
that verged on theology), and she refused to be drawn into an argument that was already en route to Paterson's destination. She
tried to get the discussion back to what she regarded as foundational premises. But Paterson wouldn't give up on her own idea of
what the foundations should be. She continued even after Rand's
associate Nathaniel Branden arrived to meet her. Branden, largely
excluded from Paterson's notice, would remember her as a "shell.
. . . All the fire had burnt out. Even the bitterness was only, what
should I say? perfunctory."[12] It had been a long afternoon.

Rand and Paterson never met again. Paterson always expressed
admiration for Rand's genius, but she had little to say to anyone
about their final encounter. John Hospers, a distinguished philosopher and, for a while, a close friend of Rand's, remembers her
saying of Paterson that "because of certain disagreements about
religion, they were no longer friends." Asked if Rand was sad about

that, Hospers replied wistfully, "Yes, she was. She had so few friends."[13]

Rand kept urging those friends to read *The God of the Machine*, and she wrote a handsome review of its posthumous republication:

> It is brilliant in the perceptiveness, the incisiveness, the power, the scope of its analysis . . . . It is a sparkling book, with little gems of polemical fire scattered through almost every page, ranging from bright wit to the hard glitter of logic to the quiet radiance of a profound understanding.

She also warned against the book's "touch of mysticism" (i.e., religion).[14]

The connection with Rand would do much to keep Paterson's name in circulation. It was of special importance, given her expertise at repelling the kind of relationships that help most authors spread their influence. After her firing from the *Herald Tribune*, she was pressed to go on circuit for the Columbia Lecture Bureau; she declined.[15] Later, she neglected to do anything to capitalize on her popularity as a *National Review* author. Robert LeFevre, head of the libertarian Freedom School in Colorado Springs, wrote to tell her that her picture occupied an honored place on the wall of his main classroom, and tried repeatedly to contract some kind of alliance with her, or at least get her book back in circulation. She wouldn't cooperate.[16] She was becoming the mystery woman of the libertarian movement. Worse: because of the gradual spread of libertarian ideas, she was no longer the only game in town. If she wouldn't speak and write, other people could. They did.

But no one who had been attracted to Paterson's ideas ever seems to have lost respect for them, or for her, no matter how much she may have surprised or hurt or angered them. A rising generation of libertarian thinkers was also becoming attracted to her, though they knew almost nothing about her personality, which was half the fun. When *New Individualist Review*, a pace-setting libertarian intellectual journal, was founded at the University of Chicago in 1961 (editorial advisors: Milton Friedman, Friedrich Hayek, Richard Weaver), its honor roll of the "eminent publicists and political thinkers" who had transmitted the libertarian faith from an earlier generation included Paterson, Lane, Garrett, Nock, and Chodorov. Three decades later, economist Murray Rothbard, the most influential figure among the radical libertarians of his generation, hailed

The God of the Machine as "by far the most profound" product of the writers "who virtually created the individualist movement during World War II." *The Libertarian Reader*, the studbook of the libertarian movement, enrolls Paterson beside Madison and Hayek and Friedman and Rand—and some others whom she might not have liked so well.[17]

Still more to the point, *The God of the Machine* has been republished several times: in 1964 by Muriel Hall; in 1972 as part of a series, "The Right Wing Individualist Tradition in America," masterminded by Rothbard; in 1983 by Robert Hessen of the Hoover Institution at Stanford University; and in 1993 as a jubilee edition in Transaction Publishers' "Library of Conservative Thought," a series edited by Russell Kirk.[18] "*The God of the Machine* had an immensely strong influence upon me," Kirk had written. "IMP stood out courageously, in defiance of the Lonely Crowd. I thought that everyone must be reading her book and her book-reviews, and could never forget her; but I was mistaken."[19] Yet neither the author nor the book had been forgotten, as Kirk's own memory stood in witness.

Paterson had said at the end of *The God of the Machine* that "it does not appear that men have ever wholly lost any important body of knowledge once attained." Her ideas were not lost; they contributed substantially to the late-twentieth-century revival of American political individualism, and they are constantly being rediscovered by people interested in individual freedom. Borrowing her own vocabulary, we can say that Paterson's ideas became part of the long circuit of intellectual energy that continually reconveys and re-enriches America's idea of itself as a nation whose highest achievement is personal liberty. Although it is now very easy to escape from the pillars of Hercules, Pytheas remains "an exemplar of the free mind."[20]

But from another perspective, equally Patersonian, it is clear that the nature of her accomplishment is not yet fully known. Her distinctive philosophy of individualism, embodied in *The God of the Machine*, presents an intellectual challenge that has not been fully subsumed either by modern libertarianism or by individualist conservatism. And beneath the philosophy lies Paterson's distinctive experience as an individual, that mysterious organization of life that lay, Atlantislike, within her, as it lies in every authentic personality. She said that Pytheas "appears to the imagination, a solitary figure framed in light," though only his name and the general nature of his accomplishment have come down to us.[21] The same might be said of any truly distinctive experience; it can never be fully analyzed, because it can never be re-experienced. Yet it can be imagined. Imagination knows that there was more to Isabel Paterson than this book can tell.

But now it is time to describe her death.

The Halls never suspected that her health was failing; they still thought she was "in command of the world."[22] Nevertheless, she had not been really well for years. Among the most obvious problems were the loss of most of her teeth (to drug-free extractions, by her own demand) and the onset of gout, from which she suffered terribly. Not one to complain, she somehow confined herself to "a little squeak" when her foot was jarred. She laughed about it. "If I know ahead of time I'm going to die," she said, "then I'm going to sit down and eat as much cheese as I want." She still expressed the fear that she would outlive her financial resources, although she continued to do all right in that way, without any aid from the federal government. She looked forward to moving into her pretty house in Greenwich, as soon as the tenants were gone.

Christmas 1960 came on, and Muriel's oldest brother Edward, the Episcopal bishop of West Missouri, prepared to visit with his wife and four children—a big group, even for a big house. After a lifetime of Christmases, many of them lonely, Paterson found the season depressing; she did not look forward to what Muriel describes as the "mob scene" in the house. Muriel advised her to stay just where she was, but if she was really uncomfortable, the Halls would put her up at the Montclair Inn, two blocks away. So she went there and paid a deposit for a two weeks' stay.

Within a few days, Paterson was sick, very sick. Muriel thought it might be pneumonia. So, ignoring Paterson's insistence that she get the remainder of the hotel deposit back, Muriel hurried to bring her home. She lay in her room upstairs, offering "rude" but also "funny" remarks about the episcopal family's conversations, heard through the intervening floor, and making little jokes about herself as a rheumatic caveman who could say nothing better than "ugh, ugh!" A doctor was summoned, discussed her gout, and suggested medicine, which she refused. A couple of mornings later, she could not rise from her bed; she was paralyzed. She could moan, but she could not talk; and she was clearly in distress.

Muriel and young John McLaren, who was in the house that day, had to struggle to help her to the bathroom. A hospital bed was brought in, and a visiting nurse. Paterson remained speechless. On the afternoon of January 10, 1960, a beautiful fall-like day, it was time. Muriel spoke to her about the blooming seasons and happy days in the past, and she seemed to understand. She stopped moaning; but her eyes were no longer in contact with the world. Muriel recalled a remark that she had made: "Frankie Spinelli tells me that after I die, he's going to buy some masses for me . . . I like that idea. I'm not a Catholic, but I think that's a nice idea." She had also said, "At the end of the Roman Empire, and as Christianity was taking hold, the old Romans still worshiped at the old altars, to the old gods. . . . I can understand old Christians still worshiping." So Muriel said, "I know you're not a Christian, but I'm going to read the prayer for the departing soul," and the dying woman seemed to assent.

Turning to the Episcopal prayer book, Muriel read,

> O Almighty God, with whom do live the spirits of just men made perfect, after they are delivered from their earthly prisons; we humbly commend the soul of this thy servant, our dear sister, into thy hands, as into the hands of a faithful Creator . . . .

It was late afternoon. Isabel Paterson was dead.

Muriel had the body clothed in a beautiful pure silk kimono that, she believed, had been a gift to Paterson from Nat Roberts—a memento of her passion for *The Tale of Genji*. Paterson had said, "Now, when I die, you just wrap me in my Lady Macbeth robe," a plain white dressing gown that she had made and that reminded her of Lady Macbeth's "out, damned spot!" But Muriel wanted her to be clothed in her best.

The body was not to be embalmed. Ted, who had reported on the affairs of labor unions, called some union men who had machinery that could open a grave quickly. Paterson had always loved machines ("I should have been a construction boss"), so that would have pleased her. Mr. Cotton, Montclair's black undertaker, provided the simple pine box that she would also have approved.

On January 11, the body was taken to the Welles family plot on the slope behind St. Mary's Episcopal Church in Burlington, New

Jersey.[23] It was a glum, overcast day. The rector, Father Wiles, came out to the grave and performed the committal service. The Halls had decided that the ceremony should be private; Muriel didn't want people who hadn't sought Pat out before she died to come and seek her now.

Muriel and Ted and the children and Muriel's brother Sam stood by the grave. At the end of the service, the sun was setting, but its light suddenly burst through the clouds and transfigured the old church and the nondescript industrial buildings at the bottom of the hill. It was "extraordinary," Muriel thought. It was the world as Isabel Paterson had wanted it to be seen.

Notes

Abbreviations

GB: Garreta Busey
HTB: *New York Herald Tribune "Books"*
IMP: Isabel Paterson
LF: Lillian Fischer
MH: Muriel Hall
T: "Turns With a Bookworm," Paterson's column in *New York Herald Tribune "Books"*
WFB: William F. Buckley, Jr.

Correspondence and Manuscripts

Unless otherwise indicated, these are the locations of correspondence of IMP with the following people:

Lillian Fischer: Isabel Paterson Letters, Manuscripts and Archives Division, The New York Public Library, Astor, Lenox and Tilden Foundations

Burton Rascoe: Rascoe Papers, Rare Book and Manuscript Library, University of Pennsylvania

With the exception of communications to author, other correspondence and manuscripts not referred to specific sources are located in the Paterson Papers and other collections of the Herbert Hoover Presidential Library, West Branch, Iowa.

Chapter 1

1. MH, interview; T 11/27/27.
2. T 9/23/28, T 2/11/34, T 1/17/43.
3. Francis L. Broderick, *Progressivism at Risk: Electing a President in 1912* (New York: Greenwood Press, 1989), provides an excellent guide to the controversies of 1912, emphasizing the "progressive" commitments of all four candidates, even the supposedly conservative Taft. By Broderick's account, which is fair enough, the Democratic candidate, who wanted government action mainly to prevent "restraint of trade," was distinctly the most conservative of the four.

4. Frederick Jackson Turner, "Contributions of the West to American Democracy" (1903), in *The Frontier in American History* (New York: Henry Holt, 1920) 267, 268.
5. T 7/13/47.
6. "Second Aerial Meet at Oakwood Heights" *New York World* (November 3, 1912) 6; "She Gets Nearer the Sky Than Any Other Woman Has," *New York World* (November 6, 1912) 20; "Brown's Altitude Record," *New York Times* (November 6, 1912) 16; "Successful Aviation," *Staten Islander* (November 9, 1912) 9; Isabel Paterson, "A Girl's Flight in Cloudland," *New York World*, Magazine and Story Section (November 14, 1912) 6. We may be sure that the title of that last article was not supplied by the 26-year-old "girl." The *Times* and the *Staten Islander* emphasize that Paterson beat both the record for high flight by a woman and the American passenger-carrying record, which was set (according to the *Times*) on September 30, 1911, by Claude Grahame White and a male passenger, at 3,347 feet.
7. *New York World* (November 6, 1912) 3.
8. *New York World* (November 6, 1912) 6.
9. T 5/16/43, T 7/26/42; Paterson, *The God of the Machine* (New Brunswick NJ: Transaction Publishers, 1993) 232.
10. Quotation: T 4/20/47.
11. Alan Brinkley, *Liberalism and Its Discontents* (Cambridge MA: Harvard University Press, 1998) 277, 296.
12. Elsie McCormick, "She Had To Be a Writer," HTB (February 12, 1933) 7.
13. IMP to Tay Hohoff, August 18, 1959.

Chapter 2

1. Paterson, *The God of the Machine* (New Brunswick, NJ: Transaction Publishers, 1993) 292.
2. T 6/6/26.
3. The standard history of Manitoulin Island is by W. R. Wightman and is appropriately titled *Forever on the Fringe* (Toronto: University of Toronto Press, 1982). See especially 4, 12-16, 44-46, 80-83, 151-52.
4. William Bowerman, "As I Recollect," *Through the Years* [Gore Bay, Ontario] 2 (January 1985) 23; T 11/24/35, T 8/29/48; birth notice, *Manitoulin Expositor* (February 13, 1886) 4. IMP added that she was born "on the banks of . . . the old Bluejay Creek" (T 7/11/26), which flows lazily into Lake Huron at Michael Bay.
5. Gravestones, Stettler-Lakeview Cemetery, Stettler, Alberta (pictures, courtesy Amy Jo Tompkins), "Dilly Tante" [Stanley Kunitz], *Living Authors: A Book of Biographies* (New York: H. W. Wilson, 1931) 317; Stanley Kunitz and Howard Haycraft, *Twentieth Century Authors: A Biographical Dictionary of Modern Literature* (New York: Wilson, 1956) 1082. The last source indicates that Margaret's maiden name was Batty.
6. T 5/2/37.
7. Letters written to IMP on October 14 and 21 by George(?), a boyfriend, are addressed to "Miss M I Bowler"; and there is an envelope, postmarked March 19, 1907, and addressed to "Miss Mary Bowler," that is inscribed on the back, "Mary is-a-belle." In IMP's certificate of naturalization, however, "Isabel" comes first (Zelda Good [sister of IMP], correspondence with IMP; U.S. Certificate of Naturalization 2673592, September 20, 1928.
8. T 2/24/35, T 5/12/29; "Dilly Tante" 318; T 10/14/34; IMP to MH, undated (June 1949); T 9/11/27; "Dilly Tante" 317.

9. T 5/19/40.
10. T 12/1/29; IMP to Nat Roberts, March(?) 1930.
11. Bowerman 24.
12. MH, interviews; Paterson, *Never Ask the End* (New York: William Morrow, 1933) 191, 192; Paterson, *The Golden Vanity* (New York: William Morrow, 1934) 99.
13. Paterson, *If It Prove Fair Weather* (New York: Putnam's, 1940) 50; Paterson, *God of the Machine* 152.
14. Paterson, *Golden Vanity* 99.
15. IMP to Burton Rascoe, December 1931.
16. T 8/9/36.
17. T 12/17/33.
18. T 5/20/34. Although IMP does not connect the anecdote explicitly with her mother, she says that it happened "[a] great many years ago" and involved "the best and kindest and gentlest of women, who had never done anything wrong in her life." She writes of no one else in terms like these.
19. Paterson, *Never Ask the End* 54.
20. IMP to GB, November, 1931(?).
21. IMP in Kunitz and Haycraft 1081; T 10/12/24, T 11/14/43.
22. T 8/15/26. A manitou is a power-spirit. Many of them haunted the Manitoulin (as they did other northern places), but IMP's romantic idea of an Indian Olympus is not confirmed by contemporary anthropology. See Theresa S. Smith, *The Island of the Anishnaabeg: Thunderers and Water Monsters in the Traditional Ojibwe Life-World* (Moscow: University of Idaho Press, 1995).
23. IMP to LF, July 20, 1926; T 8/15/26, T 9/12/26.
24. Minnie Ida Mattson, ed., *The History of Luce County from Its Earliest Recorded Beginning* (Newberry: Luce County Historical Society, 1995) 51, 53.
25. IMP to MH, June 10, 1949; IMP to MH, undated (1958); T 10/18/25; T 9/15/35.
26. T 7/17/38, T 12/29/29.
27. T 10/7/34.
28. T 2/18/34.
29. "Dilly Tante" 317 mentions Utah. At T 10/12/24, IMP discusses the "Southwest" and says that she lived "down that way" when she was "quite small"; she also describes desert flora and fauna, such as the lizards. See also T 1/12/41.
30. T 1/23/27; Jean-Jacques Rousseau, *The Social Contract*, book 4, chapter 8.
31. T 3/8/31; Elsie McCormick, "She Had To Be a Writer," HTB (February 12, 1933) 23. McCormick, who got her information by interviewing IMP, says that the episode took place when she was five years old, which would place it in Michigan; but this dating is questionable. Isabel may have inquired about free silver when she was five, as she said she did (T 12/17/33); but the fame of William Jennings Bryan dates from his Cross of Gold speech at the Democratic convention of 1896, when she was ten, and ten is too late for the little red hen. She told McCormick that she attended only two schools, and there is certain evidence that the second was in Alberta. The first was probably in Utah.
32. IMP to R. S. Henry, received January 4, 1944; T 4/13/30.
33. T 6/6/37; Paterson, review of *The Tragedy of Henry Ford*, by Jonathan Norton Leonard, *Nation* 134 (April 13, 1932) 436.
34. T 6/6/37. The staff of the Latter Day Saints' genealogical library in Cardston finds no record of Mormon baptisms in the Bowler family. When IMP's mother died, the service was conducted by an Anglican priest, "Mr. Sterbert the English church minister" (Zelda Good to IMP, October 28, 1933).

35. James G. MacGregor, *A History of Alberta* (Edmonton: Hurtig, 1972) 174; T 7/2/ 44, T 11/1/36, T 2/10/29, T 7/26/36; Bowerman 23-24.

36. T 7/2/44; MacGregor, esp. 20-22, 110-12; Paterson, *Never Ask the End* 242; T 9/ 23/28.

37. T 7/2/44, T 11/10/35.

38. IMP to MH, June 29, 1951. By coincidence, as IMP goes on to say, one of her own employers, a North Dakota banker, discovered Beresford at the train station in Fargo "on a zero day with no overcoat when he (the banker) happened to be carrying an extra overcoat for some reason." He didn't recognize Beresford, but he "tried to think of a tactful approach to a stranger in order to give him the spare coat." Unfortunately, "then the man got on the train, so the occasion passed. And that was the train that was wrecked, and by photos published my boss recognized that the object of his intended charity was Lord Delaval Beresford, who left an estate of two or three millions. Romances of the Peerage."

39. T 6/6/37, T 5/13/45.

40. Paterson, review of *I'd Live It Over*, by Flora Cloman, HTB (May 4, 1941) 3; T 6/ 6/37, T 10/7/34.

41. T 11/27/27, T 3/9/30. One of the books she read was *Robbery Under Arms*, by Rolf Boldrewood (Thomas Browne). It concerned a romantic outlaw named Captain Starlight who rode a beautiful horse named Rainbow. She read it when she had been living in the wilds of Alberta for about three years (T 2/20/38).

42. T 4/27/30.

43. IMP to GB, undated (December 1934); IMP to LF, January 3, 1931. The literal farm had changed a good deal; the Bowlers had moved at least twice in the intervening period, but the family remained the same.

44. IMP to LF, June 5, 1931.

45. T 9/11/32, T 1/5/41, T 11/24/40, T 11/1/36; interview, MH. The Paterson Papers at the Hoover Presidential Library include a number of pictures of IMP as an adult on horseback in Albertan landscapes.

46. T 4/20/30, T 8/30/42, T 9/13/42, T 9/16/34, T 7/25/43, T 3/23/47, T 7/26/36, T 11/ 13/38. IMP's preference for the paws of the bear was frequently, though not universally, shared by other frontier people; see Tracy I. Storer and Lloyd P. Tevis, Jr., *California Grizzly* (Berkeley: University of California Press, 1996) 190-91.

47. T 10/26/30, T 5/3/36.

48. T 3/20/27, T 4/11/37.

49. T 8/18/35, Paterson, "The New Morality—If Any," *McNaught's Monthly* 5 (February 1926) 90, T 3/2/47, T 8/18/35.

50. T 6/6/26; Hugh A. Dempsey, "Launching Alberta History," Alberta History 45 (Winter 1997) 2-8; W. Everard Edmonds to IMP, March 12, 1956, March 31, 1956. IMP said that she had been "educated in the public schools of Mountain View and Cardston, Alberta" (Kunitz and Haycraft 1082), a phrase that may refer either to two successive schools or to one school in the general district of the two nearby communities. At T 6/19/32, she says that the "log schoolhouse where [she] got her education, such as it is," stood "ten or fifteen miles" from the NE slope of Chief Mountain; this distance would take in Mountain View but not Cardston.

51. T 12/10/39, T 12/3/39, T 1/17/26, T 3/20/27, T 12/23/34; McCormick 23.

52. T 3/16/30.

53. T 10/27/29.

54. T 8/9/31, T 7/15/34, T 3/23/30.

55. T 6/21/31, T 6/14/36, T 8/2/36.

56. T 8/2/36.

57. T 12/21/41.
58. T 1/4/42, T 9/29/40.
59. T 9/29/40; Mark Schorer, *Sinclair Lewis: An American Life* (New York: McGraw-Hill, 1961) 9-10; Paterson, review of Cloman 3; T 7/7/40.
60. T 9/2/45, T 10/19/30, T 7/3/38, T 2/22/31, T 7/15/34. IMP never mentioned what the paper was, what the contributions were, or whether they were printed.
61. T 12/13/42, T 7/1/34.

Chapter 3

1. T 3/20/027, T 5/12/35; IMP to GB, undated (December 1934). She told Elsie McCormick ("She Had To Be a Writer," HTB [February 12, 1933] 23) that she was seventeen, which probably indicates a date of very early 1904.
2. T 2/14/32; anon., "'Books' Covers the World of Books," *Publishers' Weekly* 136 (September 30, 1939) 1341.
3. T 7/24/38, T 3/3/35, T 8/10/41, T 12/5/43; IMP to MH, October 22, 1957.
4. McCormick 23; T 7/24/38, T 2/1/42, T 8/10/41. Yet information that IMP supplied to one source has her working "with a firm of American investment bankers" after she had "a clerical job with the Canadian Pacific Railroad" ("Dilly Tante" [Stanley Kunitz], *Living Authors: A Book of Biographies* [New York: H. W. Wilson, 1931] 317; similar information in Stanley J. Kunitz and Howard Haycraft, *Twentieth Century Authors: A Biographical Dictionary of Modern Literature* [New York: H. W. Wilson, 1956] 1082). We know from her story about the sad end of Lord Delaval Beresford that she was employed at some time by at least one North Dakota banker (chapter 2, note 38). Reference to two North Dakotan "bosses, partners . . . middle-aged bankers, and presumably conservative" appears at T 11/19/44. The "almost" comment is at T 12/17/33, where, in a bizarre slip, IMP makes the job contemporaneous with the organization of "the Federal Reserve Board," which occurred in 1913, almost a decade after she started working.
5. The date is established by IMP's friend Grace Luckhart in a letter to MH, February 6, 1961.
6. T 2/3/35.
7. On Calgary in the early days and Bennett's role in it, see Ernest Watkins, *R. B. Bennett: A Biography* (London: Secker and Warburg, 1963) esp. 34-47.
8. Watkins, *Bennett* 41-42; T 8/10/30.
9. Beaverbrook, William Maxwell Aitken, 1st Baron, *Friends: Sixty Years of Intimate Personal Relations with Richard Bedford Bennett* (London: Heinemann, 1959) 25; Paterson, *The God of the Machine* (New Brunswick NJ: Transaction Publishers, 1993) 116.
10. T 8/14/32. For the flirtation: Sam Welles to IMP, May 3, 1949, recalling her report.
11. Larry A. Glassford, *Reaction and Reform: The Politics of the Conservative Party under R. B. Bennett, 1927-1938* (Toronto: University of Toronto Press, 1992) 77; Watkins, *Bennett* 256-63.
12. T 8/14/32; IMP to R. S. Henry, received May 16, 1945, May 23, 1945; MH to author, October 28, 2000. The young friend was Muriel Welles, later Muriel Welles Hall.
13. T 6/6/26. According to a letter addressed to IMP at Calgary in 1907 (? to IMP, March 19, 1907), she was with the company at that time; and she was listed as office help ("steno") for the company in *Henderson's City of Calgary Directory* for 1908. She may not have been directly involved in sales; she may simply have worked in the office (cf. Paterson, *Never Ask the End* [New York: William Morrow, 1933] 228). I am grateful to Amy Jo Tompkins for references in the *Directory*.

14. T 11/1/36, T 3/10/35.
15. IMP to LF, January 5, 1932; T 7/24/32, T 1/6/35.
16. T 2/22/31. I assume that the Mrs. Booth who figures constantly in correspondence of 1911 from Grace Luckhart to IMP is the same woman mentioned in T 2/22/31 and IMP to GB, December 17, 1928. In that letter, IMP confesses to have been so green that for years she didn't know what people meant when they "gossiped" about the two women's friendship.
17. T 4/16/39.
18. T 2/22/31, T 6/21/31, T 6/6/26. There was no Calgary "weekly" that published short stories.
19. T 6/25/33.
20. T 9/22/35; IMP to GB, November(?) 1931; T 1/16/38, T 2/6/38.
21. Marriage certificate, Paterson Papers; T 2/22/31. *Henderson's Calgary Directory* for 1910 lists Kenneth as an agent for McCutcheon Brothers, a real estate company; the 1909 directory lists him as a traveler for Donnelly, Watson, and Brown, Ltd.
22. IMP to MH, February 16, 1957; W. L. Hamm to IMP, June 27, 1918.
23. IMP, U.S. tax returns for 1956 and 1957. In earlier years, when the forms seemed to require information on this point, she was "married" but "separated."
24. Gertrude Vogt, to author, July 18, 1989.
25. IMP to GB, undated (December 1934).
26. Paterson, *Never Ask the End* 226, 63, 231; T 7/16/33.
27. Paterson, *The Magpie's Nest* (New York: John Lane, 1917) 295. Like Kenneth Paterson, the husband in this novel is also an adept of the guitar (91).
28. Gertrude Vogt, interview; T 6/20/37. T 11/16/24 refers to a honeymoon hike around Crowsnest Pass in the Canadian Rockies.
29. The telegram does not record its year. Its direction to Isabel Paterson at the *World* in Vancouver places it in the same period as two envelopes addressed to her at that place and inscribed in the hand used to write the "Pat" letters. These envelopes are postmarked January 9, 1911, and September 17, 1911. The latter postmark matches a letter dated "Sept 17." The letter originally enclosed in the January 9 envelope has not been found.
30. Grace Luckhart to IMP, early 1911(?); late January or early February 1911; and 1911(?).
31. IMP to GB, late July 1933 (see note 28, above).
32. IMP to MH, March 1, 1951; T 10/1/33.
33. Paterson, *Magpie's Nest* 187, 219.
34. T 5/30/37.
35. McCormick 23; T 11/1/36, T 5/30/37.
36. McCormick 23. The *Inland Herald* is not specifically named here, but the reported sequence of jobs makes the identification.
37. T 6/6/26.
38. Paterson(?), "A Splendid Citizenship," and "The Fight," *Spokane Inland Herald* (July 6, 1910) 4. These editorials are written in a common style, which is by no means perfect but is distinctly superior to that of the fight editorial that the paper carried the day before ("The Sane and Insane Fourth," *Inland Herald* [July 5, 1910] 4), an article less concerned with the big fight than with safe use of fireworks. Among the possibly Patersonian touches in the July 6 editorials is a reference to Spokane's having gotten through the fight without deserting "the even tenor of its way"—an allusion (to Gray's *Elegy Written in a Country Churchyard*) that could easily have been supplied by IMP's extensive reading.

39. T 11/1/36. IMP told McCormick (23) that she was "placed among the feature writers" within "a month or two."
40. Editorial, "Single-Tax City," *Vancouver World* (April 27, 1911) 6.
41. See such editorials as "Reciprocity," *Vancouver World* (April 27, 1911) 6; and "The Anti-Reciprocity Absurdity" (April 29, 1911) 6. See chapter 4, below, for discussion of *The Shadow Riders*.
42. "The Disability of Sex," *Vancouver World* (April 29, 1911) 6.
43. Paterson, "Postscripts," *Vancouver World* (April 8, 1911) 13.
44. Paterson, "Postscripts," *Vancouver World* (April 15, 1911) 3.
45. Paterson, "Postscripts," *Vancouver World* (May 13, 1911) 5; (April 29, 1911) 3.
46. Paterson, "A Question of Values," *Vancouver World* (April 29, 1911) 3. In 1933, Paterson detailed the difficult relations of people and cattle in an account of a Bowler family cattle drive (T 11/12/33).
47. In a record of IMP's conversation on the weekend of July 27, 1958, MH wrote, "Pat was fired from first job—on the Sunday World. Says it was fair enough, that she wasn't any good at the kind of things she was assigned" (MH, "Pat 1886," typescript). There is some misunderstanding here: IMP worked on the *Vancouver World* and the *New York World*, but neither of them was the *Sunday World*, and neither of them was her first job, even on a newspaper. She was fired from *something*.
48. T 11/1/36. The only documentary evidence about when this may have happened is the envelope for Kenneth Paterson's letter of September 17, 1911, which is addressed to Isabel at the *World*. The date is four months after her column and short stories ceased to appear in the *World* (May 27, 1911). But Kenneth may not have been keeping up with her address.
49. T 11/1/36.
50. Paterson, *Magpie's Nest* 194; T 9/11/32, T 11/1/36.
51. Paterson, *Magpie's Nest* 194; IMP to Mary Welles, September 10, 1936; T 6/28/31; IMP to Burton Rascoe, late 1933(?); T 8/2/31.
52. T 3/2/30.
53. At T 9/10/33, she recalls being "a proud dramatic critic on the Pacific Coast." Information published in the *Bookman* in 1916 makes her "an editorial writer" for the *Inland Herald* and the *World* but a "dramatic critic" for the *Province* ("Chronicles and Comment," *Bookman* 43 [May 1916] 242). At T 6/6/26 she mentions writing "a critical study of an Al Woods farce" for the *Province*. In a letter to LF, October 17, 1932, she says that for "a couple of years" she "did the theaters for a paper in Vancouver." Yet the two years, more or less, were probably divided between the *World* and the *Province*: she published columns under her byline in the *World* in April and May 1911, moved to the *Province* some time after, and resided in New York at the time of her airplane flight in November 1912.
54. T 6/9/35.
55. T 8/22/43, T 10/7/34.
56. T 6/6/26; Paterson, *Magpie's Nest* 198.

Chapter 4

1. T 2/15/31.
2. Obituary, *New York Herald Tribune*, January 11, 1961. The obituary, which was sent to the *Trib* by IMP's friend Ted Hall, undoubtedly transmits some of her memories. But it is not wholly accurate. It reports, for instance, that IMP "denied the existence of Social Security . . . tore up her card and refused to participate in its benefits." Only the last of those three statements is true.

3. "Dilly Tante" [Stanley Kunitz], *Living Authors: A Book of Biographies* (New York: H. W. Wilson, 1931) 318; Stanley J. Kunitz and Howard Haycraft, *Twentieth Century Authors: A Biographical Dictionary of Modern Literature* (New York: H. W. Wilson, 1956) 1082. Letters are addressed to Paterson at *Hearst's Magazine* by J. W. H. Graf, August 21, 1914; by D[orothy], August 29, 1914; and by M. Jones(?), September 25, 1915.
4. IMP to Burton Rascoe, December(?) 1931; T 6/6/26; "Dilly Tante" 318; Anon., "You Meet Such Interesting People," *Publisher's Weekly* 155 (March 12, 1949) 1250.
5. T 12/11/32. In early 1913, IMP was living at The Alcazar, 215 Manhatttan Avenue (address of letter from D[orothy] Eldridge to IMP, March 9, 1913). That may have been her best address.
6. T 10/30/32, T 6/4/33, T 11/5/33, T 1/23/38. After IMP became a well-known personality, she did her best to raise money for the library's circulation department.
7. T 1/17/43, T 6/7/31.
8. T 2/9/36; interview, Muriel Hall; IMP to R. S. Henry, received July 20, 1948; IMP to R. S. Henry, received January 4, 1944. IMP found the Lippincott plane "enormous" but the pilots "handsome" and the trip accordingly "pleasant" (T 2/9/36).
9. Paterson, *The Golden Vanity* (New York: William Morrow, 1934) 90; Elsie McCormick, "She Had To Be a Writer," HTB (February 12, 1933) 23; T 2/22/31, T 9/8/40. IMP also remembered that later, when she was working in Vancouver, she still did not "suspect [she] should some day be writing novels" (T 9/10/33). This may mean that she refused to regard the earlier attempt as serious. Perhaps "writing," however, should be read as "publishing." A letter that seems to have been written to her after she had lived in Vancouver for a while refers to her knowledge of how long it takes to write a story; another asks her, "Have you heard further about your book"—a likely reference to the first novel she submitted for publication (Grace Luckhart to IMP, two letters, early 1911 [?]). That novel may, of course, have been a later book than the one she wrote "to please a dear friend."
10. In a letter to GB, c. April 18, 1931, IMP confesses to having written a bad novel about her family but does not identify its date. At T 4/13/30, she confesses to having written a novel about her family's pioneer experience. I assume that these are the same books.
11. T 12/2/28.
12. Paterson, "The Absentee Novelists of Canada," *Bookman* 55 (April 1922) 133, 136.
13. T 2/22/31; IMP to GB, c. April 18, 1931.
14. Paterson, review of *Such Is My Beloved*, by Morley Callaghan, HTB (February 18, 1934) 4; IMP to GB, c. April 18, 1931.
15. T 3/25/34. Here IMP maintains that all civilization is "an insistence on values," and hence "a great, continuous romantic effort."
16. T 10/15/33.
17. T 11/9/30, T 4/8/34.
18. William Morrow to IMP, September 14, 1914; Henry Holt & Co. to J. D. C. Rogers, September 24, 1914; T 12/20/31; Sinclair Lewis to IMP, December 24, 1914. The manuscript that Morrow saw was still unfinished (T 2/14/26).
19. T 10/19/24, T 12/20/31; IMP to Burton Rascoe, December 1931; T 12/1/35. In 1941, IMP was still at pains to praise Lewis, even when she had to admit that she disagreed with almost everything he had said in a speech she listened to (T 12/7/41). IMP, who hated speeches, paid tribute to him simply by attending.

20. G. P. Putnam's Sons to IMP, June 2, 1915; Emma Pope to IMP, February 8, February 11, 1915.

21. Paterson, *The Magpie's Nest* (New York: John Lane, 1917) 9.

22. Paterson, *Magpie's Nest* 302. This is one of the few places in IMP's work where the protagonist's father comes off well—although the pioneer father's place in the novel is very slight.

23. Paterson, *The Shadow Riders* (New York: John Lane, 1916).

24. T 2/12/33. On "corruption in the administration of law" versus "the presumptuous tyranny of the laws themselves," see T 7/3/32.

25. Editorial, "Single-Tax City," *Vancouver World* (April 27, 1911) 6. The *World* was full of Georgeite material.

26. T 10/23/32; Anon., review of Paterson, *The Magpie's Nest*, *New York Times Book Review* (April 15, 1917) 137-38; IMP to LF, October 3, 1924; T 6/6/26. Amy Jo Tompkins, *"Investigating Civilisation': The City as Frontier in the Early Prairie Novels of Isabel Paterson* (thesis, Memorial University of Newfoundland, June 2001) 4-6 surveys the reviews.

27. Tompkins, esp. 7, 60-61; H. L. Mencken, "A Soul's Adventures," *The Smart Set* 49 (June, 1916) 151.

28. IMP to LF, October 3, 1924; T 4/8/34, T 11/9/30.

29. Cited in Alta May Coleman to IMP, 1916.

30. Letters addressed to IMP in San Francisco by W. L. Hamm, December 20, 1917, and June 27, 1918; *Crocker-Langley San Francisco Directory* (1918) 1330; T 9/ 11/32. Earlier and later annual editions of the *Directory* fail to mention IMP.

31. T 10/9/32; IMP in Kunitz and Haycraft 1081.

32. IMP to LF, June 5, 1931; T 8/13/33.

33. MH, interview.

34. IMP to Burton Rascoe, December(?) 1931; IMP to R. S. Henry, received January 29, 1944; IMP to LF, October 6, 1938.

35. T 10/22/33; IMP to MH, March 5, 1955.

36. T 8/18/35, T 3/26/33.

37. Anon., "'Books' Covers the World of Books," *Publishers' Weekly* (September 39, 1939) 1341.

38. T 12/28/30.

39. Francis Fisher Dyer, "'Why a Greek Colonnade to Lincoln?' Ask American Architects," *New York Herald* (May 28, 1912); T 6/13/26, T 2/27/27, T 9/6/31. IMP says that she worked for Borglum for eighteen months. She was still working for him in early 1922 when she found a job with Burton Rascoe (Rascoe, *We Were Interrupted* [Garden City, NY: Doubleday, 1947] 141.

40. Paterson, *The God of the Machine* (New Brunswick NJ: Transaction Publishers, 1993) 123-24; T 6/13/26.

41. Rascoe 26, 143, 15.

42. Rascoe 140-42 offers the account of his first meetings with IMP.

43. Rascoe 141-42. When this account was published, IMP asked Rascoe why he had inflated her salary, and he replied, "Because nobody would believe what it really was." She admitted, however, that she "made something extra on space rates" for her writing (T 10/12/47). The 1922 date is supplied by IMP to LF, June 5, 1931.

44. Rascoe 142.

45. Burton Rascoe to IMP, late June 1932.

46. Rascoe 136-40; IMP to Burton Rascoe, 1930.

47. Paterson, *God of the Machine* 238-39, 248-49.

48. Rascoe 142-43.

49. T 1/12/36.
50. IMP to LF, June 5, 1931; Rascoe 143.
51. IMP to LF, June 5, 1931.
52. T 9/5/26; IMP to LF, June 5, 1931.
53. T 9/5/26; IMP to LF, June 5, 1931.
54. September 21, 1924, through January 30, 1949.

Chapter 5

1. T 9/26/26, T 2/9/41.
2. T 2/9/41, T 3/18/34, T 12/11/32; Paterson, review of *Cheerfulness Breaks In*, by Angela Thirkell, HTB (February 23, 1941) 2.
3. T 8/2/42. Cerf sent her a note the next day: "The pictures were lovely" (Bennett Cerf to IMP, August 3, 1942).
4. In the late 1920s and early 1930s, she reviewed books twice a week in the daily editions (IMP to LF, June 5, 1931).
5. T 9/21/24, T 1/10/43.
6. T 1/24/37, T 4/5/31.
7. Burton Rascoe, *We Were Interrupted* (Garden City NY: Doubleday, 1947) 146; T 4/8/34, T 6/14/36.
8. T 2/19/33; Paterson, review of Louis Paul, *The Wrong World*, HTB (November 27, 1938) 2; T 9/23/28; Rascoe, *We Were Interrupted* 145-50.
9. T 7/10/32, T 8/2/36, T 3/17/40, T 7/24/32, T 3/29/42, T 12/3/39, T 10/28/34, T 4/29/34, T 10/15/33.
10. Finley Peter Dunne, *Mr. Dooley: In Peace and in War* (Boston: Small, Maynard and Company, 1899) 82-83.
11. Paterson, "Native-Born Americanism," review of Albert Jay Nock, *Free Speech and Plain Language*, HTB (October 24, 1937) 3.
12. T 7/4/26.
13. T 9/7/41, T 6/8/41.
14. T 6/14/25 (a reference to Thorstein Veblen, *The Theory of the Leisure Class*), T 8/1/26, T 1/20/29, T 12/9/45, T 2/3/46.
15. Paterson, review of *Dead Lovers Are Faithful Lovers*, by Frances Newman, HTB (May 6, 1928) 3; T 1/1/39, T 11/20/40, T 4/13/41.
16. T 12/6/31, T 10/18/25, T 11/14/37, T 1/22/33, T 10/14/34, T 6/12/32.
17. Paterson, "A Civilized Survey of This Age of Decay," review of *Memoirs of a Superfluous Man*, by Albert Jay Nock, HTB (September 19, 1943) 6.
18. T 5/3/36.
19. T. S. Stribling's *The Sound Wagon* is a good example. It was a novelistic attack on the New Deal by an important author, but IMP detested it: its style was bad, its plotting was bad, its metaphysics was bad (unsound on the free will question); it was a bad book (Paterson, review of *The Sound Wagon*, by T. S. Stribling, HTB [December 29, 1935] 3).
20. Paterson, "Mr. Forster, Cultured, Tolerant, Urbane," review of *Abinger Harvest*, by E. M. Forster, HTB (May 31, 1936) 6; T 4/11/48, T 11/25/34. IMP sent Russell's book as a gift to at least one close friend, praising it and affixing no warning label (IMP to LF, March(?) 1935).
21. T 1/23/38; Jonathan Swift, "Verses on the Death of Dr. Swift," *Gulliver's Travels and Other Writings*, ed. Louis A. Landa (Boston: Houghton Mifflin, 1960) 473.
22. T 11/2/41, T 1/23/38; Richard Kluger, *The Paper: The Life and Death of the "New York Herald Tribune"* (New York: Alfred A. Knopf, 1986) 324.

23. Swift 472; T 1/23/38, T 9/22/35, T 2/13/38.
24. T 6/24/34, T 10/1/33.
25. T 3/23/41.
26. Upton Sinclair, *Money Writes!* (New York: Albert & Charles Boni, 1927) 3, 50; T 11/27/27; Upton Sinclair to IMP, February 7, 1928; Sinclair to IMP, undated.
27. T 6/15/30, T 7/13/30.
28. T 1/17/32.
29. T 2/7/32, T 7/23/33, T 10/8/33.
30. T 5/4/30; Paterson, "The Critical Blues," review of *The Literary Mind*, by Max Eastman, HTB (November 22, 1931) 2.
31. Paterson, "Critical Blues" 2.
32. T 2/7/32.
33. IMP to Burton Rascoe, July 1933 - January 1934.
34. T 10/4/36, T 12/7/41.
35. IMP to GB, May(?) 1931; T 2/8/31; Paterson, review of *Such Is My Beloved*, by Morley Callaghan, HTB (February 18, 1934) 4.
36. T 11/16/30.
37. IMP said that she would write a book of literary criticism, but not until she could avoid devoting a chapter to Joyce or Stein (T 7/19/31). She thought that Joyce's work might "not endure because at least a part of its impressiveness depends upon sheer novelty, verbal twists equivalent to the 'conceits' which enlivened Elizabethan literature but perished in the excess of [John Lyly's] 'Euphues.'" She would "leave the verdict on Joyce to those who can read him" (T 1/28/34).
38. Willa Cather, "The Novel Démeublé" (1922) in *Not Under Forty* (1936), *Stories, Poems, and Other Writings* (New York: Library of America, 1992) 834-37.
39. T 11/18/34. IMP met Mrs. Sunday's alter ego, Miss Stein, at a party given for her by Bennett Cerf on October 31, 1934 (T 11/11/34), and found herself in luck: "She doesn't talk as she writes."
40. T 8/28/32, T 5/6/45.
41. T 2/12/39, T 2/21/43, T 12/27/36, T 1/20/29, T 2/19/33, T 11/16/30.
42. T 5/14/33.
43. T 5/19/29, T 5/28/39, T 5/14/39; G. P. Brett, Jr., to IMP, September 30, 1946; IMP to G. P. Brett, Jr., October 9, 1946; T 5/18/47. A similar censorship-defense episode happened years before (T 5/14/39).
44. T 12/29/35, T 6/25/33.
45. T 7/12/36.
46. T 3/27/32, T 3/13/32; Irene and Allen Cleaton, *Books and Battles: American Literature: 1920-1930* (Boston: Houghton Mifflin, 1937) 130.
47. For a startlingly long list of important contributors, see Lewis Gannett, "A Quarter Century of a Weekly Book Review . . . and of the World," HTB (September 25, 1949) 4-5.
48. Kluger 262. The *Trib*'s circulation, which does not include that of *"Books"* sold separately, was about 70% of the *New York Times*', putting it in second place among New York papers.
49. Mary McCarthy and Margaret Marshall, "Our Critics, Right or Wrong," *Nation* 141 (December 18, 1935) 718.
50. Frances Newman to Hudson Strode, March 10, 1928, *Frances Newman's Letters*, ed. Hansell Baugh (New York: Liveright, 1929) 333.
51. Cleaton and Cleaton 130; Ishbel Ross, *Ladies of the Press: The Story of Women in Journalism by an Insider* (New York: Harper, 1936) 405; Anon., "'Books' Covers the World of Books," *Publisher's Weekly* 136 (September 30, 1939) 1341.

52. Ross 405. See also the interview with IMP reported in "How the Critic Sells Books," *Publisher's Weekly* 122 (December 3, 1932) 2103.
53. T 6/13/26; Ford Madox Ford, *The Last Post* (New York: Literary Guild, 1928) v-ix.
54. Frances Newman to John W. Crawford, November 27, 1926, *Letters* 226; John O'Hara to Thomas O'Hara, August 16, 1934, *Selected Letters of John O'Hara*, ed. Matthew J. Bruccoli (New York: Random House, 1978) 94. The novel was *Appointment in Samarra*, and O'Hara's fears were misplaced: IMP mildly approved (T 9/2/34).
55. Ross 405.

Chapter 6

1. IMP to LF, December 26, 1924.
2. IMP to LF, July 20, 1926; MH, interview; T 3/11/34, T 3/18/34; Gertrude Vogt (who worked in the *"Books"* office), interview, speaking of IMP in the 1930s and 1940s; T 4/4/26.
3. Certificate of Naturalization 2673592, Isabel Paterson; Ishbel Ross, *Ladies of the Press: The Story of Women in Journalism by an Insider* (New York: Harper, 1936) 405; Elsie McCormick, "She Had to be a Writer," HTB (February 12, 1933) 7; T 7/25/26.
4. Eleanor Perényi, interview; McCormick 7; MH, Gertrude Vogt, John McLaren, interviews.
5. Elinor Wylie, review of Paterson, *The Fourth Queen*, HTB (April 11, 1926) 1; Burton Rascoe, "Contemporary Reminiscences," *Arts and Decoration* 25 (June 1926) 49, 80; McCormick 7.
6. Ross 406; McCormick 7; MH, interview.
7. Eleanor Perényi, interview; Ross 406; T 3/27/38, T 1/22/39. At some point, she also formed the custom of cutting her own hair.
8. T 7/4/26, commenting on observations by John Farrar, "The Gossip Shop," *Bookman* 63 (July 1926) 618.
9. Interviews, MH; T 5/15/27, T 9/10/39; IMP to GB, December 1931 or January 1932; IMP to LF, May 1, 1933; T 11/15/36, T 2/23/41, T 2/11/34; Ross 406.
10. IMP to LF, April 1938 (misdated "1933"); see also IMP to LF, October 17, 1932.
11. Paterson, *The Golden Vanity* (New York: William Morrow, 1934) 229; T 4/11/26; IMP to Mary Welles, September 10, 1936; MH, interviews; T 6/2/40. In 1954, IMP estimated her last visit to a theatre as "about 25 years" before (IMP to MH, August 20, 1954).
12. T 6/2/29, T 6/16/29, T 1/29/33, T 10/20/35, T 12/22/35. Tugboats first show up in IMP's column on February 17, 1929, when she says that she once spent all Sunday on a tugboat and would love to do it again. The Moran company immediately offered her another ride (T 3/3/29), and a lifelong friendship was formed.
13. 508 W. 34th Street, was demolished in the 1990s.
14. IMP to GB, May(?) 1931; Ross 406, cf. Paterson, *Golden Vanity* 36; IMP to LF, February 16, 1926; T 9/14/30, T 2/16/30.
15. IMP to GB, May(?) 1931; MH, interview; T 7/5/31, T 7/26/31, T 1/3/32; IMP to LF, November 19, 1931, January 5, 1932; Isa Glenn to IMP, April 10, 1932.
16. McCormick 7; T 8/9/31; MH to author, October 31, 2000.
17. T 12/16/34, T 12/29/35; MH, interview; T 5/19/40. By 1940, she had increased her speed from an earlier 1,800 words in sixty minutes (T 9/16/28).
18. T 10/1/33, T 4/2/33, T 6/20/26.

19. Ross 405; T 5/8/32. Lack of tea was a perpetual complaint; see also T 3/20/38, T 3/27/38, T 2/12/39.
20. T 11/8/25, T 1/17/37; Ross 405.
21. IMP to LF, October 17, 1932.
22. T 3/5/33.
23. IMP to LF, January 20, 1925. On her abstemious drinking habits, see also T 5/29/ 38, T 2/12/39.
24. IMP to LF, December 26, 1924; Paterson, review of *Exile's Return*, by Malcolm Cowley, HTB (May 27, 1934), 3; T 5/13/34, T 11/5/33, T 3/11/34, T 4/5/31.
25. IMP to LF, July 28, 1925, July 20, 1926, December 26, 1924, February 16, 1926; Burton Rascoe, *We Were Interrupted* (Garden City, NY: Doubleday, 1947) 242; Lee Meader obituary, *New York Times* (February 15, 1930) 17; "H. L. Meader Left $1,136,412," *New York Times* (August 13, 1930) 11; IMP to LF, May 1, 1930.
26. Paterson, *Golden Vanity* 181, 182.
27. T 7/16/33, T 1/12/41; GB to MH, December 28, 1962.
28. Paterson, *The Magpie's Nest* (New York: John Lane, 1917) 198; IMP to LF, November 2, 1927; T 7/24/32.
29. T 2/18/34.
30. IMP to LF, April 14, 1931; Rascoe, *We Were Interrupted* 140; T 7/9/33.
31. IMP to GB, c. March 29, 1930; Thomas Maeder, "Afterword," *The Decline and Fall of Practically Everybody*, by Will Cuppy, ed. Fred Feldkamp (Boston: Nonpareil-David R. Godine, 1984) 235. Maeder's biography of Cuppy (ms., unpublished) has also assisted me in understanding its difficult and elusive subject.
32. Rascoe, *We Were Interrupted* 143-44; Will Cuppy, *How to be a Hermit, or A Bachelor Keeps House* (New York: Liveright, 1929) v; IMP to LF, November 19, 1931; Will Cuppy, *How to Tell Your Friends from the Apes* (New York: Liveright, 1931) 5, 12; Cuppy pinch-hitting for IMP at T 9/1/29.
33. IMP to GB, c. March 29, 1930; MH, interview; Maeder 238-39; T 6/4/33.
34. IMP, memorandum of conversations; IMP to GB, late 1929(?).
35. IMP to LF, March 26, 1934; Paterson, *Golden Vanity* 357.
36. Cuppy, *Decline* 19 (on the Paterson-Hatshepsut association, see R. S. Henry to IMP, April 6, 1957); Paterson, review of *The Journal of Arnold Bennett: 1921-1928*, HTB (June 4, 1933) 3.

Chapter 7

1. Paterson, *The Road of the Gods* (New York: Horace Liveright, 1930) 7.
2. Isabel Paterson, *The Singing Season: A Romance of Old Spain* (New York: Boni and Liveright, 1924) 289. Cf. Revelation 6:14.
3. Paterson, review of *Ladies Whose Bright Eyes*, by Ford Madox Ford, HTB (May 26, 1935) 6.
4. Sinclair Lewis, *Babbitt* (New York: Harcourt Brace, 1922) 64.
5. IMP to LF, April 23, 1925.
6. IMP to Burton Rascoe, November 14, 1924; November 26, 1924.
7. Paterson, *The Fourth Queen* (New York: Boni and Liveright, 1926) 113.
8. Paterson, review of *Queen Elizabeth*, by J. E. Neale, HTB (February 11, 1934) 5. In this article, IMP also comments favorably on Elizabeth's understanding of money and her financially conservative way of dealing with political difficulties. IMP elsewhere calls Elizabeth "a shrew of genius" (Paterson, review of *In My End Is My Beginning*, by Maurice Baring, HTB [November 8, 1931] 4).

378 The Woman and the Dynamo

9. IMP to LF, July 20, 1926, and June 8, 1926; Stuart Sherman to IMP, in Jacob Zeitlin and Homer Woodbridge, *Life and Letters of Stuart P. Sherman* (New York: Farrar & Rinehart, 1929) 795; T 7/24/27; Harry M. Hitchcock to IMP with IMP's annotations, February 27, 1929; IMP to GB, November 1929; IMP to Burton Rascoe, December 1929; IMP to GB, January or February 1930; IMP to LF, February 15, 1930.
10. Paterson, review of *London Bridge Is Falling*, by Philip Lindsay, HTB (July 22, 1934) 2.
11. Paterson, review of *Evening of a Martinet*, by Jane Olivier, HTB (April 7, 1935) 22.

Chapter 8

1. T 3/17/40.
2. Paterson, review of *The Tragedy of Henry Ford*, by Jonathan Norton Leonard, *Nation* 134 (April 13, 1932) 435-36.
3. T 5/19/29; Paterson, "Whose Agent Is He?," *Nation* 132 (February 11, 1931) 153-54.
4. T 11/16/30. IMP is here commenting specifically on divorce laws.
5. Paterson, "Why Is Alimony?" *McNaught's Monthly* 4 (November 1925) 136-39.
6. IMP to Mark Sullivan, undated (Hoover Institution, Stanford University).
7. T 6/12/32.
8. IMP to GB, October 1931.
9. William J. Barber, *From New Era to New Deal: Herbert Hoover, the Economists, and American Economic Policy, 1921-1933* (Cambridge: Cambridge University Press, 1985) 5, 198, 41; general discussion, 1-41.
10. Burton Rascoe, *We Were Interrupted* (Garden City, NY: Doubleday, 1947) 281.
11. See T 12/31/33 on IMP's prediction. Writing to LF on February 15, 1930, she indicated that at the time of the crash she was not in the market. But her income tax returns show her eventually selling off about $11,000 worth of stock that she purchased between 1927 and the approximate time of the crash (IMP, tax returns, 1933, 1941). Perhaps she meant that she hadn't been trying to *play* the market.
12. T 10/13/29.
13. Richard O'Connor, *The First Hurrah: A Biography of Alfred E. Smith* (New York: Putnam's, 1970) 168; Walter Lippmann, *Men of Destiny* (New York: Macmillan, 1928) 6; Franklin D. Roosevelt to Ward Melville, September 21, 1928, quoted in Arthur M. Schlesinger, Jr., *The Crisis of the Old Order: 1919-1933* (Cambridge, MA: Houghton Mifflin, 1957) 127.
14. Claude Bowers, quoted in O'Connor 189.
15. IMP to GB, November 8, 1928; Paterson, "Murphy," *American Mercury* 14 (July 1928) 347-54; IMP to GB, late November or early December 1932.
16. George Wolfskill, *The Revolt of the Conservatives: A History of the American Liberty League, 1934-1940* (Boston: Houghton Mifflin, 1962) 37-55; Herbert Hoover, *The Memoirs of Herbert Hoover*, vol. 2, *The Cabinet and the Presidency* (New York: Macmillan, 1952) 202. For a contemporary perspective on this issue and on the continuity of Hoover-Roosevelt programs, a perspective that accords with Paterson's, see H. Parker Willis, "The Future in Banking," *Yale Review* 23 (December 1933) 233-47.
17. U.S. Certificate of Naturalization 2673592, September 20, 1928. Some decades later, IMP recalled that her interest in the American constitutional system had been stimulated by the reading she did to prepare for naturalization, reading that undoubtedly proceeded far beyond the necessary minimum (Muriel Hall, interview).

18. T 6/19/32; Abraham Lincoln, quoted in William H. Herndon to Jesse W. Weik, February 11, 1887, *The Hidden Lincoln: From the Letters and Papers of William H. Herndon*, ed. Emanuel Hertz (New York: Viking, 1938) 173. Paterson's ultimate position on immigration and voting was that the federal government must have control of immigration, "otherwise the nation cannot remain in being," and the states must have the "power to designate the qualifications of voters" (*The God of the Machine* (New Brunswick, NJ: Transaction Publishers, 1993) 159).

19. IMP to LF, 12/12/28. Amy Jo Tompkins *"Investigating Civilisation": The City as Frontier in the Early Prairie Novels of Isabel Paterson* (thesis, Memorial University of Newfoundland, June 2001) 121-22, 136, notes that in Paterson's Alberta novels, the Canada-U.S. border has no particular significance; "the important distinctions are between the East and the West."

20. IMP to GB, November 8, 1928, November(?) 1929.

21. IMP to GB, early 1929.

22. IMP to GB, November 1929, January or February 1930, and June(?) 1930; Nathaniel Roberts obituaries, *New York Times* (July 29, 1930) 6; (August 1, 1930) 19.

23. IMP to GB, January or February 1930; IMP to Nathaniel Roberts, August 1929; IMP to MH, June 11, 1956.

24. T 9/15/29; IMP to GB, January or February 1930; IMP to LF, September 17, 1929.

25. IMP to GB, January or February 1930; IMP to LF, May 1930, February 15, 1930; Nat Roberts to IMP, March 26, 1930, and c. April 16, 1930; Wilfred P. Meredith to IMP, June 6, 1930, and August(?) 1930. Nat Roberts died on July 21, 1930 (obituary, *New York Times* [August 1, 1930] 19).

26. IMP to LF, May 1, 1930; IMP to GB, June(?) 1930.

27. On the novel's inspiration, see Elsie McCormick, "She Had to Be a Writer," HTB (February 12, 1933) 23. On its start in September 1929, see IMP to GB, late June 1932. On its completion and publication, see T 7/10/32; IMP to GB, late June 1932; and IMP to LF, December 14, 1932.

28. T 5/18/30.

29. Times and ages in this novel can be computed by comparing pp. 63-65, 221, 296, and 300 in Paterson, *Never Ask the End* (New York: William Morrow, 1933). In one of IMP's small revisions of autobiographical detail, her trip to Europe in 1929 becomes Marta's trip to Europe in 1928.

30. For Marta's remarks on politics, see *Never Ask the End* 203, 209, 297-98, 322-23, 326-27.

31. Natalie Roberts Young to IMP, October 23, 1935.

32. IMP to LF, September 8, 1932.

33. IMP did suppose that Grace had approved the idea of the book while it was being written (IMP to GB, June or July 1933). When Grace got the book, she wrote briefly that she "had such a lovely time reading" it and added that she wanted to see "what the reviewers say of us as individuals" (Grace Luckhart to IMP, undated (c. December 28, 1932).

34. Grace Luckhart to MH, February 6, 1961.

35. T 11/21/37, T 12/28/30.

36. T 4/27/30.

37. IMP to GB, October 1931; T 5/10/36; T 10/17/37.

38. T 1/1/33.

39. IMP to LF, November 19, 1931.

40. IMP to LF, August 1930; January 3, 1931; April 14, 1931.

41. IMP to LF, April 14, 1931; to GB, c. April 18, 1931; *New York Times* (April 11, 1931) 19.
42. MH, interview.
43. IMP to GB, May(?) 1931; IMP to GB, late April 1931.
44. IMP to GB, late April 1931; IMP to LF, January 5, 1932.
45. IMP to GB, May(?) 1931; IMP to LF, June 5, 1931; MH, interview.
46. MH to author, December 22, 1999; MH, interview.
47. IMP to LF, September 8, 1932; Zelda Good to IMP, October 28, 1933.
48. IMP to Burton Rascoe, December 1931.
49. Gravestones, Stettler-Lakeview Cemetery, Stettler, Alberta; IMP to Zelda Good, February 10, 1954; Zelda Good to IMP, c. January 1, 1954; January 24, 1954; February 24, March 5, March 26, 1954; January 1959.
50. IMP to Burton Rascoe, December 1931; Paterson, review of *The Victorian Aftermath*, by Esme Wingfield-Stratford, HTB (February 4, 1934) 7.
51. T 11/3/29.

Chapter 9

1. IMP to GB, November 1929; IMP to LF, February 15, 1930.
2. IMP to GB, June(?) 1930.
3. In 1930, IMP lost $700 on stock in the Bahia Corporation; in 1931 she lost $1100 when she sold General Electric stock; and in 1933 she dropped $15,321.23 when she liquidated investments of $23,901.46 that she had made, mainly in 1930, in such companies as Texas Gulf Sulphur, IT&T, Kennecott Copper, Mack Truck, and the Harriman Investment Company. In December 1933, she put $4356.25 into Alaska Juneau Goldmining shares, apparently expecting gold to respond better than it did to the New Deal's retreat from the gold standard; in 1940, she sold most of her Alaska holdings for a loss of $2580. Nineteen thirty-four saw a loss of $1800 on a bankrupt wrought iron company. In 1941, she finally gave up on the Industries Development Corporation stock that she had purchased gradually between 1924 and 1927 with the first large capital she managed to amass, $8600—an indication either that previous investments had turned out remarkably well, or that she had been alarmingly frugal, or both. This stock sold for $43.80 (IMP, income tax returns, 1930-1941.)
4. IMP to LF, November 19, 1931; IMP, tax returns.
5. IMP to LF, June 5, 1931.
6. T 12/31/33.
7. T 10/30/32.
8. T 7/10/32 (cf. T 6/26/32, T 8/14/32); Garet Garrett, *A Bubble that Broke the World* (Boston: Little, Brown, 1932) 38-40. See also William J. Barber, *From New Era to New Deal: Herbert Hoover, the Economists, and American Economic Policy, 1921-1933* (Cambridge: Cambridge University Press, 1985) 38-39.
9. Murray Rothbard, *America's Great Depression* (Los Angeles: Nash, 1972; T 8/14/32. A recent economic historian has outlined three major types of explanations for the severity and persistence of the depression. Paterson's ideas had characteristics of them all: "short-run theories" (emphasizing the stock market crash of 1929), "theories of the depression as a policy problem" (emphasizing the failures of government action), and "long-run theories" (emphasizing factors predating the crash)—Michael A. Bernstein, *The Great Depression: Delayed Recovery and Economic Change in America, 1929-1939* (Cambridge: Cambridge University Press, 1987) 1-20. As Paterson saw it, the state encouraged and participated in the

bad investments that led to the crash, then did its best to prevent the economy from moving on.

10. Lewis W. Douglas, *The Liberal Tradition: A Free People and a Free Economy* (New York: Van Nostrand, 1935) 1-14; Stuart Chase, *A New Deal* (New York: Macmillan, 1932) 109. IMP and Chase met at the end of 1931 (T 1/3/32, 1/10/32).

11. Barber 61, Milton Friedman and Anna Jacobson Schwartz, *A Monetary History of the United States: 1867-1960* (Princeton, NJ: Princeton University Press, 1963) 298, 291. Compare economist Joseph T. Salerno's recent review of the debate on the government's inflationary policies, "Money and Gold in the 1920s and 1930s: An Austrian View," *The Freeman* 49 (October 1999) 31-40. "Austrian" does not refer to a country but to a type of free-market economic theory.

12. On the formation of the NCC and the RFC, see Barber 130-32.

13. Barber 140, 146-57.

14. Robert Higgs, "Regime Uncertainty: Why the Great Depression Lasted So Long and Why Prosperity Resumed after the War," *Independent Review* 1 (Spring 1997) 561-90, assembles evidence from many sources on this question. For figures on net private investment, see Higgs 566-67. Friedman and Schwartz (493-99) provide an outline of factors involved in the failure of private investment.

15. Lewis Douglas, quoted by Robert Paul Browder and Thomas G. Smith, *Independent: A Biography of Lewis Douglas* (New York: Alfred A. Knopf, 1986) 90.

16. Herbert Hoover, *The Memoirs of Herbert Hoover* (New York: Macmillan, 1952), vol. 2, *The Cabinet and the Presidency: 1929-1933* 203, 108 (quoting an address of May 12, 1926); vol. 3, *The Great Depression: 1929-1941* 420.

17. IMP to Burton Rascoe, December, 1931; Paterson, *The Golden Vanity* (New York: William Morrow, 1934) 235; Paterson, *The God of the Machine* (New Brunswick, NJ: Transaction Publishers, 1993) 231; T 4/23/33.

18. IMP to Burton Rascoe, December 1931; IMP to GB, c. July 16, 1932.

19. T 8/14/32. For IMP on Keynesian "deficit spending," see T 6/8/41.

20. John W. Davis, "Why I Am A Democrat," *New York Times* (October 30, 1932), section 2, 2. Chase, on the left, formed a similar view: Hoover's Reconstruction Finance Corporation was sheer "collectivism," though not the kind that conservative businessmen usually complained about (Chase 61).

21. Walter Lippmann, *The Method of Freedom* (New York: Macmillan, 1934) 32-33; Arthur M. Schlesinger, Jr., *The Crisis of the Old Order : 1919-1933* (Cambridge, MA: Houghton Mifflin, 1957) 183.

22. IMP to GB, c. July 16, 1932. See also IMP to Burton Rascoe, December, 1931.

23. IMP to Burton Rascoe, December, 1931.

24. Unemployment statistics for the 1930s are derived from U.S. Department of Commerce, *Historical Statistics of the United States* (Washington, DC: US Government, 1975) esp. 135. The best account of Cleveland's trials and triumphs is Allan Nevins, *Grover Cleveland: A Study in Courage* (New York: Dodd, Mead, 1932). IMP read parts of Nevins' book while taking a break from writing one of her columns and found it "curiously interesting in a pedestrian way"—perhaps because she already understood the subject, perhaps because she found the author's political and economic views unstimulating (T 10/16/32). The fullest economic study of the late-nineteenth-century depression is Charles Hoffmann, *The Depression of the Nineties: An Economic History* (Westport, CT: Greenwood, 1970). Hoffmann shows that wage rates fell during the depression, but that the cost of living fell at least twice as far. He believes that unemployment would have been less severe if industrial combinations and labor unions had not resisted price and wage decreases (233-69).

25. IMP to Burton Rascoe, December 1931.

26. Willa Cather, "Nebraska: The End of the First Cycle," *Nation* 117 (September 5, 1923) 238.

27. IMP to LF, March 4, 1933.

28. Galatians 6:7. Herbert Spencer, whose name is inextricably, though often rather facilely, linked with Social Darwinism, is mentioned by IMP at T 2/10/37, T 5/29/ 38, T 11/29/43, T 4/23/44, T 9/30/45, T 12/30/45, T 1/5/47, T 9/28/47, always in contexts irrelevant to this discussion. Spencer's warnings about collectivism are cited at T 7/7/40, T 2/21/43, *God of the Machine* 232, and perhaps T 8/27/44. At T 9/28/47, IMP takes a superior tone toward the influence of Spencer's ideas in America. She offers no discussion of his evolutionary social theory. She was willing to cite him in opposition to collectivism, many years after she started to attack it, but what especially interested her was the bad "advice" he had given to the Japanese, to the effect that "a high energy technology can be introduced into an authoritarian system without catastrophe" (T 1/5/47; see also T 9/30/45, T 12/30/ 45).

29. Paterson, *Golden Vanity* 232-33.

30. IMP to GB, c. July 16, 1932.

31. Paterson, *Golden Vanity* 191; T 3/26/33.

32. T 4/24/32.

33. Alexander Pope, *An Essay on Criticism* 1.88; Paterson, review of *The Literary Mind*, by Max Eastman, HTB (November 22, 1931) 2.

34. Hoover, *Memoirs* 3.30-31, 282, 17. See also Barber 82.

35. T 9/15/29.

36. T 9/15/29, T 10/20/29.

37. T 12/1/29, T 3/16/30; see also T 11/15/36.

38. Daniel Aaron, *Writers on the Left: Episodes in American Literary Communism* (New York: Harcourt, Brace and World, 1961) 339, 342; T 10/18/36.

39. T 6/22/30.

40. T 8/30/31.

41. T 8/30/31.

42. T 4/8/34, T 2/14/32.

43. Alfred E. Smith, "Notes on Technocracy," *New Outlook* 161 (January 1933) 12.

44. Lincoln Steffens, *The Autobiography of Lincoln Steffens* (New York: Harcourt, Brace, 1931) 798; T 7/6/30.

45. Thorstein Veblen, *The Engineers and the Price System*, 1921 (New York: Harcourt, Brace, 1963) 166.

46. Daniel Bell, introduction to Veblen, *Engineers* 2; Max Lerner, "Veblen and the Waste Land," *New Freeman* 2 (February 25, 1931) 567; T 1/29/33; T 1/8/33.

47. "Stuart Chase," *Wilson Bulletin for Libraries* 6 (January 1932) 336, 342; MH, interview.

48. Chase 117; T 2/13/38; T 1/29/33. When one of her readers responded to her attacks on technocracy by attacking Chase, she replied, "Well, personally we like Stuart Chase and welcome rather than tolerate him. We think some of his ideas are all wet, but feel strongly that they should be heard" (T 2/26/33).

49. Chase 136-37, 248; T 7/31/32, T 2/12/33.

50. Chase 156, 163, 248. On President Roosevelt's planning of Social Security as a mechanism that could not be removed, see Arthur Schlesinger, Jr., *The Coming of the New Deal* (Boston: Houghton Mifflin, 1959) 308-309.

51. T 7/31/32, Chase 177.

52. Paterson, *Never Ask the End* (New York: William Morrow, 1933) 191; T 3/27/32, T 4/3/32.

53. Chase 189, 48.
54. T 11/22/31, T 9/8/35.
55. T 1/8/33. For my usage of the word "relational," I am indebted to a conversation with David Kelley, who points out that economic values respond to objective conditions, which individuals *relate* to themselves when making assessments and choices.
56. T 1/8/33, T 1/29/33, T 2/2/36.
57. T 9/16/45.
58. T 1/8/33.
59. T 3/15/36.
60. T 3/15/36, T 3/10/40; Chase 1.
61. T 7/6/30. On politics as "an art and science in itself," see also T 11/16/30 and T 7/26/31.
62. T 7/6/30.

Chapter 10

1. T 6/12/32, T 3/5/33.
2. T 5/28/33.
3. Ronald Reagan, in Manuel S. Klausner, "Inside Ronald Reagan: A Reason Interview," *Reason* 8 (July 1975) 6.
4. T 4/30/33.
5. T 4/26/36.
6. T 4/30/33.
7. T 6/22/41.
8. Lincoln Steffens, *The Autobiography of Lincoln Steffens* (New York: Harcourt, Brace, 1931) 812-19.
9. Eleanor Perényi, interview.
10. T 4/12/36, T 10/29/33.
11. Leslie A. Fiedler, "Afterthoughts on the Rosenbergs," *Contemporary American Essays*, ed. Maureen Howard (New York: Penguin, 1985) 12; T 4/2/33. As for the fascists, they were "grown-up boy scouts in black and brown shirts . . . retreating to a horrible imitation of childhood" (Paterson, *The Golden Vanity* [New York: William Morrow, 1934] 300).
12. T 4/30/33.
13. Will Rogers, *Autobiography*, ed. Donald Day (Boston: Houghton Mifflin, 1949) 249. These remarks from Rogers' so-called autobiography date to July 1931.
14. IMP to LF, November 19, 1931; T 12/6/31.
15. T 3/6/32.
16. T 3/13/32.
17. T 3/13/32.
18. T 3/13/32.
19. T 3/20/32.
20. IMP to GB, c. February 26, 1932; Granville Hicks, "The Crisis in American Criticism," *New Masses* 8 (February 1933) 3.
21. T 2/16/36.
22. T 2/16/36.
23. T 3/13/32.
24. IMP to GB, June 20(?), 1932; IMP to GB, c. January 1934.
25. IMP to GB, late January or early February 1933.
26. T 3/5/33.

27. IMP to GB, late June 1932; to LF, September 8, 1932.
28. IMP to Burton Rascoe, late 1933. In December 1933, the novel was about half finished (IMP to GB, December 1933). It was completed in mid-August 1934 (IMP to LF, August 15, 1934; to Burton Rascoe, c. August 15, 1934; to GB, c. September 8, 1934).
29. Paterson, *The Golden Vanity* (New York: William Morrow, 1934) 8.
30. T 12/17/33.
31. IMP to R. S., received January 9, 1946.

Chapter 11

1. T 6/25/33, T 4/16/33, T 12/17/33.
2. IMP to LF, September 8, 1932.
3. T 3/11/34.
4. Arthur M. Schlesinger, Jr., *The Crisis of the Old Order: 1919-1933* (Boston: Houghton Mifflin, 1957) 290-91.
5. IMP to GB, late November or early December, 1932.
6. IMP to LF, May 1, 1933; T 4/23/33.
7. T 4/23/33.
8. Franklin D. Roosevelt, Fireside Chat, July 24, 1933, *The Roosevelt Reader: Selected Speeches, Messages, Press Conferences, and Letters of Franklin D. Roosevelt*, ed. Basil Rauch (New York: Holt, Rinehart and Winston, 1960) 112.
9. Roosevelt 114; Hugh Johnson, in Proceedings of the Special Industrial Recovery Board, quoted by Arthur Schlesinger, Jr., *The Coming of the New Deal* (Boston: Houghton Mifflin, 1959) 113.
10. T 4/2/33.
11. For IMP's analysis of innovation in the automobile industry, see *The God of the Machine* (New Brunswick, NJ: Transaction Publishers, 1993) 213-14.
12. T 9/16/33, T 1/28/34.
13. Schlesinger, *Coming* 7.
14. T 4/2/33.
15. T 10/22/33; MH to author, January 2, 2001.
16. Schlesinger, *Coming* 241. On gold in contracts, see Henry Mark Holzer ed., *The Gold Clause* (New York: Books in Focus, 1980).
17. T 12/3/33.
18. Milton Friedman and Anna Jacobson Schwartz, *A Monetary History of the United States: 1867-1960* (Princeton, NJ: Princeton University Press, 1963) 462-83, 496-99, place the government's dealings with gold in the context of its attempts to raise prices and offer an interesting account of rising prices and the money stock during the New Deal.
19. Schlesinger, *Coming* 247-48, echoing FDR.
20. T 1/7/34.
21. T 1/7/34. IMP found her opinion supported by H. Parker Willis, "The Future in Banking," *Yale Review* 23 (December 1933) 233-47.
22. T 12/23/34, T 3/3/40.
23. T 6/30/35. Senator Gore, who was blind, opposed most government subsidies, including and especially subsidies for blind people ("Thomas Pryor Gore," *The National Cyclopaedia of American Biography* 36 [Ann Arbor, MI: University Microfilms, 1967] 22-23).
24. T 6/30/35.
25. T 2/19/39, T 11/17/35, T 3/17/40.

26. See, for example, Garet Garrett, *The Revolution Was*, in *The People's Pottage* (Caldwell, ID: Caxton, 1953).
27. T 1/13/35, T 1/27/35. The adventures of Lewis Douglas, Roosevelt's budget director, provide many good illustrations of the president's opportunistic management style; see Robert Paul Browder and Thomas G. Smith, *Independent: A Biography of Lewis W. Douglas* (New York: Alfred A. Knopf, 1986) 84-116. I know of no *favorable* account of FDR's administration that fails to mention it.
28. T 3/8/36. IMP adds a respectful reference to the Du Pont family, Al Smith Democrats who opposed the New Deal, because "they have managed to run their own business competently. If they can hold onto it, we have no objection; that's their job; and we'd like to hold onto our own savings."
29. T 12/30/34, T 4/23/33.
30. T 9/29/40, T 5/12/35.
31. T 11/4/34.
32. MH, interview.
33. T 5/4/41.
34. T 2/4/34.
35. T 10/11/36; Joseph P. Kennedy, *I'm for Roosevelt* (New York: Reynal and Hitchcock, 1936) 103. Amusingly, Kennedy opens his book by saying, "I have no political ambitions for myself or for my children" (3).
36. T 2/5/39.
37. T 10/24/37, T 11/14/37, T 3/20/38, T 3/12/39, T 12/24/39, T 2/18/40. On the court, Black turned out to be a defender of first-amendment liberties, but there is no evidence that IMP changed her opinion of him. She did not view the Supreme Court as an asylum for political penitents.
38. William Blake, annotations to Bishop Watson's *Apology for the Bible*, *The Complete Poetry and Prose of William Blake*, revised ed., ed. David V. Erdman (New York: Doubleday-Anchor, 1988) 617; punctuation and spelling modernized.
39. Paterson, review of *Walden Revisited*, by George F. Whicher, HTB (October 28, 1945) 1-2.
40. Schlesinger, *Crisis* 202.
41. Roosevelt to E. N. Vallandigham, May 21, 1926, quoted in Schlesinger, *Crisis* 377.
42. Schlesinger, *Crisis* 276, 282-85; George Wolfskill, *The Revolt of the Conservatives: A History of the American Liberty League: 1934-1940* (Cambridge, MA: Houghton Mifflin, 1962).
43. Granville Hicks, "The Crisis in American Criticism," *New Masses* 8 (February 1933) 3.
44. T 3/13/32.
45. Lincoln Steffens, *The Autobiography of Lincoln Steffens* (New York: Harcourt, Brace, 1931) 795, 799; T 12/22/40, T 7/10/32.
46. T 3/13/32.
47. T 11/2/41, T 6/18/44, T 3/12/39, T 6/9/40, T 11/19/39, T 3/10/40, T 12/22/40, T 3/17/40, T 12/31/39, T 7/19/42, T 10/3/37, T 1/1/39, T 9/8/40.
48. T 11/27/32, T 5/28/33.
49. T 3/13/32, T 3/31/40.
50. T 3/31/40, T 5/28/33; Friedrich Hayek, *The Road to Serfdom* (Chicago: University of Chicago Press, 1944).
51. Walter Lippmann, *The Method of Freedom* (New York: Macmillan, 1934) 38.
52. Lionel Trilling, *The Liberal Imagination: Essays on Literature and Society* (New York: Viking, 1950) ix.

53. T 9/16/34, T 1/20/35. For a typical appearance of "dinosaurs," see the frank remarks about private enterprise and its exponents in Sinclair Lewis's novel *It Can't Happen Here* (New York: Collier, 1935) 441-42.
54. T 1/14/34, T 11/27/32, T 12/16/34.
55. T 5/23/43.
56. Stuart Chase, *The Proper Study of Mankind*, revised edition (New York: Harper & Brothers, 1956) 260.
57. Paterson, review of *The Victorian Aftermath*, by Esme Wingfield-Stratford, HTB (February 4, 1934) 7.
58. T 4/23/33. On IMP's partiality toward Jezebel, see IMP to Nat Roberts, early April(?) 1930.

Chapter 12

1. IMP to LF, May 1, 1933.
2. IMP to Burton Rascoe, late 1933.
3. IMP to GB, late July 1933.
4. IMP to GB, late July 1933; IMP to LF, June 21, 1933; IMP to GB, June or July 1933; T 10/1/33, T 9/10/33; IMP to LF, September 16, 1933; March 26, 1934.
5. Paterson, *The Golden Vanity* (New York: William Morrow, 1934) 84; T 9/10/33; IMP to GB, June or July 1933; T 1/2/38; IMP to LF, May 1, 1933. The property ran back from the corner of Summit Ridge Road and Hill Crest Avenue (map, Paterson Papers).
6. T 12/24/33.
7. IMP to GB, July 1933; T 12/24/33; IMP to LF, September 16, 1933.
8. T 12/24/33.
9. IMP to LF, November 15, 1933; IMP to GB, June or July 1933; MH, interview.
10. T 2/15/42.
11. MH, interview; T 11/24/40, T 12/3/39.
12. T 5/11/41, T 8/19/34, T 2/5/39, T 7/11/26, T 10/27/35.
13. MH to author, January 2, 2001. In spring, 1942, IMP was still living at Stamford (T 6/28/42). MH, interview, is the source of my speculation about the reasons for IMP's move. Her taxes at Ridgefield were a small fraction of what they had been at Stamford (IMP, tax returns).
14. MH, interviews; IMP to Edwin Way Teale, c. August 5, 1949.
15. IMP to LF, June 21, 1933; T 10/21/34. In December 1931, IMP told Rascoe about her problems in writing *Never Ask the End* and said, "You will probably have a good laugh when at long last you read the damn book. You'll wonder what two other books I told you about in my letters." This could conceivably refer to some earlier comment about *The Golden Vanity* and *If It Prove Fair Weather*, but it is probably a joke in a common Patersonian formula; e.g., "He thought he was writing to two other people" (T 6/22/41; Paterson, *Golden Vanity* 325).
16. IMP to LF, December 12, 1934; June 6, 1936(?); July 6, 1940; T 5/26/40.
17. IMP to GB, late July 1933, and late winter 1936.
18. MH, interviews; Paterson, *Golden Vanity* 83; IMP to GB, late July, 1933.
19. T 10/6/40; IMP to GB, June 1935(?). MH (interview) believes that the romance in *Fair Weather* was based on an episode in IMP's life.
20. IMP to LF, December 12, 1934; IMP, quoted by Carl Van Doren, "A Clever and Articulate Woman," review of *If It Prove Fair Weather*, by Isabel Paterson, HTB (September 1, 1940) 4.
21. Paterson, *If It Prove Fair Weather* (New York: Putman's, 1940) 274; T 9/8/40; IMP to LF, December 12, 1934.

22. Paterson, *Fair Weather* 261; Paterson, "But Nobody Wants Another's Whole Heart," review of *The Death of the Heart*, by Elizabeth Bowen, HTB (January 22, 1939) 4.
23. Paterson, review of *Death of the Heart* 4; *Fair Weather* 306; *Golden Vanity* 84.
24. In 1940, IMP received a large advance for the novel—$2500—but her additional earnings from it were only $340 in the succeeding year (IMP, U.S. tax returns, 1940, 1941).
25. Anon., "'Books' Covers the World of Books," *Publishers' Weekly* 136 (September 30, 1939) 134.
26. Paterson, *Golden Vanity* 82.
27. Anne Ford to MH, January 13, 1961.
28. T 2/1/31.
29. IMP to LF, July 26, 1940; IMP to LF, September 4, 1935(?).

Chapter 13

1. T 7/30/39.
2. Paterson, *The Shadow Riders* (New York: John Lane, 1916) 86; Paterson, review of *A Short History of Women*, by John Langdon-Davies, HTB (November 6, 1927) 4; Paterson, *The Road of the Gods* (New York: Horace Liveright, 1930) 131.
3. T 8/14/38.
4. T 1/14/34.
5. Paterson, review of *Pamela's Daughters*, by Robert Palfrey Utter and Gwendolyn Bridges Needham, HTB (November 29, 1936) 10.
6. On Paterson, Lane, and Rand, see John Chamberlain, *A Life with the Printed Word* (Chicago: Regnery Gateway, 1982) 136; on Paterson and Lane, see Albert Jay Nock to Mrs. Edmund C. Evans and Ellen Winsor, August 1943; to Mrs. Edmund C. Evans, August 7, 1943, *Letters from Albert Jay Nock, 1924-1945, To Edmund C. Evans, Mrs. Edmund C. Evans, and Ellen Winsor* (Caldwell, ID: Caxton, 1949) 181, 183.
7. Gertrude Stein, "All About Money," "Still More About Money," "My Last About Money," *Gertrude Stein: Writings and Lectures 1909-1945*, ed. Patricia Meyerowitz (Baltimore: Penguin, 1974) 333-37. Cather's ideas on the politics and economics of individualism are most clearly expressed in her novel *O Pioneers!* (1913).
8. As Mysie's origins are described by Paterson in *The Golden Vanity* (New York: William Morrow, 1934) 120.
9. Paterson, *The Shadow Riders* 205; T 3/14/37, T 4/25/37; IMP to R. S. Henry, received June 3, 1944.
10. T 9/29/35; MH to author, January 2, 2001.
11. IMP's satires of Stein and Roosevelt have already been mentioned; for her strictures on Thompson, see, for instance, T 2/18/40, T 11/24/40, T 5/18/41, T 12/6/42, T 2/14/43, T 2/21/43, T 4/4/43.
12. T 2/19/33. IMP makes many references to Woolf, but her views are best summarized in a splendidly insightful essay, "Life Caught By Virginia Woolf," a review of *Virginia Woolf: Her Art as a Novelist*, by Joan Bennett, HTB (October 7, 1945) 2.
13. T 4/26/42, T 1/21/34.
14. IMP to Burton Rascoe, July 1933; IMP to Burton Rascoe, July 1933 - January 1934.
15. T 10/13/35, T 6/21/42; IMP to GB, early 1929; IMP to Burton Rascoe, c. December 1929. *War and Peace* was "the greatest novel ever written" (T 6/3/28).

16. Paterson, "Man as Lover," *The more I see of men—*, ed. Mabel S. Ulrich (New York: Harper, 1932) 218, 222, 210-11.
17. Paterson, "Man as Lover" 211, 215-16.
18. Paterson, "Man as Lover" 210-11.
19. IMP to Burton Rascoe, c. July 5, 1933.
20. T 4/10/32.
21. T 6/16/40.
22. T 12/20/42, T 1/24/43.
23. Paterson, "Adventures in Biology and Bunk," *McNaught's Monthly* 4 (December 1925) 188-89; IMP to Burton Rascoe, July, 1933 - January 1934.
24. T 4/10/38, T 10/1/33, T 2/9/36, T 2/21/43.
25. T 8/26/34; IMP to Burton Rascoe, July 1933 - January 1934.
26. T 8/26/34.
27. T 4/17/38; IMP to GB, October 1931.
28. T 6/14/31.
29. T 6/14/31.
30. T 4/29/34. In *Joyous Gard* (unpublished typescript, p. 347) IMP turns things around and asks how the universe could be "intelligible" if it were not "a work of intellect" (see below, p. 332).
31. T 7/12/31.
32. T 3/3/40. IMP is slightly misquoting Rudyard Kipling's "The Sack of the Gods."
33. T 10/27/29, T 9/12/26; Paterson, *Never Ask the End* (New York: William Morris, 1933) 249, 295, 328, 19-21.
34. Paterson, *Never Ask the End* 21; T 3/15/31, T 7/12/31, T 10/6/35, T 11/20/38.
35. MH, interviews; T 9/20/31.
36. T 10/6/35. In 1941, IMP made similar comments about both the interest and the scientific unverifiability of parapsychic phenomena (T 11/2/41).
37. Alexander Pope, *An Essay on Man*, 1733-34; *The Universal Prayer*, 1738.

Chapter 14

1. Sheldon Richman, "New Deal Nemesis: The 'Old Right' Jeffersonians," *Independent Review* 1 (Fall 1996) 204, 202.
2. Richman, esp. 203, 211; T 4/5/36.
3. Richman 211.
4. George Wolfskill, *The Revolt of the Conservatives: A History of the American Liberty League, 1934-1940* (Boston: Houghton Mifflin, 1962) 218.
5. On the Du Ponts, see T 3/8/36, a column written during the Liberty League's campaign; cited above, chapter 11, note 28. Raskob's sharp business practices were notorious; see Richard O'Connor, *The First Hurrah: A Biography of Alfred E. Smith* (New York: Putnam's, 1970) 244-47.
6. Robert Paul Browder and Thomas G. Smith, *Independent: A Biography of Lewis W. Douglas* (New York: Knopf, 1986) 12-13. My summary of Douglas's life relies on Browder and Smith's very able account. Their assessment, however, differs sharply from my own.
7. Lewis Douglas, *The Liberal Tradition: A Free People and a Free Economy* (New York: Van Nostrand, 1935) 29, 32.
8. Douglas, *Liberal Tradition* 3-4, 104; Lewis Douglas, Newton D. Baker, and Leo Wolman, "Federal Bureaucracy Is Condemned," *New York Times* (June 3, 1936) 20.
9. Browder and Smith 126-27.

10. Browder and Smith 148.
11. Douglas's main reason for supporting Johnson was (ironically, in view of Johnson's later actions) opposition to expanding the war in Vietnam.
12. T 3/29/36.
13. T 3/23/30, T 4/10/32, T 7/31/27, T 1/29/28 (see also T 5/8/27).
14. H. L. Mencken, *My Life as Author and Editor*, ed. Jonathan Yardley (New York: Alfred A. Knopf, 1993) 361.
15. Robert Rives La Monte and H. L. Mencken, *Men versus the Man: A Correspondence between Robert Rives La Monte, Socialist and H. L. Mencken, Individualist* (New York: Henry Holt, 1910) esp. 24, 32-33.
16. T 11/23/41.
17. H. L. Mencken, "On Being an American," *Selected Prejudices: Second Series* (London: Jonathan Cape, 1927) 22, 41, 42.
18. Mencken, "Observations on Government," in *Selected Prejudices* 100; "On Being an American" 26-28. For IMP's remarks on Mencken's "yearn[ing]" for an intellectual "aristocracy," see T 12/1/29. For her sneers at his *Notes on Democracy*, see T 3/27/27, and "Full of Sound and Fury," *McNaught's Monthly* 7 (January 1927) 25, where she is amazed that "intelligence could be suspended so long without some permanently injurious result." Joseph Epstein agrees with Mencken in saying that he "was no liberal. He was a libertarian" ("Cornered by Events," review of *A Second Mencken Chrestomathy* and *Thirty-Five Years of Newspaper Work*, by H. L. Mencken, *TLS* [June 9, 1995] 14). Paterson, of course, was both.
19. Mencken, *Men versus the Man* 112-13.
20. H. L. Mencken, "The Crowd," "Sententiae," "American Culture," *A Mencken Chrestomathy* (New York: Alfred A. Knopf, 1949) 324, 623, 181.
21. T 6/15/41.
22. Garet Garrett, *A Time Is Born* (New York: Parthenon, 1944) 16, 36. Carl Ryant has written a brief biography, *Profit's Prophet: Garet Garrett (1878-1954)* (Selinsgrove, PA: Susquehanna University Press, 1989).
23. Garet Garrett, "Economic Fascinations," *Saturday Evening Post* 207 (March 9, 1935) 7.
24. Garrett, *Time Is Born* 173; *Ouroboros, or The Mechanical Extension of Mankind* (New York: Dutton, 1926) 71. The latter work is especially interesting for Garrett's theories about machines and surpluses and the limitation of economic desire. For his theories about self-sufficiency, see especially his *The Blue Wound* (New York: Putnam's, 1921) and *A Time Is Born*.
25. Garrett, *Time Is Born* 173; Garet Garrett to Rose Wilder Lane, autumn(?) 1936. The Garrett-Lane correspondence quoted in this book is in the Herbert Hoover Presidential Library.
26. Garet Garrett to Rose Wilder Lane, early November 1936; November(?) 1936.
27. Whiling away an idle hour on the deck of an Atlantic steamer, Nock was asked by a friend why he had left his wife. What was wrong with her? "Nothing was wrong with her," he replied. "She was perfect, perfect in every way. That's why I left her." (Russell Kirk [interview] told this story as he had heard it.) For an analysis of Nock's intellectual and literary career, see Stephen Cox, "Albert Jay Nock: Prophet of Libertarianism?", *Liberty* 5 (March 1992) 39-46.
28. Charles H. Hamilton, Foreword, *The State of the Union: Essays in Social Criticism*, by Albert Jay Nock, ed. Charles H. Hamilton (Indianapolis, IN : LibertyPress, 1991) xi-xxviii. Hamilton provides an excellent survey of what is known about Nock's life.

29. Albert Jay Nock to Mrs. Edmund C. Evans, September 29, 1929, *Letters from Albert Jay Nock, 1924-1945, To Edmund C. Evans, Mrs. Edmund C. Evans, and Ellen Winsor* (Caldwell, ID: Caxton, 1949) 40.
30. T 3/13/32.
31. Albert Jay Nock, *Henry George* (New York: William Morrow, 1939) 150; Nock, "Anarchist's Progress," *State of the Union* 34-51. Nock's distinction between government and state appears at large in his *Our Enemy, The State* (New York: William Morrow), 1935.
32. T 6/27/26, T 4/1/34; Paterson, review of *A Journal of These Days*, by Albert Jay Nock, HTB (March 18, 1934) 3; IMP to John Chamberlain, April 23, 1952.
33. Albert Jay Nock, "Baiting the Russian Bear," *New Freeman* 1 (March 15, 1930) 8-10. Nock was willing to sign that article. The same sentiments persist in many unsigned or pseudonymous but very recognizably Nockian pieces, in one of which he regards the Soviet Union as accomplishing Georgeite goals in a non-Georgeite way ("Journeyman," "Miscellany," *New Freeman* 2 [September 10, 1930] 610). In one signed piece (to be fair) he indicates that all this Soviet business would be "unnecessary" if the Single Tax program were adopted in its purity (Nock, "The Testimony of Marx," *New Freeman* 2 [November 26, 1930] 256-57).
34. The most convenient source for Chodorov's life and work is *Fugitive Essays: Selected Writings of Frank Chodorov*, ed. Charles H. Hamilton (Indianapolis, IN: LibertyPress, 1980), with a good biographical introduction by the editor. Quotations from Chodorov are from an essay of 1959, "Economics Versus Politics," in the same volume (79, 81).
35. Gertrude Vogt to IMP, July 18, 1954.
36. Lane first appears in the column on March 15, 1925.
37. Rose Wilder Lane, "Who's Who—and Why," *Saturday Evening Post* 207 (July 6, 1935) 30; T 3/21/26.
38. William Holtz, *The Ghost in the Little House: A Life of Rose Wilder Lane* (Columbia: University of Missouri Press, 1993), from which I have drawn most of my basic biographical information about Lane. Lane's diaries are in the collections of the Herbert Hoover Presidential Library.
39. Rose Wilder Lane, "Credo," *Saturday Evening Post* 208 (March 7, 1936) 5-7, 30-31, 34-35.
40. T 4/26/36.
41. T 5/22/38, T 6/19/38.
42. IMP to GB, August 19, 1937; T 4/17/38.
43. Rose Wilder Lane to IMP, March 26, 1942. The letter is dated "1932," but the return address establishes the correct year.
44. John Chamberlain, *A Life with the Printed Word* (Chicago: Regnery Gateway, 1982) 136.
45. Ayn Rand, taped interview with Barbara Branden, 1961. Ms. Branden kindly allowed me to hear this interview.
46. T 5/31/36. Rand would not reappear in IMP's column until June 29, 1941, when IMP discusses her escape from Russia.
47. The following information on Rand's political development and early acquaintance with IMP is derived from Barbara Branden, *The Passion of Ayn Rand* (Garden City, NY: Doubleday, 1986), 158-67, compared with Branden's tape of her 1961 interview with Rand.
48. Branden, *Passion* 161.
49. Pollock was the rare author whom IMP had never met (T 2/28/43); contrast Branden, *Passion* 163.

50. Mimi Sutton, quoted in Branden, *Passion* 166.
51. T 9/23/45; Muriel Hall (sister of Gardner Welles), quoted in Branden, *Passion* 165.
52. Chris Matthew Sciabarra, *Ayn Rand: The Russian Radical* (University Park: Pennsylvania State University Press, 1995; "The Rand Transcript," *Journal of Ayn Rand Studies* 1 (Fall, 1999) 1-26. Robert Hessen, Rand's secretary in later years, confirms what her literary oeuvre suggests, that she read relatively few books (Robert Hessen, interview). Interviews with Henry Mark Holzer and Erika Holzer, her attorneys and friends, and with her closest associate, Nathaniel Branden, also indicate her ability to form opinions based on intellectual conversation instead of reading.
53. Ayn Rand, taped interview with Barbara Branden, 1961.
54. Some of this territory is surveyed in Stephen Cox, "The Evolution of Ayn Rand," *Liberty* 11 (July 1998) 49-57.
55. Ayn Rand, *The Fountainhead* (New York: Bobbs-Merrill, 1943) 740, 741.
56. Branden, *Passion* 177; confirmed by photocopy of inscription.
57. IMP to Jasper Crane, January 9, 1946.
58. T 1/31/43; Paterson, undated memorandum.
59. T 9/23/45.
60. T 8/9/42, T 4/25/43, T 6/6/43.

Chapter 15

1. T 3/17/35.
2. T 3/17/35.
3. T 4/7/35.
4. T 2/16/36, T 11/15/36, T 12/6/36, T 4/12/36.
5. T 4/12/36.
6. T 4/12/36.
7. Mary McCarthy and Margaret Marshall, "Our Critics, Right or Wrong," *Nation* 141 (October 23, 1935) 468-69, 472; (November 6, 1935) 542-44; (November 20, 1935) 595-96, 598; (December 4, 1935) 653-55; (December 18, 1935) 717-19.
8. T 12/16/34.
9. T 10/27/35. One of those illustrators, Tom Bevans, has indicated that IMP had little or nothing to do with the pictures; the illustrators did what they wanted (Tom Bevans, interview). In this case, one cannot doubt that their taste coincided with hers.
10. IMP to LF, December 25, 1938.
11. T 12/27/36.
12. T 3/14/37.
13. T 3/15/36.
14. T 3/15/36.
15. T 7/5/36; IMP to LF, August 25, 1936.
16. T 7/5/36. When Roosevelt was indeed "drafted" by his party for a third-term campaign, IMP looked up her 1936 columns and reminded everyone that she had prophesied the event (T 11/22/36, T 7/28/40).
17. IMP to Burton Rascoe, late summer 1936; T 4/5/36.
18. T 11/22/36.
19. T 12/6/31, T 12/6/36.
20. T 12/6/36, T 2/23/36, T 3/28/37. In 1939, IMP remarked that "[f]or many years" she had kept *The Federalist* near her desk at home, using it as a "style book of clear

thinking and plain honesty" (T 2/12/39). But she seems not to have relied on it for direct political support until 1936.

21. T 3/3/40, T 5/19/40. On the timing of the latter column, see chapter 16, note 20. Other spring 1940 discussions of "democracy" appear at T 3/10/40, T 3/24/40, T 3/31/40, T 6/9/40.
22. T 6/14/42.
23. For IMP's views on Beard's theory, see T 3/13/32, T 10/7/28, T 9/4/38.
24. T 7/20/41, T 11/29/42.
25. T 6/30/40.
26. Sidney Hook to IMP, April 19, 1943 (Hoover Institution).
27. "Remembering the Cold War," *The New Criterion* 18.4 (December 1999) 1.
28. T 12/22/40.
29. T 12/22/40.
30. T 1/5/41.
31. T 1/19/41.
32. Neil Jumonville, *Henry Steele Commager: Midcentury Liberalism and the History of the Present* (Chapel Hill: University of North Carolina Press, 1999) 112, xiii, 63-68. Commager's biographer, who is often hard pressed to defend the emphases of his subject's self-avowed generosity and civil libertarianism, says that Commager "would have been considered by many to be an anti-anticommunist" (110).
33. T 3/2/41; U.S. Department of Commerce, *Historical Statistics of the United States: Colonial Times to 1970* (Washington, DC: U.S. Government Printing Office, 1975) 135, 263, 989, 1105, 1114, 1117, 1122-24.
34. To cite one important instance: she regarded *To the Finland Station*, Edmund Wilson's history of the communist movement, as the best work in its field and insisted that her audience read it (T 9/22/40, T 11/24/40, T 2/2/41).
35. T 6/24/34, T 6/7/31.
36. T 1/16/38.

Chapter 16

1. IMP to LF, September(?) 1934; T 7/25/37.
2. Paterson, *The God of the Machine* (New Brunswick, NJ: Transaction Publishers, 1993) 278; T 7/26/42. *The God of the Machine* came out in 1943; the column of 1942 is one of many documents leading up to it.
3. T 6/23/35, T 8/18/35, T 10/18/36.
4. T 8/11/40, T 5/18/41.
5. T 7/26/36, T 2/23/36.
6. Paterson, "H. M. Tomlinson's Voice in the Wilderness," review of *Mars His Idiot*, by H. M. Tomlinson, HTB (November 17, 1935) 7.
7. T 4/13/41.
8. Thomas Jefferson to John Adams, June 1, 1822, *The Adams-Jefferson Letters*, ed. Lester J. Cappon (Chapel Hill: University of North Carolina Press, 1959) 50.
9. T 7/13/41. IMP had long been an anti-interventionist in respect to Russia; see, for example, T 12/6/31, T 3/13/32.
10. MH, "Pat 1886," typescript notes on IMP's conversation, weekend of July 27, 1958. For IMP on Nehru, see T 3/16/41, T 4/20/41, T 4/12/42; on Toynbee see T 5/9/37.
11. T 7/5/42.
12. T 6/12/32.
13. IMP to LF, October 6, 1938.

14. T 10/23/38.

15. T 12/31/39.

16. T 4/14/40, T 3/17/40, T 3/24/40, T 3/31/40.

17. Anne Morrow Lindbergh, *The Wave of the Future: A Confession of Faith* (New York: Harcourt, Brace, 1940).

18. T 12/3/39.

19. T 10/8/39, T 11/19/39.

20. The three columns are T 4/21/40, T 5/19/40, and T 5/26/40. If IMP kept to her usual practice of writing her columns on the second Friday before publication date, the first of the three was written on April 12. Hitler invaded Denmark and Norway on April 9 and began his invasion of the low countries in the early hours of June 10, European time. According to the diary of Rose Wilder Lane (see below, note 21), IMP heard about the second invasion before midnight on May 9, U.S. time; for the second column, the second Friday before publication would have been the next day, May 10. But Lane has IMP spending that Friday at her home in Connecticut. IMP must have moved the deadline for her column back to Thursday, May 9 and, in keeping with her custom, have written it during the afternoon before departing for Connecticut and hearing the news from Europe.

21. Rose Wilder Lane, diary, May 10, 1940. IMP's remark about the shadbush is at T 4/27/41.

22. Rose Wilder Lane, diary, May 29, June 15, 17, 1940.

23. IMP to LF, October 6, 1938.

24. T 7/28/40; MH, interview, for IMP's emotional reaction to the world wars.

25. T 11/16/41, T 7/6/41, T 2/9/41. IMP's comment about getting down to cases appears in her notice of the anti-interventionist book *We Testify*, in which John T. Flynn recorded some ideas that she found "indistinguishable from the ideas they claim to reprehend."

26. T 5/18/41, T 7/13/41, T 4/20/41.

27. T 8/11/40. On conscription, see also T 9/15/40, T 9/22/40, T 10/6/40.

28. T 5/18/41, T 6/1/41. Meanwhile, a government intelligence and sabotage officer was helping Sherwood put together an organization for foreign propaganda. "The whole venture," according to a friendly source, "was probably illegal" (Wallace Carroll, *Persuade or Perish* [Boston: Houghton Mifflin, 1948] 5).

29. T 5/18/41.

30. T 5/18/41, T 8/11/40.

31. Wendell Willkie to IMP, September 11, 1939; T 2/5/39, T 10/6/40.

32. H. L. Mencken, *Thirty-five Years of Newspaper Work*, ed. Fred Hobson, Vincent Fitzpatrick, and Bradford Jacobs (Baltimore, MD: Johns Hopkins University Press, 1994) 329. A good published source for the Willkie-Van Doren relationship is Richard Kluger, *The Paper: The Life and Death of the "New York Herald Tribune"* (New York: Alfred A. Knopf, 1986) 325-29.

33. As emphasized by interviews with IMP's friends Muriel Hall and Gertrude Vogt, the burden of which is, "you had to like him."

34. Mark H. Leff, "Strange Bedfellows: The Utility Magnate as Politician," *Wendell Willkie: Hoosier Internationalist*, ed. James H. Madison (Bloomington: Indiana University Press, 1992) 38.

35. Robert Paul Browder and Thomas G. Smith, *Independent: A Biography of Lewis W. Douglas* (New York: Knopf, 1986) 152, quoting Douglas and John Hanes, recently under secretary of the treasury for FDR, to Wendell Willkie, July 20, 1940. Douglas and Hanes formed a highly successful fund-raising group called Democrats-for-Willkie.

36. After writing the October 6, 1940 column, Paterson went home for a vacation; her next column appeared on the Sunday after the election.
37. Rose Wilder Lane, diary, November 6, 1940.
38. Rose Wilder Lane, diary, November 6, 1940.
39. T 11/17/40; IMP to Gertrude Vogt, November 14, 1954.
40. T 12/21/41.
41. MH, interview; T 7/26/42.
42. MH, interview.
43. MH, interview.
44. T 7/5/42.
45. T 7/26/42.
46. T 7/19/42.
47. T 7/19/42.
48. T 11/23/41.
49. Paterson, *God of the Machine* 278; IMP to R. S. Henry, received March 20, 1945.
50. M. Roberts to IMP, August 13, 1945, citing IMP to Roberts, August 7, 1945 (not extant); IMP to MH, February 19, 1959; T 9/2/45.
51. T 8/26/45.
52. T 9/16/45.

Chapter 17

1. Paterson, *The God of the Machine* (New Brunswick, NJ: Transaction Publishers, 1993) 3, 14.
2. Stuart Chase, *A New Deal* (New York: Macmillan, 1932) 177.
3. Paterson, *The Golden Vanity* (New York: William Morrow, 1934) 84, 249. For the idea of the "short circuit," see *Golden Vanity* 249.
4. T 6/14/36.
5. IMP to R. S. Henry, received February 9, 1944. In late 1939, for instance, she turned down an offer from George Shively of the Frederick A. Stokes publishing house to make a book of her "Dissenting Opinions." Shively was "impressed by [her] ability," he told her, "not only to disagree with orthodoxy, but to disagree from an angle nobody else could think of" (George Shively to IMP, December 5, 1939).
6. T 2/2/41, T 11/9/41. IMP remembered that she spent three years working on the book (T 2/16/47).
7. Thomas T. Read to IMP, March 30, 1942. Read reviewed a manuscript which, at that stage, seems to have carried the argument at least through a preliminary stage of chapter 23. He made numerous suggestions. IMP made revisions and sent the manuscript back to him, whereupon he pronounced it "a genuine engineering description" (IMP to R. S. Henry, c. April 2, 1943).
8. Margot Johnson to IMP, May 13, 1942; IMP to R. S. Henry, November 12, 1942; Helen Ferrigan to R. S. Henry, March 17, 1943.
9. T 2/22/31.
10. T 5/9/37, T 5/30/37, T 8/29/37, T 4/14/46. IMP owned only the first three volumes of Toynbee's *Study of History*. Her comments on Toynbee (T 5/9/37) indicate that what she took from his historical theory was confirmation of her own view that civilizations benefit from liberty.
11. Henry Adams, *The Education of Henry Adams: An Autobiography* (Boston: Massachusetts Historical Society, 1918) 474, 484, 493. Adams speaks of a "social mind" (495, 498).

12. MH, interview.
13. MH, interview; Eugene Debs, recorded address (author's collection).
14. For a concise summary of Knight's views, see David Gordon, "Frank Knight's Mixed Legacy," *Mises Review* 6, no. 3 (Fall 2000) 1-4.
15. John Locke, *Second Treatise of Government*, esp. paragraphs 25-51.
16. James Madison, *The Federalist* 10.
17. T 3/11/34.
18. This is another collision point between IMP and Frederick Jackson Turner. He had referred, in Patersonian fashion, to "an indefinite number of parallelograms called States," states without a political culture capable of balancing the central power; but he had regarded this as an essentially benign stage in America's growth toward national democracy, a concept that IMP regarded as an evil and the root of many evils (Turner, *The Frontier in American History* [New York: Henry Holt, 1920] 190).
19. Here IMP departed from her friend Colonel Henry, who had praised government encouragement of railroads: Robert Selph Henry, *The Story of Reconstruction* (New York: Bobbs-Merrill, 1938) 365-66.
20. IMP admired Tate on purely literary grounds and strongly encouraged his writing; she made fun of his political ideas (see esp. her debate with Donald Davidson of the *Nashville Tennessean*, T 12/1/29) and she sought him out in person to ask him how the idea of the old South as "agrarian" rather than "commercial" squared "with the fact that slavery traded in human beings[.] When a 'society' will sell an infant out of its mother's arms it has gone about as far as it can go . . . in the perversion of 'commercial' transactions. Proper commercial transactions . . . are real human relations, the natural relations of productive human beings . . ." The ensuing conversation was inconclusive (T 10/5/47).
21. The sequence of Rand's expressed ideas, from a quasi-Nietzschean individualism to a rationalistic one, can be seen in her posthumously published literary notes: *Journals of Ayn Rand*, ed. David Harriman (New York: Dutton, 1997). On this see also Stephen Cox, "The Evolution of Ayn Rand," *Liberty* 11 (July 1998) 49-57.
22. Adams 476, 497, 500-501.
23. Anne Morrow Lindbergh, *The Wave of the Future: A Confession of Faith* (New York: Harcourt, Brace, 1940) 18.
24. T 6/11/33.

Chapter 18

1. Paterson, "What Do They Do All Day?", typescript, 1959; Katherine Taffert Willis, review of *The God of the Machine*, *Library Journal* 68 (May 1, 1943) 362; Anon., review of *The God of the Machine*, *The New Yorker* 19 (June 5, 1943) 87; Anon., review of *The God of the Machine*, *Atlantic* 172 (July 1943) 127.
2. C. Wright Mills, "Item for Bandwagon," review of *The God of the Machine*, *New Republic* 109 (July 5, 1943) 28-29; Lindsay Rogers, "Renovations and Revolutions," review of *The God of the Machine*, and *Reflections on the Revolution of Our Time*, by Harold Laski, *Saturday Review* 26 (July 10, 1943) 3-5, 18. Laski was a model for Ayn Rand's villain in *The Fountainhead* (Barbara Branden, *The Passion of Ayn Rand* [Garden City, NY: Doubleday, 1986] 139).
3. John Storck, "The Dynamics of Our Society," review of *The God of the Machine*, *New York Times Book Review* (May 23, 1943) 29. One Herman Hausheer, reviewer for *The Annals of The American Academy* (229 [September 1943] 180-81), liked Storck's critique so well that he used some of its phrases without attribution.

Otherwise, Hausheer was disappointed that IMP ignored "the best government in existence—the Swiss," and that she said "nothing helpful" about such features of "a socially alert liberalism" as "the disappearance of interest rates." This is a curious review indeed.

4.   Ralph E. Flanders, "It Stimulates and Chastises," review of *The God of the Machine*, HTB (May 23, 1943) 2; John Chamberlain, review of *The God of the Machine*, *New York Times* (May 13, 1943) 19.

5.   Kern Dodge to IMP, April 8, 1949; Paterson, "What Do They Do All Day?" *The God of the Machine* had a print run of 3,500 copies, of which 2,500 had been taken in the first year of publication. At that point, the book was temporarily out of stock; 250 more copies were then bound, leaving 750 in sheets (Earle Balch to IMP, April 21, 1944).

6.   Albert Jay Nock, "Isaiah's Job," *The State of the Union: Essays in Social Criticism*, ed. Charles H. Hamilton (Indianapolis, IN: LibertyPress, 1991) 124-35.

7.   Paterson, "A Civilized Survey of This Age of Decay," review of *Memoirs of a Superfluous Man*, by Albert Jay Nock, HTB (September 19, 1943) 6; T 12/12/43. IMP also recommends Nock at T 10/10/43, T 12/26/43, T 8/27/44.

8.   Albert Jay Nock to Mrs. Edmund C. Evans and Ellen Winsor, August 1943; to Mrs. Edmund C. Evans, August 7, 1943, *Letters from Albert Jay Nock, 1924-1945, To Edmund C. Evans, Mrs. Edmund C. Evans, and Ellen Winsor* (Caldwell, ID: Caxton, 1949) 181, 183.

9.   Rose Wilder Lane, *The Discovery of Freedom: Man's Struggle Against Authority* (New York: Arno-New York Times, 1972) 190.

10. Lane, *Discovery* 139, 140, 86, 87. Lane would eventually tell friends that *Discovery* was a "bad book" and that she "found more and more 'mistakes'" in it (Robert LeFevre, Foreword, and Roger Lea MacBride, Introduction to *Discovery*'s 1972 reprinting, no page numbering). However that may be, the book notably lacks the charm and perspicacity of Lane's letters and reviews and some of her works of fiction.

11. Lane, *Discovery* 41, 60.

12. Lane, *Discovery* vii-4.

13. Among the interesting similarities are the following. *The God of the Machine* makes a major issue of St. Paul's appeal to the rights of Roman citizenship: "a poor street preacher, of the working class, under arrest, and with enemies in high places, had only to claim his civil rights and none could deny him." Lane uses the same episode, although she fails to assimilate it completely to her own argument (Paterson, *The God of the Machine* [New Brunswick, NJ: Transaction Publishers, 1993] 27; Lane, *Discovery* 142-43). IMP insists that ownership of property, especially real property, is necessary to the exercise of all other rights: "How can a man speak freely if there is no spot on which he and his audience have the right to stand?" Lane mentions the fact that "no man can use his natural freedom, if he has no right to stand upon this earth . . . if by merely living he is a trespasser upon property that Government . . . owns" (Paterson, *God of the Machine* 184; see also 178; Lane, *Discovery*, 183). For many years, IMP had been comparing political systems she did not like to the inventions of perpetual-motion cranks; Lane does the same (T 1/1/39, T 8/11/40; Lane, *Discovery* 141).

14. Lane, "Credo," *Saturday Evening Post* 208 (March 7, 1936) 30, 34 (on released energy—see also an additional reference in the essay's book publication, *Give Me Liberty* [New York: Longmans, Green, 1936] 49). The 1945 revision of *Give Me Liberty* (Mansfield, MO: The Laura Ingalls Wilder-Rose Wilder Lane Home Association, 1977), adds a good deal of material on which IMP and Lane agreed and

gives slightly greater prominence to energy. A new reference to freedom as control of one's "life-energy" appears on p. 15.

15. Rose Wilder Lane, "The American Revolution, 1939," *Saturday Evening Post* 211 (January 7, 1939) 52. One of Lane's friends, the libertarian activist Robert LeFevre, claimed that Lane wrote *The Discovery of Freedom* "at white heat" (LeFevre, Foreword to *Discovery of Freedom*); but much of it—though not the bulk of the "energy" discussion—stems directly from "The American Revolution, 1939." If the emphasis on energy got in at the "white heat" stage, it got in very late. Yet "white heat" must be an exaggeration; see note 18, below.

16. See, for example, T 4/3/32, T 1/8/33, T 1/29/33, T 9/24/33, T 7/12/36 (cf. Lane, *Discovery* 61), T 7/16/39, T 4/21/40, T 6/2/40, T 12/15/40, T 7/27/41, T 11/9/41, T 1/25/42, T 2/1/42, T 2/15/42, T 3/15/42, T 5/10/42, T 8/2/42; these in addition to the central conceptual role that Paterson gives to energy in *The Golden Vanity*.

17. Lane, *Discovery*, esp. 61, 209.

18. *Discovery* may have been the book that Herbert Hoover had in mind when he wrote to Lane on July 7, 1941, "If you write a book on that subject, I will surely read the manuscript and give you any help that I can." It was certainly the book she had in mind when she wrote to Hoover on January 10, 1942, "My own book is taking much longer to write than I expected." This is the book that, she tells him, is "all but finished" on August 5, 1942, and that she finally sends him on September 5, 1942 (Hoover-Lane correspondence, Hoover Presidential Library). *Discovery* was published in January 1943, four months ahead of *The God of the Machine*—which, however, was partially finished in November 1941 (T 11/9/41).

19. Herbert Hoover to Rose Wilder Lane, September 27, 1942; Rose Wilder Lane and Jasper Crane, *The Lady and the Tycoon: Letters of Rose Wilder Lane and Jasper Crane*, ed. Roger Lea MacBride (Caldwell, ID: Caxton, 1973); Rose Wilder Lane to Roy Childs, November 30, 1967 (Hoover Institution, Stanford University).

20. Lane's biographer, William Holtz, *The Ghost in the Little House: A Life of Rose Wilder Lane* (Columbia: University of Missouri Press, 1993) esp. 324-25, 340-43, emphasizes the ideological narrowing of her later attitudes more than the resolution of emotional difficulties that her ideological interests afforded her; and he probably would not agree with me on the word "happy."

21. T 8/8/43. She adds that one can make a pretty good guess about how they will work out: "The history books have the answer already."

22. IMP to Ayn Rand, January 19, 1944, February 2, 1944; Rose Wilder Lane to Herbert Hoover, May 8, 1943; *Economic Council Review of Books* 3 (February 1946) 2. On the same day on which she wrote to Hoover, Lane wrote in the same vein to Raymond Moley (correspondence, Hoover Institution), adding Jefferson to the list of comparisons to IMP.

23. Ayn Rand, *The Art of Fiction: A Guide for Writers and Readers*, ed. Tore Boeckmann (New York: Penguin-Plume, 2000) 163. *The God of the Machine* never names IMP's chief American antagonists, Wilson, Hoover, and Roosevelt, even in places where it would be easier to name them than not. It does refer directly to Hitler and Stalin.

24. On romanticism: Ayn Rand, *The Romantic Manifesto: A Philosophy of Literature* (New York: World, 1969) esp. 81-89; Paterson, T 6/9/35. On integration: Rand, *Manifesto*, esp. 63-64; IMP to GB, May(?) 1931; Paterson, review of *They Went On Together*, by Robert Nathan, HTB (April 13, 1941) 4; review of *Sir Richard Burton's Wife*, by Jean Burton, HTB (June 22, 1941) 3.

25. Ayn Rand, *The Fountainhead* (New York: Bobbs-Merrill, 1943) 742. Datings of Rand's work on *The Fountainhead* are largely derived from the evidence in Barbara Branden, *Passion* 168-74.

26. Ayn Rand to John C. Gall, July 4, 1943, *Letters of Ayn Rand*, ed. Michael S. Berliner (New York: Dutton, 1995) 78; to Earle H. Balch, November 28, 1943, *Letters* 102, 104. See also her letter to Leonard E. Read, November 24, 1944, in which she calls *The God of the Machine* "a treasure mine" (*Letters* 171), and her letter to Frank Lloyd Wright and Mrs. Wright, November 30, 1945, noting that she has sent them a copy of *The God of the Machine*. Wright responded on January 14, 1946, saying that he had "learned from" the book (*Letters* 116).

27. Branden, *Passion* 179-84; Gertrude Vogt, interview.

28. Herbert Hoover, calendar, November 30, 1943, Hoover Presidential Library. My summary of the meeting is derived from the only account that has been discovered, IMP to Ayn Rand, early December 1943.

29. MH, interview.

30. T 12/3/33, T 9/17/39, T 12/31/39.

31. T 8/6/39, T 9/17/39. IMP objected to the characterization as "injurious" but used it to advertise her opposition to suing anyone over such things, asserting that the state should have no "power to adjudicate on points of opinion." In response, Chamberlain removed the offending statement from his forthcoming book, *The American Stakes* (Philadelphia: Lippincott, 1940). See p. 33, where Nock is still listed as an anarchist, but IMP has disappeared. The book is an undigested mass of social-democratic and limited-government ideas, the first owing to the times, the second, apparently, to IMP.

32. John Chamberlain, *A Life with the Printed Word* (Chicago: Regnery Gateway, 1982) 96, 136. For other examples of Chamberlain's comments on Paterson's work, see "The Literary Market: 1952-53," *Human Events* 10 (August 19, 1953) 1-4; and the several essays discussing Paterson in the collection of his contributions to *The Freeman*, *The Turnabout Years: America's Cultural Life, 1900-1950* (Ottawa, IL: Jameson Books, 1991).

33. Pierre Lecomte du Noüy, *Human Destiny* (New York: Longmans, Greene, 1947) xviii-xix, 40, 197.

34. Lecomte du Noüy 117, 238.

35. T 7/11/48. Kirk appears in one of IMP's last columns, T 1/9/49.

36. Russell Kirk to author, November 30, 1990.

37. IMP to R. S. Henry, received January 12, 1944, and received June 6, 1945; R. S. Henry to IMP, July 19, 1945; Chamberlain, *Life* 136; IMP to R. S. Henry, received January 9, 1946.

38. Ayn Rand to Leonard E. Read, May 18, 1946, *Letters* 275-77. Rand returned to Read the Paterson-Read correspondence that she saw and discussed in this letter. It is apparently lost.

39. Leonard E. Read to Muriel Hall, September 15, 1964; John Chamberlain, "Despair Not!" *Freeman* 14 (May 1964) 59-62.

40. H. M. Griffith to IMP, July 8, July 21, August 1, August 4, August 11, August 18, August 21, 1952. IMP's side of the correspondence has not been found, but its tendency is clear.

41. Rand, *Fountainhead* 549.

42. Howard Buffett to John Chamberlain, June 13, 1952; to IMP, August 5, 1952, and August 22, 1952; to MH, March 1, 1963; R. C. Hoiles to MH, October 19, 1962; to Bernice D. Henderson, September 10, 1943 (courtesy of Mrs. Henderson); David Henderson to author, July 11, 1991.

43. R. C. Hoiles to IMP, May 13, 1950; IMP to R. C. Hoiles, May(?) 1950; R. C. Hoiles to Muriel Hall, October 19, 1962; Alan W. Bock, "'Ours Is Liberty, Now and Forever,'" *Orange County Register*, Commentary Section (April 16, 2000) 6.

44. M. Roberts to IMP, July 27, 1945; August 13, 1945.

Chapter 19

1. Paterson, "Has the World Grown Smaller?" *Georgia Review* 2 (Spring 1948) 177-85. IMP to R. S. Henry, April 26, 1948, tells the article's history and dates its writing.
2. IMP, annotations to *Physics and Philosophy*, by James Jeans (Cambridge: Cambridge University Press, 1943) 55; John D. Barrow and Frank J. Tipler, *The Anthropic Cosmological Principle* (Oxford: Clarendon, 1986).
3. Jeans 2.
4. IMP to Ted Sprague, December 24, 1951(?); IMP, "Notes for a new mathematical approach to the order of the physical universe," typescript, undated; previous version of "Notes" (early 1952?) with long postscripts to Sprague. Sprague, who was knowledgeable in science, was a devoted friend of IMP; he and his wife Grace attended her last Monday night at the *Herald Tribune*.
5. IMP to Ted Sprague, December 24, 1951(?).
6. IMP to Ted Sprague, September 5, 1951, December 13, 1951(?); "Notes for a new mathematical approach."
7. IMP to Ted Sprague, December 13, 1951(?).
8. IMP to Ted Sprague, December 13, 1951(?).
9. IMP to Ted Sprague, December 13, 1951(?).
10. IMP to R. S. Henry, received July 20, 1948; John D. Wade to IMP, September 14, 1948; Paterson, "The Riddle of Chief Justice Taney in the Dred Scott Decision" *Georgia Review* 3 (Summer 1949) 192-203.
11. On Taney's education, skill, and sometimes courage as a jurist, see Charles W. Smith, Jr., *Roger B. Taney: Jacksonian Jurist* (Chapel Hill: University of North Carolina Press, 1936); on his gross judicial errors in the Dred Scott case, see Don E. Fehrenbacher, *Slavery, Law, and Politics: The Dred Scott Case in Historical Perspective* (New York: Oxford Univeristy Press, 1981) 183-213.
12. Fehrenbacher 193-94. Taney's involvement in popular democracy is discussed at large by Smith.
13. IMP to R. S. Henry, received September 28, 1945. Sales of *The Fountainhead* were 150,000 and still "accelerating."
14. Barbara Branden, *The Passion of Ayn Rand* (Garden City, NY: Doubleday, 1986) 218. It is noteworthy that in the first, Rand-approved telling of this story, Isabel Paterson is merely "an acquaintance" (Barbara Branden, "A Biographical Essay," in Nathaniel Branden and Barbara Branden, *Who Is Ayn Rand?* [New York: Random House, 1962] 167).
15. T 6/21/42; Paterson, *The God of the Machine* (New Brunswick, NJ: Transaction Publishers, 1993) 169.
16. Ayn Rand, *Atlas Shrugged* (New York: Random House, 1957) 576-77; T 9/17/39.
17. Paterson, *The Singing Season: A Romance of Old Spain* (New York: Boni and Liveright, 1924) 235.
18. IMP to Ayn Rand, October 7, 1943, October 13, 1943, March 24, 1948; Ayn Rand to IMP, July 26, 1945; *Letters of Ayn Rand*, ed. Michael S. Berliner (New York: Dutton, 1995) 176-77.
19. IMP to Ayn Rand, January 19, 1944, March 7, 1944, June 7, 1944, November 1944.
20. Albert Mannheimer to IMP, April 26, 1947.
21. IMP to R. S. Henry, received September 28, 1945; IMP to R. S. Henry, received September 12, 1945; Ayn Rand to IMP, February 7, 1948, *Letters* 191.
22. Ayn Rand, *The Fountainhead* (New York: Bobbs-Merrill, 1943) 710.

23. Branden, *Passion* 164, confirmed by Branden's taped interview with Rand, 1961. After IMP's death, her friend Muriel Hall went to lunch with Rand and prefaced some remark by saying, "I don't want to upset you but . . . ." Rand interrupted with the soothing comment, "Don't worry, my dear. I don't get upset with people *the way Pat did!*" (MH, interview).

24. Rand's fiction is often very funny; see Stephen Cox, "The Literary Achievement of *The Fountainhead*," in Cox and David Kelley, *"The Fountainhead": A Fiftieth Anniversary Celebration* (Poughkeepsie, NY: Institute for Objectivist Studies, 1993) 5-23; and "Ayn Rand: Theory versus Creative Life," *Journal of Libertarian Studes* 8 (Winter 1986) 19-29. But her friends testify that she sometimes could not understand even the most obvious jokes (Nathaniel Branden, Henry Mark Holzer, Erika Holzer, interviews).

25. For instance: Rand was disgusted when, as she thought, IMP referred to her own novels as less than the highest in literary quality (Ayn Rand, taped interview with Barbara Branden). To Rand, such a remark was an admission of spiritual inferiority, if not deformity. To IMP, it just amounted to seeing the truth: she wasn't Conrad or Woolf—but that didn't mean she was just playing with literature, either. Years before, one of IMP's readers had taken her to task for saying that Arnold Bennett was not of the first rank, and she had replied, "[H]e was at the head of the second raters. And that's pretty good" (T 6/18/33).

26. Ayn Rand to Leonard E. Read, May 18, 1946, *Letters* 275. Here Rand, who is angry about something Paterson had written to Read about *Anthem*, says, "I have never respected [Paterson's] literary judgment as I have her political one."

27. Branden, *Passion* 177. Rand's associate Nathaniel Branden (interview) recalls that Paterson had an especially bad reaction to the scene in *The Fountainhead* in which Dominique Francon, after a violent sex encounter with Howard Roark, goes into her bathroom and does *not* cleanse herself: "Paterson thought that was the obscenity of obscenity," because it showed Dominique's enjoyment of what had happened.

28. Ayn Rand, quoted in Branden, *Passion* 35-36.

29. Branden, *Passion* 165, 204-205; Ayn Rand, taped interview with Barbara Branden. Nathaniel Branden notes that Rand lacked an understanding of "mysticism" but used it as a general term for "irrationality." He remembers that people who tried to talk with her about even the mildest purported manifestations of ESP found that "she could not have been any more closed-minded. She knew all about how the universe ran" (Nathaniel Branden, interview).

30. MH, interviews (on IMP's view of Christian morality); T 5/28/33; Rand, *Fountainhead* 740-41.

31. Nathaniel Branden, interview, recalling Rand's view of the effects of Paterson's ethical Christianity. See also Barbara Branden, *Passion* 204, citing Rand on IMP's religious prejudice against *The Fountainhead*.

32. Rand's dismay seems especially remarkable in light of another memory, which was that she had gladly authorized IMP, who "hated a lot of footnotes," to "use [her] ideas" without attribution (Branden, *Passion* 181-82, 172; confirmed by Branden's source in Rand's interview tape). Justin Raimondo, *Reclaiming the American Right: The Lost Legacy of the Conservative Movement* (Burlingame, CA: Center for Libertarian Studies, 1993) 198, is inclined, as I am, to distrust Rand's memory and to emphasize IMP's role as teacher. He sees IMP and Rand as much closer on the contested points than I do, but he thinks it impossible to determine "who learned what from whom."

33. Ayn Rand to Leonard E. Read, May 18, 1946, *Letters* 275-76.

34. T 4/25/43, T 6/6/43. Before its publication, IMP read only the speeches in the novel, or some of them (Ayn Rand, *The Art of Fiction: A Guide for Writers and Readers*, ed. Tore Boeckmann [New York: Penguin-Plume, 2000] 163).
35. A good example is Harry Scherman, whose book *The Promises Men Live By* (New York: Random House, 1937) she was willing to laud as "the one original and important contribution to economics—which means also social and political think-ing—of the present period," simply because it showed the importance of economic commitments and "deferred exchanges" (T 2/12/39, T 3/12/39, T 1/18/42; Pater-son, *God of the Machine* 219). IMP knew how to contextualize Scherman's ideas so as to bring out their real importance, but she gave him full credit anyway.
36. T 10/1/33. Cf. T 11/19/33: "The biggest pests are the people who use altruism as an alibi." See also T 3/31/40, which is one of IMP's rough drafts for *The God of the Machine*, on the dismal results of "a century of incessant attention from altruis-tic idealists"; and *The Golden Vanity* (New York: William Morrow, 1934), 334, on the psychology of altruism.
37. T 4/14/40.
38. T 2/16/36, T 10/1/33; Rand, *Fountainhead* 743; Paterson, "Has the World" 185.
39. Branden, *Passion* 182.
40. T 2/1/42.
41. Paterson, *God of the Machine* 250; Rand, *The Fountainhead* 738, 741; Paterson, review of *Clara Barron*, by Harvey O'Higgins, HTB (March 7, 1926) 4.
42. Paterson, *God of the Machine* 239; Rand, *Fountainhead* 739.
43. T 9/27/36, Rand, *Fountainhead* 742, T 9/22/40.
44. T 11/17/35.
45. It is interesting that in a column written more than three years after publication of *The God of the Machine* (T 9/1/46), where Paterson contrasts the "sacrifice" demanded in war with the "selfish" behavior that produces the arts of peace, her quotation marks maintain the sense that the words can be variously used. In a later column she notes that "the philanthropist manages to take care of Number One" (T 1/12/47). Still later, she refers to "'unselfish beings'—a contradiction in terms" (T 10/17/48).
46. Ayn Rand, taped interview with Barbara Branden. The passage in question ap-pears in Boswell's *Life* under date of October 26, 1769. Paterson must have brought up the episode; she was a reader and quoter of Boswell, whereas Rand, so far as is known, never referred to his work in any other context. In recounting the exchange with Paterson, she also misremembered the details of Boswell's story.
47. Ayn Rand to IMP, May 8, 1948, *Letters of Ayn Rand* 211, IMP to Ayn Rand, May 13, 1948 (partially quoted in *Letters*, 214-15).
48. Rand, taped interview with Barbara Branden; T 4/2/44.
49. T 6/29/41, T 8/9/42, T 1/31/43, T 4/25/43, T 6/6/43, T 6/20/43, T 7/4/43, T 7/18/43, T 10/10/43, T 12/26/43, T 4/2/44, T 9/23/45, T 12/16/45 (which contains an account of IMP's conversation with Rand's friend Albert Mannheimer), T 8/25/46, T 11/30/47, T 1/4/48. MH (interview) is certain that IMP used her contacts in publishing to interest Bobbs-Merrill in accepting *The Fountainhead*, a book that had been repeatedly rejected by other publishers: "She was very pleased with her achievement."
50. Hiram Haydn, *Words & Faces* (New York: Harcourt Brace Jovanovich, 1974) 33. Haydn was Rand's editor at Random House.
51. Roy Childs to Nathaniel Branden, February 23, 1979; Nathaniel Branden to Roy Childs, March 5, 1979 (Hoover Institution, Stanford University). In his letter, Childs refers to a theory, which has circulated in libertarian circles for many years,

that Paterson and Lane supported Rand financially while she finished *The Foun-tainhead*. Lane's heir, the late Roger Lea MacBride, as I have heard (Michael Holmes, interview), was one of the people who conveyed this idea, but there is no other evidence for it, and much against. Rand would not have accepted charity. As for a loan, Lane says in a letter written to Paterson while Rand was working on *The Fountainhead* (March 26, 1942), "I know you do not lend money." (This letter is dated "1932," but the return address establishes the correct year.) In his reply to Childs, Branden says that Rand spoke to him "very complimentarily" of both Lane and Paterson, "and acknowledged her many valuable discussions with them." He adds, however, "I am aware, sadly, that she had been helped by friends during her struggling years," while maintaining that "'no one has ever helped me.'"

52. IMP to R. S. Henry, received May 27, 1948. IMP to R. S. Henry, received July 20, 1948, mentions "[f]lying [back] across the continent last month."

53. Ayn Rand, taped interview with Barbara Branden. The larger story of Paterson's involvement with the *Freeman* will be told in chapter 22, below.

54. Interview, MH.

55. The following information is derived from Branden, *Passion* 203-205, and Branden's taped interview with Rand.

56. IMP to MH, July 5, 1958.

57. Four brief letters sent by Rand to IMP in 1950 have been published (Rand, *Letters* 217-18).

58. MH and Gertrude Vogt, interviews.

Chapter 20

1. The young friend was Muriel Hall (MH to author, December 6, 1999).

2. Richard Kluger, *The Paper: The Life and Death of the "New York Herald Tri-bune"* (New York: Alfred A. Knopf, 1986) 172. I follow Kluger's summary of the life of the Reids, esp. 139-40, 171 ff.

3. Kluger 140, 172.

4. Kluger 408, 205.

5. Kluger's anxious defense of Gannett (who was one of Irita Van Doren's creations) merely demonstrates that he was a warm communist sympathizer (350-51, 510). Another instance is Joseph Barnes, a major fixture at the *Trib*, whom George Kennan, who knew him when Barnes was reporting from Moscow, delicately characterized as "naive" about Russia and consequently "much more pro-Soviet than the rest of us." Naiveté is perhaps not the finest qualification for journalism, but Mrs. Reid defended Barnes. See Kluger 301, 428, 286 on this and other examples of her "liberating and liberalizing influence."

6. My summary of Irita (pronounced eye-REE-ta) Van Doren's early life relies on Kluger, 323-24. H. L. Mencken indicates that Sherman was "violently" and pretty publicly in love with Irita, though "so far as I know it remained quite innocent." He credits Irita and Carl with Sherman's swerve from critical conservatism (Mencken, *My Life as Author and Editor* [New York: Alfred A. Knopf, 1993] 185). Sherman's correspondence, though published with the consent of his surviving wife, indi-cates that Mencken was right, at least about the first of his conclusions; see Jacob Zeitlin and Homer Woodbridge, *Life and Letters of Stuart P. Sherman* (New York: Farrar & Rinehart, 1929) 700.

7. Hiram Haydn, *Words and Faces* (New York: Harcourt Brace, 1974) 165. Mencken, not so easily bowled over, calls Irita "civilised" and "very charming" (185). Others

have characterized her as the classic Southern belle (Gertrude Vogt, interview). It is probable that no one ever completely disliked Irita Van Doren.

8. Paterson's correspondence shows that although they knew that Irita and Carl had recently divorced, they were confused about whether she had remarried or not (IMP to GB, July 16, 1936: Irita will soon remarry; IMP to Mary Welles, c. September 10, 1936: Irita has remarried; IMP to GB, December 4, 1936: Irita hasn't remarried after all).

9. IMP to Irita Van Doren, August 19, 1940; Van Doren to IMP, August 22, 1940; IMP to Van Doren, August 22(?), 1940.

10. Gertrude Vogt, MH, interviews. For Mrs. Reid's introduction, see Kluger 323.

11. Joseph Barnes, *Willkie: The Events He Was Part Of—The Ideas He Fought For* (New York: Simon and Schuster, 1952) 313-16; Ellsworth Barnard, *Wendell Willkie: Fighter for Freedom* (Marquette: Northern Michigan University Press, 1966) 412; "Baedeker for the Future," *Time* 41 (April 12, 1943) 24; "One World," *Life* 14 (April 26, 1943) 73-76, 79-81.

12. Wendell Willkie, *One World* (New York: Simon and Schuster, 1943) 52-54, 102; Howard Jones, "One World: An American Perspective," in James H. Madison, ed., *Wendell Willkie: Hoosier Internationalist* (Bloomington: Indiana University Press, 1992) 119.

13. Willkie 83.

14. Willkie 53, 57, 61, 102, etc.

15. Gertrude Vogt, who worked with Paterson at *"Books"* from 1935 on, was "sure" there was no censorship (Gertrude Vogt, interview).

16. T 7/19/36, 8/2/36.

17. Gertrude Vogt, MH, interviews. Even in the mid-1930s, John Chamberlain observed that Paterson and Van Doren disagreed "about practically everything" and that although Van Doren didn't try to "disturb" her, she heartily disliked her "opinions" (Chamberlain, *A Life with the Printed Word* (Chicago: Regnery Gateway, 1982) 35.

18. Schroeder Boulton to Editor, HT, July 20, 1942; T 8/2/42.

19. IMP, "'How can I get past the (deleted) conservatives?'" typescript. Paterson may have written these notes on her life at the *Herald Tribune* while preparing the account of her misfortunes that appears in "What Do They Do All Day?", her typescript review (1959) of Crawford Greenewalt's *The Uncommon Man*; see chapter 23, below.

20. Kluger 475-78. In 1951, as Kluger shows, this person was moved to another desk, with no cut in pay. He—unlike Paterson—remained at the paper for another decade.

21. TASS to Coward McCann, Inc., attention Miss Cobb, March 24, 1943; Paterson, "What Do They Do All Day?"

22. T 11/11/34, T 8/24/41, T 4/23/44.

23. MH, "Pat 1886," typescript record of IMP's conversation, weekend of July 27, 1958; Kluger 428, 470.

24. Rodney Gilbert to IMP, September 16, 1957; Kluger 428, quoting Helen Reid to William Loeb, November 16, 1945 (see also 470). Gilbert was for many years a writer of *HT* editorials and a contributor to *"Books."* He was concerned with "fellow-travelling" in both departments.

25. Kluger (427, 429) indicates that the *HT* did go so far as to refrain from "lur[ing] back" leftwing Foreign Editor Joseph Barnes, after the leftwing journal for which he had left the *HT* collapsed for lack of money. (See also Kluger 475-78.) Kluger does not mention the attack by veteran journalist Irene Corbally Kuhn—more

moderate, but more convincing than Pegler's—on the book-reviewing practices of the *HT* and the *New York Times* ("Why You Buy Books that Sell Communism," *American Legion Magazine* [January 1951]). Kuhn's article received much national attention in the popular media (e.g., "Review of Reviews," *Newsweek* [March 19, 1951] 58) and provoked anxious defenses from the *Trib*, including a six-page "Memorandum for Members of the Staff." The "Memorandum" was mainly sophistries. A more effective defense was provided by the monthly journal of the paper's American Legion post (Maurice Rosenwald, "Kuhn Article About Anti-Red Book Gag Burps," *The Guidon* 5 [April 1951] 1, 4).

26. Kluger 324; Neil Jumonville, *Henry Steele Commager: Midcentury Liberalism and the History of the Present* (Chapel Hill: University of North Carolina Press, 1999) 24; Lewis Gannett, "A Quarter Century of a Weekly Book Review . . . and of the World," HTB (September 25, 1949) 5.
27. Paterson, "'How can I get past.'"
28. Paterson, "'How can I get past'"; Wallace Carroll, *Persuade or Perish* (Boston: Houghton Mifflin, 1948) 377; review by Arthur M. Schlesinger, Jr., HTB (August 15, 1948) 1. Carroll's earlier book was reviewed favorably, but with reservations, by William L. Shirer, HTB (October 4, 1942) 1.
29. Gertrude Vogt, interview, referring to Lewis Gannett.
30. MH, interview.
31. Kluger 425-26. According to her 1948 tax return, the *HT* was paying IMP $7730 a year, up from $7084 in 1947 and $6199 in 1946.
32. MH, interview; IMP to R. S. Henry, January 24, 1949.
33. Interview, Gertrude Vogt.
34. Paterson, "'How can I get past.'"
35. See, for example, Irita Van Doren to Mrs. Roger H. Williams, May 19, 1949; Alma Josenhans to IMP, May 23, 1951.
36. T 6/14/42.

Chapter 21

1. IMP tax returns; A. V. Miller to IMP, December 31, 1954, January 12, 1955; IMP to A. V. Miller, January 5, 1955; Social Security card and envelope, Paterson Papers; MH, interview; IMP to MH, March 30, 1956.
2. IMP to MH, June 11, 1956; August 26, 1956; May 9, 1957; May 13, 1958; IMP to MH(?), undated (late 1958). "Sanner" is pronounced "Sawner."
3. IMP to MH, June 14, 1949; c. February 12, 1951; c. January 31, 1951. The woman with the housemaid was IMP's friend Mary Lecomte du Noüy.
4. MH to GB, August 28, 1962.
5. IMP to MH, May 13, 1955; Paterson, annotations to *The Duke*, by Richard Aldington (New York: Viking, 1943) 283; IMP to MH, February 1, 1955.
6. Not "relaxing" (Barbara Branden, *The Passion of Ayn Rand* [Garden City NY: Doubleday, 1986] 164), as indicated by MH to GB, August 28, 1962; MH, interviews.
7. IMP to MH, January 13, 1956; February 16, 1957; November 19, 1957; February 16, 1958; Paterson, "A Suburban Tristram and a South Dakota Saga," *McNaught's Monthly* 8 (July, 1927) 28. The earliest evidence of the novel is a letter of February 11, 1948, in which IMP tells Ayn Rand that she isn't moving quickly with her book.
8. IMP to MH, June 17, 1957. At one point in the typescript (ms. page 103), IMP crosses out an explicit reference to 1918, apparently not wanting to clarify matters too conveniently; but one gathers that the heroine, now thirty-four years of age,

was seventeen during "the war," the Great War (ms. pages 8, 9). She is roughly fourteen years younger than IMP, but her wedding, the crisis of her life, takes place only about seven or eight years after Paterson's. The typescript of *Joyous Gard* is preserved in the Paterson Papers. Succeeding references are to page numbers in that text.

9. IMP to R. S. Henry, received January 9, 1946.
10. Paterson, *The Golden Vanity* (New York: William Morrow, 1934) 84.
11. It also resembles the Welles family's Buttonwood Farm, which Paterson liked to visit; see chapter 22, below.
12. MH, interview.
13. T 2/22/31.
14. Paterson, *The God of the Machine* (New Brunswick, NJ: Transaction Publishers, 1993) 178.
15. By July 1960, the typescript had been "put away somewhere" (IMP to LF, July 18, 1960). With stubborn honesty, Paterson maintained, as she had in years past in regard to other people's books, that "the fact of a novel being rejected by publishers doesn't necessarily mean that it is good, either" (IMP to LF, August 1, 1959). But she continued to think that *Joyous Gard* was a good novel, which it is.

Chapter 22

1. IMP to MH, November 29, 1958.
2. IMP to MH, August 21, 1955; T 10/20/46.
3. Grace Zaring Stone to IMP, two letters of August 1950(?); Eleanor Perényi, interview.
4. T 6/2/46; IMP to GB, two letters, spring1938(?); GB to IMP, May 8, 1949, responding (unenthusiastically) to an earlier letter of Paterson. After Paterson's death, Busey praised her warmly and insightfully; see e.g., GB to MH, December 28, 1962.
5. Burton Rascoe to IMP, February 26, 1949, March(?), 1949 (Paterson Papers); MH, interviews. On Rascoe's political opinions and latter days, see Donald M. Hensley, *Burton Rascoe* (New York: Twayne, 1970).
6. IMP to R. S. Henry, received September 6, 1945; MH, interview.
7. Fred Feldkamp, "Introduction"; Thomas Maeder, "Afterword," to Will Cuppy, *The Decline and Fall of Practically Everybody*, ed. Fred Feldkamp (Boston: David R. Godine, 1984) 2-4, 239-41; MH, interview.
8. Ayn Rand to Nathaniel Branden (called here by his original name Nathan Blumenthal), January 13, 1950, *Letters of Ayn Rand*, ed. Michael S. Berliner (New York: Dutton-Penguin, 1995) 465; Nathaniel Branden, interview.
9. MH quoted in Barbara Branden, *The Passion of Ayn Rand* (Garden City, NY: Doubleday, 1986) 204 n.
10. Rose Wilder Lane to Robert Le Fevre, August 2, 1957. Lane, a fine story-teller, was not always accurate in her accounts of her past; see William Holtz, *The Ghost in the Little House: A Life of Rose Wilder Lane* (Columbia: University of Missouri Press, 1993) e.g. 340. IMP's last known letter to Lane was sent soon after August 16, 1945.
11. Ted Sprague to IMP, c. November 1950.
12. IMP to John Chamberlain, April 23, 1952.
13. George H. Nash, *The Conservative Intellectual Movement in America Since 1945* (New York: Basic Books, 1976) 27-28, 146-47.

14. Gertrude Vogt to IMP, November 9, 1950; John Chamberlain to IMP, April 22, 1952; John Chamberlain, "A Reviewer's Notebook," *Freeman* 2 (June 16, 1952) 625-26.
15. IMP to John Chamberlain, c. June 9, 1952.
16. IMP to MH, June 24, 1952; John Chamberlain to IMP, after June 10, 1952; John Chamberlain to IMP, notation on letter of Rose Wilder Lane to Chamberlain, June 9, 1952, Hoover Presidential Library.
17. *The Lady and the Tycoon: Letters of Rose Wilder Lane and Jasper Crane*, ed. Roger Lea MacBride (Caldwell, ID: Caxton, 1973); Gertrude Vogt to IMP, June 15, 1951; John Chamberlain to IMP, after June 10, 1952; Jasper Crane to IMP, December 26, 1944; IMP to R. S. Henry, c. August 14, 1945.
18. Jasper Crane to IMP, January 4, 1946, January 10, 1946; IMP to Jasper Crane, January 9, 1946; IMP to R. S. Henry, received January 9, 1946, January 11, 1946, c. September 6, 1946.
19. See esp. Jasper Crane to IMP, July 16, 1950; IMP to John Chamberlain, April 23, 1952; IMP to Jasper Crane, July 20, 1954 (unsent).
20. IMP to MH, c. September 15, 1958.
21. Information on the Welles family is derived from Samuel Gardner Welles, ms. history of the Welles family (written 1930-?), courtesy MH, and from interviews with MH and Mabel Welles Owen.
22. Paterson, *The God of the Machine* (New Brunswick, NJ: Transaction Publishers, 1993) 239.
23. T 2/7/37, 12/19/37; MH interview.
24. IMP to MH, May 5, 1955; MH interview. When "puzzled" by other people's conduct, Paterson said, "I always think vaguely: 'Well, of course they are Easterners, not very bright'" (IMP to MH, May 13, 1958).
25. Samuel Gardner Welles, Jr., to DeWitt Wallace, May 31, 1943.
26. MH, interview; IMP to R. S. Henry, May 16, 1945.
27. MH, interviews; Whittaker Chambers, *Witness* (New York: Random House, 1952) 483; Sam Tenenhaus, *Whittaker Chambers: A Biography* (New York: Random House, 1997) 156; Allen Weinstein, *Perjury: The Hiss-Chambers Case*, 2nd ed. (New York: Random House, 1997) 104, 296-98, 303-304; IMP to MH, February 5, 1957.
28. MH, interviews.
29. MH, interviews.
30. IMP to Edward Hall, April 21, 22, 1954; MH, interviews.

Chapter 23

1. Russell Kirk, interview.
2. In his path-breaking book, *The Conservative Intellectual Movement in America Since 1945* (New York: Basic Books, 1976) 148-51, 171-85, George H. Nash effectively summarizes the "fusion" (more or less) of libertarian with traditional ideas in the conservative movement focused on *National Review*; he also explores early libertarian opposition to *National Review* conservatism.
3. Friedrich Hayek, "Why I Am Not a Conservative," in *The Constitution of Liberty* (Chicago: University of Chicago Press, 1960) 395-411. On Trilling, see chapter 11, above.
4. Manuel S. Klausner, "Inside Ronald Reagan: A Reason Interview," *Reason* 8 (July 1975) 6. Sheldon Richman ("New Deal Nemesis: The 'Old Right' Jeffersonians," *Independent Review* 1 [Fall 1996] esp. 206-208), who takes isolationism as his

touchstone, sharply distinguishes the "Old Right" of Paterson et alia from *National Review's* "New Right." He emphasizes militarily and economically interventionist or "collectivist" elements in the program of "New Right" intellectuals. The distinction between Old and New appears less sharp when one considers the ascendancy of fusionism in *NR*'s counsels, its aggressively individualist tone and style, and its salient insistence on the virtues of a supposedly discredited capitalism (precisely the elements that facilitated the electoral breakthrough of rightwing forces in the 1980s and 1990s).

5. WFB to IMP, September 25, 1954; Gertrude Vogt to IMP, July 18, 1954.
6. WFB to IMP, September 16, 1955.
7. WFB to IMP, September 23, 1955.
8. WFB to IMP, November 17, 1955; December 15, 1955.
9. IMP, "The Southern Breakthrough," *National Review* 1 (December 21, 1955) 9-12.
10. IMP to GB, two letters, (spring 1938?); IMP to MH, September 18, 1956. Paterson was far from sharing white Southerners' racial fears and aversions. She cheerfully predicted that all Americans would eventually be one race, an attractive mixture of colors (MH, interview).
11. Paterson, "The Oracles are Dumb," *National Review* 2 (May 23, 1956) 10-13, 16.
12. IMP to MH, c. June 19, 1952; February 19, 1959.
13. IMP to MH, c. July 16, 1947; IMP to Edward Hall, March 18(?), 1955; Paterson, "Oracles" 10.
14. Paterson, "Oracles," 10-11.
15. Paterson, "A Man of Destiny," *National Review* 1 (January 4, 1956) 26-28.
16. Paterson, "Learning to Read: Child's Play," *National Review* 4 (November 30, 1957) 489-91; IMP to MH, March 5, 1955.
17. MH, interview.
18. Gertrude Vogt to MH, March 14, 1961. Buckley tried to sell the article to the *Reader's Digest*, but Eugene Lyons, the *Digest*'s sophisticated senior editor, rejected it as too "sophisticated" for his audience (Lyons to WFB, November 20, 1957). Two years later, Paterson told Lippincott's that she was planning to write a short book on "the intelligence of children" (IMP to Tay Hohoff, August 18, [1959]). Whether she received any encouragement from intelligent adults does not appear.
19. WFB to IMP, December 14, 1955; Gertrude Vogt to IMP, January 15, 1958; WFB to IMP, March 14, 1956.
20. WFB to IMP, March 9, 1956; July 9, 1956; May 8, 1957; March 14, 1956; April 2, 1956; April 6, 1956; IMP to WFB, April 4, 1956; c. April 8, 1956; William F. Buckley, Jr., "RIP, Mrs. Paterson (A Personal Reminiscence)," *National Review* 10 (January 28, 1961) 43; WFB to IMP, October 9, 1959. Most of IMP's letters to WFB have, unfortunately, been lost.
21. Among his good qualities, she listed "youth, boundless energy, determination, and I think actual business ability" (IMP to MH, December 29, 1955). "Buckley is naturally a journalist, and he just has to put it over" (IMP to Ted Sprague, November 23, 1955).
22. WFB to MH, February 6, 1961; IMP to John Chamberlain, April 23, 1952.
23. Whittaker Chambers, "Big Sister Is Watching You," review of *Atlas Shrugged*, by Ayn Rand, *National Review* 4 (December 28, 1957) 594-96; IMP to Gertrude Vogt, c. January 1, 1958 (Yale University Library); IMP to MH, January 1, 1958.
24. WFB to IMP, January 7, 1958.

25. Paterson's response did not survive, but her displeasure is indicated in Gertrude Vogt's letter to her of January 15, 1958.
26. Crawford H. Greenewalt, *The Uncommon Man: The Individual in the Organization* (New York: McGraw-Hill, 1959). Paterson's typescript account of this book is entitled "What Do They Do All Day?"
27. WFB to MH, February 6, 1961.
28. WFB to IMP, September 16, 1959; IMP to WFB, September 18, 1959; WFB to IMP, October 9, 1959.
29. Whittaker Chambers to WFB, December 16, 1954, in *Odyssey of a Friend: Whittaker Chambers' Letters to William F. Buckley, Jr., 1954-1961*, ed. William F. Buckley, Jr. (New York: Putnam's, 1969) 94. Chambers regarded Paterson's *National Review* article on Lecomte du Nouy as "enough to justify any issue of a magazine" (Chambers to WFB, January 3, 1956, *Odyssey* 114.
30. Whittaker Chambers to WFB, December 8, 1958, *Odyssey* 219-20.

Chapter 24

1. IMP to LF, January 1958; IMP to LF, August 9, 1958.
2. IMP to MH, May 15, 1959; IMP to Mrs. Knowlton, May 8, 1960; IMP to MH, August 26, 1959; MH, interviews.
3. John McLaren, interview; MH, interview.
4. MH, interview. To Ted Hall, Paterson had the best sense of humor in the world (Edward Hall to Mabel and Charles Owen, June 1, 1955).
5. MH, interviews; MH to GB, August 28, 1962.
6. MH, interviews; IMP to MH, May 13, 1958.
7. IMP to Tay Hohoff, August 18, 1959. She seems to have broached the idea of writing her "memoirs" ten years earlier (GB to IMP, May 8, 1949).
8. Zelda Good to IMP, late May(?) 1959; Zelda Good to MH, February 26, 1962; Zelda Good to IMP, February 9, 1960; June 2, 1960; August 29, 1960(?). For a while, Zelda didn't even have IMP's home address (Zelda Good to IMP, c. January 1, 1954).
9. John Chamberlain to IMP, March 17, 1959; W. Everard Edmonds to IMP, March 12, 1956; March 31, 1956; Grace Luckhart to IMP, March 8, 1957; IMP to LF, December 24, 1957.
10. IMP to Edward Hall, February(?) 24(?), 1959; first ellipsis marks in the quotation are IMP's.
11. My account of Paterson's meeting with Rand is based on Barbara Branden, *The Passion of Ayn Rand* (Garden City, NY: Doubleday, 1986) 308-309, and Branden's taped interview with Rand, 1961.
12. Nathaniel Branden, interview.
13. John Hospers, interview. Hospers ran for president on the Libertarian Party platform in 1972 and earned a vote in the Electoral College for himself and his running mate Theodora Nathan, the first woman ever to receive a vote.
14. The essay, originally published in *The Objectivist Newsletter* 3 (October 1964) 42-43, as a review of Muriel Hall's edition of *The God of the Machine* (Caldwell, ID: Caxton, 1964), was reprinted, with Rand's permission, as the Introduction to the edition of the book by Bea and Robert Hessen (Palo Alto, CA: Palo Alto Book Service, 1983). Robert Hessen had been Rand's secretary. Rand's practice of recommending *The God of the Machine* to friends is reported in interviews with Nathaniel Branden, Erika Holzer, and Henry Mark Holzer, and by Barbara Branden, *Passion* 182n, who writes that the book was one of only "a handful of books [on

economics] she recommended to us." The 1964 edition of *The God of the Machine* was distributed by the NBI Book Service, sponsored by Rand.

15. Edna J. Giesen to IMP, June 15, June 23, 1949.
16. Robert LeFevre to IMP, January 30, April 9, April 19, April 26, May 2, 1960.
17. Ronald Hamowy, "'National Review': Criticism and Reply," *New Individualist Review* 1 (November 1961) 84; Murray N. Rothbard, "Machine Politics," review of *The God of the Machine*, by Isabel Paterson, *Chronicles of Culture* 17 (December 1993) 33; David Boaz, ed., *The Libertarian Reader: Classic and Contemporary Readings from Lao-tzu to Milton Friedman* (New York: Free Press, 1997).
18. Paterson, *The God of the Machine* (New York: Arno Press and the *New York Times*, 1972), (New Brunswick, NJ: Transaction Publishers, 1993); for 1964 and 1983 printings, see note 14.
19. Russell Kirk to author, January 20, 1990.
20. Paterson, *God of the Machine* (1993) 290-91, 14.
21. Paterson, *God of the Machine* (1993) 3.
22. MH, interview. The following account is dependent on interviews with MH.
23. Because of a dispute between MH and church authorities about the nature of a monument (debate having followed Paterson to the end, and after it), the grave remains unmarked. It is number 8 in plot 121.

Index

Acton, John E. E. D., 1st Baron Acton, 260
Adamic, Louis, 199
Adams, Henry, 259-60, 275, 277
Adams, J. Donald, 226
Addams, Charles, 355
American Academy of Arts and Letters, 235
American Newspaper Guild, 228
American Writers' Congress, 223-24
Anderson, Sherwood, 59
Archimedes, 276
Armada, Spanish, 101
Armstrong, John, 61
Arthurian romance, 327
Association Against the Prohibition Amendment, 112, 206
Astor, Vincent, 130, 158, 171
Atherton, Gertrude, 196
Augustus, 105
Austen, Jane, 79, 84
Austin, Mary, 79, 203

Baker, Newton, 109, 208
Barbary pirates, 238
Barnes, Djuna, 114
Barnes, Harry Elmer, 69
Barton, Bruce, 69-70
Beard, Charles, 205, 232-33
Beaverbrook, William Maxwell Aitken, 1st Baron, 25
Benchley, Robert, 67
Bennett, Arnold, 95
Bennett, Richard Bedford, 24-26, 113, 116, 341
Beresford, Lord Delaval, 16
Berkeley, George, 342
Berle, Adolf, 176
Black, Hugo, 174
Blake, William, 65, 175

Bontemps, Arna, 200
Book-of-the-Month Club, 228
Borglum, Gutzon, 58-59, 60
Boswell, James, 311
Bowen, Elizabeth, 189
Bowler, Francis, 7-11, 116, 121-22
Bowler, Margaret, 8, 10, 18, 116, 120, 121, 203
Bowler, Mark, 10, 121-22
Bowler, Zelda. See Good, Zelda
Boyd, James, 244
Brady, William A., 59, 120
Braeme, Charlotte M, 19
Branden, Barbara, 334-35
Branden, Nathaniel, 334-35, 358
Bread Loaf Writers' Conference, 63, 88
Brickell, Herschel, 226
Bright, John, 54
Bromfield, Louis, 91-92, 226, 333
Brook Farm, 152
Broun, Heywood, 67, 228-29
Brown, Harry Bingham, 2-3, 312
Brown, Roy, 36
Browning, Robert, 89
Brunhoff, Jean de, 79
Bryan, William Jennings, 13, 109
Bryant, William Cullen, 62
Buckley, William F., Jr., 216, 343-46, 350-53
Buffett, Howard, 294
Burke, Edmund, 292
Burke, Kenneth, 223
Busey, Garreta, 91, 113, 333-34

Cabell, James Branch, 59, 67
Caesar, Julius, 105
Caldwell, Erskine, 223
Caldwell, Taylor, 336
Calonne, Charles Alexandre de, 171
Calvinism, 19-20, 293

Canadian Pacific Railway, 24, 26
Carroll, Wallace, 321
Castiglione, Baldassare, 317
Cather, Willa, 59, 77-78, 133, 195
Cerf, Bennett, 66, 319
Chamberlain, John, 218, 282-83, 290-
    91, 293, 312, 335-37, 351, 357
Chamberlain, Joseph, 25
Chambers, Whittaker, 248, 340-41, 351,
    353-54
Chase, Stuart, 127, 129, 140-41, 145,
    181, 256
Chaucer, Geoffrey, 326
Chiang, Kai-Shek, 317
Chodorov, Frank, 215-16, 312, 338, 359
Christy, Howard Chandler, 41
Churchill, Winston, 70
Clark, Emily, 229
Cleopatra, queen of Egypt, 203
Cleveland, Grover, 132-33, 206
Cluny Museum, 114, 115, 119
Cobden, Richard, 54
Colby, Henry Moore, 68
Coleman, Alta May, 59-60, 92, 116, 120-
    21, 122, 203
Coleman, Pierre, 59
Commager, Henry Steele, 233-35, 321
Conrad, Joseph, 44, 82
Coolidge, Calvin, 107
Cooper, James Fenimore, 21
Cotten, Joseph, 304
Couzens, James, 194
Cowley, Malcolm, 137, 223-24
Crane, Jasper, 337-38, 341, 351-53
Cummings, E. E., 75
Cuppy, Will, 73, 92-95, 117, 157, 183-
    84, 236, 334, 341

Darwinian theory of evolution, 210, 348-
    49, 350
Davis, Andrew Jackson, 19, 20
Davis, John W., 112, 131
Debs, Eugene, 1, 112-13, 263
Defoe, Daniel, 15
Delafield, E. M., 196, 197
De Voto, Bernard, 235
Dewey, John, 74
Dickens, Charles, 19, 55
Dinarzade. See Fischer, Lillian
Doran, George, 46
Dos Passos, John, 223
Dostoevsky, Fyodor, 220

Doughty, C. M., 79
Douglas, James ("Rattlesnake Jimmy"),
    207
Douglas, Lewis, 127, 129, 207-209, 246-
    47
Dred Scott decision, 301-302
Dreiser, Theodore, 50, 59, 79, 150, 223
Dumas, Alexandre, 19
Dunne, Finley Peter, 68-69
Du Pont family and corporation, 206,
    287, 337, 351, 353, 385n.28
Duranty, Walter, 226

Eastman, Max, 75
Eccles, Marriner, 176
Edmonds, W. Everard, 19, 357
Einstein, Albert, 74
Eliot, T. S., 75, 149, 224
Elizabeth I, Queen of England, 101-102
Emergency Banking Bill, 168
Emerson, Ralph Waldo, 71
Essex, Robert Devereux, 2nd earl of, 101

Fadiman, Clifton, 320
Farley, Frank, 92
Farley, James, 229
Farrell, James, 225
Federalist, The, 231
Federal Reserve system, 111, 128
Fergusson, Harvey, 256
Fiedler, Leslie, 149
Fineman, Irving, 139, 145
Fischer, Lillian (Dinarzade), 92, 125,
    184, 230, 240, 357
Fitzgerald, F. Scott, 67, 226, 330
Ford, Anne, 190
Ford, Ford Madox, 82, 114
Ford, Henry, 74, 107
Forrest, Nathan Bedford, 353
Forster, E. M., 72
Foster, William T., 175-76
Foundation for Economic Education,
    293, 336
Four Freedoms, The, 249-50
Frank, Waldo, 150
Franklin, Benjamin, 270
Frederick II, King of Prussia, 93
Free Company, The, 244
Freud, Sigmund, 70
Friedman, Milton, 128, 210, 359, 360
Frost, Robert, 81, 239
Fuller, Margaret, 62

Galsworthy, John, 37
Gannett, Lewis, 316
Garibaldi, Giuseppe, 70, 71
Garrett, Garet, 127, 212-13, 216, 285, 359
Gaynor, Janet, 313
George, Henry, 53, 71, 214-15, 351
Gershwin, George, 313
Gilson, Etienne, 326
Glasgow, Ellen, 59, 81, 196
Glass, Montague, 71
Gold, Michael, 227
Good, Zelda, 121, 122, 357
Gore, Thomas P., 170
Gray, Thomas, 21
Greenewalt, Crawford H., 351-52
Gregory, Horace, 223-24
Griffith, H. M., 293-94
Guggenheim family, 225

Haig, Douglas, 203
Hall, Edward Matson, 341-42, 355-56, 361-63
Hall, Muriel Welles, 26, 340-42, 355-56, 360, 361-63
Hall, Rebecca, 341-42, 355, 356
Hall, Thomas, 341-42, 350, 355, 356
Hamilton, Alexander, 281
Hansen, Harry, 126
Hardy, Thomas, 48
Hatshepsut, Queen of Egypt, 95
Hawley-Smoot tariff, 129
Haydn, Hiram, 317
Hayek, Friedrich, 144, 178, 210, 255, 344, 353, 359, 360
Hearst, William Randolph, 41, 228
Hemingway, Ernest, 62, 71, 84, 226
Henry II, King of Castile, 98, 99-101
Henry, Robert Selph, 257, 290, 304, 312, 322, 341
Herbst, Josephine, 223, 225
Hessen, Robert, 360
Hicks, Granville, 176
Hiss, Alger, 340
Hitler, Adolf, 57, 101, 137, 148, 149, 231, 240, 241, 243, 245, 249, 250, 303, 319
Hoiles, R. C., 294
Holt, Rush, 208
Holtz, William, 216
Homer, 19, 76
Hook, Sidney, 233

Hoover, Herbert: 107, 109, 110-11, 112, 113, 125, 128-33, 135, 147, 152, 153, 159, 165, 166, 171, 176, 183, 205, 208, 287, 294; meets with Paterson, 289-90, 297
Hopper, Hedda, 313
Hospers, John, 358-59
Housman, Laurence, 74
Hugo, Victor, 220

Ibsen, Henrik, 322

Jackson, Andrew, 176, 207
Jay, John, 234
Jeans, James, 202, 298
Jefferson, Thomas, 145, 151, 176, 213, 234, 238-39, 270, 342
Jeffries, Jim, 33
Jevons, William, 144
Jezebel, Queen of Israel, 182
John Reed Club, 150
Johnson, Hiram, 205
Johnson, Hugh, 167
Johnson, Jack, 33
Johnson, James Weldon, 200
Johnson, Lyndon, 208-209
Johnson, Samuel, 84, 311, 326
Josephine, Empress of the French, 184
Jowett, Benjamin, 71
Joyce, James, 75, 77

Keats, John, 12, 76
Kellems, Vivian, 336
Kendall, Willmoore, 346
Kennedy, John F., 356
Kennedy, Joseph, 171, 173-74
Kennedy, Margaret, 226
Keynes, John Maynard, 131, 175
Kipling, Rudyard, 19, 82, 202, 239
Kirchwey, Freda, 69
Kirk, Russell, 292, 343, 353, 360
Knight, Frank, 266
Koestler, Arthur, 72
Ku Klux Klan, 174

La Follette, Suzanne, 214, 215, 351
Lamont, Corliss, 152
La Monte, Robert Rives, 210
Landon, Alfred, 230
Lane, Rose Wilder, 195, 216-18, 241-42, 247-48, 268, 284-88, 289, 290, 294, 335, 336, 337, 359

Lardner, Ring, 67
La Rochefoucauld, François, duc de, 68
Laski, Harold, 281-82
Laurier, Wilfrid, 52
Lawrence, D. H., 76
Lecomte du Noüy, Mary, 292, 348
Lecomte du Noüy, Pierre, 291-92, 348-49
LeFevre, Robert, 287, 359
Lenin, Vladimir Ilyich, 100, 139, 148
Leopold III, King of the Belgians, 242
Levine, Isaac Don, 241-42
Levine, Ruth, 241-42
Lewis, Sinclair, 21, 45, 46, 59, 79, 81, 100, 138-39
Liberty League, 206, 228
Lincoln, Abraham, 113
Lindbergh, Anne Morrow, 241, 278
Lippmann, Walter, 111, 131-32, 173, 179, 208
Locke, John, 49, 144, 267
Louis XVI, King of France, 171
Luckhart, Grace, 24-25, 27, 29, 30, 113-14, 117, 202, 357
Luhan, Mabel Dodge, 196

MacLeish, Archibald, 243-44
Madison, James, 234, 269, 287, 360
Mahan, Alfred Thayer, 259
Maine, Henry, 265
Mangione, Jerre, 199
Mann, Thomas, 226
Mansfield, Mike, 208
Marcus Aurelius, 71
Marlborough, John Churchill, 1st Duke of, 70
Marshall, Margaret, 225-27
Marx, Karl, 62, 81, 144, 150-51, 212, 258-59, 263, 277, 281, 282, 289
Masters, Edgar Lee, 79
Maurois, André, 81, 91
McCarthy, Mary, 225-28
McKinley, William, 68-69
McLaren, John, 341-42, 355-56, 362
McLaren, Mary, 341-42, 355-56
Meader, Lee, 90, 92, 116
Means, Gardiner, 176
Mellon, Andrew, 135
Melville, Herman, 71
Mencken, H. L., 55, 59, 67-68, 209-12, 229-30, 246
Menger, Karl, 144
Meyer, Frank, 343

Millay, Edna St. Vincent, 59
Mills, C. Wright, 281
Milton, John, 76
Mises, Ludwig von, 144, 266, 344
Mitchell, Margaret, 196
Mitchison, Naomi, 196
Moley, Raymond, 172
Montaigne, Michel Eyquem, seigneur de, 71, 78-79, 201, 277
Moran Towing and Transportation Company, 86
More, Thomas, 102
Morgan, House of, 152
Morgan, John Pierpont, 130
Morgenthau, Henry, Jr., 169
Mormons, 13-14
Mullendore, William, 313
Murasaki, Shikibu, 79, 116, 196
Murphy, Charles F., 112
Muskie, Edmund, 208
Mussolini, Benito, 57, 100, 116, 148-49

Napoleon I, Emperor of the French, 184
Nashoba community, 152
Nathaniel Branden Institute, 334-35
National Credit Corporation, 128
National Recovery Administration, 166-68, 219
Nehru, Jawaharlal, 239
Newberry, John S, 11
New Harmony, 152
New Humanism, 75
Newman, Frances, 70, 81, 82
Nicholas II, Tsar of Russia, 58
Nietzsche, Friedrich, 210, 220, 221
Nixon, Richard, 208, 347, 356
Nock, Albert Jay, 71, 213-15, 267, 283-84, 351, 359
Norris, Frank, 50

O'Connor, Frank, 218, 289
O'Hara, John, 82
Oneida community, 152
Oppenheimer, J. Robert, 347-48, 350
Orozco, José, 149
Orrico, Patsy, 333
Ouida (pseud. of Louise de la Ramée), 19
Owen, Mabel Welles, 340, 341
Owen, Robert, 71

Paine, Thomas, 287
Pascal, Blaise, 76

Paterson, Isabel
I. Life
    1886-1900: birth on Manitoulin
        Island, 7; in Newberry, MI, 11-
        13; in Utah, 13; in Alberta, 13-
        15; education, 13, 19
    1901-1910: early jobs, 23-24;
        works for R. B. Bennett in
        Calgary, 24-26; marriage and
        separation, 28-32; journalism
        in Spokane, 32-33
    1911-1920: journalism in Seattle,
        33-38; airplane flight, 1-3, 6,
        42; first novels, 42-56; in San
        Francisco, 56; assistant to
        Gutzon Borglum, 58-59
    1921-1930: at *New York Tribune*,
        60-62; at *New York Herald
        Tribune "Books,"* 62-63; re-
        sides in Hell's Kitchen, 86-87;
        publishes three historical nov-
        els, 97-105; advocates libertar-
        ian views, 99-102, 104; critic
        of Republican administrations,
        107-113; endorses Smith for
        president, 111-112; becomes
        U.S. citizen, 112-13; visits
        Europe, 114; sustains financial
        losses, 125
    1931-1940: critic of planning and
        regulation, 136-45; critic of
        New Deal, 165-76; publishes
        Never Ask the End, *The Golden
        Vanity*, 115-20, 154-63; revis-
        its Europe, 184; builds house
        in Stamford, CT, 184-85; pub-
        lishes *If It Prove Fair Weather*,
        187-89; endorses Republican
        candidates, 230, 245
    1941-1950: builds house in
        Ridgefield, CT, 186-87; pub-
        lishes *The God of the Machine*,
        257; cosmological specula-
        tions, 298-301; writes for
        Georgia Review, 297-98, 301-
        302; dismissed from *Herald
        Tribune*, 322-23
    1951-1961: moves to Rocky Hill,
        NJ, 325; declines Social Secu-
        rity, 325; writes for *National
        Review*, 346-50; living at
        Montclair, NJ, 355; plan for

    autobiography, 5-6, 356-57;
        death, 362
II. Views
altruism: 306-11
anarchism: 264
arms, right to bear: 270
big business: 153-54, 158, 273, 327-
    28, 337-38, 351-52
business regulation: 52-53, 56, 99-
    101, 135, 185, 266, 272-73
capitalism: 50-55, 99-101, 104, 126,
    135, 147, 194, 210, 254-55, 298,
    337-38, 344, 352; and women,
    194-95
censorship: 79-80, 108, 135, 229, 249
communism: 57-58, 136, 137, 141,
    148, 149-53, 154, 158, 183, 223-
    25, 240, 318-21, 347-48
conscription: 109, 249, 291
conservatism: 50, 54, 104, 135, 159-
    60, 276, 343
democracy: 53, 70, 230-35, 260-61,
    267-69, 301-302
economic theory: 104, 127-28, 133-
    35, 142-45, 147, 167-68, 254-56
education: 57, 276, 349-50
empire: 25, 53, 239, 261
environmental resources: 143, 185-
    86, 254
fascism: 148-49, 224
feminism: 193-99
"Four Freedoms": 249-50
"free land": 1-2, 4, 14, 217, 258
Great Depression: 123, 125-36, 235
historical theory: 181-82, 194, 258-
    63
individual freedom: and diversity,
    168, 199, 211-12; and material
    progress, 4, 135-36, 142-45, 210-
    11, 262-66, 275, 346; and reason,
    276-79; and religion, 204, 263-64;
    and responsibility, 20, 135-36,
    174, 256; and strength of nation,
    2, 142, 249
    liberalism: 54, 135, 142, 147, 175-
    80, 210, 225, 229, 260, 267, 343
    libertarianism: 4-5, 61-62, 135-36,
    144, 147, 152-53, 156, 173, 211-
    12, 276, 343; and women, 194-95
limited government: 4, 231-35, 267-71
literary technique and theory: 44-45,
    62, 75-80, 119

marriage: 10, 34, 49-50, 55, 108, 187-88, 198

Marxism: 150-53, 258-59, 275, 349

men: 196-99

minimal government: 4, 15, 99, 147, 286

moral code, nature of: 292, 349

the North American West: 14-17, 20-21, 27-28, 43, 258, 271-72

physics and cosmology: 298-301, 332, 348-49, 358

planning by government: 56, 109-11, 128, 131, 133-34, 139-45, 147, 167-68, 264-66

race and ethnicity: 199-200, 259, 266, 347

religion and God: 13, 19-20, 121, 200-204, 262-64, 291-92, 300-301, 305-306, 348-49, 357-58, 362

Republican Party: 107, 109-11, 230, 246-48, 346-47, 353-54

Roosevelt's New Deal: 165-76, 194

science and scientists: 199, 250, 262, 291-92, 298-301, 347-49

slavery, in America: 266, 271, 301-302, 346

Social Security: 325

spontaneous order: 16, 255

tolerance: 13, 16

victimless crime laws: 108-109, 110, 111, 135-36, 147

wars: American Civil War, 57, 271, 301, 346; World War I, 8, 55, 56-58, 100, 102, 126, 237, 239, 297; World War II, 237-51

welfare: 61-62, 178, 273-74

women: 34, 53, 55, 193-99, 266

III. Writings

column in *New York Herald Tribune* *"Books"*: origin, 63; character, 65-82, 165; conclusion, 321-23

The God of the Machine: 4, 7, 9, 42, 141, 201, 236, 249, 251, 253-79, 281-87, 289-94, 302, 304, 307-11, 326, 330, 331, 335, 336, 339, 340, 346, 352, 359, 360

major essays: 108, 112, 197, 297-98, 301-302, 346-50

novels: *The Fourth Queen*, 101-102; *The Golden Vanity*, 9, 42, 94-95, 154-63, 187, 190, 206, 256, 273; *If It Prove Fair Weather*, 9, 187-

89, 317; *Joyous Gard*, 29, 326-32, 357-58; *The Magpie's Nest*, 29, 31, 39, 45-51, 55-56, 331; *Never Ask the End*, 9, 10, 27, 29, 115-20, 122, 142, 143, 154, 157, 184, 202; *The Road of the Gods*, 97, 102-105, 113, 159, 193; *The Shadow Riders*, 25, 34, 45-46, 51-57, 193, 195, 273; *The Singing Season*, 97-102, 107, 310

short stories: 27, 35-36, 60, 306

Paterson, Kenneth Birrell, 28-31, 48, 83, 329

Patou, Jean, 92

Patten, Simon, 176

Patterson, Joseph Medill, 59

Paul, Saint, 157, 262

Pegler, Westbrook, 320

Perényi, Eleanor, 149

Perlman, Hilda, 356

Pétain, Henri Philippe, 242

Peter I, tsar of Russia, 136

Plato, 71, 145

Pliny, 71

Pollock, Channing, 219-20

Pope, Alexander, 204

Pope, Emma, 45

Porter, Katherine Anne, 346

Pruette, Lorine, 89

Pytheas, 253-54, 257, 258, 259, 274, 278, 279, 360-61

Rabelais, François, 71, 213, 214

Rand, Ayn: 195, 196, 202, 218-22, 246, 287-89, 294, 302-14, 334-35, 336, 351, 357-59, 360; conflicts with Paterson, 302-14, 357-59

Raphael, Ruth, 91

Rascoe, Burton, 59-63, 75, 84, 91, 93, 111, 155, 334

Rascoe, Hazel, 91

Raskob, John J., 112, 206

Read, Leonard E., 293, 307, 336

Read, Thomas T., 257

Reagan, Ronald, 223, 233, 344

Reconstruction Finance Corporation, 128-29

Reid, Elisabeth Mills, 315

Reid, Helen Rogers, 315-17, 319-21

Reid, Ogden, 315, 322

Reid, Ogden Rogers, 321

Reid, Whitelaw, 315

Remarque, Erich Maria, 70
Reynolds, Quentin, 319
Rhodes, Cecil, 25
Richberg, Donald, 172
Richman, Sheldon, 205-206
Ritchie, Albert C., 112
Roberts, M., 294-95
Roberts, Nathaniel, 114-15, 117, 120, 122, 362
Rodin, Auguste, 59
Rogers, Will, 69, 150
Roosevelt, Eleanor, 171, 172-73, 196, 234
Roosevelt, Franklin Delano: 111, 127, 129, 132, 133,134, 147, 165-76, 183, 184, 206-208, 213, 219, 230, 231, 245, 246, 247, 317, 333; era of, 159, 179; "Four Freedoms," 249-50
Roosevelt, Theodore, 1, 3, 109, 277, 353
Rosenbaum, Belle, 317
Rothbard, Murray N., 205, 359-60
Rousseau, Jean-Jacques, 13, 49
Russell, Bertrand, 72, 74
Ryskind, Mary, 313
Ryskind, Morrie, 313

Salten, Felix, 79
Sanner family, 325
Sassoon, Siegfried, 74
Scherman, Harry, 401n.35
Schlesinger, Arthur M., Jr., 175-76, 321
Schneider, Isidor, 224
Schwartz, Anna, 128
Scott, Walter, 19
Securities and Exchange Commission, 173
Sévigné, Marie de Rabutin-Chantal, marquise de, 355
Shakespeare, William, 19, 76, 362
Shapley, Harlow, 201
Shaw, George Bernard, 74, 148
Sheean, Vincent, 154
Shelley, Percy Bysshe, 71
Sherman, Roger, 270
Sherman, Stuart Pratt, 63, 316
Sherwood, Robert, 244
Sholokhov, Mikhail, 69
Silone, Ignazio, 224
Sinclair, Upton, 50, 73-75
Smith, Adam, 144, 210
Smith, Alfred, 111-113, 137, 139, 159, 176, 206, 209
Smith, Napier, 27, 42

Snyder, Carl, 220
Social Darwinism, 133
Social Security, 325
Socrates, 145
Spencer, Herbert, 382n.28
Spenser, Edmund, 71
Spinelli, Andrea, 333
Spinelli, Frank, 333, 362
Spinelli, Marian, 333
Stalin, Joseph, 57, 137, 149, 240, 243, 244, 317, 318, 335
Steffens, Lincoln, 139, 148, 177, 223-24, 234
Stein, Gertrude, 73, 75, 78, 195, 196
Steinbeck, John, 81
Stevenson, Robert Louis, 73
Stone, Grace Zaring, 149, 196, 226, 333
Sullivan, Mark, 108
Sunday, Billy, 78
Sunday, Helen, 78
Swanson, Gloria, 90
Swift, Jonathan, 72
Swinburne, Algernon Charles, 82

Taft, William Howard, 1
Taney, Roger, 301-302
Tate, Allen, 275
Taylor, L. D., 33, 53
Thackeray, William Makepeace, 84
Thirkell, Angela, 196
Thomas, Norman, 176
Thompson, Dorothy, 196, 245
Thomson, James, 76
Thoreau, Henry David, 175
Tolstoy, Leo, 76, 136, 197
Tomlinson, H. M., 238
Tompkins, Amy Jo, 55
Toynbee, Arnold, 239, 259
Trilling, Lionel, 179, 344
Truman, Harry, 208, 250
Tugwell, Rexford Guy, 172, 176, 180
Tunney, James Joseph (Gene), 94
Turner, Frederick Jackson, 1-2

Utley, Freda, 243-44

Van Doren, Carl, 226, 316
Van Doren, Irita, 63, 72, 245-46, 315-19, 321-23
Van Loon, Hendrik, 200
Veblen, Thorstein, 69, 140, 144, 176, 185, 212, 265

Vogt, Gertrude, 345, 351
Vorse, Mary Heaton, 357

Wade, John, 297
Wallace, Henry, 172
Washington, George, 151, 181, 239, 270,
    325
Weaver, Richard, 359
Welles, Edward, 361
Welles, Edward Randolph, 339
Welles, Mabel. *See* Owen, Mabel Welles
Welles, Mabel De Geer, 339
Welles, Mary, 339
Welles, Muriel. *See* Hall, Muriel Welles
Welles, Samuel Gardner, 339
Welles, Samuel Gardner, Jr., 220, 339-
    40, 363
Wells, H. G., 35
West, Rebecca, 197
Wheeler, Burton K., 205
Wilder, Laura Ingalls, 216

Wilder, Thornton, 82, 225-26, 227
Willkie, Wendell, 219, 245-48, 288, 317-
    19
Wilson, Edmund, 137, 150-51, 176, 227-
    28
Wilson, Woodrow, 1, 3, 109, 110, 113,
    159, 176, 207, 246
Winsor, Kathleen, 79
Winter, Ella, 224
Wolfe, General James, 21-22
Wolman, Leo, 208
Woolf, Virginia, 62, 79, 81, 82, 119, 194,
    196, 251
Wright, Frank Lloyd, 398n.26
Wright, Orville, 180-81, 311
Wright, Richard, 200
Wright, Wilbur, 180-181, 311
Wylie, Elinor, 84, 120, 196

Yeats, William Butler, 62, 79, 82, 116
Young, Art, 137